The Opened Letter

THE EARLY MODERN AMERICAS

Peter C. Mancall, Series Editor

Volumes in the series explore neglected aspects of early modern history in the western hemisphere. Interdisciplinary in character, and with a special emphasis on the Atlantic World from 1450 to 1850, the series is published in partnership with the USC-Huntington Early Modern Studies Institute.

The Opened Letter

Networking in the Early Modern British World

LINDSAY O'NEILL

PENN

UNIVERSITY OF PENNSYLVANIA PRESS

PHILADELPHIA

Published by
University of Pennsylvania Press
Philadelphia, Pennsylvania 19104-4112
www.upenn.edu/pennpress

Printed in the United States of America on acid-free paper
2 4 6 8 10 9 7 5 3 1

Library of Congress Cataloging-in-Publication Data
O'Neill, Lindsay.
The opened letter : networking in the early modern British world / Lindsay O'Neill.—1st ed.
p. cm. — (Early modern Americas)
Includes bibliographical references and index.
ISBN 978-0-8122-4648-3 (hardcover : alk. paper)
1. Letter writing—Social aspects—Great Britain—History—17th century. 2. Letter writing—Social aspects—Great Britain—History—18th century. 3. English letters—Great Britain—History—17th century. 4. English letters—Great Britain—History—18th century. 5. Social networks—Great Britain—History—17th century. 6. Social networks—Great Britain—History—18th century. I. Title. II. Series: Early modern Americas.
BJ2101.O54 2015
302.2′244—dc23 2014013141

For my parents

Contents

Introduction. Speaking Letters 1

Chapter 1. The Perils of the Post Office 19

Chapter 2. Mapping the Epistolary World 47

Chapter 3. Networking in the Epistolary World 78

Chapter 4. Nurturing the Epistolary World 113

Chapter 5. New Networks and Letters Less Familiar 140

Chapter 6. Stirring News and the Role of the Letter 169

Postscript 197

List of Abbreviations 205

Notes 205

Index 255

Acknowledgments 263

Introduction. Speaking Letters

The letters Peter Collinson received spoke to him. For this London merchant and ardent botanist, letters held more than inked words on a page. They contained the voices of his friends and acquaintances, and when he cracked open the seal of a letter, they escaped and filled the room. As he wrote to his fellow botanist John Bartram in Pennsylvania in 1762, "I am here all alone and yet I have the Company of my Friends with Mee. This will be no paradox when I tell thee on the Table lays their Speaking Letters in that Silent Language which Conveys their most intimate thoughts to my Mind."[1] Simply by dipping his quill into his ink, Collinson joined a conversation. He might address Bartram first, but his letter responded to and created other conversations. He urged Bartram to go read the letter he had sent to Benjamin Franklin about mysterious animal skeletons found near the Ohio River and he passed on thanks to Bartram's wife for her postscript. While he may have not realized it at the time, Collinson was doing more than carrying on an extended conversation with his friends and associates. He, and the scores of letter writers like him, used their pens to maintain and extend the social networks that were increasingly tying together the wider British world.

The letters Collinson read and penned with such joy reveal how one eager correspondent used his letters to maintain relationships with individuals across the wider British world. But he was only one man, and the meaning of his epistolary efforts only comes into focus when his letters are considered alongside those of his contemporaries, for Collinson was not the only one who listened to letters. They spoke to men and women across the early modern British world. By the eighteenth century, members of the elite from England, Ireland, Scotland, and the colonies needed letters like never before. They used them to conduct business, plumb intellectual concerns, discuss family matters, run distant estates, exchange news, and ask for advancement. Changing social, economic, and geographic circumstances made face-to-face communication more intermittent and sparse at the same time that personal networks of support and exchange became more critical to the navigation of their world. The answer lay in letters. The scribbled notes scattered across their tables were the threads of the social networks they needed to survive.

Individual sets of correspondence reveal the personal passions of their creators, but when set beside, and intertwined with, the letters of multiple correspondents—when a few hundred letters become a few thousand—larger patterns of dependence and exchange surface. Then letters truly begin to speak, and they whisper of the need for large, elaborate, and multipurpose networks. This book analyzes such networks, and the letters that created them, at the critical period between the establishment of a permanent national postal system in 1660, which provided many Britons with a new and more constant way to keep in touch, and the flourishing of the newspaper press in the middle of the eighteenth century, which gave the British another way to monitor their world. More specifically, I reassemble and listen to the hum of a number of individual and interlocking epistolary networks constructed by a disparate group of letter writers whose collective efforts illuminate the structure and workings of the British world socially, geographically, and communicatively at a time when the nation was becoming a dominant world power. It was during this period that the British elite truly became a networking society.

Networks in the Early Modern World

The way Britons thought about the word "network" was shifting subtly. When John Hawkins published *The ENGLISH School-Master Compleated* in 1692, he included the word "network" in his "Tables of Common English Words," right after the term "neighbour."[2] But while "neighbour" or "neighbourliness" possessed great social resonance during the period, the word "network" did not.[3] Neither Peter Collinson nor any of the other letter writers examined here used the term. In the early modern world it commonly referred to crosshatched pieces of metal or wood, or to loosely woven pieces of clothing. The hero of Richard Head's novel *The English Rogue* referred to an acquaintance's dilapidated cloak as "that Network garment of yours."[4] His friend then asserted, "I wish it were a Net, for then I might employ my self by fishing."[5] These networks were intricate or worn creations that could also be useful. Some works of net caught fish and others ensnared. Arachne's "cunning network," an author argued, "still intangles Art (like flies)."[6] By the early eighteenth century, though, networks commonly helped British intellectuals describe the systems that pumped life through organisms. It was the "curious and wonderful Network of Veins" within man that transported one physician with admiration.[7] These networks of veins brought movement to networks. They were no longer just cunning and useful objects; blood and life now circulated through them. When early modern figures envisioned networks, they saw threads loosely woven together, gossamer spiders' webs, and they were beginning to see them as intricate systems of circulation.

However, no early modern figure invoked the word to describe groups of interconnected people.[8] Individuals made networks; they did not participate in them. Instead these letter writers had friends. As a young John Perceval declared, "Other things are but the luxerys of life, our friends are the necessarys."[9] They were necessary for their affection, for their conversation, and most importantly for the actions they could take on one's behalf. Letter writers often referred to friends in the plural. It was not a single friend that Perceval saw as necessary, but a host of friends. Peter Collinson enjoyed reading Bartram's single letter, but he was truly happy when he could scatter his multiple letters across his counter and enjoy "the Company of my friends." In his letters, William Byrd I of Virginia referred to "all our friends" eighteen times.[10] His letters sought to connect and weave together his different threads of friendship. For another correspondent, friends formed a strong tree with deep roots and vast branches. When a friend died he decried the loss of "a branch lopt off from the tree of friendship, which I have long cultivated."[11] But isolated trees these were not. One could mobilize and use the friends of others. When one of Peter Collinson's correspondents discovered that his friends had failed to repay the "so many hundred obligations" they owed Collinson, he swore "never to molest you with any more of my recommendations."[12] This grafting of friendship failed. Others, however, took root and allowed branches to intertwine, as in old growth forests, producing a canopy of friendship.

These early modern invocations of friendship do not stray far from modern definitions of networks. For one mid-twentieth-century sociologist, the term network encapsulated the idea that "each person has a number of friends, and these friends have their own friends; some of any one person's friends know each other, others do not."[13] The distance between the terms is not vast, and the meanings are similar. So, while anachronistic, the word network encapsulates the ways letter writers envisioned their social worlds. It focuses attention on the links between individuals, rather than on the individuals themselves and keeps such historically weighted terms as "friendship," "neighbourliness," and "community" in the background.[14] Those living in the early modern world strategically used these terms, and while I acknowledge and investigate their complex uses, I do not want them to dominate the discussion since they isolate rather than bring together what was actually occurring. As scholars have insisted, words such as "community" are difficult.[15] They bring in their wake layers of historiographic argument and, more important, a nostalgia that complicates historical inquiry.

The term "network" is not new to scholars, but it remains messy and vague.[16] Historians rarely interrogate its meaning, which has disguised the networking practices of the British during the late seventeenth and early eighteenth centuries. Digging into the vagueness of the term and tracing how historians have employed it pushes to the surface a vast constellation of networks of different sizes, shapes, and purposes. It is that array of networks, their role, and the place of the letter in nurturing them that is the subject of this book.

Networks first became an important word for historians in the second half of the twentieth century. By this time the term commonly evoked a set of relations between individuals, but the use of the term remained metaphorical.[17] Unhappy with this state of affairs, early modern social historians, influenced by sociologists, attempted to employ the term more precisely and use it analytically.[18] As one sociologist described it in 1969, social network analysis was to provide "non-quantitative mathematical ways of rigorously stating the implications entailed in a set of relationships among a number of persons."[19] Rigor and mathematical tools were the hopes of the day. Early modern social historians saw in this approach a method through which, using parish and other records, they could reconstruct, to the degree possible, the nature and structure of past communities.[20] Networks, for these historians, were webs of social support that undergirded the functioning of local societies. They were an especially useful way to describe kinship relations and it was their interior nature, their tight knit or loose structure, that provoked discussion.[21] Networks emerge here as constant structures deeply tied to a single location.[22] They provided the underlying hum of society.

While social historians drifted away from networks and began to focus on how early modern peoples thought about and spoke about social relationships, networks as analytical tools were not dead.[23] Historians of science and knowledge in general and scholars of ethnic and religious diasporas found networks useful. But their networks were different from those outlined by social historians. These networks were more fluid, more fragile, and more geographically expansive. They were the product of a shared belief, need, or interest. They became more important at specific points in time. The multiplication of religious identities in the Reformation, for example, pushed networks into action. With religious upheaval, persecution, and proselytizing zeal came exile and migration, which could separate individuals from secular networks of support and scatter them geographically.[24] Historians of religious networks, however, rarely consider the type of networks their adherents formed in their struggles.

Historians of science are more aware of the nature of their subjects' networks. A growing interest in the social processes of knowledge creation and the influence of actor network theory, developed by sociologists Bruno Latour and Michel Callon, inspired these scholars to look more deeply at networks.[25] These webs of connection did not determine the structure of individual lives or help an isolated community united through belief survive; rather, they processed information and artifacts. These historians focused on how their singular networks functioned. While interested in the interior nature of networks like social historians, the quality of the links, strong or weak, between networks also drew them.[26] It was these links that could help explicate the formation of knowledge and the workings of the larger intellectual world. Tracing networks also allowed them to highlight the geographic breadth of the world of knowledge. For these scholars networks were fragile, unanchored to place, and supplemental to deeply embedded social networks.[27]

The creators of both intellectual and religious networks demonstrated a disregard for national boundaries and a celebration of geographic mobility that this project emphasizes.[28] Networks allow us to follow people rather than institutions or states.[29] This concentration on people and lack of concern regarding national boundaries has drawn Atlantic historians to networks. For example, Bernard Bailyn has noted, when mapping out the concepts and contours of Atlantic history, that "there were Atlantic networks everywhere—economic, religious, social, cultural."[30] Migration, forced and voluntary, often made networks, old and new, necessary.[31] Atlantic historians have traced a number of these social and religious networks, but historians of economic networks, especially those involving trade, have scrutinized the term most intensely.[32] For David Hancock, decentralized networks played an especially vital role in trade during the seventeenth and eighteenth centuries.[33] Like intellectual and religious networks, business networks were fragile, changeable, and engaged only obliquely with dense social networks. And, as scholars of the Atlantic world are beginning to see, such networks were rarely contained within the Atlantic.[34]

Social networks, kinship networks, intellectual networks, religious networks, and business networks: according to historians, the early modern world was bursting with networks. But the textures and purposes of these networks differed. Inspired by approaches and theories emanating from sociology, and by the attractiveness of the unexamined term itself, historians have examined networks in two ways. For social historians, networks explain the texture of local society. They underpinned early modern life in total and could point to social polarization or explain political upheaval.[35] Other historians use the word network to explain how groups of individuals coalesced around an idea, belief, or interest.[36] These networks could feed off larger social networks, but their creation was independent of them. All individuals were members of a larger social network, not everyone belonged to or needed voluntary networks of interest. They were more fragile, changeable, and geographically vast than their larger cousins.

Scholars rarely acknowledge that these two kinds of networks functioned simultaneously. Those studying networks of interest make reference to the importance of personal connections to flesh out how these networks functioned, but scholars usually leave the deeply entangled nature of the two unexplored. Historians of larger social networks note the influence of religious identities on community relations and fret over the institutionalization of networks of social action and support, but they rarely touch on the interplay between the two.[37] In this book I bring these two kinds of networks together to see exactly how they worked together and against each other. This is necessary because both were in the process of being transformed. Social networks strained to cover a larger geographic world and networks of interest were multiplying and becoming more institutionalized. Looking at the two in tandem reveals how this world worked. It allows the emphasis on formation, functioning, and geographic breadth found in studies of networks of interest to become entangled with the assertion that networks defined the structure of everyday life located in studies of social networks. My use of the word network embraces both broad social networks and networks of interest. They worked together, not separately. But I keep an ear cocked for their differences and allow them to surface when necessary. The networks sustained and used by these letter writers were vast webs of personal connection that laid dormant until mobilized for action.

The early modern British world was a networking society, not a society with networks. Webs of connection were not static entities, but active and changeable organisms. This is where social network analysis becomes useful once again. With it we can visually reconstitute these different networks and explain how they functioned, worked together, and changed. It emphasizes their different shapes and sizes, their interlinked nature, and their dynamic existence. The static image of the network as a web needs to be picked apart, analyzed, and set in motion.

The British elite navigated, with varying degrees of success, their changing world by weaving, nurturing, and playing on these networks. No longer did their centers of power sit solely in the localities and the Court; they recognized that they now inhabited a more polycentric urban world that obliged them to move between different social centers.[38] Now they converged at coffeehouses, at Parliament, at clubs, and at assemblies in both London and other urban destinations before retreating to their estates. To function socially, politically, and financially, they had to maintain links with individuals in these constantly shifting centers. The nature of these links also altered as formal ties to clubs and societies and distant business partners made networks based on shared interests more necessary. The world of the British elite was widening geographically. All the letter writers examined had acquaintances, friends, family members, and interests spread across the wider British world. Members of such a society needed fine-tuned and flexible webs to play upon. But the growth and integration of the British world and the increased mobility of its elite made maintaining these networks challenging. In the pen, and the letters they produced, many Britons found an answer.

As the British elite became a networking society, they also became a nation of letter writers, a phenomenon a number of historians have recently recognized. Indeed, analysis of letter writing practices has experienced a renaissance recently. Letters, as objects of study, first attracted literary scholars in the 1980s. For these authors, the growing popularity of the familiar letter helped explain the emergence of the novel, the rise of the individual self, and the divide between the private and public world.[39] Letters revealed the interior lives of their writers, who were usually members of the British elite. Recently the field has shifted away from the relationship of the letter to the self and toward its participatory role in navigating social relationships and negotiating social power. Scholars have emphasized the growing use of letters by the middling and laboring classes and the role such letters had in their lives and in the functioning of the British world.[40] Others have turned to the need for and use of letters by those separated by the Atlantic Ocean.[41] Though networks themselves never hold center stage in these works, they make brief appearances.[42] We are shown how letters supported and complicated family ties, held businesses together, and provided a way for coreligionists to stay in touch.[43] But the way these links came together and functioned within larger networks is not central to their arguments, and hence the networking propensity of letters and the different types of networks they supported is never fully examined.

Yet networking was often the purpose of a letter. In fact, nowhere is the union, importance, and negotiation between social networks and networks of interest seen more clearly than in the letters the British wrote during the period. These networks, formed by letters, came together to create a space of social negotiation that linked local, informal, and face-to-face realms of interaction with the more centralized, institutionalized, and interest-driven forms that were emerging. It was this world of personal networks, tentatively held together by letters, that is my focus. Concentrating on and explicating this realm provides a profitable way to examine a society portrayed as straddling the gap between the premodern and modern world. Rather than accepting the sense of transformation implied by the word "modern," which allows for the pronouncement of large—if ill-defined—statements about change, I focus on the interplay of the new and the old. Letter writing and the growth of networks and related institutions can point to the emergence of a more "modern" world. Letters helped cultivate the individual self, spurred a growth in literacy, and laid the foundation for the growth of the post office, which itself gestures to governmental centralization and control.[44] But seeing letters as the sinews of networks reminds us that they nurtured communal ties as much as a sense of individual identity and that they tied together informal networks that stood outside state or institutional control. The prevalence of these personal networks reflects a world where the sense of the public sphere was not yet fully formed, where smaller publics, formed of individuals with similar interests, were beginning to surface.[45] An examination of networks blurs the borders between the modern and the premodern worlds, between public and private spheres.

Networks, as a whole, gesture to a more informal and decentralized world centered on people rather than institutions. Seeing their prominence during this period emphasizes the continued importance that informal modes of social organization had as the geographic complexion, social functioning, and means of information distribution and control altered. Tracing these multiple, mutable, and vibrant networks reveals how members of the far-flung British elite succeeded and failed in navigating the changes that were slowly transforming their geographic and social worlds. And it was their letters that provided them with the sails to set forth on these rough waters.

Writers and Their Letters

The eighteenth century was awash in letters. They survive in their original form with broken seals testifying to their perusal, they come to us as meticulous copies recorded in well-cared-for letter books, and as scribbled drafts hastily inserted into small well-worn notebooks. The letters of some individuals survive in bulk, while those of others have been mangled by time, leaving only tantalizing glimpses of an active epistolary life. It is in larger sets of letters, particularly in those kept in letter books, where networks speak to the historian most loudly, especially in collections where personal correspondence sits next to business correspondence and letters of an intellectual bent nestle next to those detailing the working of an estate. Then, if a diary holds court nearby, the network produced by letters can speak to that formed through face-to-face interaction. These are the letter collections I focused on in this project since they allow the networks of their creators to emerge the most strongly. Additionally, since this is a book about networks and distance, I also chose letter writers who were scattered across the British world and who had written to each other. I then paired them with a number of writers who had little connection to them. This way ties between networks surface, but are balanced by those who are unconnected. Most of these writers were members of the British upper classes because it is their letters and diaries that survive in bulk and it was they who needed to maintain these vast long distance networks. However, the best way to introduce these letter writers is by looking at their relationships with their letters.

John Perceval, who became Sir John Perceval in 1691 at the tender age of eight and Viscount Perceval at the not so tender age of forty before assuming the mantle of the Earl of Egmont at the advanced age of fifty, liked to keep track of his letters. This Irish peer, born in county Cork, spent most of his life in England becoming deeply involved in the politics of both kingdoms and in the religious reformation of the British world as a whole. However, it was on English soil that he began to record his correspondence and keep a diary. When he died, he left behind eight letter books filled with his personal

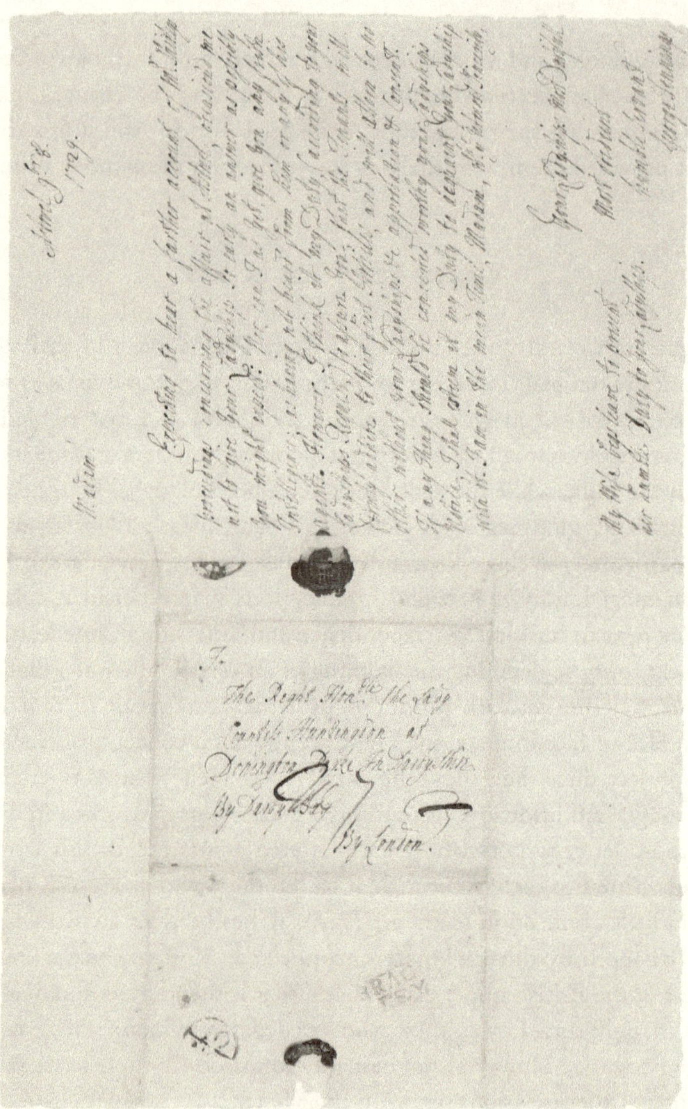

Figure 1. This rather humdrum letter from George Jennings to Selina Hastings, Countess of Huntingdon, penned in 1729, reveals the way letter writers set up their letters and how they were sent. Jennings folded the paper in half and wrote his letter on the top page, being sure to date the letter, note whence it came, leave a respectful distance between the salutation and body of the letter, and to carefully separate his wife's "duty" to the countess from the main text. Then he folded the sides of the letter to make an envelope, carefully addressed it (being sure to note it would go "by Darby Bag" once it arrived in London), and sealed it. The Post Office then left its mark by adding its postmarks.

George Jennings to Selina Hastings, Countess of Huntingdon, 8 November 1729, HEH HA 7799.

correspondence beginning in the year 1697, when he was a fourteen-year-old baronet, and lasting until 1731, when he was a thirty-seven-year-old viscount.[46] Sheltered between the covers of his letter books rest myriad voices. Some of the letters he composed himself, but most are letters written to him. He, or his personal secretary, copied these letters into a blank book in a neat hand, leaving a wide margin on the left side, and then proceeded to add elaborate indexes to most of the volumes. Perceval—it seems it must be him since many comments are made in the first person—then added a number of annotations, perhaps at a later date, to some of the letters, which noted the station acquaintances had achieved or passed judgment on their characters. (For example, Lord Dungannon was "a brave man in his person but a sot.")[47] The personal letter books end abruptly in 1731. He left the transcription of the last letter, which is from his son, unfinished, even though plenty of space remained in the book. He made no comment on why he stopped recording his personal letters and perhaps he did not; perhaps they have simply been lost. Or maybe he got caught up in keeping his diary, of which fifteen years survive from 1730 until 1745.[48] But he certainly did not stop keeping track of his letters for he also bundled up his estate correspondence into thirty-seven books stretching from 1699, when he was sixteen, until a few days before his death at sixty-five on 1 May 1748.[49] Most of the letters are actually the originals, put in chronological order, numbered, and even at times indexed. Many of them are from his agents in Ireland, although he also included a number of his own letters and those from tenants, friends, and acquaintances. Perceval's letters obviously spoke to him in diverse and treasured ways.

Few were as careful with their letters as John Perceval, but most correspondents examined attempted to keep track of their letters. William Byrd I, born in London in 1652, kept at least one letter book.[50] In 1684, when he was thirty-two and had resided in Virginia for at least fourteen years, Byrd took one of his Uncle Stegge's old account books, turned it around, and began recording his letters in it. Like Perceval he added annotations on bills and the health of correspondents, yet the book is nothing like the neat recording of letters seen in Perceval's letter books. Byrd jammed these transcribed letters together as though making the most out of the space as possible. Perhaps the short supply of such booklets in Virginia forced him to do so, but this book also hints at a man with little time on his hands, of which only a small amount could be spent neatly recording his correspondence. But while many of the letters he scrawled into his letter book detailed his business affairs, Byrd also included letters to friends and family. Recording these letters mattered too. He prospered in Virginia, the fur and tobacco trades filled his coffers, and he became a member of the governor's council (even accepting the post of acting governor at the end of his life), but he would return to the country of his birth only twice after his arrival in Virginia and this made letters his main form of communication with relatives left behind. This letter book, which spans only seven years of his life, from 1684 to 1691, accounts for over 80 percent of his surviving epistolary production. The rest of Byrd's correspondence surfaces in other collections of letters and consists mostly of official government epistles and letters of an intellectual bent that his acquaintances kept.

While the surviving letters of William Byrd I emit a sense of hurried business, those of his son sound like a man reaping the benefits of his father's labors and using them to increase his family's standing. William Byrd II was born in 1674 near the falls of the James River in Virginia, though he spent the majority of his early years in England. Before he settled permanently on his plantation, Westover, on the banks of the James River in 1726, he had spent only a shade over ten of his fifty-two years in his native land. When he entered his early thirties he prepared his first surviving letter book and diary. In the end, three of his diaries would survive, covering about twelve years of his life off and on between 1709, when he was thirty-five, and 1741, when he was sixty-seven.[51] Byrd the younger's first surviving letter book dates from the same period as his first surviving diary. This book held deeply personal letters: notes to friends who were far away and epistles that would remind him of successful and unsuccessful courtships.[52] Rather than detailing when he received his letters and who they were sent to, as Perceval did, he left them undated and at times referred to his correspondents by their nom de plumes such as "Vigilante" for the vigilant father of a marriage prospect or "Charmante" for a prospective bride. He kept more traditional letter books, like his father's, holding business and personal letters, but the surviving ones date only from his later years after his permanent return to the colonies. These, however, survive until 1741, a few years before his death in 1744.[53] Additional letter books easily could have been lost over the centuries, or perhaps it was only his arrival in Virginia that prompted his epistolary recordings. As the editor of his letters has found, bits and pieces of his correspondence surface in other locations as well; in his commonplace book, in the letter books and letter collections of friends and acquaintances, in government collections, and he himself appears to have saved a number of autograph letters.[54]

Unlike the Byrds or John Perceval, Hans Sloane, their occasional correspondent and an Irishman of Scots ancestry, who became Sir Hans Sloane in 1716, either did not keep a letter book or it has not survived. As longtime secretary of the Royal Society, however, he was a man who knew how to write and record letters. The British Library holds reams of letters to him, arranged neatly in chronological order.[55] That the British Museum bought this collection on Sloane's death in 1753 suggests that he kept these letters himself; although how he kept them or organized them is left unclear. The surviving letters date from his early twenties when he was finishing up his medical studies in London, Paris, and Montpellier in the early 1680s, follow him through his travels in the West Indies between 1687 and 1689, and hold the letters he received from the time he was made the secretary of the Royal Society in 1693 through his long tenure as the president of that august body from 1727 to 1741. Unlike the epistles in the letter books spoken of earlier, these are autograph letters where the process of writing, the art of folding and spacing, and sometimes the mode of delivery (if a postmark survives) are evident.

Some, like Hans Sloane's acquaintance, correspondent, and fellow Royal Society member Peter Collinson, placed their letters in more personal spaces. While the British Library holds two bound volumes of letters sent to Peter Collinson, many of his surviving letters were lovingly inserted into his commonplace book nestled between maps of North Carolina, records of venison received, and newspaper clippings.[56] His commonplace books appear to include pieces from throughout his adult life. The earliest piece dates from 1726 when he was in his early thirties and the last from the year of his death in 1768. Like the other correspondents, the letters of this Quaker cloth merchant and botanist also surface in the collections of others. William Byrd II, kept a number of Collinson's autograph letters detailing, he wrote on one letter, "the management of vines."[57]

James Brydges, who wrote to Hans Sloane and moved in the same circles as John Perceval, was born to the eighth Baron Chandos in 1674 and would become Earl of Carnarvon in 1714 and the first Duke of Chandos in 1719. Brydges was also a man who kept track of his correspondence. He finished the last of fifty-seven volumes of outgoing letters in 1744, the year he died at age seventy.[58] Between 1700 and 1712 he had also kept fourteen volumes of incoming letters.[59] He had begun these letter books when he was appointed paymaster of the queen's troops in his early thirties, but keeping a written record of his life was not new to him. Years before, he had kept a journal of his social rounds in London.[60] Writing letters and cultivating acquaintances helped Brydges organize his business and social world. Collecting art and the musical talents of men like Handel, who lived at Brydges's estate of Cannons for a number of years, were also ways Brydges attempted to signal his arrival in the upper ranks of the aristocracy. His estate of Cannons, so brilliant when it was finished in 1724 that Daniel Defoe declared "a pen can but ill describe it, the pencil not much better," was his almost overwrought declaration of social status.[61] However, Cannons was dismantled and demolished a few years after his death and it is his letters that remain.

The letters of Brydges's second wife, Cassandra, do not survive in the same bulk as her husband's correspondence, but she too kept letter books.[62] Cassandra Willoughby was born in 1670 to an eminent naturalist (in fact her tutor John Ray was Hans Sloane's great friend) and the daughter of a governor of the East India Company (her mother's second husband would be Sir Josiah Child, an influential governor of the East India Company). Cassandra dedicated her early years to the running of her brother's estate in west Nottingham, where she pulled together her first short letter book of seventeen pages that held letters from the mid-1690s to the early years of the eighteenth century.[63] These were outgoing letters she composed to other people; meaning that she either kept drafts she later added to her book or copied these into the book before she sent them off. It was also around this time that she began to keep a travel diary that recorded, beginning in 1695, the places she went on one side and the occurrences that blessed or befell those in her social orbit on the other. She continued to keep this travel diary for four years after her marriage to her cousin James Brydges in 1713 at the age of forty-three. Her marriage also saw her picking up the pen to begin another letter book she would keep until her death in 1735.[64] Like those in her previous letter book these were outgoing letters she seems to have copied down to keep track of her world.

Far away in Lancashire, Nicholas Blundell also kept a letter book of outgoing letters. In 1669, Blundell had been born into a long-standing Catholic recusant family in the north of England and spent time in his youth in Flanders being educated at the Jesuit college of St. Omer. This was one of the few times he would leave the embrace of his estate in Little Crosby (the other was when he went into voluntary exile in Flanders for a year after the failed Jacobite Rising of 1715). To a degree, his world was substantially different from that of the others discussed here. He was less mobile and less interested in the wider social world of London. Unlike many of these letter writers, his path would not cross theirs over the years, but like them he recorded his letters. In his early thirties he found himself the head of the family when his father died in 1702. It was at this time that he picked up a pen and began keeping both a letter book and diary.[65] He kept the diary almost daily until 1728 and recorded his letters less consistently until 1731. The diary reflects the daily life of a member of the English gentry who was deeply involved in the workings of his estate. His letter book shows a member of the English gentry reaching out beyond that local world to correspondents in, among other locations, London and the Chesapeake.

The voices of Nicholas Blundell, Cassandra and James Brydges, Peter Collinson, Hans Sloane, William Byrd (father and son), and John Perceval reverberate through this book. But theirs are not the only letters that speak. Many of these collections included incoming letters, which allow the voices of their correspondents to come through loud and clear. Friends and relatives, like philosopher George Berkeley, Perceval's great friend, and John Custis, Byrd the younger's brother-in-law, become as familiar as the main correspondents. The pen of Margaret Ray, the wife of one of Sloane's good friends, scratches loudly, as do those of Lady Petre, Peter Collinson's patron, and Helena le Grand, Perceval's witty cousin. We hear from those who were not members of the British elite, as the voices of John Perceval's tenants, James Brydges's employees, and William Byrd (I & II)'s factors and ship captains echo through their letters. Within these sets of correspondence vibrant, expansive, and elaborate networks hum with life.

The letters these writers preserved provide the raw materials to reconstruct the networks they nurtured. The form in which letters survived helps and complicates this process. Perceval, the two Byrds, James and Cassandra Brydges, and Blundell all kept letter books. These individuals chose to transcribe and retain these sets of letters. Their books tell the story of their businesses, financial affairs, government posts, and personal lives that they wished or needed to keep. Within them lay traces of their chosen networks. John Perceval, William Byrd, II, James Brydges, and Nicholas Blundell also kept diaries, which often provide a glimpse of their local networks and place their letter writing activities in a larger context. But correspondents did not place all their letters into letter books. Autograph letters, like those that make up the bulk of Sloane's correspondence, might speak with less authority about the favored networks of their writers, but they whisper important secrets about how they wrote and sent their letters. Autograph letters often contain a scribbled address, a postmark, or a disintegrating seal that still clings to the paper. The vast letter collection of the earls of Huntingdon holds many of these broken seals and scrawled addresses. The letters of the earls, their families, and those connected to them survive in bulk and usually in autograph form from the late fifteenth century into the late nineteenth century. The early letters of this family, from 1600 through the later seventeenth century, reveal the placement of seals, the wording of early addresses, and how and when their writers turned to the postal system after its introduction.[66] These autograph letters sing in a way their copied siblings cannot. They show the material reality of these letters. You can measure how much space the writers left between their salutations and the bodies of their letters, you can see where writers placed their postscripts, and you can evaluate the neatness of their hands. Their addresses and postmarks suggest how letter writers sent their epistles. Both kinds of letters, those enshrined in letter books and those surviving in their original state, have a place in this work for both, in complementary ways, reveal the workings of the epistolary world.

The lives of these correspondents also illuminate the way figures from the periphery of the British world positioned themselves. All these correspondents lived on the margins, geographically or socially, of the British elite and were relatively mobile. John Perceval, born in Ireland, spent much of his life trying and failing to gain an English title. Hans Sloane's father was a Scot; Sloane himself was born in Ireland and died in England. Sloane's father was a land agent for an earl and Sloane's daughter the mother of one. Peter Collinson was an English merchant whose interest in botany led him to share his enthusiasm with members of the British aristocracy and Pennsylvania farmers. The two William Byrds both ended their lives in Virginia, but both maintained connections to those in England until their deaths. James Brydges and Cassandra Willoughby, both English born and bred, had deep connections to powerful trading interests. In fact, James Brydges spent some time in his youth in Constantinople, where his father was the British ambassador thanks to his family ties with the Levant Company. This mobile son of a mere baron would strive to see himself crowned "Princely" Chandos. Cassandra too fought to find a place. She gained power through the management of an estate as a young woman and continued to use those skills by marrying her cousin and becoming mistress of Cannons. Nicholas Blundell did not long for an estate like Cannons. He was happy with the calm rhythms of Little Crosby, but through his letters he too found himself embedded in a larger world that crossed the Atlantic and the English Channel. These figures varied in their possession of and desire for a place of power in society. However, they show

how figures from the social and geographic peripheries of the British world were finding their way to its center. It was their letters, and the networks they extended, that allowed them entrance.

ꟿ

Each chapter of this book looks at letters and the networks they formed from a slightly different angle to flesh out the shape and workings of their senders' wider networks. I begin with a moment of change: the permanent opening of the postal service to the public. From that moment forward, letter writers no longer needed to depend on carriers or traveling acquaintances to send their epistles. They had the post and the stamp to prove it. However, the introduction of more institutional forms of organization, like the postal system, did not supplant older forms of epistolary exchange, but rather expanded their use. This made new kinds of networks more valuable. Personal postal networks mattered as much as the Post Office.

Chapter 2 analyzes where letter writers sent their epistles and how letter writers thought about and experienced epistolary distance. Mapping out the extent of the British world as seen through these letter collections shifts our focus away from a purely British or Atlantic viewpoint and allows us to see this world as correspondents did, unbounded by artificial boundaries. But not all distances were equal. A letter writer's connections to London differed from those to Paris or Virginia. And these writers rarely sat still. Both their mobility and how they thought about the distances they traversed determined how they used their networks.

Chapter 3 picks apart these networks. Social network analysis reveals that these webs contained two types of connection: a constant core of linkages and ephemeral edges. The British elite juggled multiple networks that required different forms of maintenance and altered over time. These epistolary networks were not set, unchanging, and limited, but living, moving, and mutable. They also had borders. Gender and social position affected the way individuals made use of these webs of connection. But once they had the ability to produce letters, individuals found they depended on these informal networks to keep their more dispersed and mobile worlds working.

Chapter 4 examines the words within letters. The more familiar letter of the eighteenth century made it easier to maintain distant links than the formal courtly letters of the seventeenth. However, focusing too much on the language in which writers composed their letters distracts from the elements that really built up a sense of connection and community. Many Britons distrusted the authenticity of affectionate language, and thus it was the small additions to letters that emphasized communal connections, networked ties, and time-honored forms of community maintenance that firmly anchored a correspondent to a wider network.

Chapter 5 turns to the new kinds of networks gaining strength and importance during the period: contractual and institutional networks. These networks of interest were products of formalized relationships, which often relied on communication through letters. Letters between landlords and their agents, merchants and their factors, and government officials differed from the more informal networks embedded in the vast social networks previously examined. Additionally, emerging social, religious, and intellectual societies relied on letters and the networks they formed. Both contractual and institutional forms of organization signal a more formalized and professionalized world, but these new kinds of networks relied on older ideas of connection and rested on more informal networks.

My final chapter turns to what happened when the newspaper challenged letters' near monopoly on spreading news at a distance. The blossoming of the newspaper press may have changed the way letter writers included news in their epistles, but it did not alter their importance as a form of news distribution. Like the expansion of the postal system, the growth of the newspaper press made informal networks more important. Through letters individuals could use news to nurture social bonds, establish the truth of news reports the newspapers placed in doubt, and become members of virtual coffeehouses. Examining the way news flowed through letters brings together many of the themes of this book, from the continuing importance of informal networks in the face of new institutions to the effect of the widening British world on society.

By the eighteenth century the letter had become part of everyday life for most Britons. They wrote them in their closets, their pantries, their galleries, and behind their counters during business.[67] They sent them by the post and by friends and they read them in groups and alone. These fragile, but increasingly numerous, bits of paper crisscrossed the widening British world and provided a way for the British elite to extend and monitor the fluid social networks on which their livelihoods depended. These networks provide a clear picture of the way the British elite dealt with a changing geographic and social world. Peter Collinson used his letters to convey his intimate thoughts and to make his world turn. He was not alone.

Chapter 1

The Perils of the Post Office

In 1662, during the depths of winter, John Davys found himself pelted by letters from his employer, Lucy Hastings, Countess of Huntingdon. On the night of 16 February a letter arrived from the Derby post, the next morning the carrier delivered a second one, and then Mr. Strong of Sutton handed him a third.[1] Obviously the countess did not find it difficult to send her letters the hundred miles from London to Leicestershire where her estates lay under the watchful eyes of John Davys. Her predecessors would not have found it as easy. Carriers had long taken letters for eager correspondents, as had trusted hands like those of Mr. Strong, but use of the postal system was new.[2] While the government had attempted to open the post to the public previously, it was not until after the Restoration that its bags were permanently held open to the general population.

The late seventeenth century was a time of postal possibility for the English. The government opened the royal post to the public permanently in 1660, the Penny Post began circulating letters around London multiple times a day for just a penny in 1680, and the government established packet routes to the Dutch Republic, Spain, Portugal, and the West Indies between 1669 and 1702.[3] Scholars have investigated the institutional workings of British postal systems from the Roman period to today and historians of the late seventeenth and early eighteenth centuries have cast the post as emblematic of the state's growing power.[4] However, looking at when individuals used the post, and when they did not, broadens the field of play and reveals how the British still relied on personal networks to send their letters.[5]

This chapter examines how letter writers sent their epistles and why they chose that mode of delivery. The decision hinged on many factors. Exchanging letters within the geographic boundaries of London differed substantially

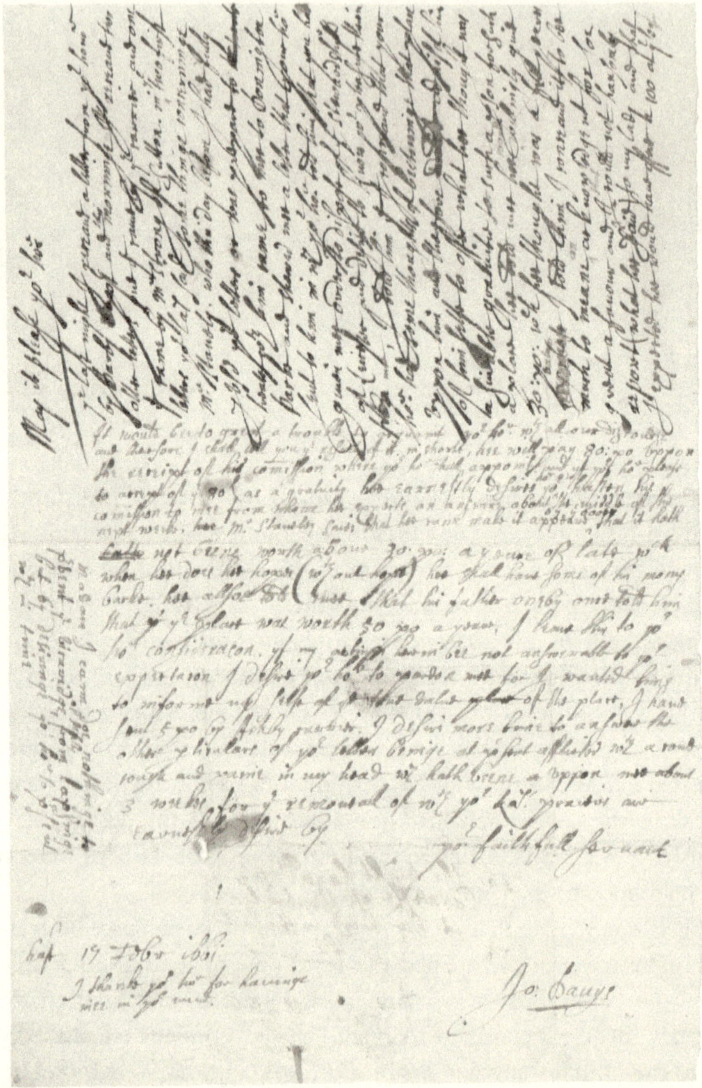

Figure 2. Letters were not always meticulous creations. This letter, composed by John Davys for his employer, the Countess of Huntingdon, on 19 February 1662, shows the hurried nature of some letters, especially business letters. The ink alters, he scribbles in changes, and squeezes additions into the margins. But he is also sure to add, right under the date-line, "I thank your honour for havinge mee in your mind." This is also the letter in which he mentioned that he had received letters by the Derby Post, the carrier, and Mr. Sutton.

John Davys to Lucy Hastings, Countess of Huntingdon, 19 February 1661/2, HEH HA 2006.

from the experience of sending a letter from London to Leicestershire, let alone Virginia. The further one traveled from the postal center of London the more important informal means of exchange became. The postal system was but one strand in a complex system of letter exchange and to understand the place of the post other forms of delivery require inspection. Writers like the Countess of Huntingdon used messengers, carriers, friends, and acquaintances alongside the post. The way letters circulated depended on place, personal preference, and opportunity. Furthermore, their circuits of exchange outline the shape of their writers' social networks and illustrate how they functioned.

By the Post

The existence of a postal system was not new to the English. One had been in use, on and off, since the Romans, but access to it and government control of it increased in the mid-seventeenth century. Charles I officially opened the royal post to the public, but growing unrest and eventually the Civil Wars curtailed the sending of letters by official means.[6] However, after peace arrived it became clear that a public postal system was too important to the security of the nation and too lucrative a business for the government to allow it to slip out of their control.[7] In 1660 the Convention Parliament passed an act "for erecting and establishing a Post Office" that reaffirmed actions taken previously by other regimes. The government shut out competing systems and thus established a government-run postal system opened to the public.

Historians have seen in the establishment and development of the postal system a force for change. In their eyes, its expansion allowed the British to make full use of their letters.[8] To James How it was behind the creation of "epistolary space," described as "spaces of connection, providing permanent and seemingly unbreakable links between people and places."[9] For Jürgen Habermas it helped push forth the bourgeois public sphere.[10] For Konstantin Dierks control of the postal system explained the difference between victory and defeat in war.[11] For these scholars the postal system was important indeed.

In many ways they are correct. Between 1685 and 1715 the volume of correspondence greatly increased and between 1686 and 1710 the number of letters processed by the Penny Post increased by 300,000 letters, from 624,575 letters to 954,283.[12] As the countess's letter illustrates, members of the Hastings family used the post as a matter of fact. Between 1718 and 1730 they, and their relations, used the post to send at least 43 percent of their letters and the true amount was probably much greater since this number is based only on the number of surviving postmarks.[13] Nicholas Blundell, a member of the northern gentry, also used the post and often referred to visits to the Post Office in an offhanded manner in his diary. On a snowy day in December 1702 he sent off seven letters and during the next eight years he visited the office at least thirteen more times.[14]

The postal system reconfigured the epistolary landscape for English letter writers. Possessing the option of delivering a letter by the post made letter sending more of a constant in writers' lives. Previously writers depended on carriers and personal letter bearers, but carriers stuck to their established routes and bearers were not always easy to find. Many letters sent by personal bearers were the product of chance. A friend or acquaintance had to be going to the exact location where the recipient resided and had to let the writer know of his or her journey. The Post Office eased this element of chance and rendered epistolary networks more permanent. It provided the British with another, more constant, mode with which to connect with those around them. As one correspondent told another, when his expected bearer canceled his trip: "I am resolv'd to make use of the common Post rather than not carry on so agreable a correspondence."[15] His decision sums up the situation: writers preferred trusted hands, but if necessary they turned to the post. Being able to use the post to send letters gave letter writers a choice.[16] They were no longer bound to bearers or carriers; now, they could turn to a government-run system. But was it an option they wanted to choose?

Painting the post as a transformative system ignores the difficulties that plagued it and places too much emphasis on its ability to open epistolary doors. Just as print technology itself did not cause a print revolution and singlehandedly create the public sphere, the expansion of the postal system did not instantly transform the epistolary world.[17] Its use depended on the needs and beliefs of its users and they knew that turning to the postal system was usually difficult, often dissatisfying, and could be dangerous since the information held within letters could be seen by prying eyes. Scholars have noted the troublesome aspects of the postal system, such as government censorship of letters, but they have not investigated the larger consequences of these problems.[18] The dangers posed by the post and its less than stellar functioning require examination, but even more attention needs to be paid to the basic difficulties faced by those sending letters, especially for those who lived far from established postal routes.[19] An understanding of these difficulties reveals that alternate modes of letter delivery were just as, if not more, important.

Sending letters by the post could be dangerous as the British were well aware. Senders knew their seals were not sacrosanct and that those running the Post Office often cracked them open and perused their contents.[20] The opening of letters was no secret. One correspondent calmly told John Perceval, the Anglo-Irish landlord and future Earl of Egmont, "To give a general opinion of things is to guess at Random, & not altogether safe by letter as times go, and the Posthouse is managed."[21] Other writers let out a sigh of relief when they realized an opened letter held no politics.[22] While there was no public outcry against the opening of correspondence, it did curtail what writers placed in letters and it annoyed many of them.[23] One irate writer grumbled "the Ministers of the Post-Office . . . had an evil eye to my Epistolary Correspondence."[24] To avoid the danger a few simply wrote in code. They replaced names and places with a series of numbers or with terms agreed upon by the correspondents.[25] These correspondents truly found safety in numbers.

But writers worried more about the rather lackluster performance of the post than they did about its dangers. Letters echo with the sighs of frustrated senders. When a letter did not arrive correspondents took it for granted that it had miscarried at some point.[26] They accounted for delayed letters by assuming that postal officials let them sit unsorted at the Post Office or simply overlooked them.[27] Such beliefs nicely shifted the blame of a late letter from the writer to an impersonal system, but it was also true. Often postal officials sent letters to the wrong place. An estate agent in Ireland complained to his employer that postal officials in Dublin often misdirected his letters because they assumed Cork meant the city of Cork rather than the county.[28] Things did not even go smoothly for the popular Penny Post. Charges of incompetence caused William Dockwra, its founder, to print a pamphlet defending his system. He reminded his readers that such miscarried and delayed letters were not necessarily the fault of the Penny Post; they could stem from human error as well: a correspondent might choose not to respond, servants could forget to deliver a letter, or a letter writer could scribble an incomprehensible address.[29]

Beyond the well-recognized snags of institutional incompetence and governmental prying stands the less frequently acknowledged fact that it was not always easy to send a letter. After the Restoration, mail still mainly flowed along six roads that started in London and went south to Yarmouth, southeast to Dover, northeast to Berwick and then Scotland, northwest to Chester and then Ireland, west to Bristol and southwest Plymouth.[30] As long as writers wished to send letters along these roads corresponding was relatively easy, but many Britons lived far from these major routes. For these individuals sending a letter and receiving one were more difficult. Nicholas Blundell, who we know went to the Post Office often, assured a correspondent he would have written sooner but "being I live some distance from Leverpoole it oft happens that letters lye some time before I recive them."[31] Even if one lived close to a Post Office, the undeveloped nature of the system caused problems. The lack of cross posts between major roads meant that a letter sent from Bristol to Portsmouth, a distance of one hundred miles, had to pass through London first, which added extra postage and an additional hundred miles to the journey. The major postal reforms implemented under the watchful eye of Ralph Allen, the postmaster of Bath who ran the bye and cross posts, revolved around the establishment of new postal routes such as these, so that by 1756 the number of cross posts had increased and there were at least two hundred Post Offices in England.[32] But even with these reforms, sending a letter by the post was not easy and many, especially those far from London, found they had to seek out alternative means.

Searching Letters

Letter writers often expressed a hope that their letters would "find" their receivers. John Perceval hoped his correspondent was up to date when "this letter finds you" and Cassandra Brydges worried that she knew not "where a letter would find" the recipient.[33] One of Peter Collinson's correspondents was more confident in her letter's abilities. After stating that Collinson was "quite lost," she expressed her belief that "this letter will find him out."[34] With such phrasing these writers gifted their letters with agency and created a picture of dogged letters intrepidly searching out their receivers like bloodhounds on a scent. Examining exactly how letters found their recipients shows how complex and difficult that process could be and how it altered according to one's geographic location. Even with an address firmly written, letters often had to pass through multiple hands to make it to their intended destination. Following four searching letters sent to or by John Perceval from London, Ireland, the Netherlands, and Virginia reveals this complexity.

With the General Post Office stationed on Lombard Street and the presence of Penny Post offices throughout the city, London was the British world's postal heart. Letters flowed in and out again, and sending a letter within London was done with greater ease than in any other area in the British world. With access to the Penny Post, Londoners could send a letter by post as easily as by messenger and many did so interchangeably. One of Hans Sloane's correspondents simply asked Sloane to send him a few lines by the Penny Post if his servant did not find him at home.[35] But even using the Penny Post could be tricky.

Between 4 and 6 November 1723 Henry Newman, secretary of the Proselyte Society and London resident, wrote four letters to John Perceval who, at the time, was living in Charlton about ten miles away. The Proselyte Society was in crisis due to the death of its treasurer, John Chamberlayne, on 2 November, which gave those who wished to reform the society an opening for change. Perceval was among those who favored reform and Newman wanted him at the Society's next meeting.[36] Luckily for Newman, sending a letter from his lodgings in Middle Temple to Perceval in Charlton near Greenwich was seemingly simple. On 4 November he sat himself at his desk, sharpened his pen, and wrote a quick letter to Perceval informing him of Chamberlayne's death and the other issues facing the Society. Once finished he probably shook some pounce on the letter to keep the ink from smearing, folded it up, wrote Perceval's address on it, sealed it with a dab of wax, and then sent it off to a nearby receiving station for the Penny Post, accompanied with two pennies to pay for its conveyance.[37] If Newman was lucky his servant would have instantly dropped off the letter, unlike some less responsible messengers whom Penny Post officials accused of destroying their letters and pocketing the money or loitering at alehouses before dropping off their letters.[38]

Once the letter was in the hands of the Penny Post, employees marked it with the two official Penny Post stamps that noted what office it left from and the time it left the office. From the receiving station the letter was sent to the Penny Post sorting house across the river in Southwark, near the Church of St. Mary Overy, from whence letters were carried twice a day, at 8 a.m. and 1 p.m., the ten miles or so down the river to Charlton.[39] Once an official carried the letter to its place of delivery in Charlton it sat waiting for collection by one of Perceval's servants, who probably checked often, or, if Newman paid a bit extra, it was delivered by a messenger to Perceval's home.[40]

In an ideal world this letter would have made it into Perceval's hands the day Newman sent it, with a response making its way back to Newman the same day if he was lucky or if he was not by the following morning. However, judging from Perceval's response penned on November 6, the system rarely achieved such rapid turnover. Perceval informed Newman that he would attend the meeting if he knew of it two or three days in advance, but Newman needed to be quick "for the letters that are put in the penny Post at London do not arrive here the same day, nor frequently the 2nd but on the 3rd."[41] The rapidity of the post pleased Newman, however, since he declared on 6 November: "I was this morning surprised to receive your Lordship's letter, when I thought it scarce possible that mine of yesterday shou'd have reach'd your hands."[42] The exchange reveals the complexity of using even the Penny Post. The writer needed to know how to address his letter and where to deliver it. He had to hope his receiver knew to look for letters or have them delivered. And all knew that the system was slower than desired. But these obstacles did not keep them from using it and London letters arrived much more quickly and regularly than those sent to other areas of the British world.

Sending a letter got harder the farther one moved away from London. Using the post was not easy or especially rapid for those residing in Scotland. Postmen traveling from Edinburgh to Glasgow went by foot rather than horse until 1717, as did those traveling to Aberdeen until 1740.[43] In 1726 one letter writer in Kent chose to send a letter by a friend to Aberdeen because "you was removed to a great Distance [and] I knew not how to send a letter to you."[44] He knew that his friend could search out his correspondent in a way the postal system could not. However, many a letter went through the Scottish post and many letters arrived in Edinburgh faster than those sent to Dublin.[45]

John Perceval's estate agent Berkeley Taylor, who watched over Perceval's estates near Cork, knew the difficulties of sending a letter from Ireland to England. On 9 December 1720, three years before Newman penned his letter, Taylor sat down to write a letter to his employer in London.[46] Since landlords wanted their letters up to date, Taylor probably acted as a future agent did and wrote his letters on the eve of post days, so Mondays and Thursdays.[47] Keeping his employer promptly informed was difficult and on this occasion Taylor was responding to letters from 10, 15, 17, and 26 November because delayed Irish packet boats had kept the letters longer than usual. Taylor began by addressing the tardy nature of the letters and then proceeded to comment on the exact items his employer had mentioned in his past letters. In fact, the last matter Taylor addressed was the final issue Perceval had noted in his last letter of the 26th: a tenant's wish to hold the church's glebe.[48] After the post boy came calling at Ballymacow he took the letter to the Post Office in a smaller town like Kinsale, two miles away, or Mallow, twelve miles away. Next, the letter traveled to Waterford or Dublin, over on a packet boat to Milford Haven or Holyhead, and thence to London.[49] However, Taylor was often suspicious of the Post Office. He knew they often sorted his letters from Perceval erroneously, sending them to the city of Cork rather than to Mallow in the county of Cork. Taylor was justified in many of his gripes, but what could one expect from an office with only a dozen employees?[50]

Taylor often tried to lower the cost of letters for his employer by enclosing them in letters to Perceval's relative who could "frank" his letters or send them free due to parliamentary privilege. This practice ended in 1721 when the corner of a letter ripped and the enclosed epistle became visible. An annoyed Perceval paid the postage.[51] Perceval franked his own letters when he was a member of Parliament, but this too caused problems. As another of Perceval's agents informed him in 1735, when Perceval asked if his letters came free, there was a complaint made in the Irish House of Commons that the Post Office in Dublin was charging for franked letters from England.[52]

However, Taylor's unfranked letter, if it was a single sheet, cost 10d.[53] Perceval bore the charge since it was usually the receiver who paid the postage. Where he paid the postage on this letter is unclear. Unbeknownst to Taylor when he wrote his letter, Perceval was no longer in London but in Bath or on his way there.[54] Luckily for Taylor, Perceval still wanted his letters directed to London. But somehow this letter did make it to Bath, for Perceval answered it from there on 28 December, nineteen days after Taylor wrote it.[55] It could have come to Bath through the post (with another 3d added to the postage) or it could have arrived with a friend or relative; Perceval does not say. On another occasion he did have his letters directed to the Post Office in Bath, and on his trip back he had Taylor enclose them to his cousin in London and direct them to St. James Coffee House.[56] When in London Perceval could receive his letters in many ways. He picked them up at the Post Office itself, at coffeehouses, or had them delivered to his Pall Mall residence.[57] Simply to send a letter to his employer Taylor had to know the ins and outs of the postal system. He had to know when the post days were, account for delayed packet boats, and keep an ear cocked to pick up on the movements of his always mobile employer.

In many ways Taylor had it easy. He and Perceval kept up a constant correspondence and Perceval attempted to inform him of his movements and provided him with directions on where to send his letters if travel intervened. This was not always the case. Many aspiring and established correspondents did not know where to send a letter: they did not know where their correspondent was or they simply did not have their address. As correspondents moved from their estates to London to Bath and to the Continent or simply between London addresses, how to address a letter became complicated. When John Perceval traveled on the Continent he moved every couple of days, making it hard for his letters to find him, and even when in England he often shifted from his house in London to his place in Charlton and to the waters of Bath, which is why he usually told Berkeley Taylor to send his letters to his cousin Daniel Dering in London whom he kept up to date on his movements. Others did the same. The Duke of Richmond told Peter Collinson to simply direct his letters to Whitehall and from there they would be sent to him.[58] However, a letter from Peter Collinson almost missed Lord Petre as he was on his way to London, which prompted him to tell Collinson that "Sir Hans had wrong intelligence in relations to my motions."[59] Collinson had obviously attempted to keep track of Petre's movements by asking his friend in London. Sometimes writers simply did not know where to send their letter until another correspondent informed them. A relative apologized to Perceval for his lax letter writing by stating, "I had given you the trouble of a line or two before now had I known what part of the world to have directed to you: My Spouse in her last letter gave me the account of your being [in] London as did my friend Mr. Wogan."[60] It was difficult to keep track of such mobile networks. At one point John Perceval simply threw up his hands and declared, "I don't know where this will find you."[61]

How one directed a letter also mattered, and with the expansion of the postal system addresses became more standardized. Gone were the personalized directions that dripped with complimentary phrasing like that gracing an early seventeenth-century letter from the Dowager Countess of Derby to the fourth Earl of Huntingdon, which read: "Right Honorable my very good L[ord] and deare frend the Erle of Huntingdon geve these."[62] In their wake came addresses that were more detailed and clear, like that written on the cover of a letter to the ninth Earl of Huntingdon in 1734: "To The Rt. Honorable the Earl of Huntingdon at Donington Park Leicestershire."[63]

Sending a letter by the Post Office could strip its address of a personal touch. By the eighteenth century the bare bones of an address consisted of the correspondent's name, their estate if they had one, the closest town, and the county. Urban addresses, especially London addresses, were more detailed. A correspondent of Hans Sloane, perhaps in jest, told him to direct his letter for him "at the sign of the Cham of Tartary's Slipper in York Buildings, next door to the Yorkshire Cushion, over against the Cinnamon Broom-stick."[64] Such a detailed address was necessary. The officials at the Penny Post insisted London writers needed "to mention the Trade and Sign, or near what Place, Lane, Church, Remarkable Public House, or Tavern, &c. which is altogether Necessary every where; but especially in long Streets, and large Places, such as are in this great City and Suburbs."[65] In the densely populated and heavily built-up city a correspondent had to include a detailed address to get a letter to its intended destination.

If a correspondent did not provide an address or if the address was not specific enough the exchange could come to a screeching halt. John Perceval complained to Berkeley Taylor that "some ordinary person" left a letter at a coffeehouse for him but included no return address so he had no way to contact him.[66] A more conciliatory Cassandra Willoughby assured her correspondent that "Had I known where to make a Letter find you, Dear Madam, you should have been thus troubled sooner, & since you are so kind as to send me a direction now, you need not doubt of such a Correspondent."[67] Even having an address was no guarantee. A friend of Hans Sloane doubted that his letter reached its destination for "it had only a loose & generall description of him in Mark Lane."[68] Others found that their address was out of date or simply wrong. One of Perceval's correspondents missed a number of his letters because he had sent them to Mr. Tooks "a bookseller near Temple-Bar" rather than to Mr. Ropers "at the black boy in Fleet Street."[69] Sometimes the sender simply forgot the address. Poor William Fisher had to admit to his employer, John Perceval, that he had forgotten what street a correspondent lived on for "he told me by Word of mouth how I should direct to him."[70] Such a danger is probably why Nicholas Blundell kept a list of addresses at the back of his letter book and why John Perceval jotted down the locations of some acquaintances at the end of one of his journals, along with the days the post left for France.[71] Many other letter writers were proactive and concluded their letters with directions on where to send a response.[72]

Writers often needed access to personal networks to send a letter by the post. When letter writers mentioned bad or forgotten addresses it was usually

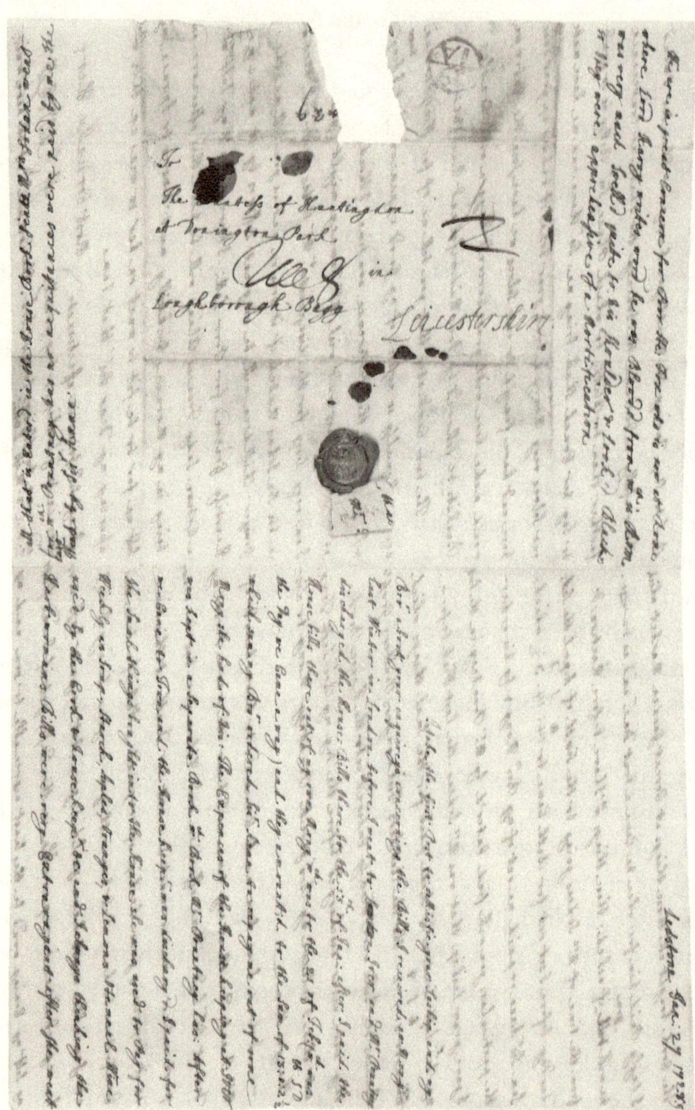

Figure 3. Letters were carefully addressed. Here Lady Francis Hastings was sure to note that Donnington Hall was in Leicestershire and that the letter should go by the Loughborough Bag. The lack of complexity of this address also shows how sending a letter to an aristocrat's estate in the countryside was easier than sending one into the maw of metropolitan London. Furthermore, Francis's scribbles on the flaps of the letter (which would have been folded inward) show her need to make use of all available space. The postal service also left its mark, which lets us know that it received the letter on 29 January, two days after Francis wrote it.

Francis Hastings to Selina Hastings, Countess of Huntingdon, 27 January 1728/9, HEH HA 4984.

because they wanted their correspondent to help them to the correct one. The Duke of Richmond sent Peter Collinson a letter to forward because he was unaware of the post town near Lord Petre's estate of Thorndon. He left a space for Collinson to fill in, but he also speculated that the estate "must be known at the post office as it is an old family seat."[73] He depended on Collinson to finish the address for him because he knew Collinson was a close friend and correspondent of the Petre family. William Fisher admitted that he had forgotten the street of his correspondent because he wanted Perceval to forward the enclosed letter. These correspondents relied on personal networks to get their letters to their destinations when their postal knowledge failed them. They also used their knowledge of their correspondents' personal habits to get letters to them. When a clergyman in Kent forgot the street his correspondent lived on, he simply sent it to another address that he knew his correspondent frequented.[74] This reliance on personal knowledge serves as a reminder that the establishment of the postal system allowed those who knew the addresses of their correspondents to send letters more consistently, but it did not make it easier for those outside a network to insinuate themselves into it. The development of the postal service itself did not make the epistolary world a more open space.

Addresses became less standardized the farther one traveled from established postal routes and personal networks became increasingly important. A correspondent of Hans Sloane who traveled to the East India Company's settlement on the island of Poulo Condor off the coast of what is now southern Vietnam told him: "If you direct for me at this Island it will come safe to hand wherever I am."[75] Perceval's good friend in Rhode Island told him to simply direct his letters to "Dean Berkeley at Rhode Island near Boston."[76] This is true of many letters sent to the Continent as well. When John Perceval traveled to Paris in 1725 he told Berkeley Taylor to simply direct his letters to "Mr Arbuthnot Banker in Paris."[77] The British populations in these locations were small compared to those of the teeming metropolis and the networks of acquaintances were often smaller. Furthermore, these writers could rarely depend on the post; they looked to merchant networks and the hands of friends.

Sending a letter to the Continent could take many hands and multiple posts. It could also take a lot of time. When a letter took over six weeks to reach him, John Perceval, who was residing in France, told his brother in Ireland on 19 September 1725, "Your Letter of 3rd August the only one I have received since my leaving England came late to hand having two Seas and a foreign Country to pass."[78] To a degree, Perceval was lucky. An acquaintance of his found himself in Barcelona in 1711 during the War of the Spanish Succession and instructed Perceval to send his letters via Genoa where a merchant friend had connections and could send them to Barcelona.[79] Perceval was familiar with the difficulties of getting letters from the British Isles when traveling on the Continent. Years before, on the first of July 1718 he was especially frustrated when he sat down to pen letters from The Hague. On this day he wrote to his cousin and brother-in-law, Daniel Dering, who was watching over his affairs from London and to his brother, Philip, who was also in London. In both letters, after addressing business concerns and giving an account of his travels (he had bought lace for both of them and found Lord Cadogan surprisingly civil), he mentioned he was sorry and troubled that he had not heard from anyone.[80] He then folded the letters, addressed them, sealed them, and sent them on their way to London.

These two letters could have made their way to London through public or private hands. As many correspondents did, he could have used a friendly messenger or a bearer to get the letter to England. However, he probably turned to the packet service operating out of Helvoetsluis (now Hellevoetsluis) in the Netherlands.[81] Helvoetsluis was about thirty miles from The Hague, so Perceval could have hired a messenger to bring his letters to the port or perhaps he used the postal system of the Netherlands.[82] Once they arrived in Helvoetsluis the letters would have sailed the next Wednesday or Saturday when the packet boats left for Harwich. Once in England the British Post Office embraced them and they made their way back to London and into the hands of Dering and Philip Perceval.

John appears to have been wary of trusting his letters solely to the public postal systems when on the Continent even though the postal system there was more mature than the English system. The family of Tour and Tassis had run the post in the lands ruled by the Holy Roman Emperor since the end of the fifteenth century, but for men like Perceval the Continental posts were unfamiliar and they often relied on personal connections to collect their letters and provide them with a central location for the delivery of letters.[83] Perceval was sure to instruct Daniel Dering to send his letters for Amsterdam to Sir Alexander Cairns in London who would forward them to an Amsterdam merchant firm.[84] Cairns, an Irish baronet and MP, had continental and mercantile connections and Perceval also sent a letter and a box through Cairns's brother Henry, a London merchant, four days before he wrote his letters from The Hague.[85] The death of the merchant in Amsterdam threw these plans into slight disarray, but while postal problems persisted throughout the trip, by 8 July, a week after his letter of complaint, Perceval appears to have begun to receive his letters, most probably because he had arrived in Amsterdam, a larger metropolis and the location where he had told Dering to forward his letters.[86] Perceval knew that letters to the Continent could easily be lost and that known hands increased the likelihood of a smooth delivery. In fact, he even had his Irish estate agent send his letters to Dering in London who summarized them in his letters to his cousin, streamlining the process.[87]

When writers sent letters across the Atlantic they followed many of the same procedures as continental correspondents. They often placed letters in the hands of merchants, and at times these letters fed into a distant postal system. While a colonial post was established later in the seventeenth century, no permanent packet service from England to the American colonies existed until the late eighteenth century. A number of individuals had attempted to develop packet services to the West Indies and New York, but none lasted.[88] Instead, some correspondents looked to government connections to get their letters across the Atlantic, but most colonial correspondents depended on merchant ships and their seasonal voyages.[89] Those living in the West Indies used the sugar ships to send letters, those in Virginia looked to the tobacco ships, and those to the north used the many merchant ships in and out of Boston or New York.[90] Once they arrived in Britain these letters could be delivered by hand or by the post to their receivers. Those living in Britain, who sent letters to the American colonies, simply reversed the process. Perceval's friend Henry Newman sent one of Perceval's letters to Rhode Island by a ship's captain bound for Boston and assured him that it would find its way to its recipient within a day by the colonial post.[91]

Like Henry Newman, Berkeley Taylor, and Daniel Dering before him, William Byrd II of Virginia sat down to write a letter to John Perceval. Byrd and Perceval had met in 1701 when Byrd accompanied the young Perceval on a trip around England and Byrd himself had almost joined Perceval on his trip through Holland and France in 1718.[92] But by 10 June 1729 Byrd was back in Virginia, dipping his quill into his ink and giving Perceval his opinion on a colonial project and telling him of his rambles through the backcountry of Virginia as he assisted in determining the border between Virginia and North Carolina. He then folded the letter, addressed and sealed it, and probably gave it to the captain of a tobacco ship docked off his plantation, Westover, along the James River.[93]

Writing a letter was a different experience for those in the colonies. The deficiencies of the postal system frustrated many a London user, but they also knew they could send a letter at almost any time of day and expect a response from anywhere in England within five days. Colonists could use the intercolonial post for local letters, but to send letters to England they depended on seasonal ships that ferried their letters across 3,000 miles of ocean.[94] For this reason colonists often wrote multiple letters at a time so they could send them by the same ship. Byrd's father wrote ten letters on 8 March 1686 and sent them all by the same ship's captain.[95] Perceval did the same when traveling on the Continent, although writing two letters on the same day pales in comparison to the ten composed by Byrd. Merchant ships, not unlike visitors, provided a convenient opportunity to send letters that many writers could not refuse. Thus it should not come as a surprise that Byrd wrote his letter to Perceval in June, a time when many tobacco ships were probably headed to London.[96] Correspondents in England with colonial connections felt a similar pressure. A loving and concerned brother living near Liverpool was "not willing to let many Ships pass with out a line or two" for his brother in the colonies.[97]

The postal pace felt slower for colonists. All their letters from England came by ship and Byrd appears to have received few letters from those in the colonies or, at least, he rarely recorded them. English correspondents, on the other hand, only waited for the few Atlantic letters that flowed into their larger pool of British letters. The Byrds did not receive letters from Britain frequently, building up a sense of anticipation for incoming letters. As William Byrd II informed a distant correspondent, "Our Lives are uniform without any great variety, til the Seasons brings in the Ships. Then we tear open the Letters they bring us from our Friends, as eagerly, as a greedy Heir tears open his Fathers Will."[98] Byrd also stated that if letters came in late in the day he would hide them from his wife so that she would sleep through the night.[99]

Once William Byrd II handed letters to ships' captains things did not always go smoothly. While neither he nor Perceval voiced any complaints about this voyage, once the ship hit the high seas a whole host of problems could hold it up, from bad weather to war to pirates. Byrd usually directed his rants at the sea captains who delivered his letters. In one letter to Perceval, almost ten years later, he blamed a ship's captain for not delivering his letter, stating, "These Tritons do now and [then p]lay us such slippery tricks, and are no more to be depended up[on than] the faithless element which they converse with."[100] While it turned out that the captain had sent the letter on, he had not gone to Perceval looking for an answer, which in Byrd's mind still made him the culprit.[101] Sometimes captains were simply slow at delivering their letters. One kept letters for six weeks after his ship docked.[102] Perceval was aware of these many dangers and made sure to send duplicates of his letters to Rhode Island, a practice embraced by many corresponding with distant locations.[103]

This particular letter, however, seems to have made it to Perceval without incident. Once in London the ship's captain might have delivered it himself to Perceval, placed it into the hands of the merchants at Perry and Lane who were Byrd's factors, or he might have sent it by a messenger to Perceval's residence, placed it into the Penny Post, or left it at a local coffeehouse where letters from Virginia accumulated. By whatever means, the letter did make it to Perceval's hands and on the third of December, six months after Byrd wrote it, he responded, declaring, "Nothing could give one greater pleasure than to hear from an Old friend of theirty years standing."[104] However delighted he was with the letter, it is likely that Perceval allowed Byrd's letter to sit a while before answering it. In the next set of letters they exchanged, he waited two months after receiving Byrd's letter to respond.[105] This rarely bothered Byrd since he usually expected only one letter a year from English correspondents. Those in the colonies delayed responding immediately as well. When Perceval's friend George Berkeley was living in Rhode Island he allowed Perceval's letter to sit three weeks before responding.[106] Unlike Perceval's letter from Newman, that from Taylor, or even that expected from Dering, these colonial letters did not require an instant response. Their purpose was to nurture a social connection and Byrd's letter did not ask Perceval to do anything but write in return when it suited him and in this he obliged.

Byrd made sure that Perceval knew how to send a response. He told Perceval to address his answer to his factor, Mr. Perry, in Leadenhall Street.[107] As Perceval was living in Charlton downriver from the city he probably sent his response via the Penny Post to Mr. Perry who then forwarded it by a ship to Virginia. If Perceval was in town he could have also left it in a coffeehouse where ships' captains often stopped to pick up letters.[108] Correspondents living in England often needed guidance in the ways of colonial correspondence. That is why both Byrd and Berkeley gave Perceval directions. An address on a letter bound for the colonies might have been simpler and less specific, but knowing what merchants or officials to turn to and when to send a letter mattered more. One London correspondent hurriedly wrote a letter to a friend in Kent, who had a daughter in the colonies, telling him that ships bound for South Carolina were leaving in less than three weeks and he should forward his letters quickly.[109] Other writers gave such notices for destinations further afield. A correspondent in Dublin reminded another that January was "the time of year for writing letters to India" and that he should forward him any he wished to send.[110] Just as using the postal system within the British Isles and from the Continent required a deep knowledge of its functioning, sending letters to the colonies required a complex understanding of the workings of Atlantic or Indian Ocean shipping. The forms of knowledge were different: users of the British post required an understanding of the institutional system, while those who sent letters further needed to understand a less centralized system, but both needed to use personal networks and knowledge to get their letters delivered.

These epistolary exchanges between different locations reveal the complex nature of communication by letter. Within London the system worked relatively smoothly. Letters might be delayed and a few might miscarry, but with the employees of the Penny Post ferrying them from the office to recipients communication was usually successful and usually completed within the fold of the postal system. The central importance of the postal system decreased and creative postal solutions increased the further from London a writer lived. When in Bath, Perceval continued to have his letters sent to London to be forwarded by his cousin who watched over his London concerns. His cousin might have forwarded them by the post or he could also have used a messenger, but he had the option to do either. Still Perceval knew he could not simply expect his letters to find him without providing them with an easier path. Similarly, he sent many of his Irish letters to his estate agent to distribute.[111] Since he kept up a constant correspondence with his agent Perceval knew his employee would watch for letters in a way others might not. By sending letters for others through his agent he guarded against such letters lying forgotten at the Post Office. This strategic use of the post colored his continental correspondence as well. He knew it was safer to have Taylor send his letters to Dering in London, rather than directly to him when he was traveling. Postal routes were only useful where they were well established and when postally savvy individuals lived on the other end. The expansion of the post created a reliable channel for postal exchange, but it frayed around the edges. This was true for correspondence beyond the British Isles as well, except that the channels were more informal. Letter writers with Atlantic correspondents knew merchant networks and used them as those in

Britain used the post. Once, when Perceval's correspondent in Rhode Island wished to send letters to England, he enclosed them to Perceval, who then distributed them.[112] Sadly one of the correspondents had died, but Perceval forwarded the other one to Durham.[113] The growth of the postal service and the expansion of shipping helped deepen these dependable channels of communication, but beyond these routes personal networks mattered more.

Careful Hands

When John Perceval's Rhode Island correspondent forwarded him the letters previously mentioned he entreated him to "send [them] by a carefull hand."[114] The careful hand turned out to be that of Perceval's only brother, Philip. Careful hands or personal bearers made the epistolary world turn: they helped the official postal system function and they increased the social meaning of a letter. To a society used to face-to-face interaction the option of a bearer was attractive. Most letter writers preferred to wait on a correspondent in person rather than to do so by letter. John Perceval's cousin apologized for a late epistolary response, but explained that he had delayed writing for he "was in hopes to have waited on you in person."[115] Sending a letter by a bearer spoke to this preference. Before the expansion of the Post Office, Britons had usually depended on bearers to deliver their letters.[116] When the Paston family sent letters in the fifteenth century they sent them by family members, trusted servants, neighbors, or hired men.[117] But the use of bearers was not just a legacy from a previous age that became irrelevant as the Post Office flourished.[118] John Eliot, a London merchant, continued to use bearers late into the eighteenth century.[119] He and other writers turned to bearers because they were easier to send a letter by, they deepened the emotional worth of the letter, and they allowed for more immediate forms of interaction. Personal postal intermediaries were an integral component of the postal process.

Many writers were seemingly unable to pass up a convenient bearer. As late as 1765 John Eliot could not resist taking, as he put it, "the opportunity" proffered by a traveling acquaintance to send a letter to his estate agent in Cornwall.[120] But it was Peter Collinson who, according to his letters, could not let a convenient opportunity pass. In 1739 it was his friend Dr. Filenius who gave him "so convenient an opportunity," in 1741 it was Mr. Biork, and in 1754 it was Mr. Smith.[121] All these hands were convenient because they were carrying letters to correspondents off the major postal routes of the world. Filenius and Biork carried their letters to Karl Linnaeus in Sweden and Mr. Smith to a friend in Connecticut. Like sending a letter across the Atlantic, the opportunity to send a letter to Sweden, as one correspondent stated, "don't occur often."[122] In many ways, these convenient bearers were merely that, easy means for getting a letter from one point to another where the postal system failed.

As they surface in Collinson's letters these bearers appear to be the product of kismet. To an extent this was probably true, but letter writers and letter bearers also created these convenient opportunities because they strengthened the web of social connection that bound them all. William Byrd II asked his friend to call on an acquaintance to see if he had a letter for him because he "is such a Philosopher that he needs a Moniter to put him in mind of his Friends."[123] By sending a prospective bearer Byrd reactivated a correspondence that had seemed to stall. Traveling friends often acted as informal postmasters and collected letters before their departures. They would come to take their leave and gather letters for brothers, sisters, and friends.[124] Here the increased mobility of the British elite helped since they had more opportunities to deliver letters. Collecting letters demonstrated a polite concern for the postal needs of a friend or acquaintance. It offered their letter a safe conveyance, saved them a trip to the Post Office, and made their letters free of charge. When the writer could not depend on the postal system a bearer who came for a letter was doubly appreciated. William Byrd II waxed poetic about the bearer of his letter to Mrs. Pitt in Bermuda who was "so very kind as to call for it, which few of his Countrymen can be perswaded to do."[125] Sending a letter by a bearer was convenient, but it was also a valued service.

Bearers fell into three categories: servants, individuals already known to the receiver, and those wishing to be known to the receiver. Servants usually received little from the exchange except perhaps a bit of change in their pocket. Unknown bearers often gained the most for they did not remain unknown for long. Bearing a letter allowed one to enter into a charmed circle of acquaintances. Often the writer was attempting to unite two individuals of similar interests. A correspondent of Hans Sloane in Amsterdam sent a letter by an "Ingenious Gentleman" who looked to Sloane for entrance into the world of London intellectuals.[126] This writer was not just looking to assist the bearer, but to help Sloane by connecting him with an individual who might serve him at a later date or enrich the quality of his intellectual conversation. But such letters most certainly also helped the bearer, especially those looking for assistance. Bearers were not shy in using letter delivery as a gateway to greater opportunity. John Perceval just happened to receive a letter from the hands of the brother of one of his agents when that young man was looking for a vicarage, and another of his acquaintances sent a letter by a young man who was looking to become Perceval's secretary.[127] Bearing a letter provided these individuals with a reason to wait on their prospective patron, giving them access that might otherwise be denied. One of Sloane's correspondents playfully admitted in a letter that he "dread[ed] the severitie of yr censure" for not responding sooner, but that his good friend Mr. Sherard had the "earnest desire to kiss yr hand, [and] desired me to favour him with some occasion of waiting on you."[128] By delivering a letter, bearers were able to serve the recipient before requesting assistance for themselves.

The sender of the letter also benefited by placing their letter in the hands of a bearer. John Boyle, Earl of Orrery, wished to write to the bishop of Oxford, but rather than simply slipping his letter in the mail, he wrote to a friend to see if he was acquainted with the bishop. To Boyle's delight he was and he convinced him to deliver the letter to the bishop for him. Sending the letter in this fashion allowed the letter to come free and it meant that this friend could tell him of the bishop's response since "a letter from him would be adding an unnecessary trouble to the liberty I have taken."[129] Boyle showed real concern for the bishop's postal welfare by not requiring him to respond. On other occasions the favor was the choice of bearer. A correspondent of Hans Sloane found that he could "not but count myself more especially ingaged to you for your last of June ye 7th which you oblidgingly contrived should be delivered me by Sir Andrew Fountaine; whose acquaintance I highly value."[130] By sending a letter by a close friend Sloane gifted him not only with his own letter but with a visit by a treasured friend. This favor increased the correspondent's sense of connection to Sloane himself. Sloane also demonstrated a deep knowledge of his correspondent's social circle. He knew by whom a letter would be welcome, and this showed the receiver how entangled in his own social network Sloane was, increasing or at least reaffirming his importance.

The use of bearers also eased the strains of epistolary distance by allowing for more immediate interaction. Writers had long used bearers to send verbal messages as well as to deliver letters.[131] As Boyle demonstrated with his letter to the Bishop of Oxford, sometimes receiving a verbal response was as desired as a letter. It cost less and, in a way, it was more personal. A young John Perceval delivered a letter and present to his guardian's friend who, rather than write a letter in return, sent his thanks and services through the protégé.[132] This was not only easier but Perceval was a physical being to whom he could extend his thanks, making the exchange feel more personal and immediate. Perceval then sent these thanks on through a letter. Having a letter delivered by an interested bearer also allowed for greater communication. Often the sender had the bearer read the letters they carried because the deliverer could then discuss the information inside with the recipient, which could lead to a more rapid resolution of the issues involved.[133] In this fashion three voices echoed in a room with only two discussants. Such an action could give the deliverer the advantage because he knew his own directions from the writer and what the writer had disclosed, or not disclosed, to the recipient. Thus he would have an idea of what to say and what not to say. The presence of the bearer also allowed the recipient to ask the questions left unanswered by the letter itself. A correspondent in Antigua thanked Cassandra Brydges for her letter by a ship's captain because it gave her "an opportunity of knowing by him more particularly your state of health."[134] Sending a letter by a bearer easily got a letter to its destination, but it also enhanced the level of interaction between the letter writer, the letter bearer, and the letter receiver.

However, there were times when receivers wished the exchange was not quite as immediate because the physical presence of the bearer was also more difficult to ignore. When one of Perceval's tenants fell on hard times after the death of her husband she did not send a letter by the post to her landlord; she sent it by her youngest son.[135] She hoped that by making her suffering visible through the person of her son she might win more leeway from Perceval. Such tactics greatly annoyed Perceval and he once declared to his agent, "when Tenants take that Course, tis only to surprize me into some concessions and impose on me by some melancholy representation of their case, of which I cannot be a competent judge," but later letters imply that he did talk to the son about the state of the farm.[136] As frustrating as Perceval found such tactics, they could work and, on the whole, welcomed bearers outnumbered the unwelcomed.

Sending a letter by a personal bearer was a necessary complement to the developing postal system. In many ways it was the more important system. It was bearers who often got letters to their intended destinations, even those sent through the post originally, and in doing so they increased the sense of personal connection between the sender and the receiver and even the bearer. Charting the way letter writers actually sent their letters insists on the importance of personal networks. Writers depended on networks to uncover addresses, to follow the movements of their correspondents, and to know who was the correct bearer to send. They also personalized the letter. These epistles flowed along deeply worn grooves of connection that held long-standing networks together. James Brydges, the eventual Duke of Chandos, received a letter from one cousin via another; John Eliot sent a letter by his sister to his uncle; and Sloane received one from his Oxford acquaintance via another intellectual connection.[137] These letters circulated through these dependable networks to reach their final destination. But to truly understand the functioning and shape of the networks that undergirded postal exchange, the way individuals circulated letters after their arrival requires examination.

Trusted Networks

Arriving at an initial destination was only the start of many letters' journeys. Bearers show the importance of personal networks in the dynamics of letter delivery and an examination of their continued circulation reveals what networks individuals depended upon.[138] After letters arrived they passed from hand to hand within a household. When discussing an affair of the heart John Perceval declared to a correspondent, "I imparted your letter to my wife, & we are at a loss what to think of the Lady's behaviour."[139] Obviously the tale puzzled Perceval and he passed the letter on to his wife and they discussed it. At times permission had to be given for such sharing. Perceval's brother told him in a letter that he could show it to their cousin. In fact, he sent the cousin over to see it and receive its news.[140] Writers knew the networks of others well enough to use them: Perceval's brother knew their cousin came by Perceval's house on a regular basis and that by sending a letter to Perceval he could also include the cousin. The sharing of letters was an acknowledged fact. Letter writers knew that the entire family read the letters sent to a single member.[141] The extended Perceval family read letters out loud among themselves. Perceval's cousin, who often watched over his children, told Perceval, "Your Proverb made us laught heartily."[142] It did not just amuse his cousin; it amused *us*. One can almost picture him sitting around the fire with his wife and Perceval's two children laughing at the proverb Perceval had sent them.

Letters were often the creations of many hands. Husbands and wives would sign a single letter to a correspondent.[143] If there was room at the end of a letter, a writer would allow another to add to it. Peter Collinson's correspondent eagerly accepted the opportunity of adding a few lines to the end of a friend's letter.[144] Some writers even thanked correspondents for these short notes of remembrance, even if they preferred a longer letter.[145] Close correspondents, especially family members, were the most frequent practitioners of joint letters. Since they saw each other frequently or lived together they had the most access to each other's letters. Daniel Dering and his wife often wrote letters together to John Perceval and his wife. Many conclude with Dering stating, "I leave my Letter open for my Wife to give an Account of her self."[146] The Derings and the Percevals were a deeply interconnected family. Daniel was John's cousin and his wife was John's wife's sister and the couple often lived with the Percevals. Thus, it seems natural that they would share communal letters.

Often correspondents simply assumed that an acquaintance's letter would stand in for their own. It was understood that close friends, family members, and other trusted eyes had access to letters. Writers would ask a correspondent to assure an acquaintance that they did not send them a letter because they knew they had access to the other letter.[147] Dering often took this route and put off writing to Perceval when he knew his wife had written either of the Percevals a long letter.[148] Perceval's other cousin assumed that one letter to the family was sufficient. She told Perceval, "I thought reading one letter at a time from one so dull as my self was a sufficient penance for the whole Family."[149] Letters were communal possessions of certain circles, especially family circles, and a letter to one was seen as a letter to all. Thus sending them by members of this circle only seemed natural and often extended the conversation.

Letters circulated beyond the family fireside as well; receivers mailed them to others who might be interested in their contents. Writers often mention returning letters composed by others and forwarding amusing or intriguing letters to other correspondents.[150] Peter Collinson sent Hans Sloane a letter "from a Curious Gentleman at Plymouth" as a present.[151] While such exchanges were an accepted practice they did cause problems, especially when receivers forgot to return letters. Collinson had to remind Sloane to return his letter from a Russian doctor on crabs' eyes because "I must write to the

Doctor answer."[152] He needed the letter by his side to compose the correct response. Sloane returned the letter with thanks and enclosed a letter for the doctor.[153] Collinson inserted this reminder not because of unauthorized sharing, but because of the logistics of sharing. In fact, such an exchange increased Sloane's own network since he added his own reply and let Collinson deliver it.

There were limits to letter circulation, however, and letter passing was more prevalent within certain networks. Identifying these networks pinpoints what groups letter writers trusted and what networks they depended upon. The three that surface most prominently are family networks, estate networks, and intellectual networks. One of the main purposes of this book is to explore the functioning and interaction of these webs of connection. Family members were quite casual about passing each other's letters around and about depending on a letter to one to account for the whole. They often lived together, socialized together, and sympathized together, so the bonds of affection, duty, and support were strong. The result of this close proximity, economic and social dependence, and affection was trust. Letters could be passed among family members and be sent by family members because they could be trusted to put letters into careful hands.

Members of the British elite had long trusted and utilized family networks, but as the circulation of letters suggests other networks were rising in importance during this period. Landlords, their agents, and their tenants often circulated letters among themselves as well. These correspondents did not inherently trust one another, but letter circulation helped create trust or at least the appearance of transparency. It also made the business of running an estate from afar function more smoothly. The same held true for absentee colonial plantation owners. The only way the increasing number of absentee landlords could keep in touch with their estates, whether they were in Ireland or Virginia, was through letters from their agents. Enclosing and passing letters helped landlords and agents stay on the same page in estate affairs: Perceval wanted to be sure that his agents in Ireland knew exactly what he wrote to his tenants so the tenants could not take advantage of the agent.[154] Agents would often show tenants their landlord's letters to prove they were not twisting his words and tenants often insisted that landlords saw their original letters, not just the agent's interpretation of them. As Perceval's slightly aggrieved agent wrote to him regarding a tenant's letter, "he desires me to forward the orginall thinking I suppose that no extract cou'd do his request justice."[155] The letters sent, passed, and enclosed by landlords, agents, and tenants illustrate the trust, strained but extant, between them: tenants had to believe that agents would pass on letters and landlords had to trust that agents would give them a fair picture of affairs on their land, a belief that was often tried by untrusting tenants. While estate letters circulated in a different fashion and for a different reason than family letters, there was a sense that such passing was allowable because the extent of circulation was known and letters could help this strained community function.

The practice of exchanging letters was even more common among members of intellectual networks like the Royal Society who, to promote their scholarly interests, were constantly circulating each other's letters. Together two members might peruse a single letter by another member and then send it on to a third.[156] At times they even lost track of who had seen a letter it had been passed around so much.[157] This kind of exchange would reach its fullest extent with the publication of *Philosophical Transactions*, the journal of the Royal Society, which drew on letters sent to the Society. Scholars had to depend on one another's knowledge and this sense of trust extended beyond experiments to include a more personal kind of trust: a belief that other scholars would treat letters, and the information in them, honorably.[158] The exchange of letters by the intellectual elite of Europe was not a new phenomenon, but it altered during the eighteenth century as intellectual thought became tied to the growth of clubs and societies, which changed the way ideas flowed and information circulated.

While letters were passed among trusted friends and networks, there were certainly places letters should not go. When a letter strayed from a trusted circle, senders worried.[159] Nicholas Blundell once recorded in his diary, "Lady Dowager Webbs Letter was given to a Rong hand by mistake and made great uneasiness."[160] This incident must have caused Blundell great consternation because usually he filled his diary only with his daily activities, not his reflections on such happenings. The way the British sealed their letters reveals the careful manner in which they guarded their privacy and from whom. Writers only sent unsealed letters to known and trusted correspondents; once trusted eyes viewed them, careful hands sealed them. On multiple occasions writers reminded their correspondents to seal enclosed letters before they sent them on. They insisted, "after you have read it pray clap a little wax to it" or "clap a Bit of Wax to the Seal."[161] Even if the letter was not going by the post it was important that it arrive sealed.[162] Usually, this emphasis on sealing stemmed from letter writers' suspicion of the Post Office, but it was also a way to keep out all prying eyes, which could be found outside the Post Office as well as in it.

Authors usually displayed mortification if their letters drifted from these trusted networks without their consent, especially if they landed in the hands of a printer. Scholars have noted that unlike on the Continent, the printing of letter collections and personal letters was infrequent in England until the later seventeenth century, with a few notable exceptions.[163] Even in the eighteenth century the publishing of personal letters could be a risky endeavor. Alexander Pope took Edmund Curll to court for publishing his letters. However, it was probably Pope himself who anonymously sent the letters to Curll so that in retaliation he could publish his "true" letters.[164] Such worries caused one correspondent to declare: "God forbid that any more Papers belonging to either of you especially such sacred Papers as your familiar Letters should fall into the Hands of Knaves and Fools."[165] The overwhelming fear was that letters could land in unknown hands. The public reading of personal letters would, in the words of one correspondent, "expose me to the misconstruction of many, the malice of some and the censure perhaps of the whole world."[166] Passing letters among known correspondents was acceptable; they knew how to interpret them, but unknown hands did not share the same skills and could cause the writer grief. Thus, while letters were communal objects, that community did not include the world at large. In many ways, this reflects Michael Warner's view of the public world before the construction of the public sphere in the later eighteenth century, where political debate occurred ideally in private and was founded on a trust in the hierarchical order of society.[167] In this world, authority was more personal and anonymity frowned upon. This view of the political realm reinforces the valuation of these personal networks; the world that mattered was small and personal.

ᔓ

Letters flowed through personal networks and sending them through these trusted webs solidified those networks. Scholars have recently placed more emphasis on the importance of the personal as a concept that softens the harsh division between private and public worlds.[168] Investigating letters, and the networks through which they circulated, reaffirms this need. Rather than examining the growth of the public or private sphere, it is more beneficial to think about the importance of smaller personal networks. The personal, with its more flexible lines of inclusion and exclusion, echoes the functioning of networks, which were neither private nor public. It was these personal networks that made the postal system work. The Post Office could not deliver letters on its own; Britons depended on their established personal networks to send and receive their letters. Allowing these networks to surface and examining how they functioned serves as a reminder that while the establishment of governmentally run systems, like the Post Office, changed the way Britons sent letters, they still relied on older modes of interaction to serve new needs. Like the Countess of Huntingdon, they knew a carrier and a careful hand were as trustworthy as the post.

Chapter 2

Mapping the Epistolary World

In a letter written in 1697, John Perceval's tutor sent his two young charges on a hypothetical journey around the world to spread the news of the Treaty of Ryswick, which settled the War of the League of Augsburg. Philip Perceval was to go southeast across the British Channel, along the coasts of France, Portugal, and West Africa until he reached the Cape of Good Hope, where, after breakfast and "a short dance with the Hottantots," he would continue on to the Spice Islands and "bid good morrow to the Japanners." John however "wou'd never endure the fatigues of so tedious a Voyage since he is so well acquainted with the short cut of the North East passage." After coasting along the shores of Denmark, Sweden, and Norway he would rent a boat and some wind from the Laplanders to take him to Peking and thence to California by way of the Juan Fernandez Islands. Their tutor ended by reminding the boys that they could easily chart their routes on the "Map of the World hanging by their bedside in Town" if they needed "to revive their Ideas of the country."[1] This playful exercise was to teach the young gentlemen about their wider world and it was a lesson well learned. While neither Philip nor John ever traveled to China or danced at the Cape of Good Hope, John did receive letters from both locations. From his vantage point in London or Dublin, he kept track of connections who traveled across the vast world described to him by his tutor.

Exotic locations beyond British shores often surfaced on the margins of Perceval's epistolary world and often piqued his interest, but he received more letters from locations closer to home: from Bath, Dublin, and Paris. Bringing together these wider connections and those closer to home reveals the true scope and purpose of the epistolary world, as well as the variations within it. It is well known that letters were the product of the need to connect over a distance, but what distances and how they differed remains unclear.[2] Following letters to their destinations and examining their writers' motivations for producing them allows us to explore the different experiences letter writers had depending on where they lived and how easy it was for them to shift locations. For besides mapping out this world, this chapter also explores the importance of mobility for these letter writers.[3] While most of them would never make it to the Juan Fernandez Islands, few remained at home.

Looking at exactly where letters originated from produces a basic outline of the shape of the epistolary world of their writers. It was this map of human connections with its hubs and peripheries that defined the world of letter writers rather than national boundaries. However, dots on a map only reveal so much; the composers of these letters experienced and expressed their sense of distance differently depending on their coordinates and their ability to change those coordinates. This map needs to be put into motion and the values of mobility and stability examined. Doing so forces us to look at the British world as a whole: to examine London alongside Lancashire and Dublin alongside Virginia.[4] It reminds us that for the British elite one's geographic origin mattered, but one's ability to maintain social connections in urban centers mattered more. For these letter writers it was mobility, or lack thereof, that determined the nature of their network, not just the specific place where they resided.

Centers and Peripheries

At the top or bottom of their letters correspondents usually noted where they composed their letters. This was a rather new development. Neither the Paston letters of the fifteenth century nor the letters written by the Hastings family early in the seventeenth century note the location of origin on a separate line. However, by the eighteenth century it was becoming increasingly important to let your correspondent know where you were. It helped ground the letters in space and provided receivers with an idea of where to send their response. This new habit allows us to map where letters were coming from, which produces a map of the geographic makeup of these writers' epistolary worlds (Figures 4–6).[5] These maps show the number of letters sent from specific locations as noted on the letters examined: on over 2,000 letters the correspondents had scrawled their location as London, 229 had placed Paris next to the date on their letters, and sixteen had noted that they wrote from Spanish Town, Jamaica. Every map of an epistolary network would look subtly different from these, since these maps reflect the lives of these specific correspondents. For example, the concentration of letters in county Munster in Ireland is due to John Perceval's estates near Cork. However, by layering the networks of twelve correspondents on each other, the concentrations that they produce reflect the general geographic proclivities of most British letter writers of their social status during the period.

The maps these letters create reveals a British world centered and embedded in England with numerous anchors on the European continent, deep ties to the North American colonies, and a smattering of connections throughout the rest of the globe. The majority of letters, 85 percent to be exact, hailed from the British Isles themselves (Figure 4). These letters deeply bespeckle the south of England and cluster around urban centers like Bristol and Bath, with an especially dense showing around London. The letters then climb their way north, clustering in places like Lancaster, and then finding their way over the border into Scotland. Westward the letters make their way to Ireland, especially to Dublin and Munster, where over a quarter of the letters originated since the group of correspondents examined had strong ties to that isle. Moving in the other direction, across the English Channel, we find that another 10 percent of the letters came from the European continent (Figure 5). These letters hailed from multiple European countries: Portugal, Spain, Sweden, the Papal States, and even Russia, but they cluster around the Low Countries and France. Fewer letters, only 5 percent, came from beyond Europe, but as we will see in many ways these links were stronger than many closer to home (Figure 6). Writers penned most of these distant letters, 79 percent, from the North American colonies, and almost 90 percent of the letters sent from beyond Europe arrived from British-ruled colonies or outposts of British trading companies. This epistolary world reached across the globe, but as the maps reveal it had its own centers and peripheries.

These letters cluster around urban centers. About 30 percent of all the letters examined originated from cities of over 100,000 inhabitants and 40 percent from cities of over 40,000.[6] Europe as a whole was not becoming increasingly urbanized during this period, but the nature of that urbanization was changing. Urban inhabitants were living in larger cities and those cities were increasingly located in the north of Europe with London, Paris, and the Dutch Randstad leading the way.[7] The distribution of letters reflects this

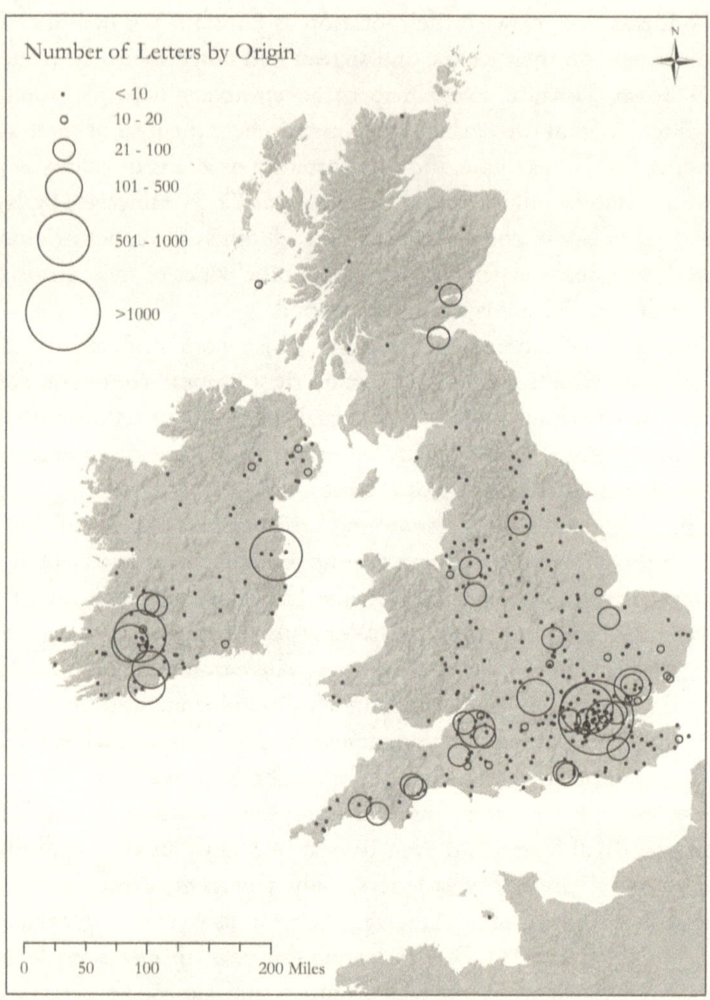

Figure 4. Number of letters originating from locations in the British Isles from the sets of correspondence examined. This map shows where the correspondents examined dated their letters from within the British Isles, allowing for larger circles around locations where many letters originated.

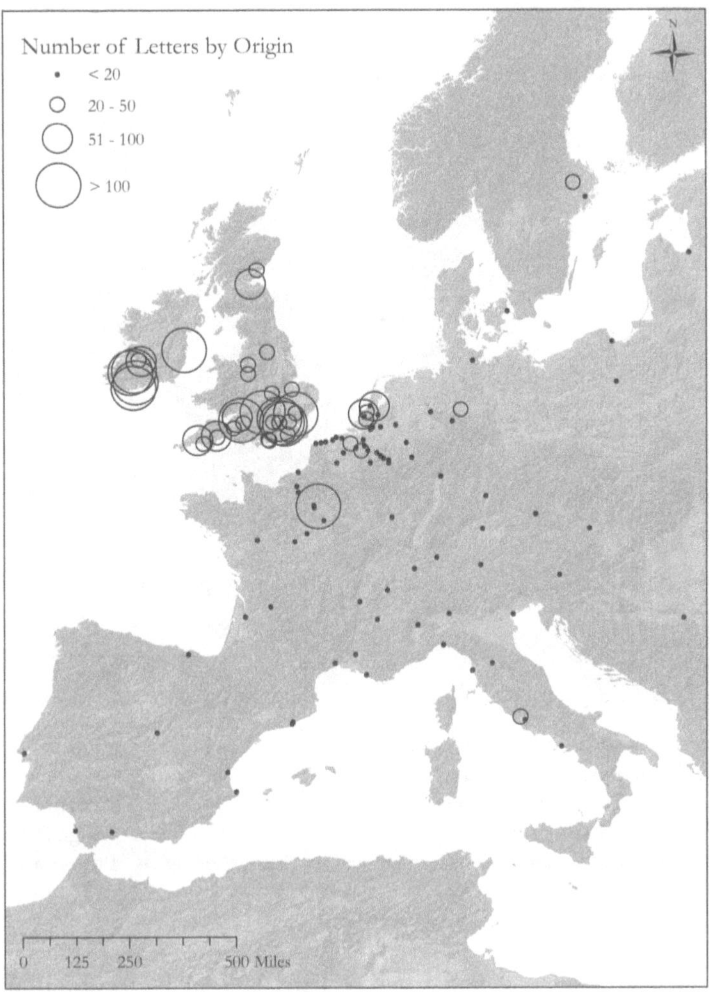

Figure 5. Number of letters originating from locations in Europe from the sets of correspondence examined. This map shows where the correspondents examined dated their letters from within Europe, allowing for larger circles around locations where many letters originated. Those emanating from the British Isles only show places from where more than twenty letters originated.

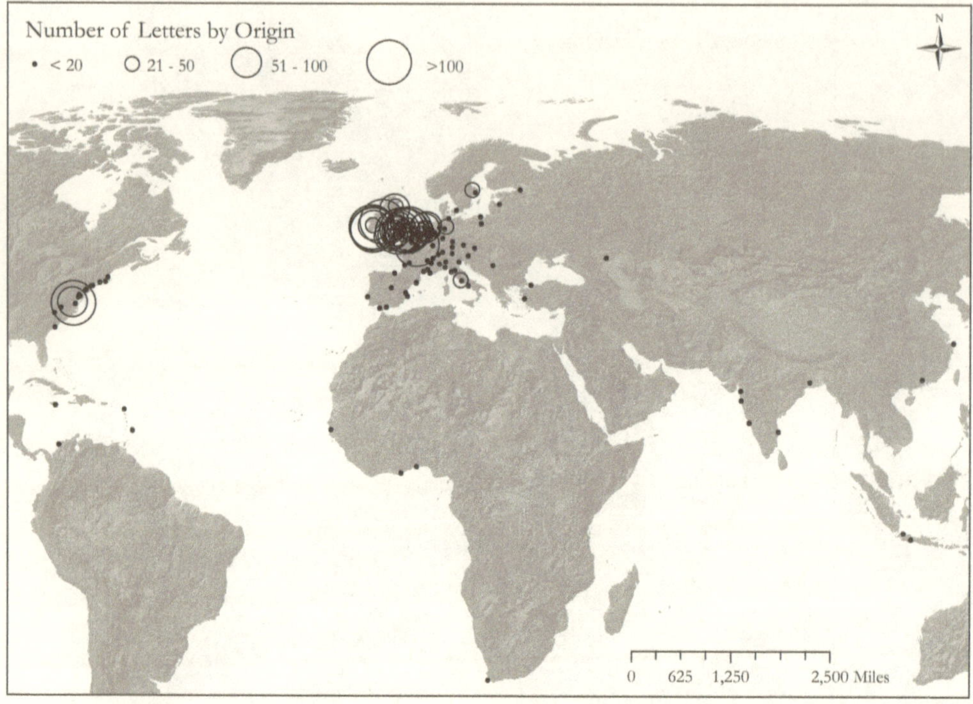

Figure 6. Number of letters originating from locations worldwide from the sets of correspondence examined. This map shows where the correspondents examined dated their letters from all over the globe, allowing for larger circles around locations where many letters originated. Only locations with more than twenty letters originating from the British Isles and the Continent are shown for those areas of the globe.

shift. The letters cluster around London, Paris, and the Dutch Randstad, and then surface around the larger cities of the Italian Peninsula: Milan, Venice, Florence, Rome, and Naples. Letters also came to and from other centers, such as Madrid, which was a growing administrative center, and Lisbon, an Atlantic port. In fact, letters originated from 68 percent of the forty-four cities on the Continent with populations of over 40,000.

This pattern holds in the British Isles as well. As the largest city in Europe and the lodestar of the British world, London dominated this epistolary world. Every correspondent sent or received a letter from the city on the Thames and half of their English letters came from there. Letters from the capital helped their receivers keep track of political occurrences, their economic well-being, and the social whirl of the season. Urban life was becoming intensified for the British elite: most spent some time in the West End of London, participated in activities that nurtured elite ties, and remained in contact with their urban connections after they left.[8] These letters also reveal England's growing polycentric nature. Social, commercial, administrative, and industrial centers were all expanding and letters flowed in from these locations.[9] Seventy-five percent of the correspondents received or sent a letter from Bath, "the queen of the spas."[10] Over half the correspondents sent or received letters from Dublin and Bristol, cities that owed their expansion to the British state's need to rule Ireland, in the case of Dublin, and the expansion of Atlantic trade, in the case of Bristol.[11] Having urban connections was important to most Britons and letters provided them with a way to keep track of these bustling centers.

These maps reflect the view contemporaries had of their own world. Writers complained when they were far from urban centers. William Byrd II of Virginia declared, "Tis a mighty misfortune for an Epistolizer not to live near some great city like London or Paris, where people play the fool in a well-bred way, & furnish their Neighbours with discourse."[12] A correspondent of Hans Sloane harrumphed that he was "buried alive" in Castle Rising, Norfolk, about one hundred miles from London.[13] Often they described their position in relation to the traditional country and city divide, popular in literary works, where the vibrant, but dangerous city was contrasted with the dull, but innocent country.[14] Authors sending letters within England put this literary device to work by referring to their residence as being generally in the city or the country. John Perceval's cousin compared John's letters to a beneficial tonic and reminded his London relative not to "neglect your Country Patient," and when Perceval resided in London his tutor hoped that he and his brother or the "court Politicians" would "have pitty on the Country ones" and provide him with news. [15] Others simply referred to their location as "the Country" rather than mentioning the specific place. When complaining about a lack of news and an excess of time, they knew that referencing their position in "the Country" was enough to explain their slim letters.[16] Thus, in their letters, writers constructed an England divided into two zones: the urban, which buzzed with people and conversation, and the rural, which only echoed with lone birdcalls. However, besides a few laments about distance and a few comments about the problems and benefits related to being in the country, place is not discussed very often in letters that stayed within English borders. The distance between rural England and urban England was not great, and it was, especially for the elite, easily traversed.

For those who saw themselves as members of a wider British elite, but lived in Scotland and Ireland, such descriptions of place surfaced more often. While both locations had flourishing urban centers, when their writers spoke of their location they usually detailed their rural isolation. While the idea of the virtuous and bucolic countryside surfaces at times, as when John Boyle declared Ireland "the land of ignorance, but at the same time, the land of milk and honey," for the most part writers derided the rural lifestyle.[17] Rural Ireland and Scotland were dirtier and duller than England. John Boyle described Cork by stating, "The Butchers are as greasy, The Quakers as formal, & the Presbyterians as holy & full of the Lord as usual: All Things are in status quo: even the Hogs and Piggs gruntle in the same cadence as of yore."[18] A similar view of Scotland emerges from a letter Perceval wrote about his brief stay there. After entering a tavern so smoky that, even though it masked "the stink," he could not see the proffered glass of wine, and after avoiding the butter, which "was of 20 colours, & Stuck with hair," he kept his gloves on to avoid the lice, ate, and promptly recrossed the border.[19] Such depictions allowed Boyle and Perceval to show their correspondents that this was certainly not a world that they belonged to; the comedy comes from the incongruity of their presence.

The world these individuals did belong to, however, was not strictly an English world, but rather one defined by a group of people usually centered in London. What concerned Boyle about Cork was its lack of excitement: everything is "as usual," "in status quo," and "in the same cadence of yore." It was "dull, insipid, and void of all Amusement."[20] Similarly, one of Hans Sloane's Scottish correspondents declared that in Dundee he was "living in a corner of the world" and that Coupar Angus was "a Country place without Converse."[21] These correspondents wanted the amusement and converse they knew flourished in London. This was a world where cultural and social distance mattered more than specific geographic coordinates. They also knew that letters were a way to reconnect with that world. They mentioned their isolation and the dullness of their surroundings to explain the lack of content in their letters, to enliven them, and to remind their correspondents of their need for letters; they were their connection to the bustling centers of elite sociability.

The fact that the same tropes surface in letters from the European continent supports the idea that letter writers saw themselves as connected by networks of sociability. Like writers in Britain, those who lived outside urban centers on the Continent worried what distance could do to their social or intellectual networks. Uppsala might have been a flourishing university town, but for Karl Linnaeus it limited his ability to join in the more lively and fast-paced intellectual discussions occurring in places like London and he envied those, like Peter Collinson, "who have a free & frequent Intercourse with your World."[22] British travelers also found the continental countryside less congenial than continental centers. On his trip to France in 1725, John Perceval and his brood went to Blois, but the dullness of the place soon sent them hurrying back to Paris.[23] These men valued ties to urban centers because they connected them to wider networks and centers of discussion.

Worries about specific geographic origins remained, however. Superficially, members of the Scottish and Irish elite faced the same situation as their English counterparts. Both groups lived in their great houses when at their estates and all were spending less time on these estates and more time in London, and both were allowing power to flow into the hands of the local inhabitants.[24] Those with lands and titles in Scotland and Ireland found their ways to the centers of elite sociability. John Boyle, an Irish lord himself, declared that Bath was "full of Poetry, of Pamphlets, of Lords and of Irishmen."[25] However, there is a reason he mentions the Irish separately. Their situation was different and much less secure than those with land in England. John Perceval continuously griped about the way the English treated Irish absentee landowners and constantly justified his English residency.[26] Men like Boyle and Perceval attempted to increase their sense of belonging by emphasizing their sense of disconnect from their location; they were not Irish or Scottish landlords, but rather members of a larger elite whose values and concerns were the same as those in London.

Those living in the colonies attempted to reaffirm their sense of belonging by expressing a desire for urban life as well. While, as a whole, the North American colonies were becoming more urbanized, Virginia and other colonies still lacked urban centers and letter writers settled there lamented the fact. [27] William Byrd II hoped that shifting the capital from Jamestown to Williamsburg would "give people a relish for cohabitacion."[28] But during his lifetime urban life in Virginia remained mostly a dream and he continued to depend on letters for urban news. From another corner of North America another correspondent in Rhode Island complained, "We have passed the Winter in a profound Solitude on my farm in this Island, all my Companions having been a lured five or six months ago to Boston, the great place of pleasure and resort in these parts where they still continue."[29] Just as writers in Norfolk, Cork, and Dundee sighed over their lack of amusement and converse, colonial writers longed for cohabitation and "places of pleasure and resort." William Byrd II attempted to close the gap by sharing the gossip of Virginia as he would have shared that of London. In one letter he delighted in telling the story of a Venetian courtesan who caused a scandal at a Virginia ball when her artificially inflated breasts deflated. However, he prefaced the story by admitting that due to the lack of gossip he often had to "lard a little truth with a great deal of fiction" when sending stories back to England.[30] The lack of urban sociability in the colonies, especially in Virginia, made it harder for the colonists to participate in a culture that defined status and belonging by one's social performance and polish.

One way to counter this concern was to make rural existence a positive trait. William Byrd II, especially, drew an idealized picture of rural Virginia.[31] He sighed over his lack of gossip and confessed, "But alas what can we poor hermits do, who know of no intrigues, but such as are carry'd on by the amorous turtles, or some such innocent lovers?"[32] Unlike Irish correspondents, Byrd could paint Virginian dullness as a positive attribute. Virginians might live like hermits, but they were innocent of many of the follies that enveloped urban dwellers. More often in Byrd's letters it was London that was the dirty and dangerous spot. He exclaimed to a correspondent there, "Tis miraculous that any lungs can breath in an air compounded of so many different vapours and exhalations, like that of dirty London." Virginia on the other hand had "pure air."[33] It was in this same letter that Byrd famously declared, "Like one of the patriarchs, I have my flock and my herds, my bond-men and bond-women, and every soart of trade amongst my own servants, so that I live in a kind of independence on every one, but Providence." Here was the ultimate pastoral retreat, detached from the pressures of the modern world and from the dependence on others that so marked the lives of Englishmen at home. The Irish could not follow suit. When John Boyle attempted to declare himself a patriarch, his friend in England replied, "Contend, my dear Lord, as much as you please for the justness of your simile, yet you are not at all like one of the old patriarchs."[34] Byrd's British correspondents lived so far distant from Virginia that they could not puncture his images as easily.

Byrd pushed the old city and country divide farther by layering colonial rhetoric about the age of America on top of it. Virginia was an untouched virgin landscape, new and innocent. The age of the Americas was long debated, but there was a sense that even if the land itself was as old as that of Europe, it had not faced intense cultivation and that the society itself was in its infant state.[35] Peter Collinson believed that in 1762 the colonies were just starting "to Walk alone."[36] Forty years earlier, Byrd insisted in his letters that if his correspondent could but smell the ground he would see it was "as if it newly came out of it's makers hands." On the other hand, English ground "has been tortured, and torn to pieces some thousands of years." In his account no one in Virginia got consumption, the water was sweeter, the fire clearer, the plants more digestible, and the fruits "more sprightly flavoured," the meats "more savoury," and he declared that when they found them he was sure that the metals would "prove all ripened into gold and silver."[37] He pushed his lavish praise to the point that Virginia became another Eden where colonists even avoided the curse of hard labor.[38] All this was hyperbole. The death rate in Virginia was high, they never found gold and silver, and Byrd's slaves certainly did not think they had escaped the curse of hard labor.[39] But Byrd's purpose was not to sell a true portrait of Virginia but to entertain his correspondent, and he also knew that since very few of them would ever come out to Virginia "larding the truth with a little fiction" was a safe venture. Due to the distanced and stylized communication provided by letters, Byrd could emphasize the better and, perhaps unconsciously, smooth over the differences between his two worlds.

When Irish letter writers used the same images, the optimistic spin was missing. When one of Perceval's correspondents declared that Ireland was a nation "in its nonage" he did not declare its land sweeter, rather he used the metaphor to bitterly portray the English as guardians "who do every thing for us, and leave us the liberty of transacting nothing material our selves . . . yet for all that we are not free from faction and discord any more than our neighbours."[40] This was not an image meant to draw souls to Ireland. Virginia was distant enough and shrouded in enough colonial rhetoric to allow Byrd to use his distance to his advantage, but doing so in Ireland was more difficult.

Still, those residing in Ireland and those settled in the colonies often saw the links between their situations. When an acquaintance of John Perceval's aired his ideas on colonial policy (he thought that the ignorance of the inhabitants, religious or otherwise, was "Englands Security") he lumped the Irish in with the Americans, but what incensed Perceval was not his linking of the two, but his condemnation of learning.[41] In fact, one of the threads that tied Byrd to Perceval was their peripheral origin. After congratulating Byrd on his success with the Council of Trade and Plantations, Perceval sighed, "How happy are you in your World compared with the Inhabitants of Ireland," as he reflected on the recent loss of the right of appeal by the Irish House of Lords.[42] Both Byrd and Perceval wanted to be enmeshed in elite social networks, but each saw themselves as protectors of the lands of their birth.[43] Byrd and Perceval were not internally torn between their colonial and English identities; they emphasized both in their letters. They saw themselves as members of a broader British elite even if they feared that they sat upon its periphery. To a degree this was a product of the greater Anglicanization of the British elite, but rather than simply a story of colonial acculturation it should be seen as one of elite formation that encompassed the entire British World.[44] Regional identity mattered, but how their location affected their relationship within larger networks mattered more. Belonging to the "world" had more to do with presenting urban polish and maintaining active social networks than with the exact location of one's residence. This is why most correspondents emphasized the city and country divide when discussing place. They knew their world was one of urban centers and rural peripheries and that letters allowed them to reconnect with the heart of their social circle.

Stability and Mobility

Urban centers and rural peripheries defined how letter writers saw their world, but their stability or mobility defined the nature of their networks. Being a stable epistolary link on the periphery could give one power in a network, even if mobile correspondents maintained more connections. Examining the stability and mobility of ties reveals the differences between most kinds of colonial connections and most types of continental ties. The majority of letters from those in the colonies came from individuals who had settled on distant shores, purchased estates, and remained tied to that place. Their letters to England nurtured constant ties. William Byrd II expected letters yearly from John Perceval and his other English correspondents. Here quality trumped quantity. Twice as many letters came from and went to those across the English Channel, but usually these letters were the product of mobile British correspondents rather than constant continental connections. Letters to the Continent usually reveal the need to maintain British connections rather than an attempt to sustain deep ties to other Europeans.

Colonial correspondents found power in their distance and stability. Members of the British elite were becoming increasingly entangled in the wider world, but few ever traversed it. The two William Byrds of Virginia and Hans Sloane, who spent time in Jamaica, were the only letter writers examined who ever crossed the Atlantic or visited the world beyond the well-worn grooves of the continental tour. Other Atlantic sojourners lay hidden within the sets of correspondence, though, for most of the letter writers had colonial ties and interests, even if they lacked colonial experience. Every correspondent examined either sent or received a letter from the North American colonies and many received letters from those in the West Indies, India, and Africa.[45] Some of these connections were family ties, like Nicholas Blundell's with his brother in the Chesapeake. Some were links with friends, like Cassandra Brydges' correspondent in Antigua. Others were of a scientific bent, like those between Hans Sloane and William Byrd II or Peter Collinson and Cadwallader Colden of New York. Correspondents back in England were interested in the colonies. John Perceval wanted to know about Bermuda because his good friend was attempting to establish a college there. He even vaguely contemplated moving there for his wife's health and the whole Perceval family had lengthy conversations about it.[46] This interest manifested itself again when Perceval became involved in the establishment of the colony of Georgia. Cassandra and James Brydges never considered a move to the colonies, but they did have an Indian king and queen from Georgia over for dinner on 18 October 1734.[47] Writers concerned with natural history and botany wanted to know more about the colonies: Hans Sloane wrote a natural history of Jamaica, Peter Collinson placed a description of North Carolina in his commonplace book, and the Royal Society was happy to receive the curiosities Byrd sent from the colonies.[48] These colonial connections were distant ties that writers wished to nourish, and colonists played on this. They, more than other travelers, used their distance to their advantage.

Byrd's distance allowed him to set himself up as an authority on colonial issues and as a reliable colonial connection. When John Perceval was pondering the establishment of Georgia he described the project to Byrd and Byrd replied with his opinions, agreeing that excluding slaves and rum would be a good idea.[49] He did not always concur, however. When Perceval informed him of the plan to build a college in Bermuda to convert the indigenous people, Byrd remained skeptical, asking him where he expected to find any Indians to convert since "There are no Indians at Bermudas, nor within 200 leagues of it upon the Continent, and it will need the gift of Miracles to persuade them to leave their Country and venture themselves upon the great Ocean, on the temptation of being converted."[50] Here Byrd's greater knowledge about the region shines through. Byrd made sure his correspondents called on him when they needed colonial assistance. When a friend of his had a difficult time settling in Virginia Perceval called on Byrd to help him and Byrd gladly obliged.[51] This was the positive side of distance and stability, for while it strained connections, it also made those links special.

William Byrd II repeatedly used his colonial status to make himself and his letters more attractive. When writing to friends in England he used colonial references to spice up his correspondence. He included phrases like "I am with a true Indian sincerity, your humble and obedient servant" or "The many favours I was so happy as to receive from your Lordship in England, stick fast in my memory in all climates, and I believe I could go thro' the ceremony of husquenawing without forgetting them."[52] Byrd then spent the next paragraph describing husquenawing, an initiation ceremony for young boys when they were to forget their youth. The description intrigued the receiver and he wrote in the margin of his letter book: "The Ceremony of husquenawing (among the Indians) described."[53] In another letter, Byrd threatened to haunt his sister-in-law with the help of an Indian magician.[54] When he found that the Royal Society had not listed him as a member in 1741, he reminded them that "I am alive, and by the help of ginseng hope to survive some years longer."[55] When forgotten, Byrd promoted colonial products such as ginseng to remind his correspondents of his colonial knowledge and thus of his importance. These kinds of descriptions did find an audience in England. Years later John Eliot's cousin wrote, "I have heard it said of the Indians in America that they always put up the first offense from the Whites, attributing it either to Mistake or Ignorance, we should do well to follow their example herein."[56] Interest in the Americas allowed colonists to slip small rarities into their letters to strengthen their epistolary connections.

However, many letter writers did not need to depend on their distant origins to maintain connections because they were but ephemeral visitors to these locations. A number of correspondents who wrote from beyond British shores were mobile correspondents, such as army officers, government officials, or traveling intellectuals who journeyed around the globe for shorter periods of time. Their residence in these strange places was finite and they could hope to reconnect with those who made up the centers of their world soon. These more mobile correspondents were like those who spent time on the Continent. For many, travel to the Continent was easier and more common than trips to the wilds of Ireland and Scotland or voyages across the Atlantic. Many members of the British elite were familiar with its social centers. Nicholas Blundell, a Catholic, had a continental education and strategically lived in Flanders during the aftermath of the 1715 Jacobite Rising.

William Byrd II spent some time training at a merchant's firm in Rotterdam and James Brydges lived in the Dutch Republic for a time when he served as paymaster to the queen's forces. Both John Boyle and John Perceval traveled throughout Europe. Hans Sloane studied in Montpellier and the only time Peter Collinson left English shores was to travel to the Dutch Republic. However, none of these correspondents settled on the European continent. They were not stable connections.

Many of the letters that hailed from the European continent were from British travelers. The Grand Tour was gaining in popularity as the eighteenth century progressed and continental countries provided British gentlemen with a counterpoint to their own society.[57] To a degree, this desire to travel to the Continent was a British acknowledgment that they did not necessarily sit at the center of the European world. As late as 1755 Londoner Peter Collinson declared Nuremburg "the Fountain of Ingenuity & Art, which flows on Every Side through your neighboring Countries" and sighed that "its Circulation is Stop'd to poor remote England."[58] Collinson was certainly flattering his correspondent, but his comment shows that many Britons still saw the Continent as a center of learning and culture and valued connections to it. British gentlemen traveled across it to gain the ability to judge their own homeland. John Perceval's early travels around the Continent were to allow him to meet and judge "Men of all Countrys, & Degrees, their Tempers, modes of living, and Employments."[59] He was to see other places, meet new acquaintances, and gather ideas he could employ when he returned. For many Britons this meant seeing all the Continent had to offer and then judging England superior or equal. As George Berkeley, Perceval's dear friend, declared in the midst of an extended trip: "I have seen enough to be satisfied that England has ye most learning, ye most riches, ye best Government, ye best people, & ye best religion in ye world."[60] In many ways, the Continent remained a troublingly alien place. There was always a frisson of danger reflected in letters from the Continent; travelers carried guns with them in their carriages and superstitious rites were always just around the corner.[61] Many travelers kept the expected journals of their movements, which signaled that they were experiencing the Continent, but were not part of it.[62]

According to their letters, British travelers spent most of their time with other Britons. When Perceval returned to England after his first trip he corresponded with Lorenzo Magnolfi, a Florentine deeply involved in the Italian art world, and the Grand Duke of Tuscany, but when he received news of his circle of friends in Florence or Rome it consisted mostly of news relating to English gentlemen.[63] On a later trip, he mixed with a number of French acquaintances, most of whom were relatives of his wife, but the majority of his letters detail his English connections in France, such as the Marquis of Blandford and the Duke of Beaufort.[64] Letters from the Continent contained travel reports on what the writers had seen and done, but the main purpose of these letters was to keep that writer in contact with his or her social world at home. The point of the epistolary links these British writers maintained with those across the Channel was not to monitor continental contacts, but to keep track of British correspondents who were at present residing on the other side of the English Channel.

Those traveling through the Continent were eager to keep track of their social network back home. They wished to know how family members fared and whether their business affairs flourished, and in return they sent welcomed continental news. When John Perceval traveled to France in 1725, he kept a journal recording what he saw and what he thought about what he saw, but his letters contain the true journal of his social world.[65] He mostly corresponded with his cousin and brother-in-law, Daniel Dering, his brother, Philip Perceval, and his cousin, Edward Southwell, three of the strongest nodes in his social network. He told them of his travels, of French news, of those he visited, and he plied them with questions about his social circle at home. The mobility of his wider network is brought home by the fact that his cousin's son, Edward Southwell the younger, was traveling in Italy at the same time. Perceval reported back on his progress to his anxious father back in England.[66] These two members of the Perceval-Southwell clan enjoyed their European travels, but the point of their letters was to maintain their larger social network centered in Britain. John Perceval knew he had little to say from Rome that would interest his aunt back in England and so he declared she should not expect many letters from him for it was "unreasonable to enact from me brick where there is no straw."[67] British letter writers had many ties to the Continent: they traveled there, fought there, and were deeply concerned about occurrences there, but rarely were their social networks centered or embedded there. The Continent mattered to the British, but it was not part of the wider British world.

As maps of the epistolary world reveal, letters poured in from all corners of the globe. But different distances called for different types of connection because the British population experienced locations differently. Colonial letter writers noted distance the most often because they were simply farther away and thus possessed strained networks, but also because distance provided them with power. It made them valuable correspondents for those with

Atlantic interests but few Atlantic ties. Colonists, due to their geographic stability, were also more likely to be constant and long-lasting correspondents. Continental ties were ever present and continued to affect British life as much as colonial affairs. It was across the Channel that the British traveled, fought, and looked for news. But the epistolary ties between the two were more ephemeral since, for those traveling, keeping their networks at home taut was more important than creating new Continental ties. They were dealing with the challenges of mobility rather than those of stability. Recognizing the importance of mobility for the British elite highlights the limitations of simply mapping the locations of origin of letters to show the way the British experienced their geographic world. Such maps are too static and undifferentiated. They need to be set into motion.

Mobile Networks and Epistolary Anchors

Places of origin can, however, gesture to the mobility of these writers. Letters sent from the Downs, a sheltered area off the Kentish coast where ships safely anchored, usually came from individuals aboard a ship.[68] Many from Chester and Bristol were from those awaiting transport to Ireland.[69] The letter noted from the Cape of Good Hope was from a correspondent on a voyage to eastern Africa.[70] One of Hans Sloane's correspondents dated his letter "From on Board the Eaton Frigatt at anchor near Banjar on Borneo July 29, 1700" and noted that his last letter had been from the tip of Africa.[71] These were men and women on the move.

This frequent mobility could alter the composition of epistolary networks. John Perceval often stopped receiving letters from one of his most frequent correspondents, Daniel Dering, because Dering had joined Perceval in Bath or because Perceval now resided in London alongside Dering. Perceval and his close correspondents would alternate letter-writing duties as they moved. From London Daniel Dering expressed his happiness that Perceval was to return to the capital from Bath and noted that "now it wil be your turn to be troubled with my Epistles," since Dering was soon to travel to the Continent for his health.[72] Each enjoyed having epistolary anchors in urban centers when they shifted away from them. Perceval's other correspondents were as mobile as he and Dering. An acquaintance, Velters Cornwall, sent him letters from London and Wales.[73] From his brother-in-law he received letters from London, Calais, Spa, Leiden, and Rochester.[74] From his good friend George Berkeley he received letters from London, Dublin,

Livorno, and Rhode Island. All this mobility made correspondents hard to keep track of, however, and it meant that writers were often absent from the centers of their concerns. But they could put this mobility to work. Sending information on common acquaintances by letter while on the move was a service many letter writers provided for their correspondents. When Perceval was in Bath, Velters Cornwall kept him abreast of political machinations in London and checked on Perceval's children at Charlton, and when he was in France John Perceval kept an eye on Southwell's son.[75]

Letter writing increased in the late seventeenth and early eighteenth centuries not only because more Britons could write and had a postal service to use but because the geographic expansion of the British world and the mobility of the elite created a need to monitor multiple locations and acquaintances. This mobility created epistolary need, but the worlds these writers wished to connect with and the frequency and direction of their mobility varied according to the individual. Looking at why letter writers chose to write to certain locations at certain times deepens our understanding of the nature of their world. Scholars often assume that writers composed letters to connect with others at a distance, but such writers did not connect with everyone they knew at a distance and not all letters traveled lengthy distances. This section looks at the epistolary networks of three letters writers from three corners of the British world over the course of a year: Nicholas Blundell, a member of the Lancashire gentry and a Catholic; John Perceval, Irish baronet and London resident; and William Byrd II, Virginia plantation owner and occasional Londoner. It examines the relationship between their local and their epistolary worlds by comparing their diaries to their letters. Approaching letters in this fashion demonstrates the geographic flexibility of epistolary networks and points to the fact that no matter how embedded in their local world writers were, they were still drawn into the concerns of the widening British world.

Nicholas Blundell, John Perceval, and William Byrd II lived far from each other, but all felt the need to keep detailed diaries and letter books. Blundell kept a "Great Diurnal" almost uninterrupted from 1702 to 1728 and kept a letter-book of much of his outgoing correspondence during the same period.[76] John Perceval kept a diary between 1730 and 1747.[77] His personal letter books, neatly copied and almost obsessively indexed, of incoming and outgoing mail from 1697 to 1731 survive, as does his estate correspondence from 1699 until his death in 1748.[78] William Byrd II's record keeping or its survival was a bit more erratic. Three of his diaries have survived from 1709–

1712, 1717–1721, and 1739–1741, and he transcribed many of his outgoing letters into notebooks throughout the period.[79] A comparison of these writers' local webs, as reflected in their diaries, and their epistolary networks, which surfaced in their letters, reveals when they turned to letters and the level of importance those letters held for them.

Each diary elucidates the texture of its author's everyday existence. In many ways, according to their diaries, the lives of these men did not differ substantially. The last day of May 1720 found William Byrd traveling home on a rainy day with two friends after a visit to a neighboring plantation and then walking over to his neighbor's for a dinner of chicken pie and the company of another set of acquaintances.[80] On the same day some three thousand miles away Nicholas Blundell visited a new barn, smoked a pipe with friends, and entertained some guests at Little Crosby.[81] Twenty years later William Byrd still participated in many of the same activities. On 25 April 1740 he awoke in Williamsburg, read his Hebrew and Greek, had coffee after his exercises, and then wrote letters before going to court. He then dined on chicken and asparagus at a local tavern, met with a ship's captain, and called on Lady Randolph.[82] In London, on the same day, John Perceval visited multiple acquaintances before dining with his brother and visiting with Mr. Vernon.[83] On the surface all their lives revolved around maintaining local ties and dealing with the trials and tribulations of running an agricultural estate or, as is clear in other segments of Perceval's diary, negotiating the webs of power that crisscrossed the capital. Differences, of course, abound. Not only did Byrd's estate produce a cash crop and depend on slave labor, but he was many miles from the centers of power in London, and Nicholas Blundell rarely left his estate or worried about London social connections as both Byrd and Perceval did. But all their diaries show the importance of being connected to others and nurturing those links.

Of the three Nicholas Blundell was the most rooted in a single locality. He was born in Little Crosby, Lancashire, in 1669 and for most of his life it was the center of his world. He was a member of a long-established and long-suffering Catholic recusant family and while he was never imprisoned like many of his forbearers he was educated abroad at St. Omers in Flanders and found it convenient to flee to Flanders after the Jacobite Rising in 1715.[84] However, as his diary and even his letters make clear, Little Crosby was his life. He watched and worried about his crops and his tenants, smoked his pipe with his neighbors, and visited and dined with other members of the local gentry. His world revolved around this core of gentry families who moved with relative ease between each other's houses. These men and women visited together, dined together, and lodged together.[85] The men drank and gamed together. These acts nurtured local relationships and neighbors noticed slights. Blundell, who rarely recorded events that did not happen, noted the failure of a local noblewoman to pay an afternoon visit.[86] This local gentry community was tightly knit and depended on face-to-face interaction to hold itself together.

John Perceval was much more mobile. He was born in 1683 in county Cork in Ireland, but Irish upheavals soon sent him to England and for the rest of his life he struggled to balance his English life and his Irish legacy. He crossed the Irish Sea on numerous occasions and he even lived in Dublin and at his estates for a number of years, but the heart of his world was in London. Even when in England, however, he was hardly a rooted figure like Blundell. He spent most of his winters in London, but he moved downriver to Charlton in the summer, and often traveled to Bath or across the Channel. In his early twenties he toured the Continent and he would return periodically throughout his life: to France, Holland, and Flanders in 1718 and to Spa in the Southern Netherlands in 1723. But like Blundell, visits with friends and acquaintances dominated his day-to-day existence. Many a diary entry noted who he visited and who came for dinner. For him these were important events to keep track of since they showed the health of his social world.

During his life William Byrd II probably traveled more miles than either Blundell or Perceval. Byrd was born in Virginia in 1674, but like Perceval he found himself sent to English shores at a young age. He spent most of the first twenty years of his life in England, moving between his relatives in Essex and acquaintances in London. Before returning to Virginia for an extended stay after his father's death in 1704 he had traveled all around England, briefly into Scotland, and across the Channel to Rotterdam. Just as Perceval crossed the English Channel and Irish Sea multiple times during his lifetime, Byrd ventured across the Atlantic seven times after his first childhood journey. But, like his two contemporaries, whether he was in Virginia or London he was deeply enmeshed in the social world around him. Like the other diarists he was sure to include whom he dined with (and often what he dined on) and whom he visited.

As their diaries show, these men depended on face-to-face interaction to run their social worlds. The less personal and less effective letter was an undesirable alternative. As John Perceval told his uncle regarding a position for his cousin: "we all know that no business, especially of such a nature is ever so effectually and Speedily done by letter as in person."[87] However, all three had to increasingly turn to letters to manage their affairs. Letters helped individuals organize their local communities and they provided greater control at a distance.

A comparison of the letter books and diaries of all three of these writers for one full year reveals the extent of the overlap between their epistolary worlds and their face-to-face worlds. In the year 1705 Nicholas Blundell dined or visited with 35 percent of his correspondents.[88] In 1730 John Perceval shared a table or visited with 37 percent of his correspondents, and ten years later William Byrd dined or visited with 9 percent of his correspondents.[89] The fact that William Byrd II, John Perceval, and Nicholas Blundell did not record all their letters could have affected these numbers, but it does show which letters these writers chose to record in their letter books as important: for some, like Byrd, letters not linked to their day-to-day social world mattered more. Investigating the overlap between these spheres shows when these writers felt the need to turn to letters and how the changing geographic landscape of the British world pushed many Britons to pick up the pen.

Blundell, Perceval, and Byrd all used their letters to manage their local worlds. About half of the letters Blundell recorded in 1705 dealt with immediate local issues like the rights to a church pew or a bill.[90] These letter exchanges were ephemeral and did not blossom into long-standing correspondences. The stoppage of letters was not taken as a slight on either correspondent's side; rather, they knew they could easily meet in a face-to-face setting. Blundell might have written a letter to Thomas Howet in February 1705, but during that year he not only dined with Howet but also with the two other men mentioned in the letter: John Plumb and Peter Ashton.[91] Similarly, he shared his time, his table, and even his house with other correspondents from that year, such as Viscount Molineux and his cousin Richard Butler.[92] Most of these correspondents lived within a ten-mile radius of Blundell's estate in Little Crosby, which made face-to-face interaction a real possibility. Letters were not the lifeblood of these relationships, face-to-face social visits were.

John Perceval and his correspondents used letters in the same fashion. When his friend Velters Cornwall was ill he simply sent Perceval a letter telling him that he could not make their appointment.[93] Perceval did not lament the loss of his company for he had invited Cornwall to a concert two days before, walked with him to a committee meeting the previous day, and he would see him at another concert a week and a half later.[94] Like this letter, most local letters dealt with the organization of meetings and the asking of favors. They streamlined social visits or opened the door to them. The letters of Hans Sloane also show the use of letters to make the local world turn. Many of his London letters were more informal requests than formal letters. In one a friend wanted to meet him at the Grecian Coffee-house; a second to set up an afternoon visit; and a third, sent by Peter Collinson, asked if he wanted a hermaphrodite goat Peter had found on an incoming ship.[95] London letters helped John Perceval and other city dwellers organize their face-to-face social world.

It was more difficult for William Byrd II to send letters to those nearby because longer distances separated him from others in his locality, so it is not surprising that his letter book and diary overlap to a lesser degree than either Blundell's or Perceval's. He only mentioned four of his correspondents from 1740 in his diary and he only dined or visited with two of them. He shared a table with Dr. Samuel Tschiffely twice early in the year before sending him a terse letter in November responding to the doctor's complaints about a land deal.[96] He regularly dined with Governor Gooch when he was in Williamsburg in 1740, and he only turned to the pen once when he could not attend a meeting of the council. And he soon had the opportunity to share his opinions in person since he dined with Gooch two weeks later.[97] And while Byrd never recorded them in his letter book, his diary does make reference to six letters he wrote in 1740 to his overseers at the Falls near present-day Richmond where he had land, over twenty-five miles away from his plantation.[98] He also mentioned writing letters home to Westover from Williamsburg twice, a thirty-mile distance.[99] Thus he did use letters to run his local world more than his letter book would suggest, but he was still a much more isolated figure than either Blundell or Perceval and his local world stretched much farther, thirty miles in either direction in fact.[100]

These local letters show that distance alone did not prompt letters and not all letters were products of long-standing and long-nurtured correspondences. Letter writers sent epistles to those nearby to negotiate local social situations and to ease communication, but such letters held varying importance for their writers. Local letters take up a lot of space in Nicholas Blundell's letter book because he had fewer distant connections and possessed deep ties to his local community. John Perceval often turned to letters to manage local affairs because, residing in London as he did, it was easy for him, and because his life in London revolved around social visits and the fast-paced negotiation of political issues, which letters could make simpler and more rapid. William Byrd II may have sent more letters to those around him than he recorded in his letter books, but these were not the letters Byrd valued enough to record. He needed connections to the wider world.

The lack of overlap between William Byrd II's diaries and letters points to the importance correspondence with distant places held for him. He had to keep track of two worlds: one centered in London and one in Virginia. After he permanently returned to Virginia in 1726, he could not visit or dine with his London connections, but through letters he did try to maintain contact. Over half of his surviving letters from 1740 crossed the Atlantic and all but two went to London. They included letters to old friends, his wife's family, merchants, and those with whom he wanted to conduct land deals.

When in Virginia Byrd wanted and needed to connect with London more than any other location. He braided together his letters from the capital to form a lifeline to London polite society. It was a rope created of relationships formed in the crucible of face-to-face interaction. As a young man in London he had formed long-lasting relationships with John Perceval; Edward Southwell, the secretary of state for Ireland; and Charles Wager, who was eventually the First Lord of the Admiralty. In 1701 he had traipsed across the English countryside with a young John Perceval and during his time in England between 1717 and 1721 he visited and dined with the more mature baronet, with Edward Southwell, and with Charles Wager. In fact, on one day he sat with Perceval for an hour and then with Mrs. Southwell for half an hour before dining with Charles Wager on roast beef.[101] Twenty years later, in 1740, he was still writing letters to Wager and Perceval to maintain his social position and his importance as a colonial link. He even penned a letter to the son of Edward Southwell in a desperate attempt to restart a correspondence with that family.[102] In these letters he rarely asked for things, but rather gave news and congratulations and hoped in return they would provide him with information on family affairs and news. These ties kept Byrd up to date on London social and political affairs, but, at times, he also turned to them for assistance. When he found himself struggling with debts to his London factor in 1740 he turned to his long-standing acquaintance, Charles Wager, and asked him for a loan.[103] He also put his English connections to work solving Virginia problems. The next time he wrote Charles Wager he did not ask for a loan, but for his support in providing Mrs. Spotswood, the widow of the former governor of Virginia, with a royal bounty.[104] London letters kept his social connections taut and active both in England and Virginia.

He also looked to family living in London for information and assistance. He wrote three letters to members of his wife's family in London in 1740, which gave news on Virginia and family affairs.[105] In return, these family members and friends sent "domestick news": information on the marriages, births, and deaths in the community surrounding them.[106] In this fashion he could remain part of the community. Byrd also turned to them for help. His sister-in-law began one letter by blaming her late reply on her uncertainty about what goods to send to her sister.[107] These letters added another layer of London connections to his social network, giving it greater strength and flexibility.

Just as important for the functioning of his world on a practical level were Byrd's connections with overseas merchants. In 1740 he recorded three letters from merchants. These letters were critical to keeping his financial world afloat. He wrote to John Hanbury of London about broken merchandise, to Thomas Chamberlayne of Bristol about beginning a possible trading relationship, and he asked Captain Christopher Smith in London for a favor.[108] Through these letters Byrd could keep track of his economic well-being, but they also had a social value. Captains of ships provided him with vital links to London. In his diary he frequently mentioned dining with ships' captains and it was by them that he often sent letters.[109] Thus it should come as no surprise that he often turned to a select number of them to do his bidding in England. In his letter to Captain Christopher Smith he asked him to resolve a misunderstanding regarding a debt when John Hanbury did not respond quickly enough.[110] Byrd's need to connect with London was a financial necessity, but he could also activate his merchant connections to make his social world run more smoothly.

Byrd had not always managed his London life from Virginia; for an extended period in his youth he had to watch over his Virginia concerns from London. When Byrd resided in London, which he did for more than twenty years of his life, he longed for letters from Virginia just as he would later long for those from London. When he resided in England between 1715 and 1720 he used letters to deal with local issues like his courtship of Mary Smith and his negotiations with the commissioners of trade and plantations, but the majority of the letters that survive are to his brother-in-law, John Custis, who watched over his Virginia affairs, and to Philip Ludwell, who shared concerns about Governor Spotswood with Byrd.[111] Custis promised to watch over the shipping of his tobacco, to visit his plantations when he could, and to collect his rents.[112] Even when Custis was ailing and could not be as vigilant, he assured Byrd: "You are not destitute of friends to see your affairs do not suffer here, though indeed I can give you little intelligence of them at present, not knowing my own."[113] In return Byrd watched over Custis's English concerns. He sent him a watch, a map, and prints he desired and looked into a legacy left to Custis's son by his grandfather.[114] The fact that Byrd had interests in two different and far distant locations meant that he had to cultivate different epistolary webs depending on where he resided. Epistolary networks were rarely constant entities; their specific makeup transformed depending on the location of the correspondent.

The need to monitor multiple worlds was not just an Atlantic phenomenon. Many members of the British elite who lived in England needed to turn to letters to connect with those at a distance just as often, if not more often, than their colonial counterparts. Absenteeism was on the rise across the British world as landlords residing in England, Ireland, Scotland, and the American colonies heeded the siren call of the town.[115] So, while John Perceval's Irish estates might have been closer geographically to London, he had to be sure to monitor them as carefully as Byrd did his lands in Virginia. Perceval had to keep track of his Irish estates when he was in London or even in Dublin. In fact, while he never visited Ireland in 1730, almost 20 percent of his correspondence from that year hailed from that isle.[116] Visits and meals with his Irish estate agent, William Taylor, who lived in London for the first six months of the year, augmented the information found in these letters.[117] They often discussed affairs pertaining to his Irish lands, and most of their information came from Irish letters. Taylor himself kept a correspondent in Ireland during his absence who kept him informed, and he, in turn, told Perceval of events.[118] Perceval probably heaved a sigh of relief, however, when his agent returned to Ireland since his information would be more direct, immediate, and trusted. As Custis was Byrd's trusted anchor in Virginia, Taylor was Perceval's in the Cork countryside.

Perceval needed to keep track of political events in Dublin as well and in 1730 he depended on Marmaduke Coghill, the commissioner of the revenue in Ireland and a privy councillor, for information. The two men exchanged political news throughout the year; Perceval providing information on English debates and Coghill on Irish concerns.[119] Perceval valued this correspondence to the extent that he recorded drafts of his letters to Coghill in his diary and in a letter to Coghill he gave him "hearty thanks for the trouble you have given your Self to inform one who has indeed a very great affection for Ireland and a Zeal to Serve her, but had not a knowledge equal there to."[120] This correspondence was vaguely similar to Byrd's correspondence with Philip Ludwell when he was in London presenting his views to the commissioners of trade and plantations on Virginia affairs. Byrd kept Ludwell apprised of English affairs and Ludwell kept him up to date on Virginia happenings. Perceval and Byrd both had to monitor their multiple financial and political worlds. Often they did so by establishing reciprocal relationships with anchors in each location who were usually trusted family members, friends, or employees.

Just as Byrd longed to maintain his London social ties from a distance, Perceval too kept a close eye on London occurrences. When he traveled on the Continent it was letters from London he longed for. Such letters would tell him of the welfare of his family, the occurrences within his social circle, and alert him to important political and economic affairs. Even when he traveled to Bath he had to monitor occurrences in London and thus over 20 percent of his correspondence from 1730 came from acquaintances in London.[121] These letters kept Perceval up to date on the social and political happenings in the capital. In December 1730, while he resided in Bath, he learned of the death of his cousin, Edward Southwell, in London, via a letter, he corresponded with Horace Walpole about obtaining a place for a suppliant, he negotiated his role as a trustee for "D'Alone's legacy for converting negroes," and he received news of a rumor about his son's marriage and quashed it.[122] As a member of Parliament, a member of multiple charitable institutions, and a patron, Perceval needed these connections. He could easily nurture them since he was rarely absent from London for long and he usually resided near a reliable postal route.

John Perceval was the most mobile of the three correspondents. In 1730 alone he changed location four times. He rang in the new year at Charlton, spent the next four months in London, and then traveled to Bath for two months. He then returned to London for the next two months before heading off again to Bath for the last four months of the year. Other years found him on his estates in Ireland, in Dublin, and traveling across the Continent. This mobility, along with his political responsibilities and social desires, made him more dependent on letters than someone like Nicholas Blundell, but his more constant mobility, which often touched upon urban centers, allowed him to keep his social ties taut. He rarely wrote letters to individuals living near him. Between January 1710 and December 1712 only about 3 percent of the almost three hundred letters he exchanged arrived from those residing in the same area.[123] Similarly, only 5 percent of the letters, five of over two hundred, which survive from the year 1730 came from those residing in the same location as Perceval.[124] Even expanding his London world to include Charlton, ten miles down the river, only increases the number to eleven of sixty-five correspondents. Yet, he still mentioned visiting or dining with over 30 percent of his correspondents in his diary for the year 1730. He was able to do so because of his mobility. As he shifted from location to location he reaffirmed his social links with his correspondents through meals and visits.

William Byrd II could not do the same when he was in Virginia and here his distance hurt his social connections. While he managed to maintain his connections with Perceval and John Boyle to the end of his life, other connections quickly faded. His correspondence with the Southwell family sputtered. He declared to John Perceval that they were "so unkind as to drop me, distance beng in their Reckoning the same as Death."[125] Later attempts to establish a correspondence with Southwell's son do not appear to have flourished.[126] His wife experienced similar problems. Her sister admitted to Byrd that she did not include much news in her letter to his wife since "there is such an intire new generation of people sprung up since she left England that were I to give her an account of their actions, it would be rather tiresom than otherways, as she knows nothing of them."[127] Mobility mattered if one wished to keep in touch with a whole social world.

Nicholas Blundell did not share Perceval's or Byrd's desire for London life, and after 1717 he nested happily in Little Crosby. Yet he did write to other locations. Letters to London pepper his letter book. In 1705 he wrote letters to John Gelibrond, Henry Eyre, and Mr. Cole, all of whom resided in London and were among his most constant correspondents.[128] These men helped Blundell deal with money issues and organize his accounts. Cole was his agent for his affairs in Rouen, but Gelibrond and Eyre were closer connections; both were distant cousins who visited Blundell in Little Crosby and partook of his hospitality there. He probably dined with both of them in 1705.[129] London correspondents helped him deal with his more far-flung concerns, but these writers possessed deep ties to his local world and he could still meet them face-to-face and cultivate their friendship with visits and food. He did not need to travel to retain these friendships because his friends came home and visited him. Their mobility made maintaining the connection easy.

But even Nicholas Blundell's correspondence exhibits the need for wide-ranging connections. While he himself rarely traveled beyond Lancashire and he did not have estates or political connections elsewhere, he was an anchor for others. Many of his brothers and sisters settled far from the environs of

Little Crosby. For generations the women of his family who did not marry settled in convents on the Continent. At least two of his aunts lived across the Channel, and his mother settled there late in life, joining four of his sisters. Eventually his two daughters spent time in a continental convent as well before their marriages. This is the reason many of his letters went to Mr. Cole in London, his agent for Rouen. Blundell monitored the financial situation of his aunts and sisters and he supplied them with information on the world they had left. In 1705, when he was busy maintaining his local community through drinks and visits, he also received a letter from his sister Margaret taking him to task for not writing her a letter. He defended himself by declaring that he had thought that the oral account by her servant would satisfy her, but he quickly told her of his daughter, wife, aunt, brother, and other local connections.[130] When his mother entered a convent in Ghent in 1707 he began to send her similar letters. It became his "old custom" to send "domestick news."[131] His letters told her of the deaths, births, and marriages that marked their small community and even of the "sad misfortune" of an undermaid who died from severe burns after falling into boiling water.[132] Even when he began to fear that their religious vocations made such "trifles" distractions rather than desired bits of news he continued to send them.[133] Blundell looked to letters to stay connected with his mother, aunts, sisters, and daughters on the Continent, but they depended on his letters to stay connected with the world they had left behind.

Richard Blundell, Nicholas's brother in the Chesapeake, relied on his sibling to an even greater extent than his sisters. One of the first letters in Blundell's letter book is to his brother and in it he declares that one of the purposes of his letters was to "set down many things that happened, to acquaint you with & let you see I am not forgetfull of you."[134] The four letters to Richard that Blundell recorded before his brother's death are full of both personal details and business dealings. In the first, sent in September, he informed Richard of their father's death and then proceeded to produce a lengthy letter detailing the different goods he had gathered for his brother. He was sending him hats, thin wigs, "ye lightest I could find," a "Plush saddle & cavat with Gold Fringe," black stockings, gloves, some shot and lead, and ink, among other things.[135] Gathering such goods was not a simple task. He visited local craftsmen and the Chester and Liverpool fairs looking for just the right goods. The rest of his letters follow this pattern. The next, sent in January, told him of changes on the estate, recent deaths and marriages, and that Nicholas was sending him butter and cheese, which he heard "will be a good Commodity."[136] The other letters held advice on how to deal with his employers in Liverpool and news about the clogs he was sending.[137] Squeezed within these records of business help were tidbits of "domestick news." In fact, he noted in his letter book at the end of the last two letters that he had not transcribed the whole of the letter for it was "not materiall relaiting chiefly to oure Neighbours & Frends."[138] Nicholas did not need these details for his records, but his brother needed them to keep track of the world in Lancashire.

Unsurprisingly, John Perceval was also an anchor in the networks of those far from English shores. In 1730 he received three letters and sent three letters to the American colonies. He exchanged two letters with his old friend George Berkeley who was living in Rhode Island and one with his friend William Byrd II. In his letters to Berkeley he provided him with updates on Berkeley's financial affairs, the activities of the Perceval family circle, whom he knew well, and on the success, or lack thereof, of his scheme for erecting a school in Bermuda for "the Spreading of Religion and learning in America."[139] In his letter to Byrd, Perceval told him of the fates of his old acquaintances, the state of international affairs, and sent him information on "the Kanna Root that grows among the Hottentots," which reminded him of the ginseng Byrd had mentioned in his previous letter.[140] Both Byrd and Berkeley depended on Perceval to keep them up to date on English social affairs, international news, and, in the case of Berkeley, on the fate of their joint projects. While the cutting of either of these threads would not have disabled Perceval's larger network of correspondence he did make use of them. In letters to both he introduced James Oglethorpe and his project for settling part of the Carolinas, the colony that would eventually become Georgia. Such a project would deeply appeal to Berkeley's interest in charitable plans with Atlantic dimensions, and Byrd, with his colonial knowledge, could provide information on its feasibility. Thus, like Blundell, Perceval served as a font of news for his distant correspondents and he too benefited from the exchange.

The geographic needs of these different correspondents illuminate the nature of their social worlds and the place of the letter within them. All three men nurtured their local relationships through face-to-face interaction, but increasingly the geographic expansion of the British world and the growing mobility of the elite made many Britons turn to letters to nurture their social, political, and economic ties. Scholars consider the significance of distance seriously when inspecting the lives of colonists, but as the letters of John

Perceval and Nicholas Blundell show the need was much wider. John Perceval's concerns may not have often stretched across three thousand miles of ocean, but he too had to monitor occurrences both in Ireland and England to keep his financial, political, and social worlds afloat. Even the isolated Nicholas Blundell got caught up in these far-reaching webs. His world could function without long-distance connections or letters, but that of his sisters and brothers could not. He served as their anchor in Lancashire, just as John Perceval served as one of William Byrd II's in London.

However, as these networks suggest, it was easier for some to spin these webs and to nurture them. The epistolary networks of John Perceval and Nicholas Blundell overlapped more with their face-to-face networks than did that of William Byrd II. In Blundell's case the difference stems from Blundell's own immobility; he had few far-flung ties to nurture and no wish to connect with London society. The overlap of John Perceval's networks, on the other hand, is due to his mobility and that of his social circle. He was constantly moving between different centers and meeting with epistolary ties as he went. William Byrd did not have this luxury and thus the overlap was less. He had to rely on his letters themselves to maintain his far-flung social world. Perceval was more in demand as an anchor than Byrd or Blundell because of his central positioning, which gave him a denser epistolary network, but fostering such a network was a group effort and Perceval too depended on his connection with Byrd. These correspondents still preferred face-to-face interaction, which kept relationships active and fresh, and power emanated from the center of the British world in London, but their epistolary networks show that the importance of long-distance connections was growing and with it the importance of networks.

ᔕ

Letters writers could and did sent their epistles on journeys all over the globe. Their increased mobility called for it, as did their expanding interests. But more often they sent letters to those close to home. Their main goal was to maintain a large and functioning social network even when they were far from social centers. However, their own mobility or lack thereof affected their ability to do so. The British elite could easily travel from Norfolk to London, but a trip from Virginia to London was more onerous and thus the letters from these places dealt with distance differently. Those living near the centers of the British world like London, Bath, and even Dublin moved between these worlds with greater ease and could send their letters more easily. Their mobility gave them power and made the maintenance of their epistolary networks less of a trial. But stability mattered as well. Mobility allowed the British elite to travel across the Continent, but little held them there. Their epistolary ties to that part of the globe were more ephemeral. On the other hand, while colonists often saw the number of their ties to London withering, those that remained were stronger and more long-lasting than many ties held by Britons in England.

Most letter writers worried more about distance from social hubs than they did about their specific geographic position. Writers from Virginia, Uppsala, Dundee, Cork, and Norfolk all worried about distance in a similar way and for similar reasons: they needed to connect with those in urban centers. In these cities the members of their social world congregated and to keep their socials worlds spinning they needed to keep in touch with them. Luckily for some distant letter writers, those at the center needed those on the periphery to watch over their affairs as the scope of their interests and concerns widened geographically. These writers wrote to hold their multiple worlds together. Understanding the way the British dealt with and experienced distance means looking beyond the way they thought about empire or how those in the three kingdoms negotiated their relationships. All these distances need to be examined as a whole. This allows us to place the Irish experience next to the Virginia experience. It serves as a reminder that the Continent exerted a strong draw for the British. And it simply shows the geographic world that the British elite experienced: a world that was fluid and changing, but which had specific centers around which its different peripheries revolved. The young John Perceval could take a tour of the world by looking at a map on his wall, but the more mature Perceval knew he toured his true world through his letters.

Chapter 3

Networking in the Epistolary World

William Byrd I of Virginia was not one to let a convenient epistolary opportunity pass him by. When he knew of a ship heading eastward, he would hurriedly write multiple letters on a single day to send by the ship's captain. On 20 May 1684 he wrote nine letters and sent them by Captain Wynne. On 31 March the next year he again penned nine letters to go by a different ship. The following March found him dashing off ten letters to give to Captain Ruddes to carry.[1] In this last batch of letters he informed his brother and his three brothers-in-law in England of the birth of his son Warham and thanked them, and his father-in-law, for their care of his daughter "Little Nutty" whom he had sent across the ocean the year before.[2] His letters reached farther into their overlapping social circles and sent messages from Virginian acquaintances and asked after friends and relatives left behind in England. His letters did more than nurture social networks, though. He dealt with the estate of his sister who had passed away in England, attempted to unravel a misunderstanding about an estate of an acquaintance, and discussed business arrangements with his factors.[3] Byrd used these letters to nurture multiple networks that overlapped and intertwined.

Letters were the connective tissue that held together widespread networks. However, while scholars note the networking possibilities of letters, they rarely inspect how letters functioned within networks.[4] As the previous chapter has shown, epistolary networks were fluid creatures whose shape changed depending on the needs of their creators, but not all was fluid. Two different kinds of networks surface in letters. The first are constant networks that were made up of epistolary connections that writers maintained over time. The second were more ephemeral networks that manifested themselves only when writers needed to solve a specific problem. Both kinds of networks worked together to make the social worlds of their creators function. But not everyone had equal access to these networks. Women and those lower in social rank had their networking possibilities curtailed due to their position in society. Analyzing these webs of connection illuminates not only their basic connective ability but also how that connective ability functioned to include and exclude.

To understand epistolary networks it helps to draw them out (see Figures 7–13, 16–18).[5] When accomplished, such networks show the two layers of connection embedded in letters: links to those written to, represented by large symbols, and ties to those written about, denoted by smaller symbols.[6] Those who received letters were usually close acquaintances deeply intertwined with the writer's world. But if a correspondent mentioned other individuals by name within a letter the receiver most likely knew them. By mentioning them the correspondent allowed the receiver to keep abreast of the actions of those connections as well as those of his direct correspondents. One did not need to send or receive a letter to be part of an epistolary network. Acknowledging this second layer of connection broadens the scope of the epistolary world and helps reveal how it functioned.

While the exact composition of these networks changed over time, the nature of the ties they consisted of rarely did. When coded by shape for different types of relationships these networks shade into different subsidiary clusters. The webs become the densest where nodes of friends and family cluster. Then they form subsidiary groupings created by the need to monitor an estate, transatlantic trade, or general business dealings. Many correspondents also had a network that embraced intellectual or institutional ties to individuals or emerging clubs and societies. Inspecting the makeup and functioning of these different clusters shows exactly how members of the British elite controlled their increasingly dispersed world. This chapter focuses on the more traditional networks formed by letters between family members and friends and between supplicants and patrons because these two types of networks highlight the different ways letter writers used their epistles to network and how they continued to depend upon traditional social ties. Usually ties between family members and friends were the most constant and strongest part of epistolary networks, while those between supplicants and patrons were more ephemeral. They illustrates how these two kinds of networks helped the worlds of their creators function and what kinds of connections the British elite valued and why.

"Tyes of Blood and Intimacy": Epistolary Constants

During a discussion about moving to Bermuda the Percevals, unintentionally, revealed the importance of "tyes of Blood and intimacy." John Perceval had sent his brother an account of Bermuda, where a friend of his was trying to persuade acquaintances to settle and Philip playfully responded. They had talked about it, he said, and he, his wife, his daughter, his son, and other relations, specifically, Kit Usher and Mrs. Donnellan, were for it, but his daughter Kitty was against it, and sister Usher thought they were mad. Kitty thought "it a strange thing to leave ones Friends, when after all very few can be called realy so beyond ones own family who have the tyes of Blood and intimacy of many years Standing to induce them to be so."[7]

To a degree Kitty's declaration is a paean to friendship, but it also reveals that friends who were not relatives were hard to find and those with "tyes of Blood and intimacy" were usually family members. Those who participated in the discussion about Bermuda were family. They included Perceval's brother's nuclear family and relatives of Philip's wife, the Ushers and the Donnellans. But what worried Kitty were friends, and she obviously connected those with the lively and diverse family group in which the discussion raged. These family members were friends. Historians have noted the thin line between the two relationships and linked it to the definition of friendship.[8] One's actions, not one's inherent ties, made one a friend. It was this group, which acted for each other and watched over each other, that provided the foundation upon which the worlds of the British elite stood. Certain segments of epistolary networks remained constant and reliance upon family members and friends was such a feature.[9] This is one of the densest parts of John Perceval's network. Figure 7 shows his whole network with his friends and family members highlighted. He wrote to a lot of friends and family members, they wrote back, and they all mentioned one another in their letters. Links between family members and friends were woven into a stable web of support. In fact, without Perceval's presence the network remained strong (Figure 8). Perceval's brother even finished his story by stating, "Thus you see we are something divided as most communitys great or small are."[10] It was the group of family and friends who made up his community.

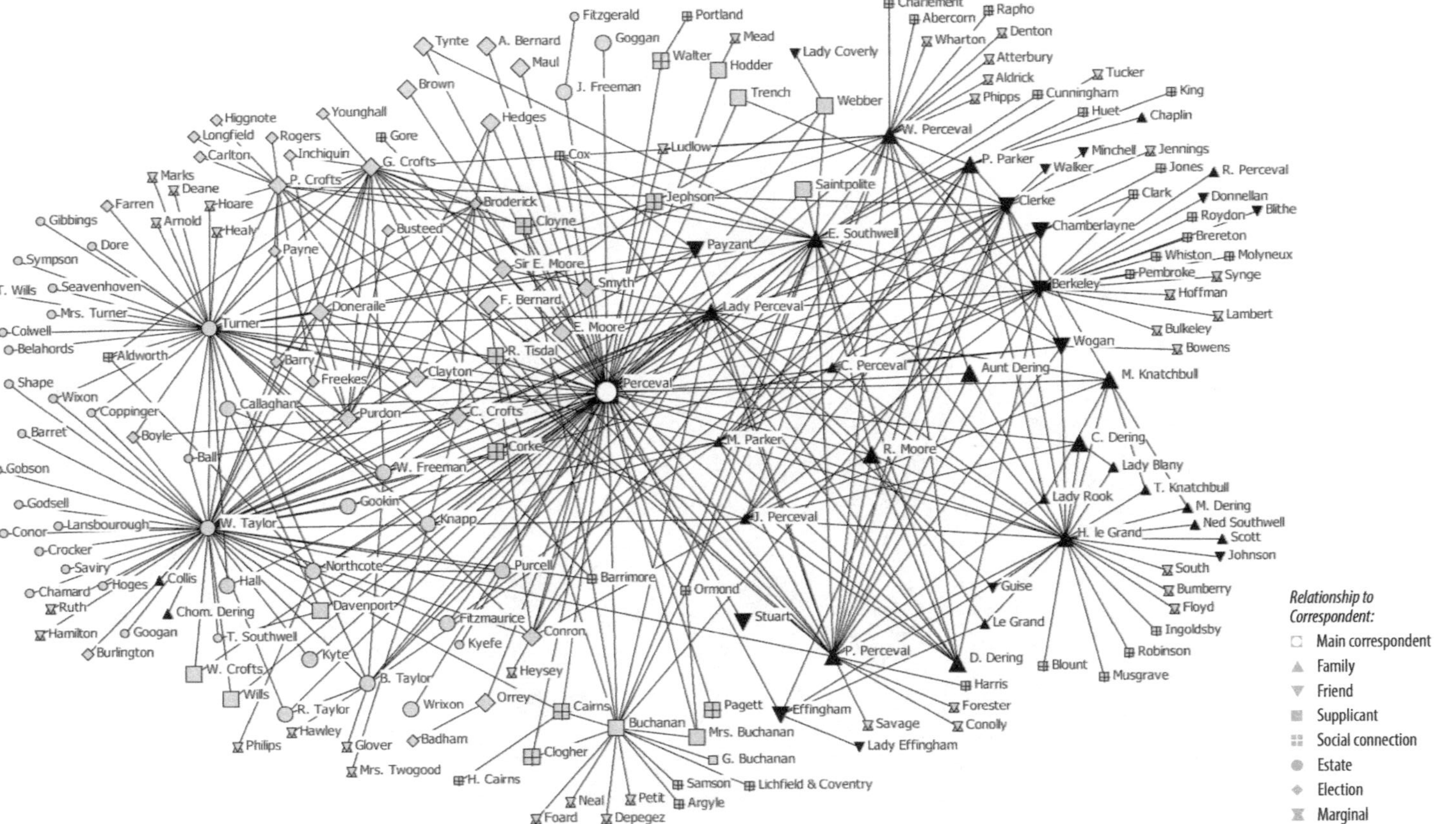

Figure 7. Epistolary network of John Perceval, 1710–1712, with family and friends highlighted. Large symbols represent individuals Perceval wrote to or received a letter from between 1710 and 1712; smaller symbols denote people mentioned within letters. The symbols themselves designate the individual's relationship to Perceval. In this network those who were designated as family members or friends are highlighted in black.

Network courtesy of Borgatti, S.P., 2002. NetDraw Software for Network Visualization. Analytic Technologies, Lexington, Kentucky.

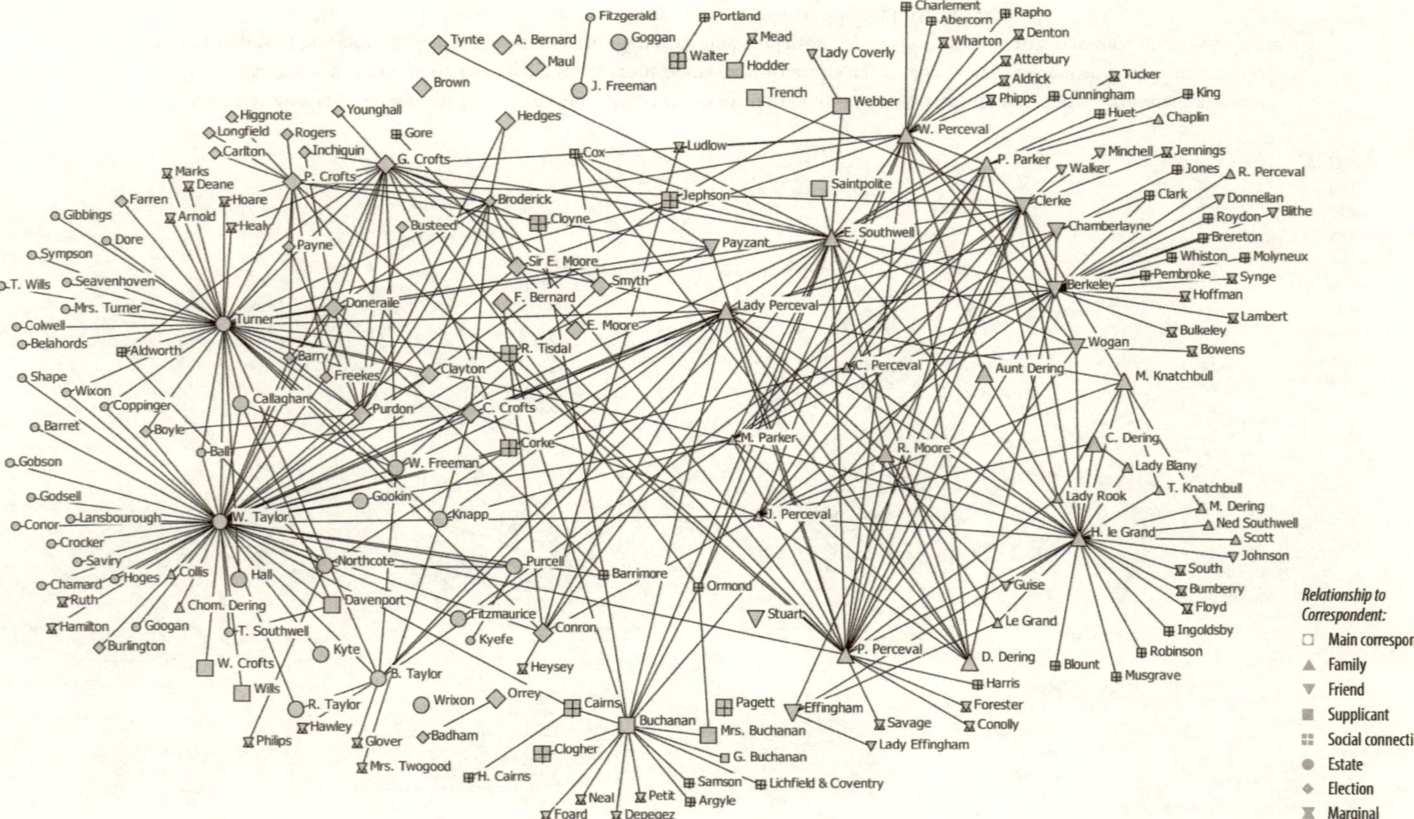

Figure 8. Epistolary network of John Perceval, 1710–1712, with John Perceval taken out. This network is the same as Figure 7, except that Perceval's ties to the network have been erased and no relationships highlighted.

Network courtesy of Borgatti, S.P., 2002. NetDraw Software for Network Visualization. Analytic Technologies, Lexington, Kentucky.

Family Ties

In Perceval's network family members dominate. He wrote to his wife, his brother, Philip Perceval, and his brother-in-law, Philip Parker. He also corresponded with a slew of distant and not-so-distant cousins during this period: Daniel Dering, William Perceval, Edward Southwell, Helena le Grand, Emmanuel Moore, and Robert Moore. Letters flew in from the older generation as well. He fielded epistles from his uncle Charles Dering, and his aunts Helena Dering and Mary Knatchbull (née Dering). These extended relations were especially important to Perceval since his nuclear family was small. All of his immediate family, besides his brother, Philip, had died by the time the young baronet was ten years old. His father passed away when he was three, his elder brother when he was nine, and his mother when he was ten. However, he had a lot of uncles, aunts, and cousins. The family of his guardian, his uncle Sir Robert Southwell, embraced John and his younger brother. Throughout his life Perceval relied upon his connection with Southwell's son, Edward, and his daughter, Helena le Grand. The profusion of Derings in his network came from the deep ties both the Southwells and Percevals had to this family. Perceval's mother, Catherine, and Robert Southwell's wife, Elizabeth, were two of the six daughters of Sir Edward Dering, who also had four sons, so there was never a shortage of cousins. It was this extended family that Perceval depended upon and wrote to.

Perceval was not alone in his entanglement with an extended kin network. Both William Byrds of Virginia kept in touch with their relatives back in England and, in the father's network especially, a dense web is produced (Figures 9 and 10). William Byrd I wrote letters to his brother, his sisters, and their husbands back in England and corresponded even more frequently with his wife's father, her sister, and her sister's husband.[11] Epistolarily, William Byrd II depended heavily on the network formed by his second wife's family, the Taylors, Pratts, and Otways, and even attempted to cultivate a correspondence between his son and his nephew in England, but for William Byrd II, as will be discussed later, friends were as important as family members.[12] For both Byrds family members provided them with anchors in England. This same need for an anchor tied the relatives of Nicholas Blundell to him and vice versa. Unsurprisingly, the most entangled segment of Blundell's network consists of family members (Figure 11).

This reliance on family networks often created and strengthened geographically far-ranging connections. Helping a relative could mean watching

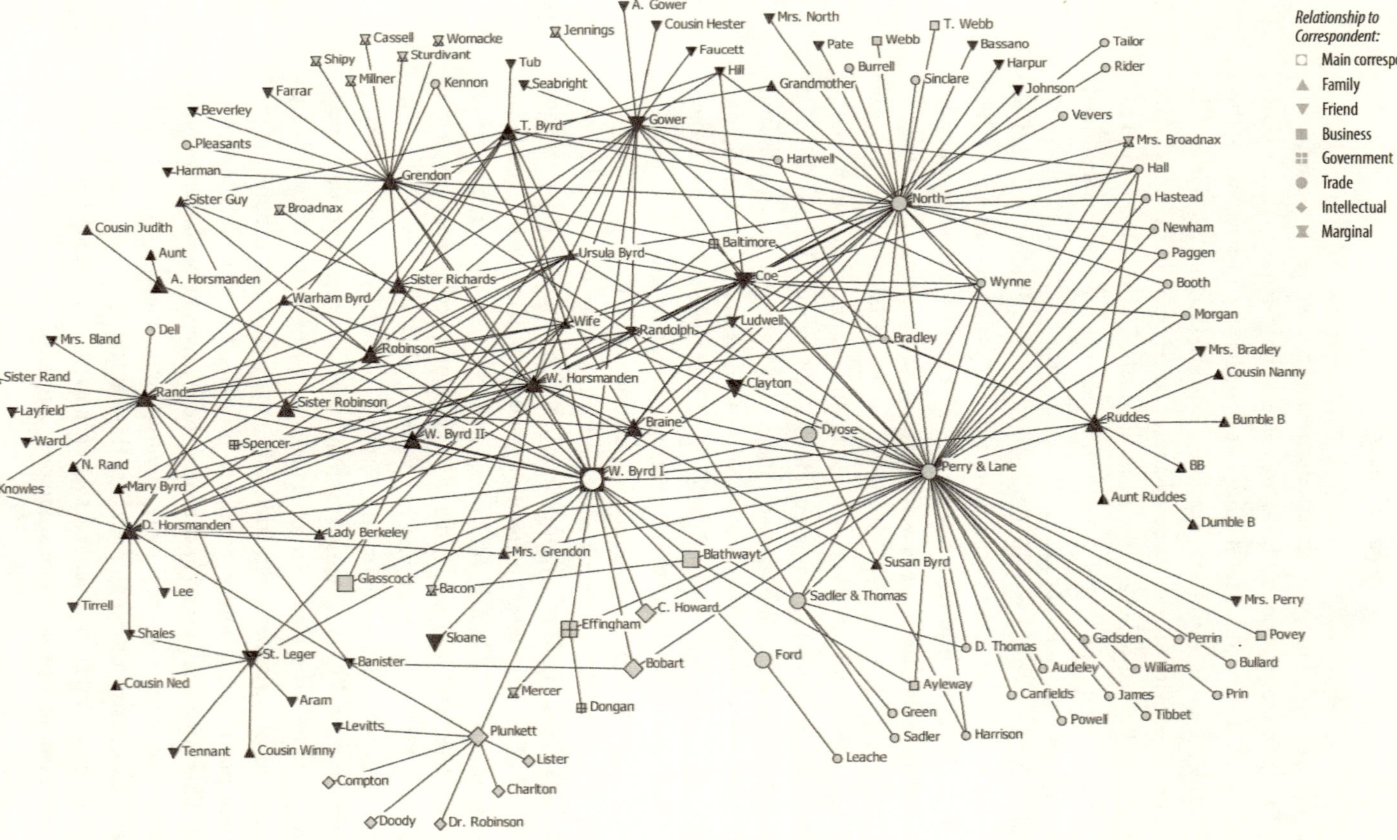

Figure 9. Epistolary network of William Byrd I, 1684–1688, with family and friends highlighted. Large symbols represent individuals William Byrd I wrote to or received a letter from between 1684 and 1688; smaller symbols denote people mentioned within letters. The symbols themselves designate the individual's relationship to Byrd. Those who were marked as family members or friends are highlighted in black.

Network courtesy of Borgatti, S.P., 2002. NetDraw Software for Network Visualization. Analytic Technologies, Lexington, Kentucky.

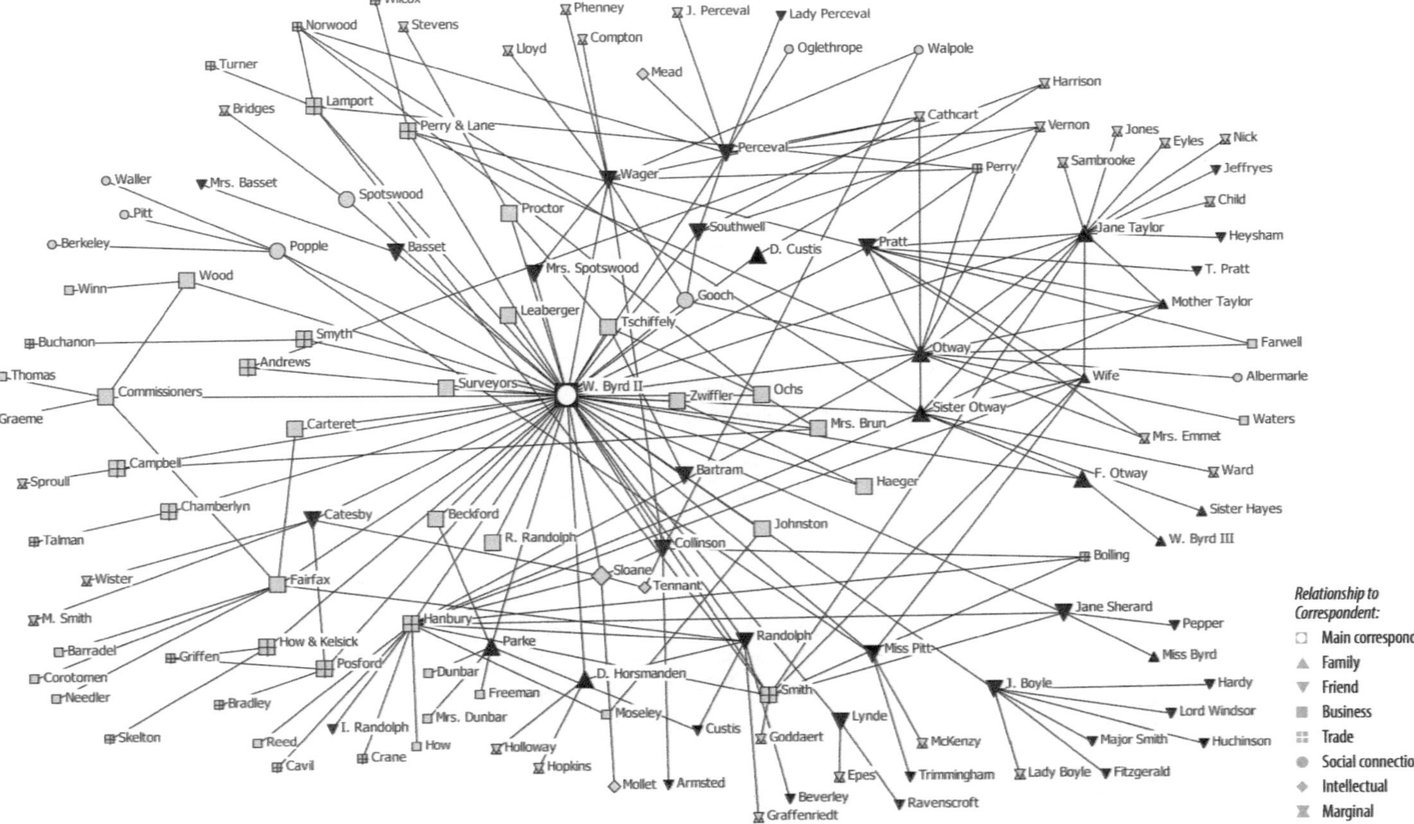

Figure 10. Epistolary network of William Byrd II, 1735–1742, with family and friends highlighted. In this network large symbols represent individuals William Byrd II wrote to or received a letter from between 1735 and 1742 and smaller symbols denote people mentioned within letters. The symbols themselves designate the individual's relationship to Byrd. In this network those who were marked as family members or friends are highlighted in black.

Network courtesy of Borgatti, S.P., 2002. NetDraw Software for Network Visualization. Analytic Technologies, Lexington, Kentucky.

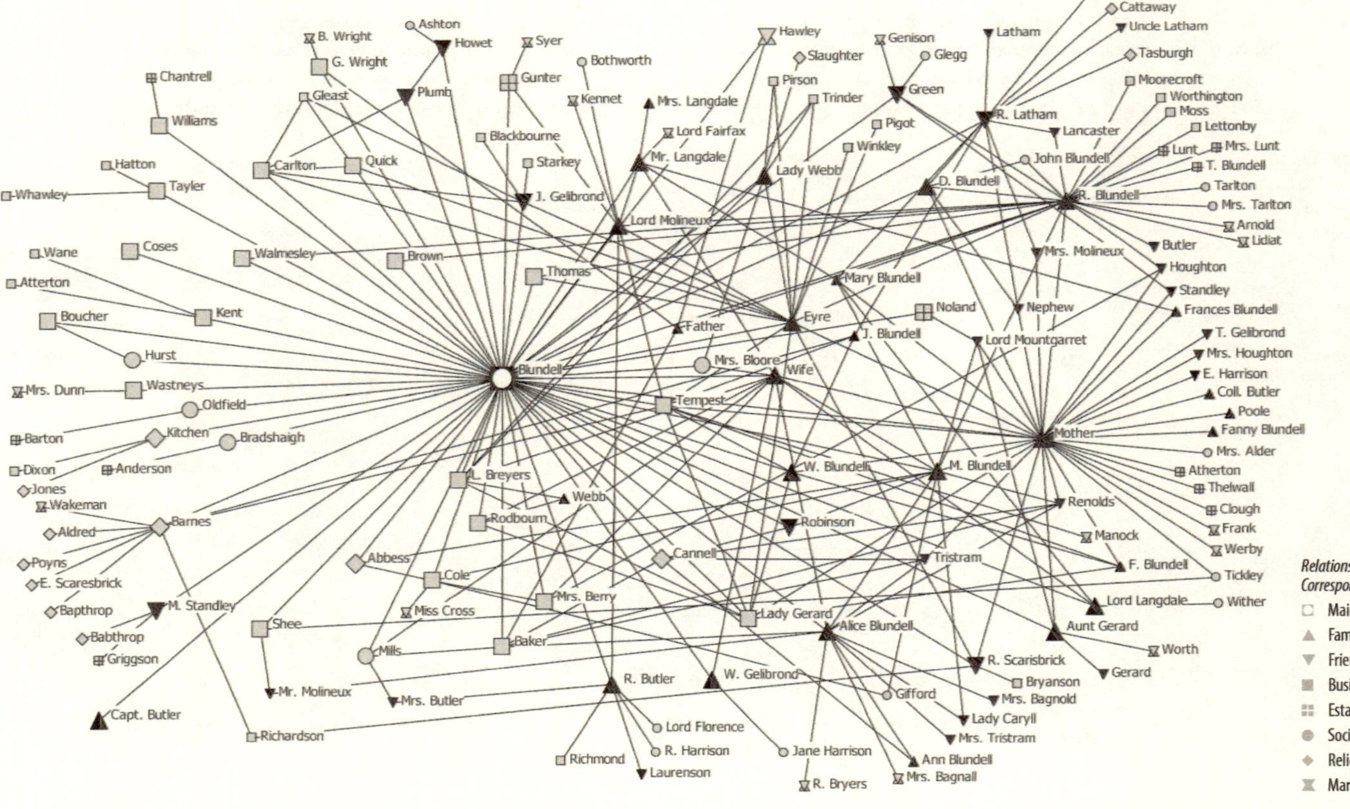

Figure 11. Epistolary network of Nicholas Blundell, 1702–1710, with family and friends highlighted. Large symbols represent individuals Nicholas Blundell wrote to or received a letter from between 1702 and 1710; smaller symbols denote people mentioned within letters. The symbols themselves designate the individual's relationship to Blundell. Those marked as family members or friends are highlighted in black.

Network courtesy of Borgatti, S.P., 2002. NetDraw Software for Network Visualization. Analytic Technologies, Lexington, Kentucky.

over their children or finding them a place in a distant corner of the British world. John and Philip Perceval came to London from Ireland due to their connections with the Southwell family. James Brydges and his wife took in multiple nieces and nephews.[13] John Eliot, a London merchant, attempted to send his cousin to Quebec and Newfoundland. The Byrds would not have arrived in Virginia if it were not for the childless uncle who took in William Byrd I, and both Byrds' familial networks would have weaker if William Byrd I had not sent his son and daughters to England under the care of their maternal grandfather. Family members took such exchanges for granted. Without warning, William Byrd I simply sent his daughter Ursula to London and hoped his father-in-law would "please to excuse the trouble." He invoked the code of familial obligation, almost ominously, stating to other English relatives, "I doubt not your kindness."[14] Children traveled across the Atlantic in the other direction as well. William Byrd II provided a home in Virginia for the children of his widowed sister Susan Brayne. Individuals automatically turned to family members for support and in doing so they reaffirmed ties and created geographically dispersed webs. In turn, letters allowed them to use and maintain these networks.

Extended kin networks existed and mattered well into the eighteenth century. Leaning upon family connections was a familiar social action, but these extended families stretched farther across the globe and, to a degree, the forms of obligation were less formal than they had been in past centuries. The transformation of the family has long interested historians, especially since it sits at the center of debates about social change in the early modern period.[15] While the initial discussion revolved around the emergence of the nuclear family, more recently scholars have recognized the continued importance of extended networks of kin.[16] As one historian has put it, family offered "a sort of readymade network."[17] The functioning of this "readymade" network altered throughout the early modern period. Increasing urbanization meant that the services offered by relatives could change. As one scholar has noted, elite men provided relations with less venison and more stock tips.[18] Also, as mobility increased the need to have trusted anchors in many locations expanded. Letters helped family members deal with distance, but it did strain relations, causing letter writers to increasingly use family rhetoric in their letters.[19] However, most letter writers did not openly fret about their kinship networks—they were too busy using them. Family members provided careful hands to carry letters from one location to another and they could also be trusted to provide support and information about a changing world. Focusing on networks of kin allows us to escape an argument about the shape of the family and enter into a discussion about how it functioned. These letters show that families were active networks, which provided necessary support for individuals dealing with an expanding world.

The exact composition of familial epistolary networks altered depending on the needs and familial status of the writer. Some members rarely sent or received letters unless certain events activated the latent network and pressed them to reaffirm their ties. When children were born and when loved ones married or passed away, family members picked up the pen. When Richard Blundell died on colonial shores, Nicholas wrote to relatives to remind them to pray for his brother's soul, and when John Perceval married Catherine Parker, letters of congratulation poured in from Dublin and Kent.[20] But some family members were constant cogs in a writer's epistolary network. The two correspondents that surface most frequently in Perceval's letter books, with over two hundred letters each, are Daniel Dering, his cousin and eventual brother-in-law, and Philip Perceval, his only brother. They both appear in the network formed by his letters between 1710 and 1712. The threads that spring from their nodes burrow deep into the cluster of connections formed by letters from friends and family. Perceval knew both could assist him, he trusted them, and he possessed a deep affection for both. They, besides having a real affection for John, also knew they were dependent on his goodwill for their livelihood.

Daniel Dering was deeply enmeshed in Perceval's kinship network. His mother was Perceval's father's sister, Helena, and his father was Perceval's mother's brother, Daniel. He, in turn, married Mary Parker, the sister of Perceval's wife. So it was a case of a pair of siblings marrying another pair of siblings and the products of those unions marrying another set of siblings. However, compared to his cousin, Daniel Dering was not well off. His father was a younger son and Daniel was dependent on his wealthier relatives throughout most of his life. Dering first surfaces in Perceval's letters in 1708 during a discussion between Perceval and his other cousin, Edward Southwell, about getting the eighteen-year-old Dering employment.[21] Dering would never find himself independent of these two relatives. In 1720 he evidently managed to make ten thousand pounds through the purchase of South Sea stock, which enabled him to marry Mary Parker, the lady whom he "long wished for," but until his death in 1730 he still often watched over Perceval's children and his wider concerns when Perceval was away.[22] And upon his death Perceval moved fast to find support for Dering's widow and daughter since all Dering's income came from the positions he held.[23] Perceval also had a deep affection for Dering. When he died Perceval lamented the loss of "the wisest, most experienced, faithful, generous, honest, sober and affectionate friend and relation I had."[24]

Perceval felt as attached to his brother. Philip was only three years younger and the two had been brought up together. When life later separated them, as John settled mainly in England and Philip in Ireland, they often lamented the distance. In one letter Philip declared that he often wished "the Gulph between us removed" and the news, a few years later, that Philip was to visit England gave John "the greatest pleasure imaginable for we have been many years Separated, to my great concern."[25] In fact, John named his second son, who died young, Philip, and Daniel Dering stood as his godfather. But, like Dering, Philip was dependent upon his brother. Born the youngest son he struggled to find a position and, in fact, most of the letter in which Edward Southwell and John Perceval discussed Daniel Dering's fate is taken up debating that of Philip. In it John mused that perhaps Philip should simply manage his Irish estates or join the army to give him some polish.[26] Philip eventually found a place in Irish society and married a wealthy widow in 1712, Mrs. Martha Usher Donnellan, but his service to his brother never ended. These two men were integral to Perceval's network because of their sense of duty to it and him.

While the distance that separated these relatives from Perceval often bothered them, it also made both Dering and Perceval valuable correspondents. The reason these two men surface in Perceval's network between 1710 and 1712 is because they could provide him with news and monitor his Irish interests when he was in London. During this period both Philip Perceval and Daniel Dering resided in Dublin and John was glad to make use of them. Philip visited his estates in Ireland for him and informed him that many in Ireland speculated about his coming over.[27] When John later spent time at his estates in the countryside, Daniel Dering told him of the welfare of his children whom he had left behind in Dublin.[28] These two were among Perceval's Irish anchors, correspondents who remained immobile as John moved from London to Dublin to the Irish countryside. Throughout most of his life Philip would remain one of John's Irish anchors and after his return to England Dering would become one of his London anchors. It was Dering who watched after Perceval's interests and children as Perceval traveled around England, Ireland, and the Continent, and he kept John informed through letters. Philip and Daniel were not the only familial connections Perceval looked to: the brother and sister pair of Edward Southwell and

Helena le Grand loom large in his network, as does his distant cousin, William Perceval, upon whom he depended more during this period than he did on the younger Philip and Daniel, a fact illuminated by the greater number of unconnected links emanating from his node. These unconnected figures were individuals, not deeply tied to Perceval's network, whom William Perceval mentioned either to keep Perceval up to date on changing governmental and ecclesiastical positions in Ireland, in the case of Aldrick and Phipps, or because he wished Perceval to serve him by contacting two individuals, in the case of Charlement and Abercorn. Again, it is often the location of these correspondents that made them valuable. Southwell and le Grand both resided in London during this period and William Perceval lived in Dublin.

The strong presence of Perceval's kinship links in his epistolary network was a reflection of the social world that most Britons inhabited during this period. Family mattered because family members acted in support of kin. Letters echo with families attempting to be of use to one another. As already mentioned, John Perceval spent many years trying to find positions for his brother. In 1716 they set their sights on the position of the master of the rolls, and to this end Perceval sent a letter to the Duke of Grafton and also recommended that Philip write to his cousin Edward Southwell.[29] He did, but the response was less than he hoped. As he told his brother, Southwell did not play the game of patronage well. In Philip Perceval's words: "he is so tardy and squeamish in his Solliciting for his friends that his manner of application is a sort of consequentiall refusal . . . he hears you with a hum and a ha, says, tis, or would be, very well if it cou'd be done, but, &c."[30] But for all his failings Southwell would remain a critical link in Perceval's web, for as secretary of state for Ireland, he held the key to many possible positions.

The Percevals were not alone in looking to family for support. John Eliot, the London merchant, also looked to assist his kin and spent years trying to help one of his cousins. He helped him with his debts and tried to send him to Quebec and Newfoundland, but in the end all his efforts failed.[31] James and Cassandra Brydges often cared for his sisters and their families when they fell on hard times. When her second husband deserted her, Brydges's sister looked to her brother for help, both for herself and for her sons from a previous marriage. Brydges responded and gave her an annuity, paid her debts, and attempted to help her sons, both of whom proved disappointing.[32] But this was not just a case of strong connections helping weaker ties. Correspondents with less social clout were useful because they too provided information on public and private affairs. The letters between Philip and his brother John sent during 1710 spoke of finding a place for Philip, but they also contained descriptions of the attitude of the populace toward the trial of Henry Sacheverell, an Anglican clergyman whose fiery sermons, condemnation of toleration and calls of "Church in danger" angered the government who called for his impeachment.[33] The same subject appeared in the letters between John and William Perceval. John sent him an account of the trial and in return William declared he would give John an account of Dublin occurrences as long as he was in town.[34]

Perceval's cousin, Helena le Grand, was especially good at sending information, which explains why she is so prominent in Perceval's network. Her links sink deeply into the family network and then shoot forth like a firework to unconnected nodes. Between the years 1710 and 1712 she wrote Perceval seven letters in which she mentioned twenty-five individuals, over half of whom were family members. No other correspondent of Perceval's examined during this period mentioned more people. She provided him with news on royal movements, stocks, deaths in their social circle, and family monetary affairs. But most of her information regarded family members. In one letter she informed Perceval that his son's teeth were coming in, that a cousin had given birth to a daughter, and that another relative was pregnant.[35] In a letter a month later she told Perceval that she would be godmother to his next child if it was a girl, that their uncle was dead ("God be thanked"), that another relative had a daughter, that her brother should be returning from Ireland soon, and that she did not think their aunt needed condolences sent on account of her husband's death.[36] Most of her other letters follow this pattern and with them she made herself an important hub in Perceval's network. Single women often put themselves forth as informants to curry favor with the head of the family and, as le Grand's correspondence shows, so did well-off married women.[37] Family members were constant correspondents because they valued each other, but also because they needed to nurture wider networks by tracking those around them.

The need for family letters to keep the recipient up to date on the lives of other relatives accounts for the weblike nature of this segment of Perceval's network: since they all talked about each other they all show up linked to each other in his network. It was a web the entire family relied upon to keep themselves informed. Perceval's aunt, Mary Knatchbull, wrote to him after hearing through Helena le Grand that his wife was ill and might miscarry, and it was through le Grand's letter that she sent her congratulations on the birth of his son.[38] William Perceval also made himself a more valuable correspondent by passing on information he gathered from his military brother's letters on the British campaign in Spain during the War of the Spanish Succession.[39] This is why it is important to note the second layer of epistolary connection. Perceval's aunt, Lady Blaney, and his cousin, Lady Rook, did not write to him during this period, but they were part of his epistolary network. Lady Blaney surfaces in letters from Charles Dering and Helena le Grand.[40] As for Lady Rook, John Perceval mentions her in a letter to his brother, and Helena le Grand, Philip Parker, and Mary Knatchbull all refer to her in their letters to Perceval.[41] They were certainly part of the family circle.

Nurturing and using these epistolary networks became more important as the distance separating family members grew. To a degree, as scholars have noted, this distance and instability worried letter writers.[42] Philip wished the "gulph" between him and his brother removed, and John had to assure his cousin in Cheshire that "the uneasiness to know extends itself to any distance."[43] The worry grew if loved ones lived on the fringes of the British world. Nicholas Blundell insisted to his brother in the Chesapeake that "notwithstanding I am married & likely to have a Family of my own I shall ever look upon you as my own Dearest Broo."[44] From Virginia, Byrd the younger often had to press his wife's sisters and their husbands in England to write. He began one letter stating, "Well I perceive my dear cousen Taylor begins to treat me for all the world as she do's injurys, that is to forget me," and another opened with the declaration, "I have lookt out as sharp all this year for an epistle from my dear sister, as a broken gamester dos for a dinner, or St. Sibastian privateer for a prize, but alas to no manner of purpose."[45] In their letters to him they give excuses for their tardiness, but do not press him to write again.

However, those in England worried about their Atlantic connections as well. Concern vibrates throughout Blundell's letters to his brother. When ships arrived with no letters he became uneasy and even enclosed instructions to the ship's captain delivering the letter on what to do in the case of his brother's death.[46] This was a justifiable worry for Richard died on that faraway shore months before his brother was aware of it.[47] However, for the most part a sense of confidence infuses letters between family members no matter the distance. It was a relationship that could not be denied. William Byrd II might playfully insinuate that his wife's relatives had forgotten him, but they wrote back and the correspondence lasted until Byrd's death in 1744. The link itself remained strong enough that William Byrd II's son sent three of his children to live with his aunt and uncle in England.[48] Distance strained familial networks, but they remained useful and, in fact, as the British world widened they became more critical and valued.

Compared to Perceval, William Byrd II's familial ties made a more muted showing in his epistolary network, but family connections do surface. He often wrote to his brother-in-law John Custis through his first wife, and to the family of his second wife. However, he had no steadfast brothers and cousins like Nicholas Blundell, Philip Perceval, and Daniel Dering that he depended upon. Byrd's only brother, Warham, died young, and his sisters, two of whom were dead by 1710, spent most of their later lives in Virginia, making correspondence relatively unnecessary. He seems to have lost track of his cousins as well. No reference is made either in his diaries or his letters to his relatives on his father's side with whom his father corresponded (the Byrds, the Richards, the Robinsons, or the Guys). He did visit with his mother's relatives, the Horsmandens and the Rands, when he was in London, but little evidence of any correspondence between them survives.[49] In 1736 he did record an affectionate letter to his cousin Daniel Horsmanden, who had immigrated to New York, which implied an ongoing but lax correspondence. His letter began, "There is some danger of my being in disgrace with my dear cousen for having been so sleepy a correspondent, but I can tell you I did awake about six months ago & wrote you a long letter."[50] However, if an extended correspondence continued with his Horsmanden or Rand relatives Byrd did not record it with the same rigor as he did the letters of his second wife's family after his permanent return to Virginia in 1726. The family members who dominate Byrd's correspondence are those who could be useful to him. His second wife's family, who included the Taylors, the Pratts, and the Otways, resided in London, unlike the Horsmandens or the Rands, and could provide him with London news when he was in Virginia. This is why they surface so strongly in his network between 1735 and 1742 (Figure 10). Similarly, John Custis, his first brother-in-law, passed on Virginia news when Byrd was in London. Like Perceval, Byrd mainly nurtured ties through letters with family members who could provide him with the information he needed. However, unlike Perceval, it was more difficult for him to maintain his wider kinship network in England after he permanently settled in Virginia since his network, as a whole, was less interconnected.

Active Friends

Luckily for Byrd, letter writers did not depend solely on family connections; they also relied on their friends. In fact, when family members helped each other they were acting as friends. Their support or correspondence made them active friends or active members of the network. When Philip complained of Edward Southwell's less than admirable patronage techniques he did not frame his complaint using the rhetoric of family, but of friendship: "he is so tardy and squeamish in his Solliciting for his friends."[51] And when Cassandra Brydges could no longer help her cousin she wrote, "tho I cease to be an active friend for you, [I] will not to wish well to you & yours."[52]

"Ties of intimacy" without "ties of blood" do surface in these networks. As Perceval's web illustrates, embedded within his familial network were friendly connections. George Berkeley, the philosopher, managed to become an intimate tie as Perceval's description of him in an annotation in his letter book shows. To Perceval he was "a man of the noblest virtues, best learning and temper I ever knew."[53] Beside Daniel Dering, Philip Perceval, and his estate agents, Perceval corresponded more with Berkeley than anyone else.[54] Berkeley would become a famous Irish clergyman and philosopher, but when he met Perceval he was simply a newly minted fellow at Trinity College Dublin. Their correspondence, which initially focused on intellectual matters, began in 1709 and would last until Perceval's death in 1748. While only one member of Perceval's family mentioned Berkeley in a letter between 1710 and 1712, he mentioned five family members and his deep involvement in Perceval family life, even this early on in their relationship, surfaces in his letters. He relayed the greetings of Perceval's relatives to him by letter and went to Philip's house to drink with two of Perceval's cousins.[55] Berkeley was also a main conduit for information about Perceval's children when Perceval himself was away. He told Perceval that his son still kissed with an open mouth, could make a comical sneer with his nose, and that he had made up his own language.[56] His connection was close enough for him to state, "To be plain the Child seems not to care a farthing for you both."[57] The divide between friends and family could be quite thin and the two often made up one intertwined network because writers relied on them to perform similar tasks. In fact, most of those labeled friends in Perceval's network have connections to the rest of the Perceval family.

Friendly correspondents dominate William Byrd II's network even more strongly than they do Perceval's web of correspondents. In Byrd's network downward facing triangles, representing friends, are more prevalent than upward facing triangles, denoting family (Figure 10). They helpfully filled the gaps left by his weaker family network. Byrd's family connections, made up of the Horsmandens, the Rands, the Otways, and the Taylors, did not hold the same amount of social power as the Southwells and the Derings. They could not serve his needs easily and perhaps did not wish to do so. Besides the Taylors, his family connections did not reside in London and he did not have ties "of many years Standing" to deepen the relationship with the Taylors. He could not depend on them to help him to governmental positions or to deliver the gossip he desired in the same way Perceval could depend on his family connections. To resolve this issue Byrd used his friendships with figures of higher rank in London to increase the usefulness of his web.

His most valued and constant correspondents were John Perceval himself, Charles Wager, and the father and son pair of Charles and John Boyle, the fourth and fifth earls of Orrery. He met these men early in his life while living in London, began exchanging letters with them in the 1720s, and continued to do so until his death twenty years later. Perceval, Wager, and John Boyle all surface in his network between 1735 and 1742. Through these men he could continue to cultivate his knowledge of English affairs and provide them with all the information on Virginia they desired. John Perceval informed Byrd of the bursting of the South Sea Bubble and John Boyle of the English reaction to the death of George I.[58] In turn, Byrd told them of the failure of the British attempt to take St. Augustine in 1740 and shared with Perceval his worries about the feasibility of George Berkeley's Bermuda scheme.[59] At one point he apologized to Charles Boyle for the amount of American news in his letter, but defended himself by insisting that such news now mattered to all Britons.[60]

But just as Berkeley provided Perceval with information on his absent children, these men exchanged more personal information. John Boyle, throughout his letters, provided Byrd with a running commentary on their old set at Wills Coffeehouse on Downing Street, as the appearance of Lord Windsor, Major Smith, Captain Fitzgerald, Archebald Hutchison, and Mr. Hardy in his network reveals. However, the news became rather sparse by his last letter of 1742 when he admitted that "the groupe you used to meet in Downing Street is mouldered away to a single figure."[61] Byrd, like George Berkeley, also inserted himself into Perceval's larger network. He was never as successful as Berkeley, but he did make sure to ask after Perceval's wife and children and to gesture to his connections with the Southwell family.[62] To a degree he succeeded in becoming a distant link in Perceval's larger web. When Perceval traveled across the Continent in 1706 his relatives assumed he would want to know of Byrd's marriage to someone "as handsome as the Dutchess of Bolton" and in 1718 Southwell contemplated bringing Byrd along on a journey to visit Perceval on the Continent.[63] Perceval's continued interest in Byrd's life led him to add in the margin next to the letter about his marriage that the bride's name was Lucy. Even ten years later Perceval assumed Byrd would want to know the fate of his wider network and informed him of the deaths of both Edward Southwell and Daniel Dering.[64] Byrd was able to create one of Kitty's ties of intimacy since his ties of blood could not fulfill all his needs.

Epistolary networks reflected and rested on strong extended networks of family and friends. The support of such connections had long undergirded social networks and the continued dependence upon family and friends highlights the strength of this older form of social organization, a strength that was actually growing in importance. Not only did the rhetoric surrounding family relationships become more vocalized, but, as these letters show, using such connections became more necessary. The specific members who become important in these networks rose to prominence not simply because of their close relationship to the correspondent but due to their strategic placement and abilities. Perceval valued Edward Southwell's letters because, like Perceval himself, Southwell had connections to individuals with power; Philip Perceval was ever present because, besides being a beloved brother, he helped watch over Perceval's Irish estates and interests; Daniel Dering was a constant presence first for his Irish news and then for his ability to keep Perceval abreast of his English interests when he was at a distance. In Byrd's case, John Custis watched after his concerns in Virginia, John Boyle and John Perceval kept him informed of English occurrences, and his sisters-in-law provided him with English news and a place to send his children if he so desired.

The importance of well-maintained networks of family members and friends increased as the world of the British elite became more mobile and geographically expansive; the value of these networks rested not on the affection they could provide, but on the actions they could perform. But one's position in these networks could be fluid. Sometimes the closest epistolary bonds were not between immediate family members, but with those connected through marriage. On other occasions family networks allowed friends entrance to their charmed circle. This was especially useful for those like William Byrd II who had weaker family networks and thus desperately needed such connections. It was these constant connections with friends and family that formed the foundation of epistolary networks, but they were not the only connections formed through letters; many more exchanges were ephemeral.

"For Each Others Use and Helpe": Ephemeral Networks

Some epistolary links began with a problem and Mr. Steiger had a rather large one. His wife's brother had "lost his understanding" and was becoming increasingly violent. Steiger had tried to get him accepted at Bedlam, the famous psychiatric hospital in London, but the authorities told him there was no room. So he turned to his old acquaintance Ambrose Godfrey, a skilled chemist who knew many members of the intellectual elite of the British world including, most importantly for Steiger, Hans Sloane, the secretary of the Royal Society and president of the Royal College of Physicians. Sloane had connections to most of the hospitals in London and so Godfrey decided to help Steiger by writing to Sloane.[65] He thought that perhaps a letter from Sloane would create room in Bedlam for this troubled soul and so Godfrey penned the letter, sealed it, and placed in the hands of Steiger to deliver. Getting a man with violent tendencies into Bedlam was not easy, simply going to the powers that be was not enough, one had to have a network to play on and a knowledge of the networks of others.

The network Steiger created hoping to get his brother-in-law into Bedlam was what sociologists refer to as a "problem-anchored" network.[66] Such networks are the result of individuals in need of assistance determining the best way to solve their problems through their available resources and putting them to use. The networks these actions produce are ephemeral. Steiger never resurfaces in Sloane's network again and Godfrey only does sporadically.[67] But such ephemeral networks mattered to those who created them and they show how epistolary networks functioned from another angle. The ties in Perceval's network connecting supplicants and patrons, and, to an extent, those relating to local Irish issues, like elections, were ephemeral problem-anchored networks. Most of these correspondents were not integral to Perceval's epistolary network; like Steiger, they wrote to simply get something done and then disappeared.

The problems writers looked to solve through letters were many, from admittance to Bedlam, to desired governmental posts, to abatements in rent. This was a society in which people were used to assisting one another. As Godfrey reminded Sloane when he wrote his letter, "we are not born for our selfs but for each others use and helpe."[68] This was not a new idea. The sense that ties of mutual obligation and reciprocity held society together had long held weight. Previously, historians depicted this ideal as under siege by the early modern period, arguing that as a capitalist economy became more embedded it brought with it an acceptance of self-interest over communal well-being, but other scholars have modified this view by demonstrating that these older forms of social relations were not lost, but that "a reconfiguration of webs of duty and mutual obligation" occurred.[69] This reconfiguration surfaces in the way letter writers monitored, nurtured, and used the relationships held within the folds of their letters.

Historians have examined changing ideas of social assistance by looking at how modes of help, both formal and informal, altered and, for the elite especially, at the role and interpretation of patronage. Recently scholars have pointed to the continued importance of informal networks of assistance and argued that informal chains of reciprocal obligation expanded during the early modern period even as the world became more centralized and institutionalized.[70] Furthermore, there is little doubt that British society during the later Stuart period depended upon patronage, but the source and nature of patronage was changing.[71] The Tudor period saw power and patronage shift from the locality to the Court. This created a more centralized elite, often dependent upon the good will of the monarch. By the later seventeenth century the centers of patronage had moved once again. The growing centralization of the state and the expanding bureaucracy tied to it shifted the focus away from the Court to those who held positions of power in this more dispersed system and to the state itself.[72] But state centralization did not mean that social power became more centralized. What mattered by the later seventeenth century was not gaining a position that would allow you access to the pinnacle of power in the form of the monarch, but gaining a position within the growing bureaucratic web that would provide you with an income and your own connections. Helping friends and family members gain these positions through patronage was more than a political tool or a manifestation of corruption. In this new world, patronage linked new structures of governance to older webs of obligation and expectation. It also changed the nature of these webs. Connections to the center mattered, but there were more people in the center to connect with and thus maintaining broad webs of acquaintances was more critical than ever. Previously to rise in society, find a place, or resolve an issue, a connection to the local magnate would have been enough or developing connections to those close to the monarch would have sufficed. Such linkages were still highly valuable, but by the later seventeenth century it was the possession of a vast web of connections that mattered most. The emergence of a British Atlantic world intensified this need. Bureaucracy needed to stretch further and so did patronage. One way to deal with this new world was through the cultivation of extended epistolary networks that served as a base from which to reach out.

Many letter writers in Perceval's network were supplicants. Those labeled as family members or friends also asked for favors, but doing so did not define their correspondence with Perceval; for those labeled as supplicants it did. They rarely wrote multiple letters and had little interest in becoming part of Perceval's wider network. Figure 12 represents John Perceval's epistolary network between 1710 and 1712 with his supplicants highlighted in black. Daniel Webber composed only one letter to Perceval that survives.[73] He wanted Perceval to use his influence with Southwell to clear up a misunderstanding; after they resolved this issue, no further correspondence was necessary. Similarly, Thomas Hodder wrote eight letters to Perceval, but they all concerned one bill he wished to see presented to the Irish parliament about promoting the constant residence of Protestant ministers in Ireland and they mentioned very few other individuals, and thus he is not deeply embedded in the network.[74] Letters from tenants often followed the same path: their epistles might reflect the local networks of power and neighborliness surrounding them, but they wrote letters to resolve a single problem, not to maintain an epistolary connection. Hanna Wills, William Crofts, and William Davenport wrote to Perceval to ask for abatements on their rents and that was it.[75] As Hanna Wills's pained signature attests, she had to find someone to pen the letter for her; composing a letter was not an easy task. To a degree, the higher your rank the easier it was to ask for assistance since your power to give was greater. Lord Chesterfield, the eminent writer of polite English letters, defined equal connections as "those, where the two connecting parties reciprocally find their account, from pretty near an equal degree of parts and abilities."[76] Members of the British elite were able to exchange favors since they had equal "parts and abilities," but, like Perceval's tenants, they did not always wish to join the constant core of the network.

However, while they were looking for a single favor these correspondents could rarely depend upon a single connection; they needed access to a web. When an Irish correspondent of Edward Southwell wanted to become a commissioner of the revenue (he noticed that a few were looking rather unwell) he wrote to Southwell to help him obtain the viceroy's favor, not by speaking directly to the viceroy, but by recommending him to his friends in England.[77] Similarly Byrd wailed to an English connection, "Can nothing be done for an old friend of forty years acquaintance to help him at this dead lift? . . . I wish I could perswade you to take a [lit]tle upon my account, by speaking a

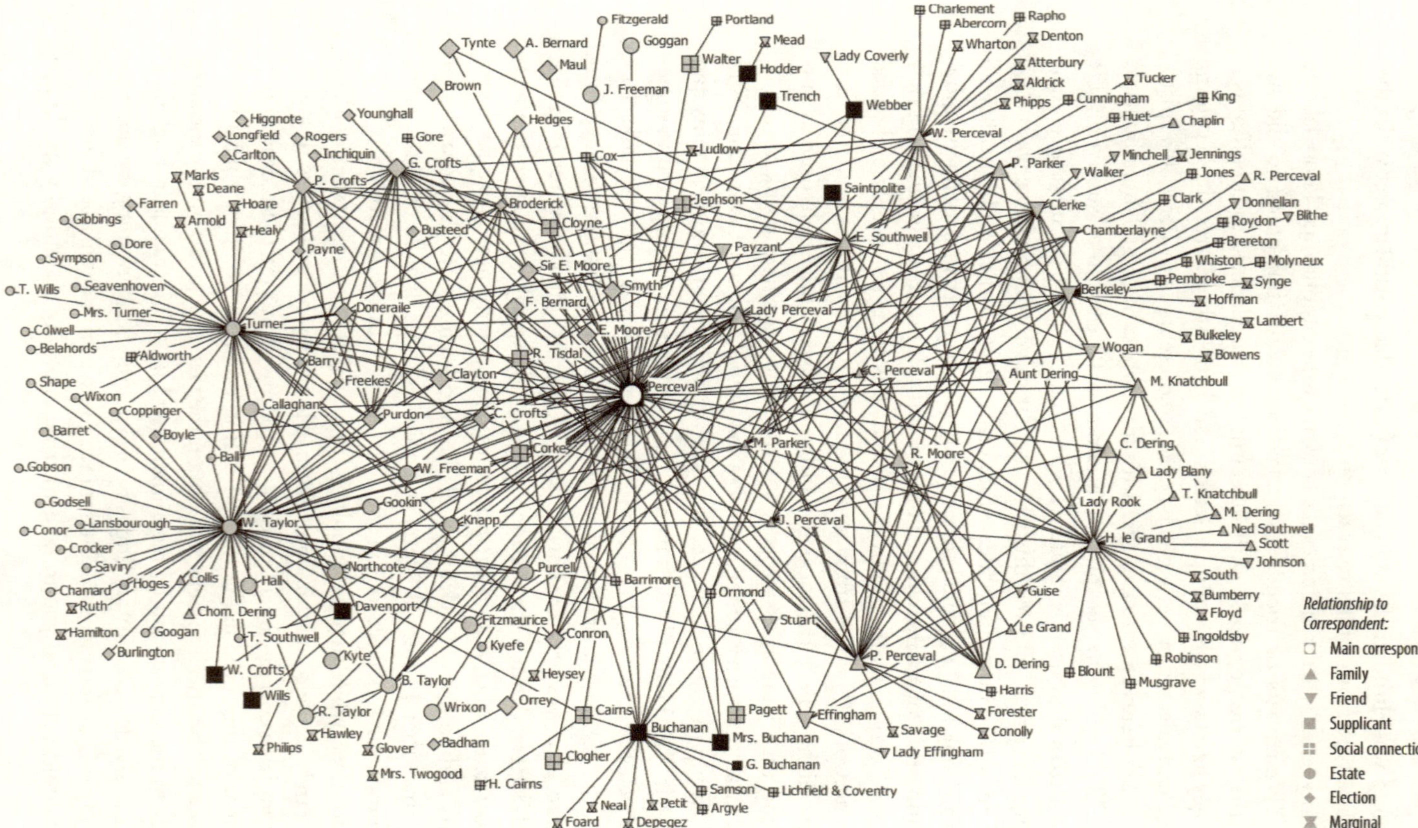

Figure 12. Epistolary network of John Perceval, 1709–12, with supplicants highlighted. This network is the same as Figure 7, except those who could be considered supplicants are highlighted rather than friends and family members.

Network courtesy of Borgatti, S.P., 2002. NetDraw Software for Network Visualization. Analytic Technologies, Lexington, Kentucky.

good word for me to your friend Sir Robert."[78] Byrd was not looking for his connection to get him a position; he wanted him to talk to his "friend" Sir Robert Walpole. Both these cries for help depended upon links within their own network of acquaintances and their correspondent's web of connections. The same was true of Webber's letter to Perceval. He did not ask Perceval to get him the position, but to contact Southwell about it. Like Webber, supplicants knew the networks of their patrons, and patrons often turned to their more constant epistolary networks to get favors accomplished. When Cassandra Brydges attempted to get an acquaintance the post of master of Balliol College she wrote to her Cousin Robinson to ask her to get her husband to talk to an acquaintance of his to get his vote for her connection.[79] Here she activated her constant family network for an ephemeral need. A single link was never sufficient; supplicants needed many connections and the power to send a vibration throughout a whole web of linkages.

For men like John Perceval, plucking at wider networks to solve his problems was not difficult and it was an action he often had to perform. One of the expectations placed on the British elite was the maintenance of an interest or the cultivation of a circle of supporters who could be relied on for assistance, especially political support. Possessing an interest demonstrated one's power and allowed one to help others. Nevertheless, keeping up an interest was not easy. A peevish James Brydges, Duke of Chandos, confessed that "tho I have long since made a Resolution to have nothing to do with the world & that Bustle which attends the Folly of what is called keeping up an Interest, yet I would not be wanting in doing every thing that's proper for one in my Station."[80] An interest did not simply come with a title. As Perceval's guardian, Sir Robert Southwell, told him in a letter, "to have fit Interest in Ireland, there needed 3 strings to the bow, Acres, Education, and friends."[81] Acres were not a problem for Perceval; he inherited 22,000 of them in Cork and Tipperary. Education he acquired through tutors, travel, and time at Oxford. Friends were harder. To a degree his "friends" in the district remained whether he cultivated them consistently or not—his acres and the promise of his patronage saw to that—but some nurturing never hurt.

Perceval, and other members of the British elite, maintained their interest in multiple ways. Positions, gifts, and recommendations kept friends happy, but letters mattered when elections loomed. Perceval sent many letters to his supporters to show that he personally appreciated their help. The lack of a letter at this juncture could erode a connection: Perceval's friend and estate agent informed him that he had met with a captain who was "very hearty in your interest," but then warned him that another acquaintance took it amiss that Perceval had not written him for his support.[82] Since Perceval was not there in person his letters had to be. When he needed support Perceval could turn to this latent local network, but unlike his networks of family and friends it was not one he regularly connected with through letters.

During the period mapped out in Perceval's network, 1710–1712, his interest was under cultivation as elections loomed.[83] Each year a flurry of letters marked the need to produce a functional interest and the ties they produced have been highlighted in Figure 13 in black. In 1710, on the heels of a politically supportive message from his cousin Emmanuel Moore, came two letters, one from Henry Maul, a Cork acquaintance, assuring him of the massive support he saw around Cork, and another from Viscount Doneraile, a neighboring peer, suggesting that Perceval's presence in Ireland would be beneficial to his interest and that he would canvas two other Irish peers for their assistance.[84] A few days later, Perceval received another pair of letters from two prosperous tenants. One, from Christopher Crofts, his grandfather's footboy and now an alderman, assured him that he had delivered Perceval's letters to his "friends" regarding the election, and the other, from Francis Bernard, Irish MP, lawyer, and eventual solicitor-general of Ireland, informed Perceval that he was fast at work developing Perceval's interest.[85] A little over a week later a letter from another prosperous tenant, Philip Crofts, came into his hands and laid out who embraced the Perceval interest.[86] Such letters flowed in and out throughout the winter and helped nurture Perceval's interest.

These men were not Perceval's constant correspondents. In his surviving letters their epistles surface only a few times: one from Henry Maul, two from Doneraile, six from Francis Bernard, eight from each of the two Crofts, and twelve from his cousin Sir Emmanuel Moore, but during this moment they formed a subsidiary network within Perceval's larger web of connections. The majority of these letters provided Perceval with information on his interest. Four of Perceval's letters from Moore revolved around his interest, the rest cultivated their familial ties, but the weight of the correspondence fell upon organizing Perceval's interest, an act Moore knew Perceval appreciated.[87] Similarly, while Bernard surfaces often in letters from others (Perceval had others contact him for legal advice), his letters to Perceval only regard elections and a favor he did for Perceval.[88] The same could be said for the letters of Philip Crofts, Henry Maul, and Viscount Doneraile. It was the

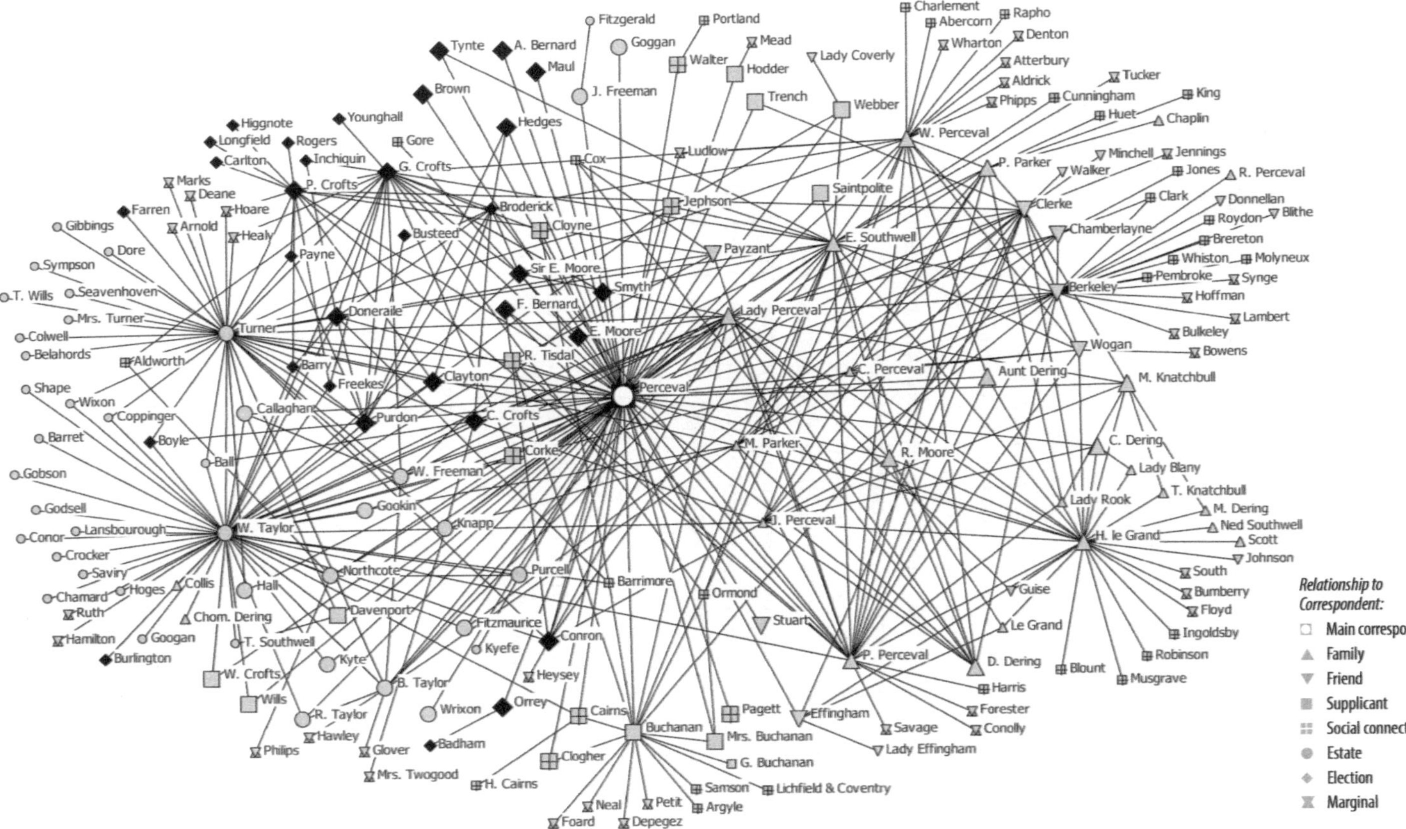

Figure 13. Epistolary network of John Perceval, 1709–1712, with election connections highlighted. This network is the same as Figure 7, but those involved in Irish elections are highlighted rather than friends and family members.

Network courtesy of Borgatti, S.P., 2002. NetDraw Software for Network Visualization. Analytic Technologies, Lexington, Kentucky.

need to keep up Perceval's interest that solidified these links, and when the need faded so did the epistolary ties. Like so many other letter writers, Perceval knew how to use letters to activate a network when he was in need.

For Perceval this was easy, but others possessed weaker networks, which limited their ability to access the networks of others. Such a lack of access could mean a slow social and economic death. This fear echoes in a letter sent to Southwell: "Sir I have no friend or interest in this kingdom so depend holy on you."[89] One wonders if the use of the word "holy" was wholly a spelling mistake. Relying on a few or fragile lines of connection was dangerous. Such supplicants often tried to integrate themselves into wider networks, but often had a hard time proving themselves worthy of the larger web. Henry Trench was a history painter whom Perceval met while traveling in Italy in 1707. Trench attempted to cultivate an epistolary connection with Perceval not long after the young baronet returned to England.[90] He first sent a letter of compliment, but quickly the messages became more desperate as he continuously asked Perceval for help in remedying his sickly and debt-ridden state. Perceval's responses to these pleas go unrecorded, but the fact that he noted Trench's death in his letter book suggests that he kept track of the connection.[91] However, Trench's need and inability to give something in return or to provide other connections made it unlikely that a sustained correspondence would ever have flourished.

Slightly more successful was Matthew Buchanan, an Irish clergyman who was a ne'er-do-well and an incorrigible optimist as well as Perceval's most persistent supplicant. Like Trench, Buchanan was often at a distance from Perceval and other lines of support, so he turned to letters to make his needs known. Perceval recorded eleven letters from Buchanan and three responses in his letter books. Letters from him arrived from Ireland, Naples, Barcelona, and Bordeaux as he searched for a living. He even pondered going to Turkey and South Carolina. Throughout these travels Buchanan kept track of Perceval and attempted to use him as a major thread in his web of patronage. Some of these attempts can be witnessed in John Perceval's network for the period between 1710 and 1712 (see Figure 12).

He first surfaces in January 1711 with a letter from Naples asking Perceval to send news to his wife in Ireland and looking to have some of the funds from his living sent to him.[92] By August of that year he was in Spain and asking for letters of recommendation to three peers with power in the army (Ormond, Argyle, and Barrimore).[93] At this point he wanted to be a deputy chaplain to a garrison, but, a few letters later, he decided he would prefer to be the head chaplain rather than just the deputy.[94] A month later he revealed that he was now set to go to Turkey and wanted Perceval to write letters to merchants with Turkish connections to be kind to him. He ended this letter by asking Perceval to send his son to Eton and Oxford if he died.[95] By January of 1712 he was in Bordeaux requesting money from Perceval and telling him that one of Perceval's acquaintances (Samson) had already helped him.[96] In September he was back in Ireland and looking for a letter to the bishop of Clogher to lease him a farm.[97] By the end of 1712 he seemed satisfied with life in Ireland and no letters from him appear for almost another ten years.

But in 1721 he suddenly resurfaced to warn Perceval of a popish plot. Being the bearer of such information could place him back in Perceval's circle of patronage. It was a rather misguided attempt, though. Perceval responded, "you mention your own opinion of the Pope being in alliance with other Princes to hurt us at a time when you cou'd not but know the Pope was dead and no new one Elected, which was not so accurate as a person ought to write who offers intelligence."[98] Such a set down did not dissuade Buchanan however and five years later he tried again. He referenced Perceval's letter of 1721, defended his past opinion and sent him, "because I believe your Lordship to be Curious," an account of his hearing music from the ground, which he thought Perceval could share with others of an intellectual bent in London. He ended by asking Perceval to recommend him to the lord lieutenant, lord primate, or the lord chancellor, to find his son a position as a tutor to a nobleman, and his daughter a place as a lady's companion.[99] For Buchanan hope sprang eternal. But three years later he was dead and his family in low circumstances; however, attempts at patronage had not died with him. Almost a year after his death Buchanan's wife wrote Perceval asking him to recommend her son to the bishop of Killala so he could support her and his six sisters.[100] Whether Perceval granted the request is unknown for after this letter the saga of the Buchanans falls silent.[101]

Buchanan's correspondence with Perceval was usually problem-anchored. Often he wrote when he wanted things and he penned letters to Perceval because he knew Perceval had a vibrant network that could assist him. He knew Perceval could write to the Bishop of Clogher and that he had connections to those with positions of power. Often he was correct. Perceval did respond to many of these demands. He did not write to the peers requested, but he did send a letter to officers in the army recommending Buchanan on his word and that of his cousin, hence the links to Colonel

Depagez and Brigadier Petit in his network. He sent Buchanan a few guineas in his time of need and he wrote to the Bishop of Clogher.[102] Perceval did know when to draw the line, however, and told Buchanan's wife he would not write to the captain general of the Queen's Forces.[103]

However, Buchanan wanted more than a few favors; he wanted to make himself an integral part of Perceval's permanent network. He tried to return Perceval's favors and act as a good correspondent should. He sent things to Perceval and his family. Lady Perceval received a "naked dog" and a "munkie" and Perceval a box of Italian books.[104] These were exotic gifts that spelt out his distance and perhaps, he hoped, made him a more important correspondent. He attempted to increase his standing in Perceval's eyes by sending his services to those high in the church hierarchy, like John Hough, Bishop of Lichfield and Coventry, and to Perceval's acquaintances, like John Chamberlayne, which insinuated that he was deeply connected to Perceval's wider network.[105] He knew it boded well if could embed himself in Perceval's web of connections, which is why so many of his links run deep into the network, but he never truly achieved that goal. Perceval replied to his requests, but he never voluntarily wrote a letter to Buchanan or offered him news of either a public or private nature as he did to Berkeley and Byrd. Buchanan's ties to Perceval remained parts of ephemeral problem-based networks even if Buchanan wanted them to be more; constant networks remained privileged spaces.

Still, Buchanan's livelihood depended upon his ability to play upon Perceval's web of connections, especially since his mobility disconnected him from other centers of support, but Perceval was not his only connection. His letters suggest that he plucked other strings as well. Throughout his correspondence with Perceval he mentions Sir Alexander Cairnes, another of Perceval's acquaintances, who also appears in the network. Cairnes lived near Buchanan when he resided in county Monaghan.[106] When Buchanan had moved on to Barcelona it was Cairnes who forwarded his letters from London, later testified to the virtuous nature of his children, and finally informed Perceval of Buchanan's death.[107] Buchanan knew how to use multiple networks and he knew whose networks overlapped. He was not deeply embedded in either of these webs, but he used them to make his life function for a time. All Buchanan's straining may not have left his wife and children in a pleasant position at the time of his death, but he knew how to use letters to activate different networks of assistance when he was in need. Buchanan's network, like many ephemeral networks, demonstrates what sociologists call "the strength of weak ties."[108] They have argued that new information spreads more easily through networks that have ties to other networks that are not deeply intertwined with their own. Here it is not information, but social support that flowed through these weak ties. When one looked for a specific form of assistance it was just as useful to have many weak ties to multiple networks as it was to be embedded in a single one.

As Ambrose Godfrey stated, this was a society in which individuals were born for "each others use and helpe." Sometimes one could help an acquaintance directly by abating their rent or delivering a letter, but more often it was the individual's network that was of "use and helpe." As the British elite became more mobile geographically, their need for help at a distance expanded and so letters became a medium through which they asked for favors. Additionally, since many were looking for assistance in obtaining specific positions or specific favors their connection could rarely directly assist them, but often they knew someone who could. To help their friends most Britons had to turn to their other connections. Those with more acquaintances, especially in high places, had more power, but while the power to give grew with social status, the power to ask was open to all. The letters they wrote did not signify a deep epistolary bond with the recipient and usually lasted only a few letters. These webs were ephemeral, but they did rely upon more constant epistolary networks. They attached themselves to these webs and played on them. The entanglement of these two types of networks highlights the importance that connections had for this society. To keep their multiple or even singular worlds turning one had to know others and be known. Their ephemeral networks also suggest that the most useful ties were not always the strongest; weak ties were just as important and useful. Problem-anchored networks show this in action. Godfrey was not deeply embedded in Sloane's network and Steiger was but an "old acquaintance" of Godfrey's, but together they could hope to accomplish things they could not do alone. Permanent and long-lasting epistolary networks formed the foundation upon which this society depended, but it was the ephemeral networks that show these epistolary networks at work.

Epistolary Borders

As the trials and tribulations of Matthew Buchanan illustrate, not everyone could easily enter these networks and there were different levels of involvement and belonging. Social status and gender mattered. Those further down the social scale saw their ability to write letters growing throughout the eighteenth century, but in the letter collections of the British elite examined here they usually appear briefly as creators or members of more ephemeral networks. Social status was more of a determinate of epistolary belonging than gender, but the place of women in the epistolary world was more limited than the place of men and becoming more so. They usually wrote their letters in the same style as men and put them to use in the same fashion, but as the borders of the public world became redefined to exclude them in the eighteenth century many women found their epistolary powers curtailed.[109]

During the eighteenth century the letter-writing ability of the middling sorts expanded, complementing their growing social strength.[110] They used letters, derived power from them, and changed the way the British composed letters. Even the laboring classes were beginning to turn to letters. Nicholas Blundell often wrote letters for his tenants and most Britons could find a secretary to write a letter for them.[111] But collections of letters written by members of the British laboring classes are relatively sparse, especially before the later eighteenth century.[112] Nevertheless, letters from this social group surface within collections of elite letters and most of them are part of problem-anchored networks.

The majority of letters found in these collections from nonelite writers are from tenants and they often take the form of letters of petition. Such letters relied upon the language of deference and its connection to the rhetoric of good lordship. Tenants knew how to present themselves to their landlord to get the results they desired and it was not through a letter resplendent in eloquence, but one steeped in deference.[113] Such use of traditional language helped remind absentee landowners of their duties. With the landowning elite spending more time away from their estates, tenants found it difficult to connect with their landlords and to perform deference. Now tenants had to go through the landlord's agent or write to the landlord themselves. Many chose to write. They could place their pleas in two different forms: letters or petitions. John Perceval received both. Formal petitions had no easy salutation or date at the beginning, only a formalized introduction stating who the receiver of the petition was and the name of the petitioner. They were much more formal documents than letters and their language was deeply deferential. The petitions Perceval received from his tenants used the same rhetorical strategies found in poor relief petitions. One tenant, who wanted to pay her arrears in installments, began by laying out who she was:

she was the daughter, granddaughter, and sister of old established tenants. As she knew, long-standing ties and loyalties called for consideration. She then played on the emotions by noting her destitute state, her widowhood, and her five children. All of these elements emphasized her status as a defenseless woman in need of support.[114] Such a presentation reminded Perceval of his need to practice "good lordship."[115] Some tenants found the more traditional form of the petition more comfortable and probably more effective than a letter of petition. A letter implied effective equality; a petition acknowledged hierarchy. It was inherently humble and looked for brief assistance, not a long-lasting connection. Tenants relied on a sense of connection tied to older structures of power, not new.

The line between letters of petition and formal petitions was thin. The form was different, but the content was the same.[116] In an almost direct echo of the petitions, a tenant begged "your Lordships charity to a poor charge of motherless children."[117] Another used one letter to throw himself at his landlord's feet and another to highlight his ties of connection to his landlord.[118] He was his lord's "most Dutifull Most Obedient & most humble servant."[119] These authors highlighted their weakness, their landlord's power, and his obligations. He should help motherless children and his dutiful tenants. It was his expected role. These gestures of deference could work, although Perceval's response often depended upon his agent's view of the situation. Perceval's distance from his estates worked to his tenants' advantage. He rarely knew the truth of a situation. As he complained to his agent, "they know that at this distance it is not easie for me to disprove a great part of what they advance & so composing a melancholy story with great exaggerations they expect continually to be favour'd in their demands."[120] But Perceval's awareness did not keep him from considering such stories. An old carpenter received some yearly charity after writing to Perceval and having his story verified.[121] The composers of these letters, like the petitioners they echoed, did not seek to form a long-lasting epistolary exchange with their landlords; rather, they looked for assistance or understanding that, like the networks they briefly brought to life, was probably of short duration.

The epistolary divide between those of the laboring classes and the British elite was larger and more definite than that between men and women. Elite women and men actively exchanged letters. William Byrd II forwarded a story about a male friend from "One of my Female Correspondents" and married women wrote to male friends, especially those who were relatives or friends of the family.[122] In fact, by the late seventeenth and early eighteenth centuries the epistolary abilities of women had grown. Men increasingly composed their letters in the vernacular and used an italic hand, which meant that, unlike previous generations, women no longer needed to know other languages or exotic hands in order to read or write letters.[123] Additionally, the period 1600 to 1800 saw an expansion of educational opportunities for women of the upper and middling classes and a growing number of works catered to a female audience.[124] In many ways, the epistolary experience of women of the British elite differed little from that of their fathers, brothers, or husbands. Young girls and boys learned to write letters in a similar manner.[125] Catherine Perceval, like her brother, sent letters to relatives when she was a child and her mother even commented on the deficiencies of her hand, calling it "a begging Scrawl."[126] Nicholas Blundell copied over a letter for his wife and helped her write others, but she constantly wrote letters.[127] Women wrote letters and used letters, but their field of action was becoming increasingly constrained.

The first half of the eighteenth century saw women's political and economic options contract even as their epistolary abilities grew.[128] Dena Goodman argues that the two shifts intertwine: that as more women picked up epistolary habits, letter writing became depoliticized and relabeled as a feminine art.[129] This supports Mary Beth Norton's view that the early eighteenth century witnessed the creation of the "feminine private," which increasingly barred women from the public realm.[130] However, during the early eighteenth century these shifts were not yet set in stone. Informal networks continued to give women a source of power, even if it was curtailed to networks of friends and family. Keeping the power of informal networks in mind shows that letters did more for women than provide them with spaces uninhabited by men and places to explore their own thoughts and identity.[131] They also gave them spaces in which to act, albeit in a constrained fashion: they could be members of the constant core of a network, but forming problem-anchored networks consisting only of women was often difficult.

The failed attempt of John Perceval's son to enter Parliament in 1736 shows the power and the limitations of a female network at work. To get the younger Perceval a seat his mother and her acquaintances, Lady Marlborough and Lady Burlington, joined forces. The correspondence began with Lady Marlborough's response to a letter from Lady Egmont informing her that while she had written to the peer requested in favor of the young Perceval, she thought others had more of an interest in that area and so she had asked

Lady Burlington to write a letter to those more influential.[132] Marlborough must have also sent Lady Egmont a copy of the letter written to the requested peer for it is recorded next in the letter book. In that letter she informed her correspondent that her friend Lady Egmont "a Woman of great Merit" had discovered, via a letter from her brother, that the seat in Marlborough might be free and thus wished for his interest since she desired the seat for her son.[133] A few days later the young John Perceval wrote to thank both ladies because his mother had shown him the letters they had written.[134] These machinations resulted from the close connection the Duchess of Marlborough felt for the female members of the Perceval family for she had corresponded with Lady Egmont's mother as well.[135] Friendship between women could operate just like friendship between men: both could have personal and political elements.[136]

The incident also reveals that these three women, especially Marlborough and Burlington, understood the political landscape and how to use letters to traverse it. They knew whom to write to and how. The Duchess of Marlborough even knew which specific individuals could help. In an earlier letter John Perceval revealed his wife's political web when he noted that his information on the 1715 Jacobite Rising came from his wife, who got it from the Duchess of Marlborough, not from his own network.[137] These women could activate their webs speedily. Lady Burlington had already written her letter when Lady Marlborough responded to Lady Egmont and Marlborough sent her letter to the post office at one in the morning so as to not miss a post.[138] Yet, they did not, and probably could not, operate without turning to men: Lady Egmont knew of the parliamentary seat because her brother told her, Lady Marlborough implied in her letter that she wrote only because Perceval was in Ireland, and all the letters these women wrote were to men. This gestures to the curtailed position women held in elite society—they had to act through and for men, rather than as independent political beings. Still, they helped the social, political, and economic world turn: they too wielded power and could help form an interest using the same tools as men. The nature of epistolary power allowed women a place to function in this society. For them letters were not simply places of self-reflection, but tools that helped them participate in larger active networks. Yet their power usually emanated from their embedded position within family networks and the ability to reach beyond those boundaries was uncommon.

The structure of social networks directed the way social status and gender affected letter writers. Ties of blood and intimacy made up the inner core of these networks. Those who possessed such ties were automatically part of the larger network, be they men or women, but joining them without such ties was difficult and required enough connections to the inner network to gain entrance. For those lower on the social scale access on those terms was often blocked, but women who possessed ties to a network were instant and active members. However changing ideas about the basis of political power increasingly kept women from shifting that power outside these inner networks. Vast epistolary networks such as those outlined here were possessions of the British elite, both male and female, and while men could reach beyond them, both genders guarded entrance to them jealously.

The epistolary networks of the British elite were complex creatures that reflected the needs and workings of that social group. The fluid makeup of the networks was a reaction to the increased mobility of the elite. Their constant cores, dependent as they were on their extended kinship networks and embedded friends, reveal that the relationships they valued and relied upon possessed deep ties to older forms of community maintenance reformulated to deal with new needs. And their more ephemeral webs illustrate that all connections were valuable, but all were certainly not equal. Both strong and weak ties mattered, but they had different places within these epistolary networks. Separating these two components helps us move beyond how letters served the needs of specific individuals or how letters between certain sets of relations altered, to reveal how epistolary networks connected webs of individuals and helped the British world as a whole turn. They also reveal who could belong to this world and how. Epistolary borders had less to do with the ability to write a letter and more to do with what the writer could expect to do with that letter. All writers of all genders could hypothetically maintain an epistolary network made up of family and friends, but entering deeply into the elaborate networks of the elite was only open to a few and the ability to use them in public affairs was increasingly restricted. When William Byrd I sent off his nine letters on 20 May 1684, he was both nurturing the constant core of his network and making it work for him. He was fine-tuning a network that hummed across three thousand miles of ocean and when he played upon it he was usually pleased. He was a member of a society that took networks seriously and one that increasingly found in letters the ideal tool with which to weave them.

Chapter 4

Nurturing the Epistolary World

In his early twenties, Sir John Perceval set out "on his travels abroad and saw a good part of Europe."[1] During his trip he collected paintings, statues, books, busts, medals, drawings, and acquaintances. One of these acquaintances was Lorenzo Magnolfi, who had deep roots in the Florentine art world and in the Grand Duke of Tuscany's service. Once Perceval returned home in 1707, he maintained his relationship with Magnolfi through letters. Magnolfi was delighted to continue the correspondence and in a letter informed Perceval of the social circle he had left behind, kept him abreast of business dealings, and requested a gift of some usquebaugh, Irish whiskey.[2] Perceval responded with a letter and a flurry of gifts, including the whiskey and some Kerry stones (crystals found in county Kerry), not just for Magnolfi but also for his employer, the Grand Duke of Tuscany.[3] All these elements pleased Magnolfi for they showed he was "still in your memory," and he promised "we shall drink your health in the liquor & the stones will be a continual memory of my obligations to you."[4] The letter and gifts reassured Magnolfi of his personal relationship with Perceval and the liquor oiled the wheels of Perceval's wider community through a toast.[5] The gift to the Grand Duke of Tuscany resulted in a letter of thanks and an offer of service embedded in another of Magnolfi's epistles, which further strengthened Perceval's network.[6]

While these letters ring with personal affection, their social power stems from what Magnolfi and Perceval sent along with or inserted into these letters: gifts, references to toasts, and professions of obligation. By relying on such insertions, the exchange drew in those surrounding Magnolfi using traditional forms of social obligation. He shared the whiskey with Perceval's other acquaintances in Florence and the gift and letters reminded the Grand

Duke of Tuscany of Perceval's regard without Perceval having to trouble him with a letter.[7] While scholars have focused on the changing tone of letters, what made these slim pieces of paper effective social tools was what writers placed within them or alongside them: tried and true tools of social maintenance.[8]

When scholars of the epistolary world consider the role of letters in processes of social and political change they cast them as crucibles for the creation of the individual self, as stepping-stones toward the rise of the public sphere, or as symbols of literate authority—all signs of an increasingly modern world that was shifting from a communal, face-to-face society to one based on the power of the literate, rational individual. In this epistolary world isolated letter writers strove to nurture individual ties through intimate phrasing and displays of rhetorical prowess placed on frail pieces of paper. But if we scratch the surface of letters, this vision of distanced letter writers striving to create intimate connections disconnected from larger social networks and dependent on the phrasing of their letters fades away. Rather, letter writers proved their value as correspondents by highlighting their networks of connection and their ties to local communities through the use of traditional forms of social maintenance. In doing so letter writers were able to ease the sense of change that enveloped them. This chapter highlights the role these older forms of social maintenance, like gift giving, the offering of service, and the inclusion of toasts, had in letter writing and how the development of the familiar letter opened doors for their inclusion. Tracing how and why letter writers folded these more traditional forms of social bonding into their letters illustrates how letters actually nurtured connections and reveals a more complex view of how this society dealt with its own transformation.

The Flexibility of the Familiar Letter

How to best phrase a letter was always in doubt. Since the Renaissance, writers struggled with what kind of letter to compose: a formal letter or a familiar letter. The valuation of the classical letter style by humanists had brought the familiar letter to the fore. Celebrated Romans like Cicero emphasized the importance of plain and open letters that fostered a sense of intimacy. But alongside the wish to write open familiar letters stood the *ars dictaminis*, which provided classical structure for letters and put forth sets of rules about how writers should compose them.[9] Following such rules allowed a writer to compose the correct kind of letter without worry, but such a letter packed less social punch. Familiar letters could create a deeper sense of connection, but they could be dangerous if sent to the wrong correspondent. These worries still concerned the correspondents of the late seventeenth and early eighteenth centuries, but the choice was not as stark. More formalized letters had begun to lose their strict sense of structure during the course of the seventeenth century. By the 1620s writers begin to separate salutations from the body of the letter and the compliments that opened a letter became more varied. It also became more customary to date letters, note from whence they came, and to place these details, detached from the body, at the beginning or end of the document.[10] The form of the letter had begun to mutate into a structure that served both formal and informal epistles. The growing use of letters in everyday life and the reliance by the elite on their own hands, rather than those of their secretaries, led to this more casual letter.

Writers still played with the phrasing of their letters. How they worded, or even structured, a letter signaled the kind of relationship they had or wanted to have with the receiver. One of John Perceval's correspondents took him to task for his overly formal letter, declaring that "till I read your name [I] was at a stand to know whether it came from a friend, acquaintance, or from an Enemy. My thoughts gave me that a friend would have writ less like a Courtier, less formall & more sincere."[11] The playful tone of the whole letter reveals that the correspondent was not overly concerned about Perceval's stilted tone, but the fact that he could use the example to playfully tease Perceval illustrates that expectations existed and language could signal the status of a social bond. The tone of a letter mattered most for those unknown to or of lower social rank than the receiver. As letter manuals insisted, a familiarly worded letter from a social inferior could rankle.[12] A correspondent of the Earl of Huntingdon noted the dangers of familiarity when he thanked the earl for a favor, writing that he was wary of "slip[ing] into indecencyis & unseemly familiarityes."[13] Not everyone could use the more open and intimate tone fostered by the familiar letter. However, the letter to Huntingdon was quite familiar; the correspondent simply removed the possible impropriety by noting his difficulties. Since the divide between the two forms was no longer as clear, it was easier for more peripheral letter writers to engage their correspondent on more familiar terms. The increasingly blurred line between formal and familiar letters expanded epistolary possibilities even as it caused writers to tread carefully.

It is also true that the tone of the familiar letter altered as it shifted from a more formal, elaborate, courtly style to a more open and plain style. Such shifts were never universal. Writers had composed plain letters previously and writing with a courtly flair still mattered. In fact, letter manuals promised that their readers would come to "express their minds and thoughts . . . in a most Elegant manner" like "learned and Ingenious Men."[14] By the later seventeenth century the dominance of the Court in elite culture had begun to fade, but the power of polite sociability had risen.[15] Speaking in an elegant manner and being skilled in the giving of compliments showed that one belonged to that world, but it took skill to walk the thin line between an elegant and an overwrought letter or a sincere and artful one. While courtly and elaborate letters still flourished, the dominant trend was to more open and plain ones.

Children's letters demonstrate this shift away from the elaborate courtly style. Most elite letter writers learned their skills at home by sending letters to relatives who then critiqued them, so such letters surface here and there in adult letter collections. These letters, since they had no real business to transact, show what elements the critics expected. The six-year-old Earl of Huntingdon began a letter to his sister in 1656 with elaborate declarations of service, then waxed poetic about his love for her (he loved her more than sweetmeats and jewels), and ended by complimenting her beauty.[16] By the early eighteenth century children were still writing letters at age six to discerning relatives, but the letters had changed. The daughter and son of John Perceval, age six and seven respectively, both wrote to their father in 1718, but rather than filling their letters with compliments they simply thanked their father for his letters, swore to follow his instructions, expressed pleasure in his imminent return, and sent their greetings to the relatives with him.[17] By the early eighteenth century elegant turns of phrase were still acceptable, but they were not expected. Later in the century correspondents turned to sentimental language instead, but before then letter writers looked suspiciously at both elaborate courtly compliments and deep cries from the heart.[18]

These alterations in style were the result of shifts in elite socialization and in the makeup of the letter-writing population. As the centers of elite culture in Britain moved from the Court to urban centers, civility became valued over courtesy and elaborate compliments were no longer as necessary.[19] Paralleling this process was the proliferation of letter writing. With letters becoming increasingly frequent and more deeply embedded in everyday life, the need for elaborate displays of compliments faded. The composition of the epistolary community had altered as well. Those beyond the elite wrote letters and the elite wrote letters for more reasons. Those of the middling and laboring classes were not as well versed in the language of compliments and everyone needed fewer flourishes when conducting business.

Members of the British elite were sensitive to the uses of language. Speaking correctly and picking the correct topics of conversation were critical if one wished to be a member of polite society.[20] And as in their conversation, members of polite society expected each other to "make each Line of their Letters sparkle."[21] Scholars of the early twentieth century viewed this period as the pinnacle of the epistolary art.[22] Facility with language and the ability to use it politely grew in importance as the British elite allowed those with less vaulted lineages into their social world in a limited fashion.[23] Membership in the upper classes was no longer judged solely on birth, but on the ability to know the proper social norms. It was how you dressed, spoke, and even wrote a letter that mattered. But the fact that it was the pinnacle of epistolary *art*, not epistolary *sincerity*, concerned some. They worried that polished exteriors hid inner evil or, less nefariously, that with overuse words lost their meaning.[24] As Peter Collinson lamented, it was a "time of day that pretensions & offers of friendship are so common & become so fashionable that they are used on every occasion with but little regard to sincerity."[25] Even letter manuals acknowledged that " 'Tis true, that Style and Phrase of a Letter ought not be too Elaborate or Over-strain'd yet it usually begins, and is ushered in with some handsom, but brief Complement, to insinuate into their favour to whom 'tis directed."[26] Writers included compliments to get the favor asked for, not because they sincerely meant them. In a society where social webs determined one's ability to function, such compliments ran wild and for that reason became paltry testaments to affection.

Scholars have picked apart these subtle changes in epistolary style. They have followed the increasingly affectionate tone of letters, the influence of the more informal mercantile style, and the increasing importance of sentimental language.[27] Such alterations in style mattered. The language used could ease the strain of distanced communication.[28] Such alterations in style also allowed letters to be more flexible. It would have been difficult to place offers of service as a postscript or tell of a toast in a more formal courtly epistle. By the early eighteenth century it was easier to signal to a deeper social bond without questionable professions of affection.

These more informal letters allowed writers to mimic face-to-face encounters in their letters. As previous chapters have shown, letter writers almost always preferred face-to-face interaction to epistolary correspondence.[29] The residents of the British world could judge a facial expression as well, if not better, than a written expression.[30] William Byrd II playfully asserted that his absence from England caused his correspondents to place him among the ranks of the dead "because we are in truth little better than dead to them. We can please none of their sences at this distance and what signifies a Fellow to Them that cant please their sences?"[31] Distance denied a sense of touch and connection and without it social death could follow. But Byrd resurrected his presence through letters; in his words he "haunted" his correspondents.[32] These thin sheets of paper allowed writers to project a spectral self or absent presence. Letters could become their physical representatives and assail the receiver with conversation and bodily presence.[33]

Correspondents often referred to their physical selves in their letters. References to hands were especially popular. Writers often included some variation of the phrase "I hope this finds its way safe to your hands."[34] Letters were safe only when they had reached the physical body of the receiver. The reference to the actual body created a more immediate bond. Writers even allowed letters to perform physical deeds. They kissed the hands of the receiver.[35] William Byrd II insisted, "This kisses your hand by my friend Dr. Tscheffely."[36] Sometimes writers conveniently forgot to include the letter in the exchange and simply said they themselves kissed the hand of their correspondent.[37] When Peter Collinson stated in a letter to his spouse, "I kiss thy hand," he directly touched his wife.[38] Kissing the hands of an acquaintance was an expected act of courtesy, albeit an antiquated one by the eighteenth century.[39] But references to hands emphasized connection. The hand negotiated most of the contact individuals had with the outside world: acquaintances kissed them in greeting, the hand lifted up food or utensils, and it picked up the pen. Correspondents preferred letters written in the composer's own hand, for it physically linked them to the sender.[40] It was a sign of intimacy and connection. By the eighteenth century the desire for direct physical contact had lessened, but bodily deportment still situated one socially.[41] The posture of the entire body spoke volumes and if writers could invoke it in their letters they eased the strain of written communication.

In the hands of some writers, letters and the words within them displayed human characteristics and replaced the need for the physical self. Peter Collinson was a master of this approach. As we have seen, his letters spoke to him, but they also allowed him, or at least his soul, to directly connect with his correspondents. To his wife he wrote, "Thine gave mee more satisfaction than I can express, the very sight of thy Dear Characters made my heart leap for joye, but when I read the contents where love and tenderness flows in every Line how did my soul spring to thee in extasies of love."[42] His wife's letter replaced the need for a physical body and allowed the souls to spring to each other. But this is an extreme case; most letters hid blushes rather than exhibiting them.[43]

More common than having a letter physically represent a correspondent was having a letter literally speak for a correspondent. Even when teaching how to write a letter, manuals instructed students "to imagine the Person we write to, present; and then to set down in our Letter what we would say to him if he were by."[44] Writers composed letters while imagining a conversation. However, letters were rarely free and easy discussions—the form of a letter was too important, but it functioned as a useful trope since the line between the written and the oral in a letter could be relatively thin. While less common by the later seventeenth century, some correspondents composed their letters orally by reciting them to a secretary and many letters assumed oral form when read out loud.[45] Conceiving of letters as conversation was not new; Cicero himself had made the reference.[46] But these epistolary conversations took place in a different historical context; in this society being able to converse well was a social necessity.

Writers often referred to letters as conversations in an off-handed manner.[47] In letters they claimed that "Brother Virtuosi's must converse" and one was "never better pleased . . . than when I am conversing with you."[48] On other occasions writers implied that they actually forgot that they were writing.[49] One writer dramatically declared, "but what am I doing? Forgive me, I entreat you, for I thought myself conversing with you, and was willing to detain you as long as possible under my roof."[50] The question mark and the begging of forgiveness create the feel of a true spoken conversation, so much so that the writer transports the receiver to his house. Other writers were less creative and simply treated letters like continuing conversations. Letters could start mid-thought, like William Byrd II's, which began, "I cannot be of your opinion that wine may not be made in this country."[51] After the salutation, this letter had no formal greeting, no reference to past letters, it simply responded to the receiver's last letter as though no time or distance had intervened.

But besides softening the divide between the face-to-face and written worlds, writers could also play with the form of a letter to signal a close relationship.[52] Most letters, even those between close relatives, began with the salutation of "Sir," "Madame" or "My Lord." Letter manuals insisted that dire consequences would result if the writer deviated from such formulas.

A letter writer should only include the name of a correspondent in the salutation when he or she wrote to one of a "mean Condition," but often those with close ties ignored this rule.[53] The Duke of Richmond referred to Peter Collinson as "Dear Peter" and Peter Collinson addressed a correspondent as "My Curious Friend."[54] Only those with solid relationships could cross this line. Lord Richmond held a much higher social position than Peter Collinson, but the letter referred not to a necessary cloth order, but to the offer of a carriage so that Collinson could visit Richmond's estate. Their botanical interests united them and made their relationship less formal. The second letter was between brother naturalists, who further broke the prescribed letter formula by playfully addressing one letter, "From the bottom of a Coal pit at Swanwich Derbyshire 135 feet deep," since he had promised "to date you a Letter from some subterranean work."[55] Playing with form in this fashion allowed letter writers to show affection while avoiding the production of overly emotional or detached letters, both of which could harm the relationship.

Others simply rejected epistolary formalities. One couple decided not to send services since "Its only a matter of form and serves only to fill up letters."[56] This was due not to a lack of affection, but to the simple belief that they no longer needed "matters of form" to maintain their relationship. As we have seen, some correspondents excluded the salutation and began letters in full flight.[57] Jettisoning the formal structure of a letter was a risky proposition, but within trusted communities it was acceptable. It allowed the writer to emphasize the social bond and matters of form did not mar the feeling of direct communication. By employing a playful or dismissive attitude toward formal letter structures writers gestured to a closeness without relying on the language of affection or compliment. However, such breaks in form were rare; most letter writers needed the formal structure to signal their status to others and show an understanding of their place in the world. These writers had to find other means of maintaining their epistolary networks.

If a writer could not rely on complimentary language or breaks in form to sustain a sense of connection with their correspondents, they could lean on the basic reciprocal nature of letters.[58] One of the most frequent words used to describe a letter was "obliging."[59] Writer after writer expressed their thanks for the "obliging" letter they had received.[60] Referring to a letter as obliging was a rhetorical flourish, but only because it had meaning. Furthermore, letters themselves were becoming obliging by the later seventeenth century for the first time. When members of the Hastings family and their correspondents mentioned being obliged to a sender early in the seventeenth century it was for favors offered them or venison sent to them; rarely was it for letters. This remained true later in the century; many different acts obliged writers, but it became more common to refer to the sending of a letter as obliging. The first time a member of the Hastings family called a letter obliging was in 1671.[61] By the end of the seventeenth century letters had become important items of exchange in and of themselves because more Britons wrote them and because they were becoming critical tools of social negotiation. Since letters were easier to send, acting on this sense of mutual exchange became expected. Keeping up an exchange of letters was no longer a feat; it was a requirement.

Writers were keenly aware of the reciprocal nature of letters and kept a careful eye on their exchanges. As scholars have noted, writers employed the language of credit and debt frequently.[62] This language was not casual; writers knew exactly how many letters they could get on credit and how many letters in debt they were.[63] Perceval's cousin playfully gave him a 3-for-1 deal: "Tho I think, dear Sir John, I am not a letter in your debt, yet having much more leasure than you, I may afford two or three for one."[64] The words "debt" and "afford" give her letter a sly monetary tilt and Peter Collinson blatantly linked the two: "I must soone Become a Banckrupt, but that I may not prove the Worst of Debtors, I wou'd gladly make some Composition In hopes of future Credit."[65] Allusions to credit and debt in letters were not new. A merchant's letter from 1545 made the same connection.[66] But the strict accounting of letters grew, especially as the excuses for not sending a letter decreased. Perceval's correspondent knew precisely how many letters he owed her. Earlier correspondents were rarely as specific. In 1654 a correspondent thanked the Countess of Huntingdon for her letter and a series of verses, declaring, "it is glorious for me to be so endebted, it would be unpardonable to hope or desire ever to be quit."[67] He luxuriated in his indebtedness, but later writers would expect a return both because it was more easily given and because credit was increasingly weighted with economic and social significance.

Since the economic expansion of the sixteenth century, lines of credit had expanded and by the eighteenth century those lines of credit were reaching across a wider geographic area. Reputation rested on successful dealing with debt.[68] This was especially true for merchants who increasingly relied on correspondence to manage their businesses. Merchants did not often use the word debt in reference to their letters, but they almost always referred to what letters they had received and a lapse in such a correspondence would be bad business and lead to the loss of credit. Beyond the docks and counting houses, other Britons worried about the strength of their credit and the depth of their debt. By the early eighteenth century the letters of the British elite had adopted the mercantile habit of being specific in their epistolary accounting because such debts had become easier to pay and because such language was familiar and powerful. But its importance in these letters lies not in the way it reflected mercantile influence or even the way it reveals the reciprocal nature of letter exchange, rather it illustrates the increasing expectations writers had of letter exchange: More than ever before a letter written called for one in return.

But sometimes receivers ignored the obligation letters placed on them and most writers needed epistolary credit because they would not reply to all the letters they received. Many a letter writer lamented the loss of a correspondence and felt the sting of rejection. William Byrd II of Virginia complained of the "profound silence" that met many of his letters and, after waiting two years for a response, Peter Collinson reprimanded a correspondent for his silence, reminding him that such an action was "not Friendly."[69] The ideal of reciprocal exchange was powerful, the new flexibility of language gave writers more ways to nurture ties and invoke face-to-face interaction, but relying on the power of an individual letter to assure oneself of a social tie was a dangerous proposition. Gifts or other traditional forms of social bonding that gestured to actions taken outside the folds of a letter, but inside a correspondent's network, could be more powerful.

Gifts That Give Back

Sending gifts alongside letters or referring to gifts in letters was one way to strengthen a social tie in a traditional fashion. Scholars have long recognized the centrality of the gift in social relations.[70] Initially scholars believed that the importance of the gift economy faded during the early modern period since it was incompatible with the rise of a market economy, but recently scholars have looked more closely at the way gift economies actually expanded and became entangled with market economies during the period.[71] The fashion in which letter writers grafted gifts onto their letters reinforces this claim: gifts augmented the social power of letters and letters added a new layer of complexity to the way gift giving operated. Letters as social tools cannot be understood without the books, hams, and herbs sent alongside them.

Gifts of many hues accompanied letters. Some of the most popular and time-honored gifts were items of food and drink.[72] Correspondents received venison, that most traditional of gifts, partridges, and scallops. Others gave tea or something of a more intoxicating variety. As Perceval's gift of Irish whiskey illustrates, these offerings were powerful because they could be shared and nurture multiple ties. Many consumed the food and partook of the drink. But like Magnolfi's Kerry stones, gifts could also be more permanent and individualized: books, busts, sheets of music, and even jewels made their way alongside letters, as did more lively cargo like monkeys, mockingbirds, and rattlesnakes. Other gifts were easily inserted into letters. News, simple verses, and intellectual information could easily pad a letter and increase its social worth.

News was a highly valued gift because it eased anxiety and allowed letter writers to keep track of their world.[73] The actions of two of John Perceval's correspondents show that news could act like a gift. They both often sent Perceval news in letters, but when they had none to send one sent "the celebrated Tragedy of Cato" and another some verses provided by "a little nymph of about 5 or 6 year old, drest all in flowers and myrtle."[74] A good tragedy or verses could replace news, insinuating that it was the giving that was important. These gifts augmented the feeling of connection created by a letter: they served as reminders that more than a simple and perhaps ephemeral epistolary link bound these correspondents.

Letters themselves, as has long been recognized, could be gifts.[75] Writers presented ornately decorated epistles to correspondents, but more often recipients treated everyday letters as presents or favors.[76] This was a new development. Earlier in the seventeenth century the Hastings family and its correspondents rarely referred to letters as favors; sending cloth was a favor, sending venison was a favor, but during the second half of the century letters themselves became favors, especially when they allowed the receiver to "repe without sowing," that is, to receive without sending.[77] Because letters were becoming more common and more easily sent, they became frequent tokens of esteem. They, and not just the actions they informed recipients of, became the gift. Peter Collinson assured his correspondent that "the kind token of your Respect has not been lost in Oblivion, but often perused with Pleasure."[78] Collinson emphasized the physicality of the letter; he picked it up and read it repeatedly. Others reportedly slept with their letters.[79] Letters gave the gift of connection; they showed remembrance and could be revisited for reassurance.

Givers thought long and hard about what gifts to give because the choice showed the status of their relationship.[80] Many members of the elite continued to give venison. Receivers knew that venison told of aristocratic landowning power and nobles knew that how they distributed venison was a test of their own power and reputation.[81] Giving venison amplified and reaffirmed prestige; it smelt of good will and good lordship. But for those looking to nurture close personal bonds, status mattered less than the desires of the receiver. Tailoring a gift to a specific individual increased the social bond automatically created by the gift. Unsurprisingly then, the gifts mentioned in letters show careful consideration. John Perceval gave his estate agent books on husbandry, and Perceval's brother sent him four stucco busts because he was "a lover of such things."[82] John Perceval enclosed, in a letter to William Byrd II, "a Picture of the Kanna Root that grows among the Hottentots with a description of it extracted from Kolbens present State of the Cape of Good Hope." He did so to allow Byrd to "judge whether this and Ginseng be the same."[83] Perceval's gift reflected his remembrance of Byrd's interest in ginseng and promoted further conversation. Senders chose gifts that highlighted the recipients' place in their social network.

Gifts also came to reflect the widening world the British inhabited as gift giving became specialized due to location. Receivers looked to Londoners for pamphlets and music that could only be found in the metropole. Those in Ireland sent Irish whiskey and Kerry stones.[84] Lord and Lady Perceval received small boxes of tea from China.[85] William Byrd II of Virginia gave the Royal Society ginseng, a rattlesnake, and an opossum.[86] His father sent the rector of Crofton Wakefield in Yorkshire an "Indian habitt," moccasins, shells for around the neck, a cap of wampum, and a bow and arrow set for his son. In return, he asked for some treatises on minerals and stones.[87] Interest in colonial rarities was high and provided colonists with a special place in the world of gift exchange. This vaulted position came burdened with expectations. Nicholas Blundell assured his brother in Virginia that no one expected him to send curiosities, only to retract this statement two years later because "Lord Moleneux doth still desire you'l procure him a mock-bird."[88]

The purpose of most gifts was to form a social bond between the sender and receiver and, as Marcel Mauss and others have insisted, receivers had to act in return. Gifts were inherently reciprocal. Some writers tried to insist that their gift came without strings. One correspondent insisted that his gift came "ex toto carde as a sincere token of friendship."[89] However, most writers worried about returning such favors. Cassandra Brydges was ashamed when her Antiguan friend showered her with orange water, but never asked anything from her.[90] Similarly, Peter Collinson exclaimed to a Virginian correspondent, "When I sum up all these repeated Instances of great Friendship, the Balance Due on my side is so great . . . I am Confused & att a Loss What Returns to Make."[91] Gifts could lock writers into a web of reciprocal exchange more strongly than letters. Receivers knew that the bond of obligation created by a gift was not easily cut. Collinson found "no Greater pleasure then to be Communicative & oblige others. It is Laying an obligation & I seldome fail of Returns."[92] He treasured the bonds these gifts created. He might playfully call into being a balance sheet of giving, but he knew the true value of a gift could never be determined. The measure of good will a gift engendered was not something a simple return gift dissolved.[93] It was the thought, not the specific gift that counted. For this reason, attaching one to a letter made the connection more binding.

The fact that these gift givers sent a letter along with their gift provided them with an extra tool in the game of gift exchange. Letters allowed givers and receivers to control their gifts: they could track them, explain them, and renegotiate their meanings. Peter Collinson kept track of the venison he expected to receive, and if it did not materialize he took the senders to task through letters.[94] Senders also used letters to organize and control their gift giving from afar. In 1724 James Brydges worried about the venison he sent after an acquaintance notified him that his gifts of venison had gone astray and were cut in an unseemly manner.[95] Brydges was not pleased. To remedy the problem he wrote to his agent and had him send a list of those who had received venison. Brydges then proceeded to tell his agent, name by name, who got venison and who did not. The dead, those in the city, those who had declined it, or those who had been "sufficiently complimented" received none.[96] Since Brydges lived away from his estates he had to depend on letters and his agents to divide up his venison. As gifts began to travel farther and more frequently, letters helped senders and receivers keep the system functioning.

Even more important, letters allowed writers to place their gifts in the correct light. When a tenant sent the Earl of Huntingdon twenty partridges he also made sure "to tender to your Lordshpps hand these rude lines," which explained that he had sent the partridges only because Huntingdon had liked them before.[97] His "rude lines" let him explain the nature of his gift and present it in the correct deferential manner. Describing a gift in a letter could also increase the value of that gift. When John Perceval received fourteen pots of scallops, the sender, Emmanuel Moore, was sure to inform him that they "past through my Wife's and Daughters' hands" for he hoped it would persuade him "to eat 'em with a better realish."[98] He wanted Perceval to know that these were not just any scallops: they had a physical link to the senders. The use of letters benefited receivers as well. Through letters they could send their thanks, show they accepted the bond of connection, and frame the gift as they wished. When Peter Collinson received shells from Hans Sloane he assured him that it was not their rarity that pleased him, but their ties to Sloane.[99] He emphasized the personal connection embedded in the gift and used it to signal to Sloane his interpretation of their relationship.

Letters' ability to provide a space for the negotiation and renegotiation of gifts was necessary at a time when receivers often became confused about the meaning of goods sent to them. As trade expanded and more goods crossed the wide breadth of the British Atlantic world, the gift economy became increasingly entangled with the market economy. To an extent, some gifts became simply purchased goods, possibly devoid of ties of obligation.[100] This forced receivers to wonder if certain objects were gifts or simply commodities.[101] A frustrated James Brydges took his correspondent to task for charging him for wine he thought was a present. In Brydges's eyes, this was no simple gift, but one he was to receive because he had dismissed the giver's debt.[102] Webs of friendship and networks of money bound Brydges and his correspondent and the two, at this point in time, stood at cross-purposes. Brydges also attempted to use money to disentangle himself from a gift relationship. In one exchange he offered to pay for two large casks of Madeira because he knew "of no Service I am capable of rendering you considerable enough to entitle me to Presents of such a nature."[103] The growing power of the market economy added another register to the language of exchange, but it did not signal the end of the gift.

However, usually the discussion raged around what a gift meant, not whether it was a gift. Givers often tried to downplay the value of their gifts. Their favors were always unworthy of the sender, "not adequate to your civilities," or but a "small token."[104] Such rhetoric pressed the receiver to embrace the gift and allowed the sense of obligation to continue.[105] Gifts were intentionally difficult to repay and it was much better to give than receive. The giver held the power in the relationship and the receiver had to be grateful. In a society where the receiver often had to act in favor of the giver, some tried to avoid certain ties by redefining the nature or value of the gift in a letter. Before he became Duke of Chandos, James Brydges tried to increase his standing with the Duchess of Marlborough by sending her a gift. He had found a jewel, once owned by the Duke of Orleans, with a picture of the dauphin inside. He replaced that picture with one of her husband and attempted to present it to her grace. She refused. The jewel, she explained, was too valuable.[106] Brydges declared it a trifle and hoped "your Grace entertains a better opinion of me than to think I am so insensible of ye obligations I have to your noble Family as to imagine they are capable of being paid by a mean present." The only repayment possible was by "ye Services of my whole life."[107] Both the duchess and Brydges reframed the gift in their letters. The duchess knew that she could not simply reject the gift since she wanted to keep the connection, but she also knew that she did not want to be tied to Brydges by such a strong chain. In response she augmented the monetary value of the gift and implied that Brydges wanted out of her web of patronage. This was not what Brydges wished for at all. He countered by revaluing the gift in his letter and insisting that the value stemmed only from the duke's picture. He shifted the negotiations away from monetary worth and centered them on personal value. This was his major goal, to tighten the personal bond between himself and the Marlboroughs, and he needed a letter to do so. The fate of the jewel is unknown, but the tussle it engendered in 1706 illustrates that letters provided a place where individuals could negotiate the value of a gift and the social bond it created.

Gifts also altered the nature of the letter. Adding a gift to a letter augmented the level of obligation placed on the recipient. A letter had many purposes, a gift but one. Writers composed letters for pragmatic purposes as well as to nurture social bonds, but they only sent gifts to foster a relationship. When Perceval's cousin at Fort St. George in India sent him tea from Canton, he wrote a letter informing him of the gift and thanking him for his help and letters of recommendation.[108] The gift gave his thanks depth. Gifts also gave correspondents a reason to write. Many of the letters that accompanied gifts had no purpose but to introduce the gift and the reasons behind it. When Brydges first sent the jewel to the Duchess of Marlborough, his letter concerned only the jewel, and when Emmanuel Moore sent John Perceval the scallops, the letter revolved around the gift and nothing else. But gifts also eased the strain caused by epistolary communication. Scallops, tea, and jewels were tangible representations of esteem, unlike words penned in letters.

By sending gifts in or alongside their letters, writers imbued the letters with the same sense of obligation and power that ran through traditional forms of gift exchange. This gave their letters more power as social tools.

However, letters also tweaked the world of gift giving. They provided a new space where givers and receivers negotiated the meaning of their gifts and provided the means to do so from afar. Letters complemented gifts; both oiled epistolary ties and increased in number due to the expansion of the British world. As historians have argued, the expansion of gift giving was a response to the growth of the market economy and the institutionalization of society, but it was also a response to the needs invoked by the increased mobility and geographic range of the British elite.

Such alterations made simply serving or helping an acquaintance a gift. Performing a favor was often as important as giving a correspondent jewels, shells, or tea. John Perceval asked an acquaintance to gather music and pamphlets in London for him and his cousin requested that he search out new maps for him.[109] Neither party stated whether he had reimbursed the other for these goods. But either way, they were willing to purchase them because they wished to serve the receivers, for in return they became active members of their webs. The same process accounts for Richard Blundell's acquisition of the mock-bird from Virginia for his brother's acquaintance. He was a node in that individual's web. Increasingly the British relied on these wide webs of association to perform economic and social acts of service. The growth of trade, the expansion of the British world, and its urbanization added another layer of gift giving. Social visits, colonial goods, and services given at a distance became as important as venison. Letters organized these exchanges and imbued them with meaning. Letters depended on gifts and gifts on letters, and examining their intersection reveals that both depended on webs of service.

Sending Services

At the end of one letter to John Perceval, his cousin inserted that "The Duke of Ormond gives his service to you," and in a different postscript, years later, another cousin reminded him that "Harry is your most humble servant."[110] Like gifts, offering services through a letter was a traditional way to show a sense of attachment. And, unlike words of affection, services implied action. But even more important, services could nurture whole networks and, as we have seen, maintaining a larger network was the goal of many letter writers. Informal offers of service increasingly surfaced in letters during this period and their presence points to a society that was growing ever more dependent on promises of service and assistance that were less formal but more widespread.

Writers saw the sending of services as an accepted element of the letter form and as a traditional way to maintain face-to-face communities.[111] Letter after letter concluded with some variation of "my humble and unfeigned duty & service to your Lordship and the most noble Ladyes, your honorable mother and sisters."[112] While letter writing manuals never mentioned sending services, they did recommend that writers close their letters by declaring themselves, "Your most humble, or most Oliged Servant," especially when writing to social superiors.[113] Such statements did not always have a larger significance. Each offer of service was not tied to a specific action, but such an addition implied an understanding of the ways in which ties of mutual obligation held this society together.

The exchange of services was not new, but letter writers began to use them more frequently. Declarations of service do not pepper the Paston letters of the late fifteenth century, but they do surface in the Hastings correspondence of the early seventeenth century and became more common later in the century.[114] Their place in the language and practice of courtesy ensured their popularity. Like face-to-face encounters, letters usually began with "hearty commendations" and ended with services.[115] But services were more than gestures of courtesy; they were reminders of social obligation. Ties of service had long held British society together. Throughout most of the medieval and into the early modern period most Britons served others. They lived either with masters of a trade or, if they were members of the upper class, with a great lord who trained them. These were legal and formal bonds. By the sixteenth century these more formal attachments faded and the nature of the relationship altered.[116] The men and women who proffered services in their letters were not formally in the service of a lord or master, but their livelihoods still depended on serving others and being served in return. The nature of service had altered with the expansion of the state and the market economy in a fashion that made informal acts of service more important than previously. Offers of service not only linked older forms of social maintenance to new social, economic, and political structures to make them more familiar, they actually helped those emerging systems to function.

When letter writers sent their services they were offering to serve the receivers, to act for them. These services took tangible form and were part of a patronage society in which Britons actively served one another. Serving might mean finding a position for a connection, watching over an acquaintance's interest, or sending rarities. It could also entail assisting the friend of an acquaintance. One served the individual and the network. When writers sent their services they were rarely offering a specific service; rather, they were offering the promise of service. At times, however, one can find offers of service manifesting themselves as tangible services. When John Joynes offered his "humble and unfeigned duty & service" to Theophilus Hastings, the seventh earl of Huntingdon, he meant it.[117] He was a prebendary at Lincoln and had been the sixth earl of Huntingdon's chaplain; after the earl's death, his service to the family continued. He offered to help the new earl find a wife and, in turn, the young earl asked him if he desired another vicarage and declared he could find a place for Joynes's brother.[118] Perhaps this was not the specific service Joynes meant when he offered his services in his letter, but he was ready to perform it because he knew the young earl would assist him in return. It was being a member of the social network that mattered, not any specific service offered. As has been seen, acquaintances could rarely provide the service asked for, but they could help petitioners find someone who could. Offering one's service in a letter gestured to the writer's wish to be part of a wider network.

Usually those of equal social stations exchanged services among themselves. But even within the elite community gradations existed. Receiving the services of the Duke of Ormond meant that Sir John Perceval had the support of a man who, at least until his fall from grace in 1715, had the ability to procure positions both in Ireland and in the army. On a smaller scale, Perceval's cousin reminded him of a relative's service because he wanted Perceval to help him find a position. Both Ormond and Perceval had social power and could easily provide services. This power emanated from the social webs they possessed. Their networks included many powerful nodes they could activate. While the ability to assist was never equal, all services were necessary. How an estate agent helped his employer differed from how his employer assisted him, but both kept the social wheel turning. Offering to serve also allowed those of a lesser rank to create connections while retaining a deferential manner.[119] When writers offered services they did not demand, they gave, often humbly. This made such offers of service hard to reject, but receivers knew that if they acted on such offers they had to serve in return, no matter their rank. Services, reciprocity, and obligations walked hand in hand.

Correspondents knew that offering their services in a letter enhanced its worth. Often writers detached them from the body of the letter and included them as postscripts.[120] Postscripts often contained the ideas that writers forgot, but they also held the elements they wished to emphasize. Rather than suggesting unimportance, this positioning implies that they were necessary, so much so that writers marred the form of their letter with lines scribbled on the bottom or side. Services inserted as postscripts owed their existence to their value; without them the letter was incomplete. Additionally, readers did not easily skim over postscripts; their distance from the body of the letter directed the reader's attention to them. Even their very specificity illustrates their importance. In 1706 John Perceval received a letter that ended, "Mr. Emmerson returns you his Service, as dos Sir Rowland Gwim. Mr. Frankland gives you his respects."[121] Perceval's correspondent had to remember that Mr. Emmerson and Sir Rowland Gwim were returning their services and that Mr. Frankland was simply sending his respects. These details implied that Perceval's acquaintances had accepted his offers of service and were returning their own, reaffirming the reciprocal bond. The acknowledgment of services was so critical that writers even told correspondents that they had sent on services.[122] This was not a simple formality. The sending of services was less crucial between close correspondents, like those sent between a husband and wife. Such correspondents saw each other on a regular basis and formal expressions of service were not necessary. However, for those at a distance or those with tenuous links, an acknowledgment of a bond strengthened their network. In fact, by offering their services individuals were almost volunteering to become a node in an ephemeral epistolary network.

Services surface in letters in three ways, which emphasize their networking tendencies. The most common and most connected to the letter form are those sent between the sender and receiver of the letter. These services could be formal gestures of courtesy, added because they were the right way to end a letter. Multiple letters end with such declarations of service, but they were not always simply conclusions to a letter. Writers could use such services to emphasize their link with the correspondent. James Brydges wrote to his cousin, "I can't any further forebear giving you this trouble to assure you of my humble service and how very much I reckon myself obliged to you for the honour of your correspondence."[123] Brydges took the traditional offer of service and exaggerated it to make it noticeable. He leaned on services and a sense of obligation to keep the correspondence functioning. These offers of service were common due to their strong ties to epistolary expectations, but other types of services give a clearer picture of the networking possibilities of letters.

Writers also sent services to acquaintances outside the epistolary fold. A Jamaican correspondent wrote to Hans Sloane and asked him to present his services to Lady Wright and Pudsy.[124] In this letter he maintained his

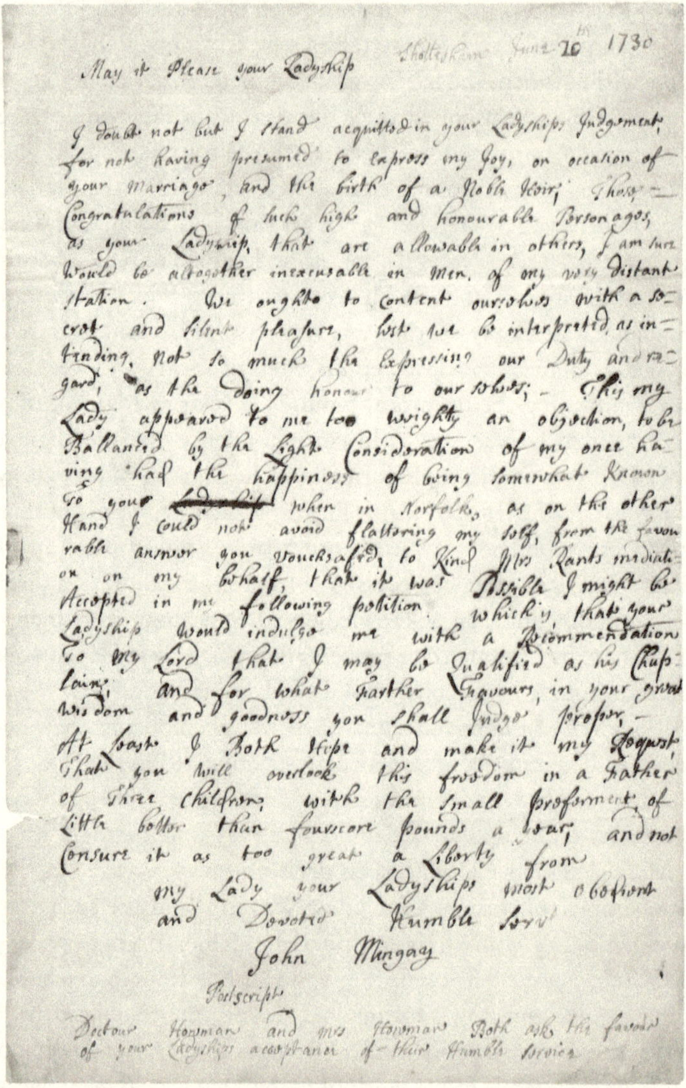

Shottesham June 20th 1730

May it Please your Ladyship

I doubt not but I stand acquitted in your Ladyships Judgement, for not having presumed to express my Joy, on occasion of your Marriage, and the birth of a Noble Heir; Those Congratulations of such high and honourable Personages, as your Ladyship, that are allowable in others, I am sure Would be altogether inexcusable in Men, of any very distant Station. We ought to content ourselves with a secret and silent pleasure, lest we be interpreted as intending, not so much the Expressing our Duty and regard, as the doing honour to our selves; This my Lady appeared to me too weighty an objection, to be Ballanced by the slight Consideration of my once having had the happiness of being somewhat Known to your [illegible] when in Norfolk, as on the other Hand I could not avoid flattering my self, from the favourable answer you vouchsafed, to Kind Mrs Rants mediation on my behalf, that it was Possible I might be Accepted in the following petition, which is, that your Ladyship would indulge me with a Recommendation to my Lord that I may be Qualified as his Chaplain; and for what farther Favours, in your great Wisdom and goodness you shall Judge proper, — At least I Both Hope and make it my Request, That you will overlook this freedom in a Father of Three Children; with the small preferment of little better than fourscore pounds a year, and not Censure it as too great a Liberty from

my Lady your Ladyships most obedient
and Devoted Humble Servt

John Mingay

Postscript

Doctour Howman and Mrs Howman Both ask the favour of your Ladyships acceptance of their Humble Service

Figure 14. Services were often added as postscripts to letters to separate the moment of social bonding from the issues dealt with in the body of the letter and to emphasize them. In his letter to Selina Hastings, Countess of Huntingdon, John Mingay boldly writes "postscript" and then adds the humble services of Dr. and Mrs. Howman. In doing so he reveals how a letter could tie groups of people together rather than simply the sender and receiver.

John Mingay to Selina Hastings, Countess of Huntingdon, 20 June 1730, HEH HA 9297.

relationship with Sloane and with two additional acquaintances. Such statements allowed letter writers to nurture connections with correspondents and the communities surrounding them. Those living near letter writers were not passive receivers either; if they knew a writer was penning a letter they asked the composer to include their services. William Byrd the elder ended a letter composed in Virginia to his brother-in-law in England: "Capt. Randolph & Mr. Banister, present their service to you, whom wee always remember when wee meet."[125] This letter reconnected the two acquaintances with Byrd's brother-in-law, and Byrd included their declaration to assure him that he, Randolph, and Banister remembered him when together. In some cases writers included these services to give their letters an aura of intimacy. They often sent services to the wives or husbands of correspondents. This gesture drew in the domestic world and signaled to a relationship with the correspondent's whole family. Writers expected such additions in letters between family members and friends, but when added to a business letter they could deepen the relationship by adding a link to the domestic world.[126] Sending services to others and from others gestured to the writer's social power. When writers received services from those surrounding their correspondent they knew their own social web was strong and reliant on more than a single thread. Furthermore, senders knew that including multiple services revealed that they possessed a strong network themselves and knew that of their correspondent.

Letter writers could also be simply middlemen; they neither sent their own services nor received any. In these cases those near a letter writer asked the writer to send services not to the receiver, but to those around the receiver. A friend of Perceval's cousin simply requested that he ask Perceval to present his service to Perceval's wife.[127] Often these types of services rode on the backs of the other two forms. Those wishing to send on services usually asked the writer to first proffer them to the receiver of the letter and then to send on additional services. Before asking Perceval to give her husband's services to his wife, a relative presented hers to him, and before requesting that Cassandra Willoughby pass on services from the correspondent's sister to three more relatives, her correspondent assured her that both she and her sister presented their services to Cassandra herself.[128] These letters were simply links between different social circles. A letter formally connected two individuals, but inside their folds letters could connect many more. The services sent between the Perceval cousins involved four people, and those involving Cassandra Willoughby included six individuals. Sending such services relied on knowledge of the writers' social networks. Cassandra

Willoughby's correspondent and even her correspondent's sister had to know that she had easy access to the other relatives. This knowledge allowed them to send services more easily and it showed their correspondents that they possessed links to their own social world. Someone with deep ties to one's own social network was hard to cut loose.

Letter writers knew that offering services through their letters was an ideal way to nurture their widespread networks, but the way they did so presses us to look beyond the letter itself. First and foremost, these writers wanted their services sent, and they delivered them any way they could, whether written or oral. When John Perceval's cousin wrote him that "Mr. Southwell has promised to make your compliments to Mr. Scroop," the service passed through four people, two joined by a letter and two by word of mouth.[129] Often a service had to travel through multiple letters. A correspondent of John Perceval's informed him that "The Marquis du Quene sends his humble service to your Lordship by a letter I received from him at Jamaica."[130] This service passed through two letters to reach its receiver. Britons received their services orally as well. A young John Perceval met with his guardian's friend and "fail'd not of remembering yr Service as you commanded me."[131] Whether his guardian made this command in a letter or verbally is unclear, but Perceval did deliver it orally and informed his guardian of it epistolarily. When a writer sent multiple services in one letter they were usually to members of the same household, who probably received these services when the receiver read the letter out loud. Writers relied on oral and written chains equally. The Grand Duke of Tuscany corresponded with Perceval himself, but when he walked in on his secretary writing a letter to Perceval he asked him to include his services.[132] If one had no time to write or if a close acquaintance was writing, a simple service through a friend would suffice.[133] Sending a service through a close acquaintance could even be a mark of respect because it did not waste the receiver's time or money on an entire letter. One correspondent was happy simply to ask Perceval's cousin to thank Perceval for mentioning him in a letter.[134] Services given directly, either verbally or in a letter, formed a tighter, more personal link, but in the end the service itself held more weight than the form it took. Letters ferried reminders of social connection to distant correspondents and the communities around them, but they were only part of a complex chain of communication. They facilitated the process rather than being its sole determinant.

Correspondents sent services through networks that included family members, friends, patrons, business contacts, and intellectual acquaintances.

These writers valued services as much as they did the wording of a letter. If a writer produced a letter that was too formalized or whose language of affection they suspected, an added service that linked them to those surrounding the receiver could relieve the tension. When writers added services to multiple connections, their worth depended not on their own suspect being, but on their ties to a wider known community. This is why letters of introduction were important. They linked the unknown to the known. Sending services also cast relationships in the right light. A promise to serve meant that the individual would act for you. By sending the services of others in a letter a correspondent could increase his standing even further. He could serve the correspondent and so could his network. Letters were places of individual connection, where language mattered and where writers could explore their own individuality, but in the late seventeenth and early eighteenth centuries they were first and foremost places to nurture wider networks that relied on letters to keep them intact and functioning.

Toasting at a Distance

Besides gifts and offers of service, writers also used the flexibility of the familiar letter to insert reports of toasts given in their local communities into their epistles. Referencing a toast in a letter both reminded the receiver of a shared social tie with the sender, as the sending of gifts did, and that their single tie was entangled in a network of acquaintances, as offers of service did. While not an integral part of the letter form, writers often described toasts or healths given in their local communities to the absent receiver.[135] Toasts were a traditional form of community maintenance that was growing in popularity during the period and like services they invoked a sense of reciprocity and obligation, and tied together wide networks in a familiar fashion. Letters also increased the power of toasts. Now they could be heard beyond the dining table or tavern; they could echo across oceans.

Shifts in the purpose of letters and the language used in them opened the door for these toasts. Medieval letters, such as those written by the Pastons, did not include references to toasts because the purpose of those letters was to speed business and to communicate critical information. The letters of the late seventeenth and early eighteenth centuries performed these tasks as well, but since letters were more easily sent and writers increasingly depended on them to nurture social relationships, what one could add to a letter expanded. While the courtly letters of the early seventeenth century did not rely on toasts, the more informal letters of the later part of the century could include such chatty, informal details. Peter Collinson could write to a correspondent, "In our Temerate Cupps Wee pour a Libation to the Memory of our Worthy Friend the Governor of N. York wishing him Health & prosperity."[136] His playful style probably provoked a smile. The growing freedom of language caused concerns, but used in the right way it could also cultivate networks, for the value of toasts lay not in their phrasing, but in the social webs that words invoked.

The British had long toasted others to bind communities, and by the seventeenth century it was considered impolite to sit down at a table without offering up a toast. In fact, the period between the Restoration and 1750 saw the tradition of public drinking reach its zenith as those lower on the social scale began to have enough expendable income to frequent taverns and toast each other as the elite already did.[137] Toasts were declarations of remembrance, respect, status, and generosity.[138] The British toasted others in taverns and clubs, they lifted their glasses to monarchs and whole nations, but they also voiced them in households in remembrance of individuals they held dear.[139] These were the toasts usually mentioned in letters.

Even more than services, toasts in letters embraced networks. Giving a toast required that at least two individuals be physically present, and when reported in a letter the writer drew in the recipient. Each reported toast included at least three people and usually embraced more. John Perceval's uncle wrote, "Lady Blany, my Brother Auditor & I din'd yesterday at Mr. Le Grands where we drank your health, & wish'd you with us as you may believe."[140] This toast included at least five people. Dining was a communal activity and dining at the homes of others reaffirmed social ties. When these elite families toasted those at a distance they drew them back into their circle. These distances could be vast. When an English correspondent's relative visited William Byrd II in Virginia, Byrd assured his correspondent, "Your health goes religiously round whenever he and I retire together and tho' the circle be not great, yet it expresses what a circle always dos, a great deal of love."[141] This toast crossed the Atlantic and Byrd's invocation of "a circle" makes it clear that toasts pulled together a network and not two individuals. Usually toasts joined those already linked through letters. Over half the individuals who participated in the toasts mentioned in letters also wrote or received letters from the individual toasted. Toasts were one tie among many that helped hold together networks of friends and family.

When correspondents referenced a toast in a letter the piece of paper suddenly echoed with many voices. It linked the reader to the social world described. This was new. Previously toasts may have bound those present for the toast, but not those toasted. They had no knowledge of the event. Letters allowed recipients of toasts to feel remembered and treasured. The value of being toasted was so great that correspondents would tell each other if they even heard of the other being toasted. Daniel Dering made sure to add a postscript informing Perceval that their cousin Edward Southwell and five others had raised their glasses to him, most probably filled with claret sent by Perceval himself.[142] Writers often assured their correspondents that when their families or acquaintances met they spoke of their absent friends, toasted them, and wished them present. Telling them of a toast could place their remembrance in a particular space and time. The receiver could know when and where their friends toasted them. The specificity of reported toasts could lessen the feeling of distance. Reports of toasts often included those present, where they were, and what they consumed. Readers knew these groups and places and could imagine the setting. It drew them into the toast and allowed them to hear it. Sometimes participants even signed the letter themselves. Six signed one letter that told Daniel Dering of a toast.[143] Even less specific details could reassure. Some letters simply included the day the toast took place or simply stated, "All here drink your healths daily."[144] While these references lacked the imaginative quality of the other toasts, they still reminded the receiver that those at a distance remembered them on a regular basis.

Placing toasts within letters served the needs of senders as well. If a toast went unreferenced it lost its reciprocal value because the receiver did not know to respond in kind. Unlike services, toasts were not inherently reciprocal. They were supposed to be spontaneous displays of remembrance and loyalty. However, they usually functioned as part of a larger exchange. Diners often raised their glasses to show gratitude for a gift. Perceval's cousin informed him that, "Phil and his Wife, Dr. Clayton and his, with Nancy Donellan dined with us to day upon a very fine Haunch of Venison which Uncle Long sent us last night. We all drank his health, and did not forget our friends at Tunbridge."[145] A gift of venison provoked this toast. Writers often reported healths given in exchange or in thanks for gifts, especially food.[146] Such toasts showed gratitude for the gift and revealed to the other diners the largesse of the giver. All the guests now knew they dined on Uncle Long's venison. More than venison could lead to a toast. Some supplied the liquor. Lorenzo Magnolfi, after receiving Perceval's gift of whiskey, promised "we shall drink your health in the liquor."[147] Some Britons simply paid for them. Many writers mention sending "tokens," small amounts of money, back and forth to pay for some of these toasts. William Byrd the elder received many a "kind token" from an English acquaintance, which allowed him and his Virginian friends to be "very merry" and "remember your good health."[148] Nicholas Blundell was sure to give ten shillings to his business associate's clerks so they could drink his health.[149] This was money well spent because unlike a personal gift of money, a gift of liquor bound a whole network and the generosity of the gift called for a return. But without letters knowledge of these toasts would have been lost.

Letter writers told of these toasts and sent such tokens back and forth across the Atlantic and beyond because they needed to base their sense of social connection on solid, familiar forms that embraced networks and a sense of mutual obligation. Those at a distance needed to connect with others in a familiar fashion that did not rely only on the flimsy words placed in a letter. Like gifts and offers of service, referencing toasts in letters provided writers with a way to do that. Toasts reported in a letter reaffirmed a social bond and highlighted the larger network the writer was a part of. While toasts acted like gifts and services in this fashion, their writers found them most effective in nurturing close ties. To be toasted one had to be known to those at the table and often they were close friends or family members. Offering services and sending gifts were more useful for those outside of their circles. But like those other forms of traditional social bonding, the placing of toasts in letters altered the way they functioned. Toasts had greater resonance in a letter and demonstrate how writers used older forms of bonding in new ways to deal with a changing social world.

ɞ

Sending a letter was an attempt to create or sustain a bond with the receiver. Some bonds were more important to maintain than others, but as we have seen when advancement and sometimes survival depended on who you knew and the strength of your larger web of connections, cultivating and keeping social ties mattered. Charting the changing ways the style of the letter nurtured relationships is revealing, but letter writers of the late seventeenth and early eighteenth centuries relied more on their ability to insert older forms of social maintenance, such as gifts, offers of service, and toasts, to bind their networks together. These additions nurtured the kind of ties they needed to negotiate the expanding British world and they allowed them to do so in a familiar fashion. Gifts made the social function of a letter obvious and made the connection dependent on an object besides the letter. Offers of service promised an active social bond and allowed writers to nurture and highlight their wider networks, which held more social power than the individual connections that letters themselves often nurtured. Toasts made letters more intimate by allowing the networks that writers were part of to surface in a letter. All of these forms reinforced the social bond created by letters and they did so by inserting elements that anchored writers to more concrete social ties. Letters functioned well as social connectors because they had the ability to facilitate wider communication: they allowed oral communication to flow farther, they allowed gifts to be negotiated, and they gave toasts the opportunity to echo across long distances. These writers folded older forms of social maintenance into their letters because such forms nurtured the kind of ties and invoked the types of webs that they desired. However, these older forms altered as well for, with the letter, they could reach farther geographically and become more interactive. The way writers nurtured their epistolary networks serves as a reminder that beneath the exquisite tailoring and sparkling conversation, the members of the British elite still strained to hear warm offers of service, clinking glasses, and the steps of those bearing a well-chosen gift.

Chapter 5

New Networks and Letters Less Familiar

June 1734 found John Perceval, by now the Earl of Egmont, ransacking his houses for lost letters. He confessed to his agent in Ireland, "I am under the greatest uneasiness about the three volumes of letters relating to my Estate years 1730, 1731 & 1733. I have looked over and over both in town and Country and cannot find them."[1] His agent was in Dublin at the time and could not look for the volumes, but assured Perceval, "I put them all into the Chest of drawers in the room where I lay . . . there I am confident they are being since I put them all safe up."[2] In the end, this correspondence was unnecessary; Perceval found his letter books in his London residence.[3] He probably breathed a sigh of relief for these letters were important to him. He worried about them and carefully bound them into volumes. By his death he had produced thirty-eight books of estate correspondence, mostly between himself and his estate agents.[4] In contrast, he filled only eight letter books with personal letters, for the most part to and from family and friends. While the sheer numerical dominance of the estate letters may not have outweighed the emotional value of the familiar ones, they held a special place in Perceval's epistolary world.

What prompted many letter writers to keep letter books was the need to preserve letters of business. Nicholas Blundell, the Lancashire gentleman, began his letter book when his father died and he came into his inheritance. John Eliot, a London merchant, started to keep a letter book when he reached his majority and took responsibility for his patrimony. James Brydges seriously cracked open a letter book in 1705 when he became paymaster to the queen's troops. Most of the epistles in the letter book of William Byrd I of Virginia were to and from London merchants. Writing letters to retain social connections was important, but writing letters to keep businesses and estates functioning was critical and required the conservation of letters on a scale unnecessary for more familiar letters.

The growing associational world of clubs and societies also depended on letters. Most of these institutions maintained correspondences and had secretaries who kept track of letters. In fact, it was the first secretary of the Royal Society who suggested they preserve their letters.[5] This phenomenon stretched beyond the Royal Society. One secretary for the Society for Promoting Christian Knowledge wrote 6,340 letters between 1708 and 1713 on behalf of the institution.[6] Like business letters, institutional correspondence filled volumes and called for careful regulation.

These types of correspondence were newly intensified in the late seventeenth and early eighteenth centuries. Merchants, landlords, government officials, and even intellectuals depended on letters more than they ever had before.[7] Long distance trade, and the number of Britons involved in trade, was increasing. More landowners spent time away from their estates. Sir John Lowther resided at his Cumberland estates only nine years out of thirty-two.[8] And while many outwardly frowned on absenteeism within Britain, the most reviled absentee landlords were those of Ireland.[9] In the late 1720s Parliament attempted to fine absentee Irish landlords, which caused John Perceval to explode in a rather lengthy diatribe on the subject.[10] The eighteenth century also saw the rise of the fiscal military state, and the cost and organization of extensive wars led to the creation of a larger bureaucracy.[11] It also opened up more governmental positions. This caused more letters to flow across the Channel as the government attempted to hold together the many threads that made up a war and organize its growing bureaucracy at home.[12] The types of connection these relationships called for were different from those underlying informal personal networks, and they usually surface as separate clusters of connection in epistolary networks. These letters were usually more straightforward and plain in style, like the nature of the connection they nurtured. Corresponding was not just useful or pleasurable, it was absolutely necessary. It was the only way to conduct business or hold together an associational body at a distance.

The increase in contractual and institutional correspondence resulted from the expansion of trans-Atlantic trade, the centralization and urbanization of the elite, and the growth of bureaucracy. How the British approached these kinds of letters shows how they interpreted and dealt with these alterations. These different types of letters need to be treated as a whole because

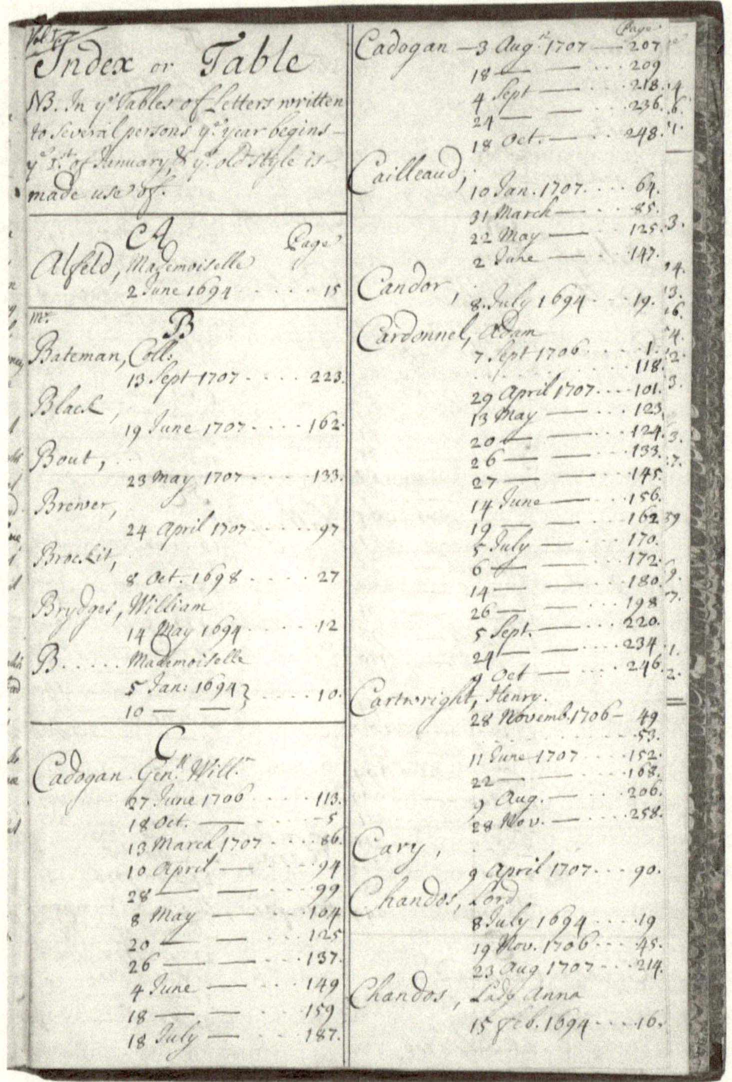

Index or Table

NB. In ye Tables of Letters written to severall persons ye year begins ye 1st of January & ye old Style is made use of.

A — Page

Alfeld, Mademoiselle
2 June 1694 15

B

Mr. Bateman, Coll.
13 Sept 1707 .... 223.

Black,
19 June 1707 .... 162.

Bout,
23 May 1707 .... 133.

Brewer,
24 April 1707 97

Broc. Lit,
8 Oct. 1698 27

Brydges, William
14 May 1694 12

B.... Mademoiselle
5 Jan: 1694
10 — — .... 10.

C

Cadogan Genl. Willm.
27 June 1706 .... 113.
18 Oct. 5
13 March 1707 .... 86.
10 April 94
28 99
8 May 104
20 125
26 .... 137.
4 June 149
18 159
18 July .... 187.

Cadogan — 3 Augt 1707 207
18 209
4 Sept .... 218.
24 .... 236.
18 Oct. .... 248.

Cailleaud,
10 Jan. 1707 .... 64.
31 March .... 85.
22 May .... 125.
2 June .... 147.

Candor,
8 July 1694 .... 19.

Cardonnel, Adam
7 Sept 1706 .... 1.
.... 118.
29 April 1707 .... 101.
13 May .... 123.
20 .... 124.
26 .... 133.
27 .... 145.
14 June .... 156.
19 .... 162.
5 July .... 170.
6 .... 172.
14 .... 180.
26 198
5 Sept. .... 220.
24 .... 234.
9 Oct .... 246.

Cartwright, Henry.
28 Novemb. 1706 49
.... 53.
11 June 1707 .... 152.
22 .... 168.
9 Aug. .... 206.
28 Nov. .... 258.

Cary,
9 April 1707 .... 90.

Chandos, Lord
8 July 1694 19
19 Nov. 1706 .... 45.
23 Aug 1707 .... 214.

Chandos, Lady Anna
15 Feb. 1694 .... 16.

Figure 15. Many letters survived because they were copied into letter books. Here, the index of the eventual duke of Chandos's first letter book of outgoing correspondence, created around 1707, shows the care lavished on these books and suggests that they were meant to used in the future, not simply stored away.

Letter book of James Brydges, HEH ST 57, vol. 1.

they are representative of a larger shift in social negotiation as networks less dependent on personal or personalized links began to emerge. These networks often revolved around a shared interest, rather than an individual social need. However, the way these new letters and networks fit into their writers' larger webs shows that the distance between the two worlds was thin and often exploited. But these newly intensified networks do mark a moment of change as more traditional social webs began to support networks that had different social goals and gestured to the emergence of new kinds of social relationships. This chapter looks first at contractual networks, those formed by the needs of merchants, absentee landlords, and officials, before turning to the institutional networks brought into being by clubs and societies.

Contractual Networks

Networks based on social connections, family, and friends were familiar. They helped writers keep track of their dispersed worlds and could be put to work when problems arose. However, all their actions, at least on the surface, were voluntary. No contract bound them, only a sense of mutual obligation and a wish to keep their social networks humming. Letters between estate agents and landlords, between merchants, and between government officials were not voluntary, they were contractual. Authority figures required their correspondents to send letters often and for a specific purpose. For them maintaining a larger web that could be activated was not the goal; instead they wanted to keep an estate, office, or trading venture going. These webs were constant problem-solving networks, but they usually solved the problem in their own contained network rather than by turning to extended personal networks. They were, to an extent, professionalized relationships.[13] But such ties still relied on the expectations established by more familiar forms of correspondence.

Most letter writers possessed a contractual network. Letters regarding trading matters dominate the surviving correspondence of William Byrd I of Virginia. Merchants in London were his most frequent correspondents, and those letters reveal the tightly knit world of trade. The commercial connections in Byrd's epistolary network form a distinct web between the years of 1684 and 1688 (Figure 16). His different trading links are connected to each other and to his wider network. Similarly, John Perceval's letters regarding his estate form a distinct cluster within his wider network; numerically, his

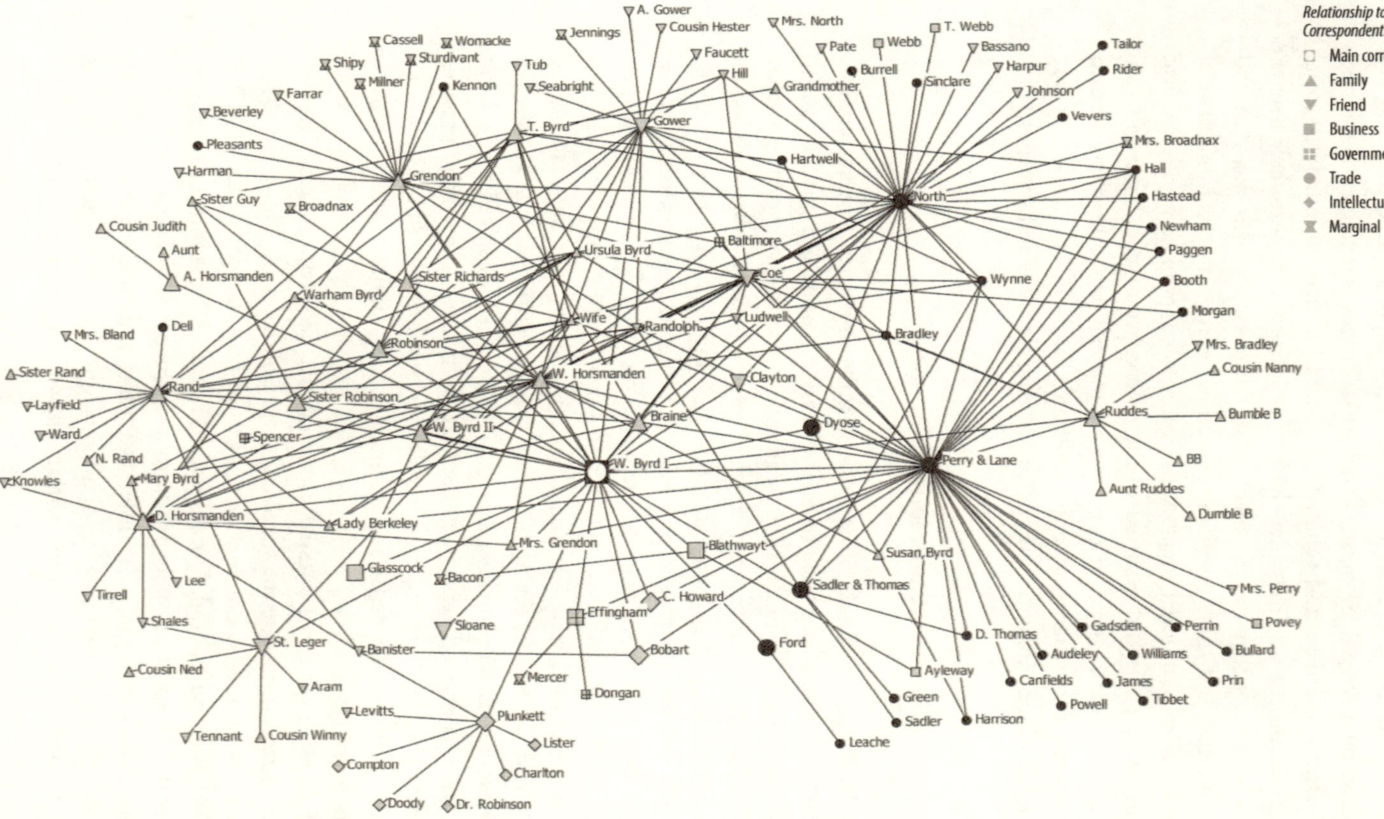

Figure 16. Epistolary network of William Byrd I, 1684–1688, with trade connections highlighted. This network is the same as Figure 9, but Byrd's trading connections are highlighted rather than his friends and family members.

Network courtesy of Borgatti, S.P., 2002. NetDraw Software for Network Visualization. Analytic Technologies, Lexington, Kentucky.

agents, at this time William Taylor and William Turner, were his most important and frequent correspondents (Figure 17).[14] For James Brydges, much of his early surviving correspondence stemmed from his position as paymaster to the queen's troops and revolved around his need to coordinate bills, keep track of exchange rates, and deal with distant but impatient army commanders. At times, the contractual networks of these men were woven into their wider social networks, but they also had rules of their own.

Constructing Contractual Letters

Contractual letters rarely drip with declarations of affection, echo with warm offers of service, or offer news on distant family relations. These letter writers picked up the pen to get things done. Writers sent them more regularly than familiar letters and structured them more particularly. Scholars have pointed to the more open and plain style of writing used to compose merchant letters, but this style also infused other types of contractual correspondence, such as letters from estate agents and government placeholders.[15] Receivers expected their correspondents to compose their contractual letters in a specific fashion. As the early modern period progressed letters became more standardized and universal in form. This made business easier, especially for those involved in long-distance trade, and helped its expansion.[16] Letter writing manuals often included exemplary business letters or directions for those composing them.[17] One author instructed that "after beginning with suitable Complements or Respects, as the Party's Degree or Quality is to whom you write, come to the Matter designed, as the proper Subject of your Writing."[18] These letters might open with compliments, but that was not their purpose. Most important, composers had to write a clearly structured and explicated letter. As Lord Chesterfield wrote his son, "The first thing necessary in writing letters of business, is extreme clearness and perspicuity; every paragraph should be so clear, and unambiguous, that the dullest fellow in the world may not be able to mistake it, or obliged to read it twice in order to understand it."[19] Unlike familiar letters, writers did not treasure these individual epistles. They would not be read multiple times to bring the absent correspondent to mind. Ideally the receiver would quickly read them, process them, and perhaps record them in a letter book for later reference.

There were expectations about how a writer should compose these clear letters. There was an unwritten agreement between landlords and agents that

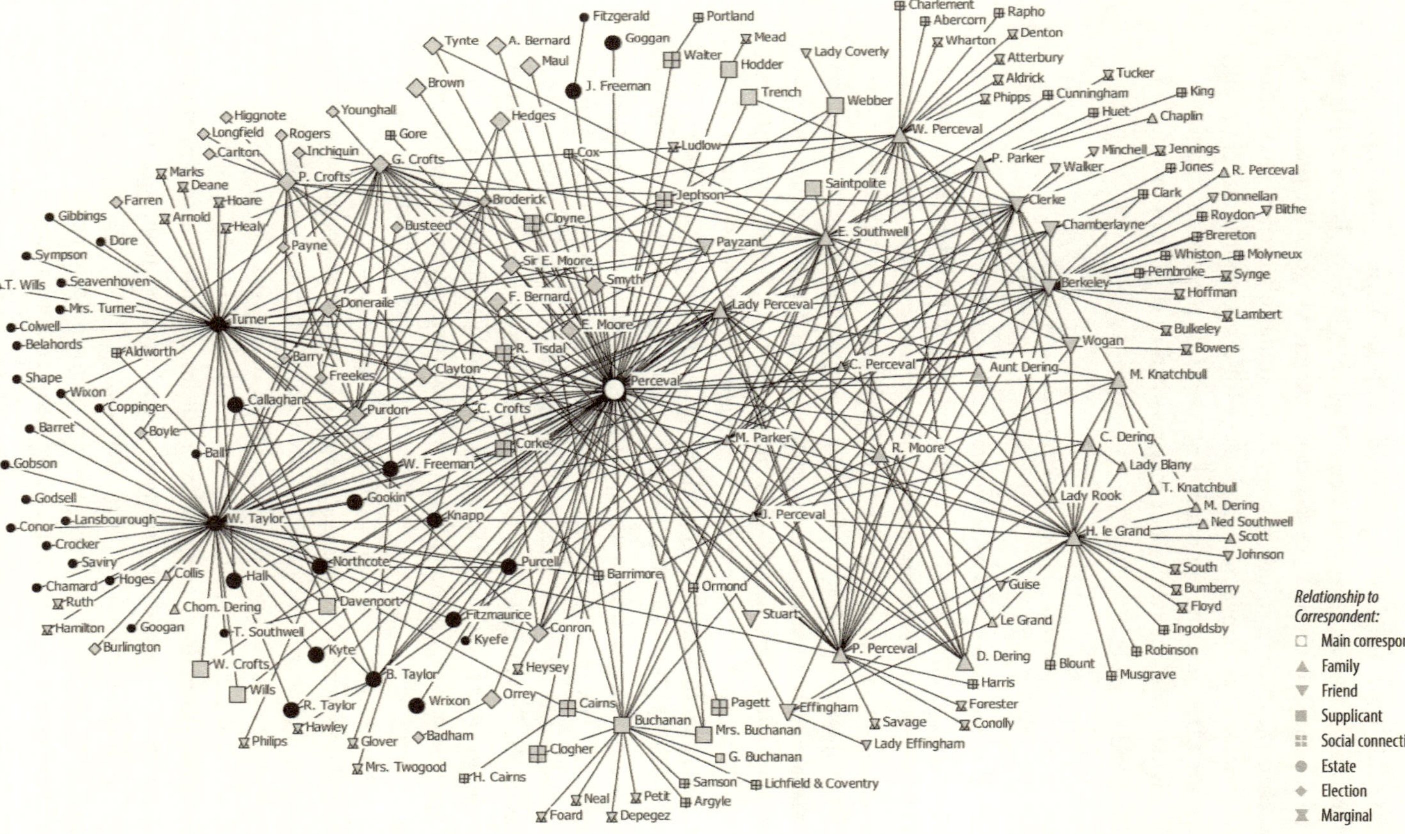

Figure 17. Epistolary network of John Perceval, 1709–1712, with estate connections highlighted. This network is the same as Figure 7, but those whose main link to Perceval was through his estates in Ireland are highlighted rather than friends and family members.

Network courtesy of Borgatti, S.P., 2002. NetDraw Software for Network Visualization. Analytic Technologies, Lexington, Kentucky.

the agent should be exact and answer his employer's letter paragraph by paragraph. One agent's response to a tongue lashing by his employer was: "I have endeavoured not only to answer Paragraph by Paragraph but sentence for sentence your Lordship's Letters."[20] While few of the letters from Perceval's agents answered his letters sentence by sentence, many of them did cover the details addressed by Perceval in the order he mentioned them, and in return Perceval usually referenced the issues noted by his agent. The goal was to resolve issues quickly. If either one forgot to mention an issue, then it would have to wait until the next set of letters and thus resolution would be slow in coming. Actually, more names usually appear in merchant, estate, and governmental correspondence than in more familiar letters because writers needed to avoid confusion. By mentioning the names of those who were going to receive money, by noting exactly which ship's captain transported goods, and by keeping track of which tenants owed money, these writers clarified their business dealings. This is why Perceval's agents, William Taylor and William Turner, and Byrd's factors, Arthur North and the firm of Perry and Lane, have so many unconnected links and so many ties to other areas of the network (Figures 16 and 17). Unlike many familiar letters the important information in an estate letter or official letter lay in the body of the letter, not in the gestures of inclusion that danced along its margins or were inherent in its arrival.

These writers also fiercely monitored their correspondence. Landlords and agents were the most consistent in noting when they had sent their last letters and when they received an answer. Most letters began with an accounting of past letters sent and received. Berkeley Taylor, Perceval's agent, usually began his letters by noting the last letter that had arrived. His employer obviously paid close attention because he noted when letters seemed to be missing. After noting the last letter he received from Taylor, he worriedly recorded that he could tell "you have not received some letters which I writ you and ought to have come to your hands before the date of it (22 Dec)."[21] Agents informed Perceval of such gaps as well. One agent, William Taylor, anxiously closed a letter by stating to Perceval, "Your not mentioning mine of 18th September makes me fear it has miscarried I therefore send a coppy."[22] These references allowed the agent to show his employer that he was not lax in his correspondence, but most importantly it revealed to both sides the gaps in their knowledge. Since these letters were so precise the loss of single letter could confuse the running of an estate or a war. Brydges also referred to the letters he received from his employees in his letters to them. On 14

March 1706/7 he let Mr. Sweet know that he had received two of his past letters and informed Mr. Drummond of the three he had received from him.[23] Such references kept the lanes of communication clear. It allowed the receiver to know whether he had all the information he needed to act correctly.

Merchants similarly kept track of their letters. In one of his first surviving letters to the firm of Perry and Lane, William Byrd I of Virginia began by stating, "Yours by Bradly, Paggen & Culpeper received & was in hopes [to] have heard from you by Wyn[ne] ere this, but hope it will [not] bee long ere hee arrives."[24] Like Perceval and Brydges, he was interested in keeping track of his contractual letters, but monitoring epistolary correspondence that crossed the Atlantic Ocean was different from organizing letters that ships ferried across the Irish Sea. It usually took letters two to three weeks to travel between John Perceval in London and Berkeley Taylor in Ireland. The letters between William Byrd I and Perry and Lane took much longer. When he wrote to them in late June 1684 and mentioned a letter he had sent about a month before, he could only hope that it "will get safe to your hands"; he knew a month was probably not enough time to reach English shores.[25] Due to the distance between him and his factors and the uncertainty of transatlantic correspondence, Byrd sent letters when he could rather than waiting for the next letter from Perry and Lane to arrive. In fact, he knew ships that left earlier could at times arrive later, and that some letters might overtake others.[26] The tight and organized back and forth correspondence Perceval had with his agents and Brydges had with his employees was not possible for Byrd. This was not a comfortable position for someone whose livelihood depended on these exchanges. He was constantly worried about his lack of knowledge regarding the state of the market for tobacco or the state of his accounts with Perry and Lane. In his first surviving letter to the firm he acknowledged that he deferred writing in the hopes of receiving his accounts from them, which would let him know if he had exceeded his credit.[27] He soon gave up this practice and simply hoped that his balance would hold. The lack of knowledge was not all on his side either. Byrd often informed Perry and Lane of the fate or status of their ships. Once, he told them when he heard that one of their ships was not sighted in Barbados over a month earlier, which would delay its arrival in Virginia.[28] Because transatlantic mercantile correspondence was so slow and uncertain, the correspondence itself depended less on the organization of details negotiated through letters and more on general commentary and trust.

Byrd often referred to the letters he had sent Perry and Lane, but he rarely referenced the letters he had received from them. Byrd was not an employee of the firm and was more concerned that they were replying to his stated needs than about letting them know if he had received their requests. Furthermore, this exchange involved goods, not actions, and the goods could talk for themselves. Byrd referred to the letters he sent and received by the ship or ship's captain they came from, not by the day he sent them. This is how he categorized his letters in his mind. Often he sent his letters on the same ships as his goods, and he sent most of these letters because they referenced the goods he was sending. Many letters begin like the one he sent to the firm of Perry and Lane at the end of March 1685: "This serves to accompany Captain Bradly with sixty one hogsheads of tobacco & 6 skins, which I hope come safe to hand."[29] The main form of correspondence between Perry and Lane and Byrd was not the letter itself but the goods it accompanied. The letter made sure goods did not go astray and helped the two sides keep track of the tobacco, furs, and English goods they passed across the Atlantic, but it was more important for both sides to receive the goods than the letter itself. Finding out what accounts Perry and Lane had of their exchanges interested Byrd more than their individual letters.

Trusting Contractual Networks

Due to the distance separating them, the relationships between employers and employees or corresponding merchants often became strained. Goods did not arrive or were of less than stellar quality. Agents did not follow directions or acted for their own good over that of their employer. Tenants undermined the reputation of the agent in their letters, either to gain their own ends or because he was actually in the wrong. One agent complained to Perceval, "I live in the midst of people, who are apt to make malicious & invidious misrepresentations."[30] Perceval, however, knew, or hoped, that the time and money he had put into gaining a trustworthy agent had paid off and usually reassured his agents.[31] Absentee landlords could misplace that trust, however.[32] William Taylor died in debt to Perceval, who showed his ire by declaring in an appendix to his letter book, "William Taylor died in Debt to me and all the world."[33] West Indian absentee landlords often had a hard time with their agents embezzling funds.[34] Due to the distance between the West Indies and England, keeping track of estates was more difficult, and on a slave plantation the agent did not have to worry about tenants complaining of his actions by letter; many took advantage. Distance could create other kinds of problems. Byrd expressed concern about a postscript included in a letter from Perry and Lane: "I am sorry any private discourse here (for write-ing I dow not find my selfe concern'd) should be so ill represented . . . & if we did (at this distance) misapprehend the measures you tooke I hope the error may be pardonable."[35] He knew he controlled the written information Perry and Lane received, but oral rumor could chip away at this relationship constructed mostly through letters. In fact, he appears uncertain as to the nature of the actual problem. But while distance could make resolving these issues more difficult, Byrd could also use his distance to argue that it was all a misapprehension rather than a troubling issue. Still, the suspicion of unknown wrongs voiced at a distance could wear away these relationships.

Estate correspondence echoes with arguments over interpretation as tenants attempted to alter an agent's assessment of their situation. Tenants knew they could use their landlord's distance from his estate to their advantage and they often insisted on writing the landlord. What Perceval said of one of his wealthier tenants held true for many: "he has a good Pen & loves to use it."[36] By telling the agent that they were going to write the landlord, tenants could delay the agent's ability to take action. While waiting for Perceval's response, his agent could do nothing. Perceval was well aware of this ploy, but he could do little to stop it.[37] He simply thanked one agent for "keeping off Tenants clamours" when he could and admitted that he was "under a necessity (tho' a very pleasing one) of depending on your information, which I shall always do with the greatest confidence."[38]

But landlords and agents also used the letter as a tool of power in their negotiations with tenants. Agents knew they held a precarious place between the landlord and the tenants. Maneuvering between the two sides could be tricky, so the agent often tried to cut himself out of the process by using the lord's letter as his employer's representative. One of Perceval's agents read his letters from Perceval to the tenants.[39] By doing so he proved to them that the commands were not ones he could ignore or demands he himself had created. It was the landlord's fault, not his. Savvy agents requested that the landlord write specialized letters for them to show tenants. One agent wrote, "if your Lordship will be pleased to write such a Letter as I may shew him to me, (not enclosed in another as the last to be shewn him was, & which therefore had no Postmark) and therein to declare your Resentment at his Refusal to give up the Land . . . I hope he may be thereby intimidated into an Act of Justice to your Lordship."[40] The agent knew the power of a well-written letter from the landlord, but the tenant too understood the workings of the Post Office and their landlord's agents: no postmark, no confidence. These letters held the voice of the landlord for the tenants, a voice with which it was hard to argue since it was so far removed. Being able to harness that voice gave the agent the extra power he needed. As an agent once triumphantly wrote, "The letter wrote as a Spurr to the Tennants has had a pretty good Effect & has furnishe'd me with an Excuse for using severities to some that I cou'd not otherwise well do."[41] Letters had great power in these negotiations and they enforced submission as often as they created trust.

Trust was necessary between these correspondents, however, and many fostered it by emphasizing the deep personal ties they had to one another. One agent highlighted his emotional connection to Perceval when he lamented the death of Perceval's daughter. He wrote that he felt any blow that fell on Perceval for "with my very early Food I imbibed a great Veneration and Respect for your Lordship, which has been heightened by the many Honours and Kindness which I have received from your Lordship and my Lord Perceval."[42] He weighed this letter well, expressing a personal form of sorrow over the death of a daughter, but retaining a sense of deference: he imbibed "respect" and "veneration," not love and affection. James Brydges tightened the bonds between himself and his employees by adding services to their wives in his letters.[43] Embedded in these declarations of affection and personal connection was a sense of obligation.

Writers strengthened this sense of personal obligation by employing the language of friendship. John Eliot informed one merchant firm that he wished to work with them because "I know by a long Experience in the Counting House of Misters Godhard Hagen & Son with what Cordiality & punctuality you serve your friends."[44] He knew a trading relationship between friends led to "cordiality & punctuality." The use of the language of friendship and obligation made business over long distances personal and punctual.[45] Being disobliging or not acting like a friend decreased business and trust.[46] John Custis exhibited his distrust of Micajah Perry, whom Byrd declared a friend, when he stated, "no one thinks but the securing his own debt was his chiefest view."[47] Putting oneself first was not friendly. Landlords and agents also used the language of friendship to tighten their relationship. Perceval reported to one agent, "I not only have the fullest satisfaction in your services, but esteem you a real friend."[48] And he signed his letter to one agent: "Your friend to serve you."[49] Such assertions of friendship shifted the relationship from a solely professional level to a personal one, which was more dependable. However, it should be noted that it is the employer who used the language of friendship, not the employee. These were far from equal relationships, but the language did bind. Brydges even altered his epistolary tone to signal an attempt at friendship: "you see I write very plain & free to you, wch I do because I think I may depend upon your Friendship as you shall always be sure of mine."[50] Such references reinforced the relationship and reimagined it. Bonds of friendship, not just bonds of contract, linked them.

But, as we have seen, bonds of friendship also implied bonds of service. James Brydges insisted to one correspondent that "the friendship you have shown me upon this as well as severall other occasions have made so just an impression in me that you shall find I will never be wanting to shew my gratitude for it."[51] These statements of friendship were not simple declarations of affection; they stressed the reciprocal nature of these relationships. Brydges would "shew" his gratitude. These were active friendships from which one benefited, but for which one had to pay. Writers employed the language of friendship to personalize contractual connections, but it did more than that: it connected contractual relationships to more traditional networks of assistance. Members of contractual epistolary networks did not need to assert their friendship or insert services, gifts, or toasts into their letters to keep their networks intact, but doing so could make these networks more trustworthy and functional.

Writers often acted for their contractual correspondents. Like Byrd's relatives, his merchant connections, Perry and Lane, helped to watch over his children when he sent them to England; in regards to his son, he only instructed them to "put him into business, or if hee wants any thing to accomplish him I desire hee might learne itt there."[52] Here they acted not only like friends but like family members. In return Byrd the elder drummed up business for the firm. In 1691 he informed them that due to his encouragement Col. Christopher Wormeley "designes to write to you, & hold a correspondence."[53] He also sent Arthur North, another constant merchant correspondent, tokens, news, and services to distribute to common acquaintances.[54] Landlords cultivated the loyalty of their agents by extending special privileges to them as well. Perceval allowed one agent to tweak his leases and both Perceval and his son helped find positions for the sons of another agent. Perceval knew that an agent who shared in his concerns and basked in his friendship was more likely to return the favor by being an effective representative. One agent with multiple sons, nine in fact, confirmed this theory, stating, "My Lord Percival has been pleased to become his and my third son's Patron, and I must be ungratefull if I will not make it my Study and Care, to the utmost of my Power, to serve his and your Lordship faithfully & diligently."[55] As in most relationships, the language of affection was never as potent as actions of service.

As these actions imply, contractual epistolary networks were never disconnected from writers' larger networks, as can be seen in the networks drawn out. Trading and estate networks were always linked to the more personal segments of the network. In his letters to Perry and Lane and Arthur North, Byrd I mentioned his father-in-law, his siblings, and other family connections. He even possessed personal connections among the captains. To one ship's captain, who was also a relation, he wrote, "All our friends here in health; B.B. is as you left her, and soe is Bumble B. [and] Dumble B."[56] Members of these formal contractual networks had connections to Byrd's more intimate personal networks and were sometimes members of them. The same was true among landlords and agents.[57] Perceval employed three generations of Taylors as agents, all of whom were vaguely related to him and whom he truly valued. Perceval even informed William Taylor of his son's engagement, stating, "for a relation and friend as you are shall know more than others ought to know."[58] Bloodlines did not connect James Brydges to his employees, but they did become embedded in his personal world. He even dined with his former employees, Mr. Stratford and Capt. Cartwright, years after their employment ended.[59] Contractual correspondence relied on more constructed letters and it often formed distinct clusters within writers' larger epistolary networks, but links to personal networks remained and helped anchor these increasingly important subnetworks.

These links and anchors to personal webs helped employers monitor their contractual networks. Byrd's need to defend himself to Perry and Lane over "ill represented" reports reveals that the firm was listening to what others had to say about Byrd and they let him know it.[60] Perceval did the same with his agent. He often spoke with his contemporaries about their Irish lands and would subtly question his agent's laments. He once wrote, "I am sorry to hear my Tenants are so backward at a time when by other accounts I hear they pay well, and was yesterday informed that Lady Barrimore says her Lords Tenants do pay well."[61] A month later his agent countered Lady Barrimore's accusation, insisting to his employer that the tenants on his estates could not pay. Perceval took the middle ground: "As to Lady Barrimores mistake abut the good payment of Rents, she ought one would think to know, being so much concerned, and my friend Mr. John Temple who has an Estate in our County says he is well paid: but be that as it will, I am confident there is no neglect by you with respect to my Rents."[62] Perceval warned him that others said differently, but that his agent still had his trust. Perceval did not need to win this argument; in fact a victory would have damaged him. He meant to caution his agent, not prove him wrong. If an agent was untrustworthy he would lose his job. Rather, Perceval wanted to keep his agent on his toes by letting him know he was not blind and he used networks and letters to do this. The same could be said for Perry and Lane's complaint about Byrd. They did not want to lose his business, but they wanted to be sure the Virginians were not taking advantage of them and so they listened carefully to what others said and wrote. Byrd himself helped them monitor their business by reporting to them about their ships' locations and their ships' captains. Little did these captains know, but the letters they carried to their employers along with hogsheads of tobacco often carried reports on their activities.[63] Trust was never simply given in these relationships—employers tested and monitored their employees and they used their personal networks, both oral and epistolary, to do so.

For landlords and merchants private networks helped guard their private well-being, but for government officials the situation was more complex as the idea of public oversight grew. Government post holders often treated their posts as personal possessions and private money often mixed with public money in the purses of post holders. When officeholders left their post, their letters books often left with them.[64] They saw them as their own possessions, not the government's. James Brydges did not think twice about holding back payments to make a profit from a better exchange rate.[65] As long as most of the money could be accounted for in the end, post holders were free to make a profit, although after Brydges amassed his vast fortune the government did investigate him.[66] But within their letters these post holders signaled to a wider recognition that their actions within these posts might be held up to public scrutiny. In their letters they note a division between private and public business. Brydges wrote to one of his underlings, "Pray when you write any thing of private business I desire you'l write it in a loose piece of paper by it self enclosed in ye letter of Publick matters."[67] Brydges did see a separation between the two forms, even if he allowed both to be enclosed in the same letter and performed by the same individual. Another correspondent spoke of "his publick letter," which he was sending along with his more private letter. Both were short, he informed his correspondent, so he would "come off cheap by this Post."[68] Here separation occurs as well, but the close proximity between the forms gestures to their overlap.[69]

Attempting to separate the two kinds of letters was important since what one penned could be used to justify one's actions. When Brydges worried that an employee's actions might spoil his own reputation with the Duke of Marlborough he enclosed old letters to a friend to justify his decisions.[70] It was best if these letters showed the post holder in the best possible professional light. Writers knew that letters shown to justify their positions had to be carefully considered. Lord Bolingbroke, when he was secretary of state, told Charles Boyle, the envoy to Brabant and Flanders, to "Write to me some time hence a Letter which I may read to the Queen concerning your Coming over."[71] In constructing such a letter Boyle would be creating a public letter that his queen could evaluate. Such letters show a growing recognition of a separation between the private and public realms of government. While the tendency to mix private and public continued to prevail, the growth of a structured bureaucracy that demanded an accounting of actions and competency in employees made the personal less powerful.[72] The British would continue to mix the two because it helped to nurture relationships, but they recognized the strain.[73] Official networks differed from personal networks; a larger entity monitored them, not individuals embedded within the network. Those who wrote official letters knew an overarching power might judge their actions and their letters.

When William Byrd I picked up a pen to write to the firm of Perry and Lane, when Berkeley Taylor sat down to compose his letters to John Perceval, and when James Brydges sealed his letters to his employees, they all were sending letters that sounded different and functioned differently from the more familiar letters that held together their informal personal networks. Contractual letters fostered more distant and disconnected social ties. Their existence points to the emergence of more professionalized relationships that did not need to be anchored by personal ties of affection. This was a time of transition, however, while these contractual epistolary networks created separate clusters within their writers' larger networks; the separation was never complete and the intersection was necessary. They are without doubt part of the larger network. Informal personal networks made contractual correspondence more familiar and dependable. However, beyond the world of trade, estate and government management, social, intellectual, and moral desires were pushing writers to use their letters and networks in new ways.

Institutional Networks

During the late seventeenth and early eighteenth centuries new forms of socialization blossomed for the British elite. They witnessed and participated in the "urban renaissance," flocked to the coffeehouse, joined institutions like the Royal Society, and read newspapers. These new forums for sociability caused the British to come together in new ways that fostered the public sphere and pushed forth new ideas about national identity.[74] The British world was seeing further, including more, and becoming more centralized. Even the meanings of community and society shifted: "Society—or at least 'civil society'—had become both general and abstract; community, while it retained some sense of institutional organization, was local, specific, and explicitly related to place."[75] The abstraction of the word "society" runs in tandem with the growth of the public sphere. As the British became aware through trade, political upheaval, and migration that their social world had expanded beyond their locality, they could embrace this larger definition of society, but, at the same time, retain a more specific idea of community. Clubs and societies were one form of specific community, but they were based on interests rather than places. Such organizations were the solidification of the multiple publics that emerged at the time, which a pair of scholars have described as "the active creation of new forms of association that allowed people to connect with others in ways not rooted in family, rank, or vocation, but rather founded in voluntary groupings built on the shared interests, tastes, commitments, and desires of individuals."[76] These new conceptions of community and association marked a shift in the way many Britons structured their social world. As Craig Muldrew has argued, in the sixteenth century most individuals lived within "negotiated" communities, based on immediate interpersonal exchange, but by the nineteenth century many Britons embraced "architectural" communities, where individuals placed their trust in larger institutions.[77] In the late seventeenth and early eighteenth centuries the divide between the two forms was indistinct, but many Britons found themselves negotiating between these transforming ideas of social organization and often using letters to do so.

Among epistles to family members, social connections, and employees lay letters to societies or institutions. Two institutions in particular dominated the epistolary networks examined here: the Society for Promoting Christian Knowledge (SPCK) and the Royal Society. Both had their origins in traditional forms of social bonding. Religious affiliation had long structured British lives and communication with other scholars was integral to intellectual life. Yet during the late seventeenth and early eighteenth centuries certain religious and intellectual networks shifted in form and became more institutionalized, usually in the form of voluntary societies. The shift from personal networks to formal societies was a long, complex, and unfinished process in which the letter played a critical role. These societies separated themselves to a degree from personal networks and could disconnect themselves from private needs or goals. They were increasingly outward looking and interested in both the expansion and improvement of the British world.[78]

Societies, Clubs, and New Networks

During this period as many as 25,000 different clubs and societies emerged across the English-speaking world.[79] These societies were the result of quickening urban growth, increased migration, lack of state intervention, and growing interest in sociability.[80] In a world where kin moved farther away, where the wider world loomed larger in interest, and where the elite gathered in urban centers, societies provided a place for companionship and a center from which to coordinate activities.[81] Joining a society could bring status and provide a social foothold in a rapidly urbanizing world.[82] The size and importance of these societies varied: there were small local clubs consisting of groups of friends or those sharing a similar interest and national societies with large memberships and branches in multiples cities, such as the Freemasons. All these societies had different purposes: some held together county or ethnic identities, others provided financial support, and many gathered knowledge and wished to reform society. Some groups were socially defensive: the Freemasons, even though they practiced philanthropy, were secretive and focused on creating and maintaining social contacts. Other societies were more proactive: the SPCK used social connections to reform the world around them. It is this second type of society that surfaced the most often in these letter collections.

The SPCK, along with the Royal Society, featured most prominently in the correspondence of John Perceval and Hans Sloane. It is hardly surprising that the Royal Society dominated Sloane's letters since he was the secretary and later the president of that body. Many of his surviving letters are from other members and regard the activities of the Royal Society. The institution that most strongly infused John Perceval's correspondence was the SPCK.[83] Two of his more frequent correspondents were Henry Newman and John Chamberlayne, both men deeply involved in the SPCK and each served as its secretary at some point in their lives.[84] As a Protestant Irish landlord Perceval found the SPCK a noble institution. Proselytizing Catholics was a great interest of his and he even established a charity school on his estate to promote that goal.[85] The SPCK supported such activities. While these societies surface the most strongly in the letters of these two men, they were not the only ones with such contacts. Letters between Perceval and the secretary of the SPCK mention Perceval's wife, his friend George Berkeley, and his cousins Daniel Dering and Edward Southwell. Also, many letter writers who surfaced in this study were members of the Royal Society, including Charles and John Boyle, William Byrd II, James Brydges, Peter Collinson, John Perceval, Edward Southwell, and obviously Hans Sloane. Moreover, the Royal Society and the SPCK shared many of the same members.[86] Perceval and Henry Newman of the SPCK discussed how they would support Hans Sloane when he was nominated as president of the Royal Society, while Royal Society members Hans Sloane and James Brydges participated in a scheme to send a pair of African princes back to Africa, a project involving many SPCK members. This was not a world of isolated networks, but one in which different networks intersected and worked together. The emergence of these societies was part of a larger shift in modes of socialization, not merely an indication of changes in scientific or religious thought.

In many ways these two societies were the crystallization of older, more informal networks; the SPCK had its roots in societies for the reformation of manners and the Royal Society was the heir of the "Republic of Letters."[87] Both societies were relatively early voluntary societies. The Royal Society, formally established in 1660, was one of the first societies to emerge, and the SPCK's establishment in 1698 places it in the earlier period as well. It was not until the end of the eighteenth century that societies became truly formalized and institutionalized, so these early societies provide a glimpse of social forms in transition: they can show how the British dealt with and thought about voluntary institutional organization at its onset. Both the founding members of the Royal Society and the SPCK believed that a group of formally linked individuals could transform science or reform society better than an official governmental body and better then the informal networks they had relied on before. The personal networks focused on earlier were not enough. Members also reacted to a need to stabilize society and to a general enthusiasm for plans, projects, and public bodies. The creation of the Royal Society was the result of both social and scientific concerns.[88] The instability of the Civil Wars helped create a longing for stability and, as a whole, the British began to embrace organized public bodies over informal organizations.[89] Concerns about stability also prompted the creation of the SPCK and its sister organization, the Society for the Propagation of the Gospel in Foreign Parts (SPG). The seeming deterioration of morals in society and the lack of state intervention in such matters worried their founder, Thomas Bray. He and his colleagues wanted to alter society as a whole by setting up schools, distributing morally edifying books, and supporting missionaries throughout the wider British world.[90] These early societies were the result of a countrywide shift toward formal public institutions that strove to stabilize and improve society.

And both societies looked beyond British borders. Discoveries from the "New World" intrigued the Royal Society.[91] In his *History of the Royal Society* (1667), Thomas Sprat gave America a whole section and stated that America still had unplumbed depths for "it had not yet bin shewn above *Two hundred years*: which is scarce enough time, to travail it over, describe, and measure it, much less to pierce into all its secrets."[92] This interest stood the test of time; as late as 1744 Peter Collinson, FRS, wrote a New York correspondent, "I expect Something New from your New World, our Old World as it were Exhausted."[93] The society also had correspondents all over the globe: from the American colonies, to Sweden, Russia, and beyond. A correspondent of Hans Sloane told him in a casual manner that he wanted to send a letter and a specimen to Moscow, Danzig, Hamburg, Leiden, and "other forreign Places."[94] Due to these vast geographic interests Sloane's letters came from a much larger portion of the globe than the letters of any other correspondent.

Unlike the Royal Society, the SPCK cared less about colonial curiosities and more about colonial souls. Bray organized the SPCK after he become interested in the reformation of Maryland, originally a Catholic colony, which had lost its right to be a Catholic haven after the Glorious Revolution.[95] The SPCK and the SPG sent missionaries over to lead wayward colonists back into the Anglican fold. They also looked to the fringes of their own isles and attempted to convert the Catholics in Ireland and set up correspondents throughout Wales. They even had links to groups helping converts from the Continent. There is also a telling overlap between members of the SPCK and the Georgia Society.[96] The ideology of social and moral reform that led to the formation of the colony of Georgia found many sympathizers in the ranks of the SPCK. This was a group attempting to pull an increasingly dispersed British world together under one Anglican awning and the Royal Society was trying to increase its members' knowledge by gathering objects and ideas from around the world. To reach these goals they needed well-organized institutions, not just the loosely linked friend networks or the informal organizations that had sufficed previously. They also required letters.

Institutional Organization and Correspondence

A dependence on letters was not born with the Royal Society. In the beginning participation in experiments, not discussion through letters or meetings, had been the focus of its activity.[97] The emphasis on correspondents and discussion grew over the course of the eighteenth century. During the presidency of Hans Sloane, correspondence, especially foreign correspondence, received more support. In 1727 the society hired a new assistant secretary to take care of foreign correspondence and Sloane attempted to gain more and better contacts.[98] However, from its inception in 1660 the society had depended on a secretary, the first being Henry Oldenburg, and one of his jobs was to organize the correspondence of the society. Oldenburg wrote, on average, 250 letters a year for the society and he began to place that correspondence into letter books.[99]

The SPCK looked to letters from its onset. In one of its early meetings in 1699 John Chamberlayne, the secretary of the SPCK until 1702, recorded that they "Resolvd . . . to find out some one particular person who shall give an Account once a month to this society of the state of progress of Reformation and of Christian Knowledge in yr respective countys."[100] And by the next week they had decided on fifty-five different correspondents in counties throughout England and Wales.[101] A few months later they added a correspondent in Germany and then Barbados and then Bengal.[102] These correspondents took their positions seriously and a sense of formality permeates their letters. They served specific regions and when a correspondent left, members made motions to find successors.[103] In fact, the society had two kinds of members: residing or subscribing members who paid dues and had a vote and corresponding members who did not pay dues or vote, but who were supposed to support the society's designs in their own community.[104]

Maintaining such official webs allowed members of voluntary societies to monitor projects. In 1724, John Perceval suspected that a convert had deceived the Proselyte Society, a set of commissioners deeply entangled with the SPCK and charged with distributing money from the Royal Bounty to support converts from Catholicism. To investigate his suspicion he suggested that Henry Newman, secretary of both the SPCK and the Proselyte Society, should write to their correspondent in the area where the convert had died to see if he had "persever'd in the Protestant religion to the last" and what character he held there.[105] Correspondence also played a role in keeping the heart of the SPCK beating. Not everyone could be at every meeting, but letters could keep business flowing. In fact, multiple letters to Newman ask him to forward their thoughts to the SPCK because they could not be present at the meetings in town.[106]

These societies were attempting to form networks that linked many correspondents across wide expanses for specific purposes, and this called for more centralized control. These groups had central meeting places (although these shifted), permanent secretaries, committees, and even publications.[107] This formality gave their members a way to control their networks in a fashion that was impossible in more informal structures. Such organization gave them a set meeting point and a constant center in their secretary. Having a secretary or writing to a secretary was not a new phenomenon for these writers—many a gentleman had a secretary, but a secretary for an institution was different. These men had to coordinate the activities and letters of many members, not a single individual, and letter writers saw their position differently. These men were not simply employees, even if they were sometimes paid. They were directors of networks. These secretaries provided correspondents with permanent central contacts: members knew whom to write to when they had an idea or a concern and they usually knew exactly how to reach them. They did not have to track them down or follow their movements like they did their more mobile individual correspondents. This made communication and connection simpler and easier.

The epistolary networks of secretaries show their central place in these networks. There is no question when looking at Figure 18 that Hans Sloane was the linchpin of his network.[108] Without his presence the network falls apart. With a few exceptions, these correspondents were not greatly interconnected among themselves; they depended on Sloane to receive knowledge and then disperse it. Sloane's centrality is even more striking when Figures 18 and 8 stand side by side. Perceval's network holds strong without him;

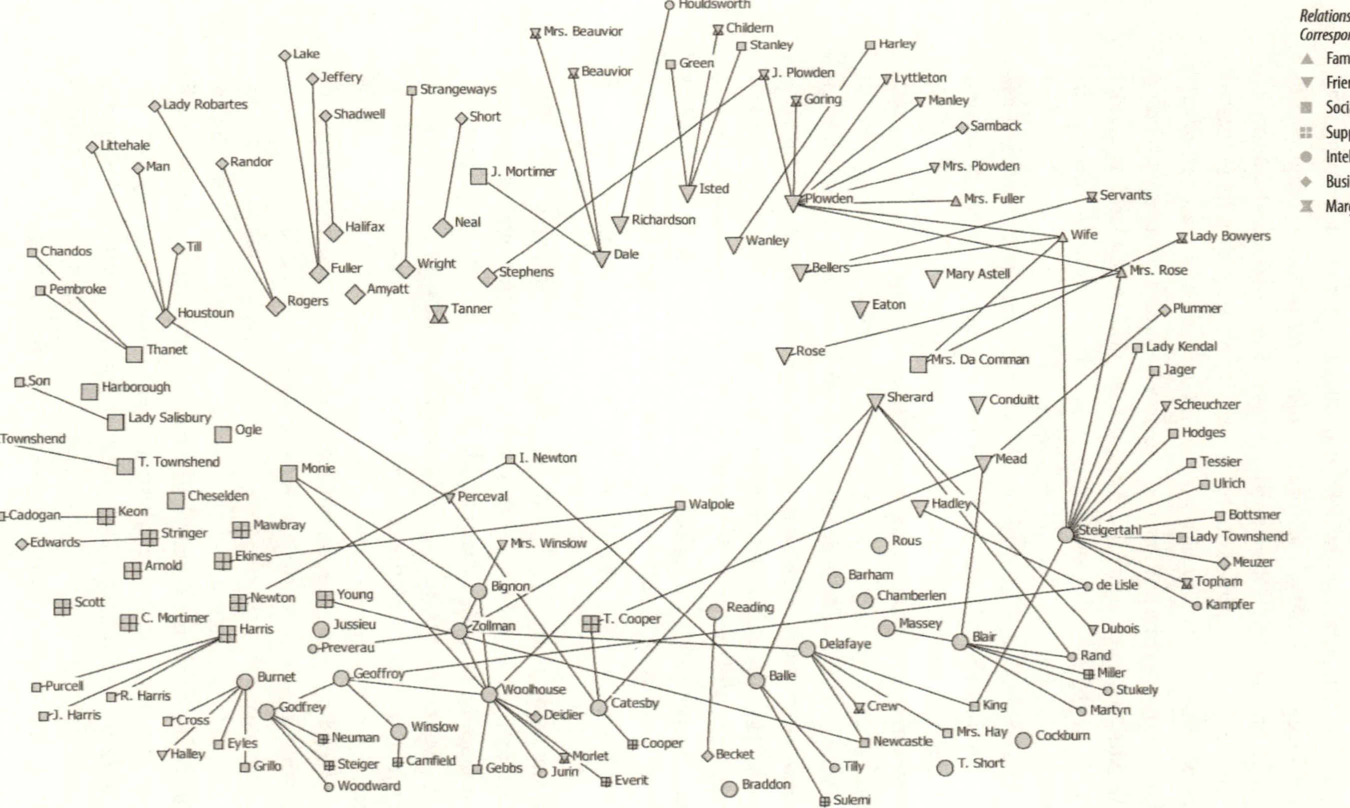

Figure 18. Epistolary network of Hans Sloane, 1724, with Hans Sloane taken out. Large symbols represent individuals Hans Sloane wrote to or received a letter from during the year 1724; smaller symbols denote people mentioned in those letters. The symbols themselves designate the individual's relationship to Sloane. In this network, however, the ties to Sloane have been left out to show the lack of interconnection within the network.

Network courtesy of Borgatti, S.P., 2002. NetDraw Software for Network Visualization. Analytic Technologies, Lexington, Kentucky.

Sloane's does not. That Perceval's network covers a longer period of time explains some of this difference, but Perceval still wrote three letters per correspondent to Sloane's two, which suggests that he had a more tightly bound network. Perceval's and Sloane's powers were different. Sloane achieved his centrality not from his individual social power, but due to his depersonalized position as secretary of a larger institution: correspondents sent him letters because of who he represented, not because of his individual power.

Secretaries knew correspondents wrote not to them but to the society, and they usually made a point to assure their correspondents that the letters they received were read by the society as a whole. Henry Oldenburg made it a point to let his correspondents know that the entire Royal Society read their letters and that they, not he, judged them.[109] The SPCK took their letters seriously as well. During one meeting the members decided that they would allow "no Letter be sent to any person as from this society until the said Letter be read and approved of by the Society" and they appear to have read abstracts of the letters received from their correspondents and then had a committee draw up answers.[110] Correspondents wrote to whole bodies of men and those organizations tried to respond in kind.

As the eighteenth century progressed, intellectuals began to believe that a connection to the Royal Society was more profitable than ties to mere individuals. One acquaintance confessed to Sloane that his correspondence with a scientific acquaintance would function better if that individual "had the honour of corresponding also with some other of the ingenious members of that honorable society."[111] Correspondence with multiple members of the Royal Society was more beneficial then a simple exchange of letters between individuals. No longer did informal personal networks hold the key. But these new kinds of networks led to questions about letters. Letters were usually addressed to a single individual and the ties they nurtured were personal. Societies were made up of many individuals and the ties they relied on were less than personal. This proved a quandary for many a letter writer.

Institutional Language?

When composing institutional letters writers often employed the same kind of language they used in more familiar letters. Both bound their correspondents through the rhetoric of friendship and through gifts and services. Some members addressed each other as "Curious Friend," "curious friends & Patrons," and "learned friends."[112] Such declarations promoted a feeling of trust and connection, which could help nurture belief in their correspondents' statements about intellectual concerns. These natural historians based their trust as much on the ability of their colleagues to act as gentlemen, with honor, as on any solid empirical proof.[113] Writing the correct kind of letter and using the rhetoric of friendship helped to define who was gentle, honorable, and trustworthy. Gestures of friendship helped bind the members of the SPCK as well. Perceval assured its secretary that he liked to hear of his particular cares and in return he asked after the health of Perceval's family and even once provided a story for the children.[114] Such personal connections mattered: it was through them that most Royal Society members received their membership, and an active member of the SPG did not approach John Perceval about joining until they had known each other for a few months.[115] Henry Newman, secretary of the SPCK, even helped his correspondents connect with their personal networks. In 1720 he sent one of his correspondents in India a letter from his wife since he was "not able . . . to tell you how your Family does."[116] These institutional networks intertwined with vast social webs. However, these new webs also called for a different kind of connection, and this often perplexed writers.

Correspondents were never sure how to address Hans Sloane when he was the secretary of the Royal Society. They often felt the need to separate his official position from his place as their friend. Some writers insisted that the curiosity or the letter they sent was for their friend Hans Sloane, not the secretary of the Royal Society. One correspondent was sure to tell Sloane that the stone he sent "is only to a comarade, not to a secretarie of the Royal Societie."[117] This could be attributed to the fact that he wanted to make sure Sloane kept the stone for himself, not for the Society, but Ralph Thoresby made the same distinction. He wrote, "I long for the favour of a line from you, not writing this to you in the Quality of Secretary of the Royal Society but as to an Honored friend and kind Benefactor."[118] These men wanted Sloane tied to them *personally*; such a connection was more valuable to them. Others worried less about the type of connection. One correspondent simply hoped to "be serviceable to you, or the Royal Society."[119] Most members felt as deep an obligation to the Society as they did to Sloane. At another point Ralph Thoresby, who once needed Sloane's assurance of personal friendship, changed his tune and wrote, "I am ashamed to be so unprofitable a Correspondent to so kind a friend, had any thing occurr'd in these parts worthy the notice of the Royal Society, it should have been communicated."[120] Here, being a good friend to Sloane meant serving the Royal Society.

Members also began to refer to and treat the Royal Society as a friend. An aspiring member asked Sloane, "If the Society should chuse me pray be so kind as to let me know whether it be customary to return a Letter of thanks & what stile & title I shall give them, that I may not commit any error."[121] This correspondent wanted to be chosen, not by Sloane or a group of named gentleman, but by the Royal Society. However, he was unsure how to deal with this new type of friend. Was a letter of thanks, as one would send a friend for services rendered, due to an institution? And if so, how did one address it? John Perceval experienced a similar confusion when writing to the SPCK. Sometime he would send his services to particular members of the SPCK, highlighting personal connections, and on other occasions he gave his services to the SPCK itself, gesturing to his loyalty to the institution.[122] The secretaries were sure to return services from the whole society.[123] Members found it natural to pick up a pen and write to a society, but whether that letter should contain the same elements as a personal letter made them pause; the line between the two was vague, like the boundary between the two types of networks themselves.

Still, like contractual correspondence these letters were more interested in getting business done than in cultivating a connection. The secretary of the SPCK and John Perceval were friends and they talked of personal matters, but the content of their letters usually regarded the Society's business. Most of their letters concerned two events: an attempt to send two African princes back to Africa to proselytize their followers, and whether a supposed convert had hoodwinked them.[124] They wrote these letters to get things done, not to nurture their relationship. When Perceval identified the secretary in his letter book it was by his formal position as "Secretary to ye Society for promoting Christian knowledge," not as a friend.[125] The majority of acquaintances mentioned in letters between Perceval and his SPCK correspondents were not family members, but other SPCK members. Their involvement in the SPCK created and contained their friendship. Newman too was careful to separate his correspondence and directed members to send their letters to the treasurer's residence where they often met "for the convenience of keeping those on a public account from those on a private."[126] The same is true of the Royal Society: those labeled as intellectual links in Sloane's network owed their classification to the lack of personal connection exhibited in their letters. While affection obviously linked members, it was their religious or scientific schemes and participation in the SPCK or Royal Society that defined their interaction. Common interest rather than blood, location, affection, or even business affairs held these networks together. Maintaining an interest was superior to constructing a wide-ranging network, and that interest had a formal institution coordinating it. Neither ties of family obligation nor those of friendship bound these networks, although such ties could help cement their trust in one another. Instead, involvement in the same schemes, shared goals, and a common perception of social good linked them together.

Societies also began to establish correspondences with other institutions, rather than just with other individuals. The French Academy of Sciences wished "to intertain correspondence with the Royall Society."[127] The Academy wanted to connect with the Royal Society, not just some of its members. This way they could reach a larger audience and gather more information. Over the course of the eighteenth century more scientific societies or academies were beginning to interact with one another as societies and to form one large scientific network. The societies began to have more foreign members, to exchange instruments and publications, and to embark on common projects.[128] In fact, during the early eighteenth century the Royal Society was often at the forefront of such collaborative efforts.[129] Likewise, the SPCK formed links with similar bodies. In 1700 their minutes declared that they wanted to encourage a "Good Correspondence" with "other Societies for Reformation of Manners & the Religious Societies," including those in Scotland and Ireland.[130]

These societies were slowly making the shift from trust in friends to trust in institutions, from "negotiated" to "architectural" communities. These networks relied not on individual connections, but on shared ideas and desires. But members still valued and used their informal social networks. The British were learning to balance the two forms and allowed them to work together. Personal networks opened doors to institutionalized networks and fellow members could act as friends. Peter Clark elegantly stated, "society members often provided the sinuous highway of communication, on to which, other looser or more informal branches were grafted."[131] Societies like the SPCK and the Royal Society had slightly shifted the center of social networks; the interest could be more important than a personal web of informal correspondents. They created new permanent centers for those concerned with science or religious reform. However, individual contacts still mattered; it took personal connections to get into the Royal Society or the SPCK. Being a member of an institution added another layer to writers' networks, a layer that worked differently and foretold things to come.

The creation of a center of activity for a certain interest also opened the door for other types of interaction, especially through print. While the SPCK did not have a journal, one of their concerns was the printing of books to educate the populace. Print was a way they reached out to the world. Print also helped the Royal Society communicate. The Royal Society's first secretary began *Philosophical Transactions*, the Society's journal, in 1665 and maintained it until his death in 1677.[132] *Philosophical Transactions* printed many of the findings of the Royal Society and allowed the members who lived beyond London to have access to that information.[133] Many of these reports came from the letters the secretary received. Print, especially ephemeral print, was the next step in connection. A periodical facilitated the spread of information more effectively than correspondence and more quickly than printed books.[134] It also made participation less dependent on personal connections and distributed the information to a larger segment of the population.[135] The secretaries were hubs of epistolary networks who lifted a burden from their own shoulders through the use of print. Members who received *Philosophical Transactions* no longer had to write to the secretary to find out the happenings of the scientific world, but often knowing was not enough. These members wished to participate. Thus it should come as no surprise that while William Byrd II of Virginia kept a set of *Philosophical Transactions* on a shelf in his library, he also kept up his correspondence with Hans Sloane.[136]

ᔕ

Contractual and institutional letters point to the changing social landscape of the British world and the place letters held within it. Throughout the later seventeenth and early eighteenth centuries more writers picked up the pen to hold together their expanding social networks, but they also knew that letters could help them negotiate new needs. The same mobility that prompted many to send letters to friends and family members at a distance created the need for more formal epistolary relationships, both intellectual and professional. Letters kept estates running, trade flowing, and the government functioning. They also allowed emerging clubs and societies to expand their reach and fulfill their goals. Such letters rarely overflowed with affectionate phrases; they focused on getting things accomplished. An interest, be it a distant estate or the need to reform a distant people, propelled these networks and held them together. The network mattered, but the goal mattered more. But those invested in these networks could never totally untangle them from their personal social webs, nor did they want to. Personal networks helped monitor these more formal webs, existed beside them, and, at times, intermixed with them. They also provided correspondents with the tools to make such networks trustworthy. The occasional insertion of devotion or personal connection anchored these networks in the familiar and eased the transition between the types of relationships. But these networks created different kinds of bonds that point to a British world that was organizing its social relations in new ways as its economic, political, and social concerns began to reach across a wider segment of the globe. It is no wonder John Perceval became so worried when his estate correspondence had seemed to stray.

Chapter 6

Stirring News and the Role of the Letter

For the British of the late seventeenth and early eighteenth centuries news was more than words on a page or events told by a friend, it was a living thing. It stirred and made noise. In their letters they referred to it by its state of motion: "You won't fail to send me what news you have stirring," "What is Stirring I here send you," "here is nothing of News Stirring."[1] Such movement made noise: "there has happen'd nothing that has made any noise," "I think at present the affairs of Ireland make more noise than any thing on this side."[2] This noise could overwhelm. One correspondent declared, "we hear the sound of News, News on Everyside."[3] Even the lack of news implied movement and sound: "To have *no Newes* is *good Newes*, it is a symptome of a *placid* and *quiet* state of affairs."[4] News moved briskly and loudly, and caused vibrations that individuals felt throughout the wider British world, and letters played a critical role in creating and controlling such stirrings.

Ignoring the news was increasingly difficult for men and women in the late seventeenth- and early eighteenth-century British world. News was available in numerous forms and worried about to an unprecedented degree. The Civil Wars had increased news distribution, produced the first newspapers, and instilled in many a wish to know about the world around them.[5] The expansion of commercial activity strengthened this need to know as did British mobility and migration.[6] It was also simply easier to get news by the early eighteenth century: more newsletters circulated, more newspapers emerged in towns across the British world, the postal system sent them further afield, and increased shipping allowed information to travel faster. News was becoming part of the daily diet of the British. While this shift worried many, especially the elite and those in government, and they made attempts to stem or at least control the flow of news, there were fewer attempts to rein in distribution and circulation.[7]

The mobile, noisy, threatening, and necessary nature of news both drew and repelled its readers. On the positive side, news promoted sociability. Everyone wanted to know what was making noise and talk about it. But too much noise could surround and confuse. This made news a little dangerous. Interested individuals also had to monitor this suspect chatter as it shifted locations. At times places were "placid and quiet" and on other occasions they were the scene of noise and movement. Finding a way to balance these different characteristics challenged newsreaders and one way they controlled and made use of this world of news was through their letters. Letters, and the networks they formed, helped their readers not only to spread but also to stalk, and to an extent, cage the news.

The forms encasing news have long drawn scholarly attention. First and foremost scholars have looked at the newspaper. In the view of some scholars, the newspaper brought more news to more readers, which caused a "news revolution."[8] However, increasingly, other forms like the newsletter and oral networks have garnered attention.[9] By adding these different layers of distribution, the intersections between the mediums surface and scholars have begun to note the need to examine networks of news and the process of news creation.[10] Scholars, like the newsreaders of the eighteenth century, have seen that news stirred on its own and that this affected the news culture of the period. Letters had a significant role in this process and news had an important epistolary purpose.[11] Pulling together the informational and social resonances of epistolary news shows how both forms ran through the same networks and how personal networks had power beyond the personal world. Watching the flow of information through these networks illuminates where news was stirring as well. News made more noise in some places than others and the manner in which individuals could hear news varied according to location. Tracing the desire for news and how it was exchanged over long distances helps illuminate the increasingly important role social networks played in helping the British elite navigate the changing contours of the expanding British world.

"Nothing of News Stirring But What You Find in the Papers . . ."

In 1730 Philip Perceval ended a chatty letter to his brother by stating "here is nothing of News Stirring but what you find in the papers so I shall only add my best wishes to all with you."[12] Letter writers often added news to their letters, but the blossoming of the newspaper altered the role news played in letters. The way letter writers added, or did not add, news to their letters shows the role letters played in news distribution. It also emphasizes the role public news had in private affairs and private letters had in the public realm. When Jürgen Habermas outlined his theory for the emergence of the bourgeois public sphere, news circulation played a critical role, but news also affected the private world as well.[13]

Letters and news have a long history of interaction that the emergence of the newspaper transformed, but did not erase. In the fifteenth century the Paston family often sent news or "tydyngs" through letters. Agnes Paston revealed the importance of epistolary news when she wrote her son, "I praye yow to sende me tydynggis from be-yond see, for here thei arn aferde to telle soche as be reportid."[14] A letter provided her with news from "be-yond see" that her oral networks would not. Centuries later, correspondents still expected to receive news in their letters. While no manual demanded its presence, their authors often included a sample letter devoted solely to the asking of news.[15] But very few actual letters were so devoted. Rather than being letters of news, most were letters with news. Correspondents usually placed news at the end of a letter, as though it was an expected component, but one divorced from the letter's initial purpose. Peter Collinson added a playful postscript that began, "Sir Joseph Jeykill is laid in his Tomb & Dudley Rider is to come in his Roome." He then proceeded to tell of the robbing of the northern mail and the possible coming of war, all in rhyming couplets.[16] Obviously correspondents thought news should close a letter and Collinson used that expectation to have a bit of fun. Similarly, James Brydges felt a little sheepish in hurriedly closing up a letter to get it to the post, but defended himself by stating that "the rest was only publick news."[17] News had become such a mainstay of the letter form that writers commented on its absence, ending many a letter with the simple statement: "No News."[18]

Letters were a traditional way to receive news, but change was in the air as the amount of information available, the forms that packaged it, and the need to have it grew. During the early seventeenth century the earls of Huntingdon relied on letters to obtain their news. Henry Hastings, the fifth earl of Huntingdon, learned the details of the Gunpowder Plot of 1605 via letters and then spread the news the same way.[19] Later in the century, his ten-year-old grandson, Theophilus Hastings, the seventh earl, received letters full of news from a family dependent. By the time the earl was about fifteen, though, this dependent turned his duty over to another, for, as he wrote, "I have not the least designe in giving you those frequent troubles as to presume to bee your Intelligencer I know that is done by a better hand."[20] By age nineteen, in 1669, Huntingdon was reading newsletters from professional news writer Henry Muddiman; this was his better hand.[21]

The circulation of professional newsletters increased during the late seventeenth century and remained a way to exchange news throughout the eighteenth century. By the later seventeenth century, and especially after the lapsing of the Licensing Act in 1695, which opened the door for more newspapers to flourish, the news the young earl received came from sources beyond the oral or the epistolary—it came from newspapers as well. Muddiman's newsletters themselves attest to the widening informational world. His news came from gazettes and newsbooks as well as oral and epistolary channels. He even directed his client to these alternate sources. In 1670 he told his lordship that "Of the arrival of ye Lord Falconberge and Sir Tho: Allen the newes book gives you an Account."[22] This expansion of the news world altered the way news in letters functioned.

Before newspapers and newsletters flourished, personal letters were the main way to receive nonoral news. This had changed by the mid-seventeenth century and letters attest to the fact. Multiple letter writers heaved a discontented sigh after informing their correspondents that the news in the printed papers would hold more or better information than their epistles.[23] Letters were no longer necessarily the fastest or most detailed way to send news and for this reason some correspondents began to leave it out or refer the receiver to the papers. These writers assumed that they had no need to add to the news flowing through their correspondents' news networks. They had already picked up a steady current thanks to the printed papers.

Newspapers were places for what contemporaries called "public news." For eighteenth-century readers, the term "public news" or "public prints" was often synonymous with the newspaper. George Berkeley assumed that "the publick papers" would tell Perceval all he needed to know of the "publick news."[24] And Perceval himself told a correspondent that he found information via "ye publick news and other accounts."[25] For these letter writers "public news" meant information that was generally available. Since this news was printed and sold, it was automatically public. John Brewer also contends "the proliferation of such terms as 'public knowledge' and 'public information' reflects a widely held desire to push out into the open—into the public sphere—knowledge and information previously arcane, obscure or

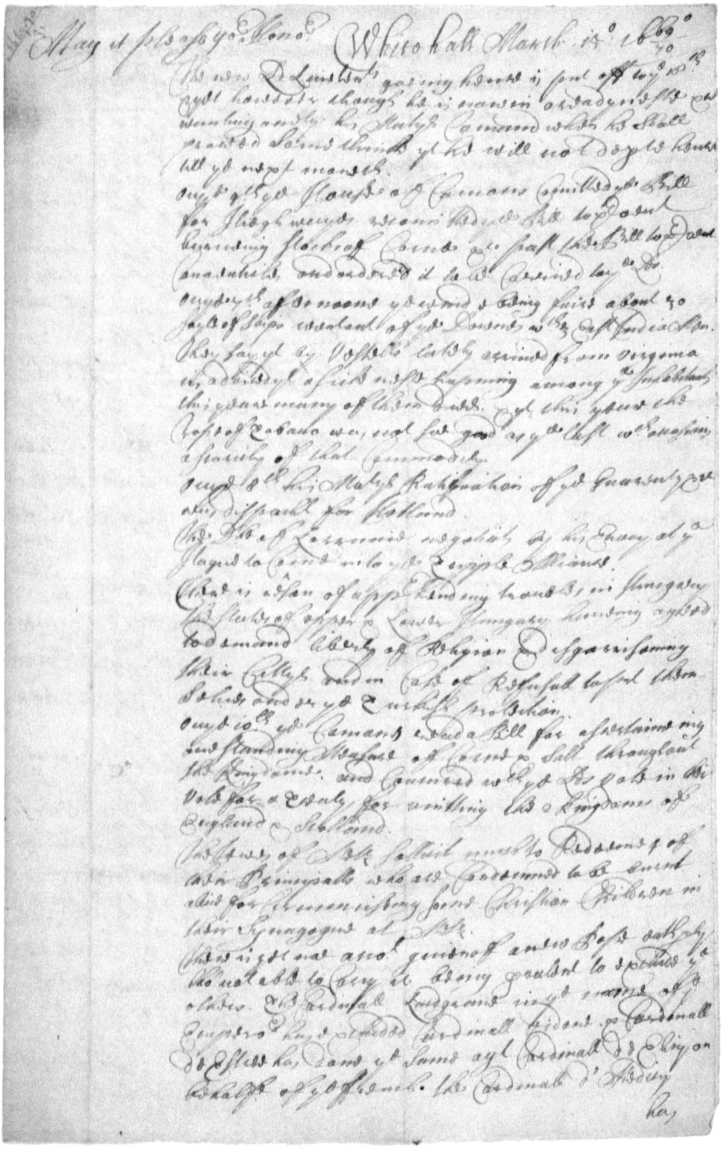

Figure 19. Newsletters, like this one sent by Henry Muddiman to the Earl of Huntingdon in 1670, looked like traditional letters. They were dated from their place of origin and had a salutation, but rather than beginning with compliments they began with news and no humble services or signatures marked their end.

Henry Muddiman to Theophilus Hastings, seventh Earl of Huntingdon, 14 March 1669/70, HEH HA 9603.

private."[26] The desire to make information more available was growing and, to a degree, everything termed as news was assumed to be public. Letter writers referred to "private letters," emphasizing their curtailed audience, but never "private news."[27] The closest a correspondent came was "private intelligence."[28] Certainly some news needed to be handled with care, and making it public would have grave consequences, but letter writers did not refer to this as "private news." The terms public and private often denoted access rather than content.

Public news could refer to news we would consider quite private. William Byrd II's correspondent provided him with the details of George II's coronation but added, "the more publick news such as death and marriages, the papers will convey to Virginia."[29] Deaths, marriages, and stock prices were public news because they were readily found in the papers. An examination of the newspapers from the period quickly affirms this fact. Papers from London, Newcastle, and Boston, Massachusetts, often included promotions in the army, clergy, or government and usually closed with a list of stock prices.[30] It should not come as a surprise, then, that letter writers regularly told their correspondents to see the prints for news on stocks, promotions, and positions.[31] Thus while all news could be public, certain kinds of news were regularly reported on, which made them categorically public news found in public prints.

To a degree, content did matter. Public affairs often dealt with information detailing state and international issues—events that might affect a larger public. Private affairs revolved around family and individual business interests. In one letter, after describing the health of his family, Perceval stated, "This is what I have to say regarding my private affairs. As to the Publick we are alarmed with an apprehension that Spain is Actually in march to invade Portugal."[32] Years later, his son termed information on lease negotiations "private inteligence" and the actions of the Irish House of Commons "public news."[33] Using the term "public news" then often had more resonances than simply wide-ranging access. The "material article of publick news," which Perceval added to a letter to Byrd in 1729, turned out to be the signing of the Treaty of Seville, which concluded the Anglo-Spanish War.[34] Fifty years earlier, a letter referred to the "publick newes of ye nation" and then referenced talk about the dissolution of Parliament during the Exclusion Crisis.[35] Public news, then, could refer both to the level of access and to its content, and while it often found its way into private letters, the need for it there was decreasing.

Some correspondents celebrated the jettisoning of public news and public affairs from epistolary channels. George Berkeley, John Perceval's constant correspondent, wanted letters to tell him about hearth and home, not king and country. He told Perceval that he could read in a newspaper about the bishop being made primate or the Lord Chancellor's displeasure, but not of "my Lady's health, your Son's learning, your daughter's beauty, Mrs. Parker's being married, Mrs. Deering's being recover'd of the Gout, or Mrs. Percival's breeding, or Mr. Deering's getting a good Employment."[36] Over a year later he was voicing the same opinion, declaring, "I would much rather correspond with you on the beauties of latin authors than on the subject of news of which the publick papers tell you all that's certain and for other surmises they are hardly worth troubling."[37] Since the public prints could keep correspondents informed of public news, letters themselves could become a venue for intellectual discussion and family affairs. One of Perceval's relatives agreed with Berkeley and reminded Perceval that a lack of news was not an acceptable excuse for the lack of a letter. As he told the young Perceval, it was "the greatest Satisfaction Man can have to hear of the welfare of his friends."[38] With the advent of the newspaper the letter could become a more personal space. When Berkeley sighed from Genoa, "I long to hear some News from your fireside," he wanted news of family not international affairs.[39] However, deaf to all his protestations, Perceval's next letter to Berkeley included political news and Berkeley's in return were often overflowing with the latest occurrences.[40] Rather than illustrating the triumph of the more intimate letter, these actions show the continued importance of public news in letters. Berkeley was fighting an uphill battle and Perceval knew that a lack of news could serve as an excuse for a delayed letter. Newspapers had only lessened the dependence on letters for news, but in letters individuals found another source to exploit for their informational world.

Public news found its way into letters time and time again and newspapers and letters worked together to keep correspondents informed. When composing a letter, writers still often felt the need to point their readers toward newspapers for certain kinds of news. Perceval's cousin reminded him: "You see how the stocks are by the publick prints."[41] Correspondents also allowed newspapers to expand on their own information. Perceval's brother-in-law directed him to the papers for "the Villanous doings in Straffordshire" and his friend informed him "the News papers will tell you" about the details of the victory at Preston during the Jacobite Rising of 1715.[42] At other times, they would send the newspapers along. John Perceval received at least three newspapers with one letter: the *Flying Post*, the *Postman*, and the *French Gazette*.[43] The interdependence worked in the other direction as well. Correspondents often knew more than the brief report in the paper. One of Perceval's correspondents told him of riots in Worcester and Stafford because "the particulars whereof are not publish'd in the papers."[44] So when gathering news on the riots in Staffordshire in 1715, Perceval's brother-in-law first directed him to the papers and then a later correspondent filled in the details with his own letter. William Byrd II's correspondent may not have wanted to waste his time with news on deaths and marriages, but he told him of George II's coronation in detail and ended by stating that he "hope[d] your other correspondents will supply my deficiencies."[45] Even though letters no longer needed to include public news, they remained a critical player in the news world.

Beyond the need to wrestle with the fluid world of news, letter writers also inserted news in their letters because it fulfilled epistolary needs. Including news strengthened a correspondence.[46] News was an expected element in a letter because it was a gesture of good will. It also simply gave writers something to discuss. John Perceval admitted to his cousin that "since compliments are by mutuall agreement cast out of doors, news can be the only article that will swell my Epistles."[47] He had proved this in an earlier letter when he sent his cousin news about the possibility of the French joining the Great Northern War, providing his cousin with the chance to expound on his belief that the French could not do much harm to the Swedes.[48] Such news fed debate, filled letters, and gave connections worth. If a place was "barren of news" the correspondence could wither.[49] Letters full of elegant compliments were acceptable, but those overflowing with news were better. It could make a correspondence not based on deep friendship or important business valuable. Matthew Buchanan, the Irish clergyman who regularly tried to integrate himself into John Perceval's network, tried to increase his status by sending news.[50] He soon found that he had to send believable news to be embraced, but the attempt is telling.

Public prints also served epistolary needs by helping to hold together social networks. The papers often provided news on private affairs. The Perceval family looked to the papers for a relative's election results.[51] Cassandra Brydges declared to her stepson, "The Prints have I believe told you that your old acquaintance Dr. Hunt is dead," and then preceded to tell him which relatives had been offered Hunt's post.[52] On another occasion, years later, she read in "the publick papers" of an acquaintance's good fortune in finding a position and asked her correspondent to tell her if the news was true and "if it is, pray make my Compliments to him & let him know I congratulate him upon it."[53] Newsreaders looked to newsletters to keep track of their personal connections as well. James Brydges recorded in his journal that "Lady Drax gave me my Unkle Lake's newsletter, in wch there was an account of Hennadge Montagues death."[54] Hearing such accounts could provoke action and cause readers to pick up their pens and reaffirm a connection. After reading accounts in the paper, multiple friends wrote to congratulate Hans Sloane when he became a baronet and when he took on the position of physician general to the army.[55] Other writers wrote to congratulate or console after learning about weddings or deaths through the newspaper.[56] Waiting for printed reports did not mean the correspondents were not close, but letters did not always carry all the details. William Byrd II assumed his correspondent did not write about his election to Parliament because he was too modest to include it in a letter.[57] The prints could keep more personal knowledge flowing quickly and they could reinvigorate ties by giving distant correspondents something to discuss. Often public news served private needs.

Looking at news distribution through letters reveals the intersection between public and private access and public and private spheres. Private letters may have often dealt with private affairs and public prints usually expounded on public news, but the divide did not dominate. Instead it is their overlapping nature that reveals the way this world functioned. News did help in the formation of the public sphere during this period, but it also helped nurture the more personal realm and personal affairs often affected the larger public. Correspondents used the word "news" to refer to both public and private affairs. Nicholas Blundell complained to his mother that his last letter "was so full of News you can not expect much in this" and proceeded ("to keep up a good custom") to tell her of the premature death of a neighbor's child and the illness of another.[58] Here news was of a domestic nature. But on other occasions the sending of news meant the inclusion of information on foreign affairs. To letter writers, the term news was a flexible one that encompassed distant battles, parliamentary disputes, stock prices, marriages, and the health of close relatives. Letter writers had little interest in dividing up their news. They needed all kinds of news to solidify their knowledge of the wider world and to keep their personal networks functioning. Newspapers took away the monopoly letters once held over the written exchange of news, but most correspondents welcomed the change for they needed more information than letters could supply. Private letters and the public prints worked together to inform their readers of events that affected their worlds on all levels. However, with the expansion of the world of news, letters received another role. Through letters correspondents could come to trust the news that was flowing unchecked through these many mediums. Private letters made public news trustworthy.

"Tis Credibly Reported"

Letter writers often felt the need to preface their news with the phrase "Tis credibly reported" for many news readers were incredulous about what they read, and for good reason.[59] The news flowing through letters, newsletters, and newspapers was often false.[60] In a world where most news was second, if not third or fourth hand, veracity could vary. False news was the product of both the increased amount of news flowing through the wider British world and the fact that news had become a commodity. It had become something to buy and sell, and truth came second to profit. As a contemporary stated of a newsmonger, he was but "a retailer of rumour, that takes up upon trust, and sells as cheap as he buys. He deals in a perishable commodity, that will not keep: for if it be not fresh it lies upon his hands, and will yield nothing."[61] For the newsmonger news was a commodity whose value hinged on its freshness, not its truthfulness. To make the news desired it had to be fresh for "A Piece of News loses its Flavour when it hath been an Hour in the Air."[62] Editors often had to publish unconfirmed news to turn a profit, which increased the inherent instability of news.

Profit motivated some newsmongers, but others had more nefarious plans; some spread false news to influence the markets or to persuade others to their causes. The editor of the *Newcastle Courant* warned readers that they should not credit a story about the imprisonment of the Spanish queen for "this Story is raised only to fall the Stocks."[63] Those familiar with the news world expected such manipulation. William Byrd II was not surprised "that false news shoud be spread, either to gain a Point, or shew the good inclinations of those that made it currant."[64] The writer of a newsletter agreed that "some make it their business to instill suspicions and uneasiness in the minds of people."[65] Many elements could make news suspicious. At times the national origin of news made it untrustworthy. Philip Perceval doubted the truth of a report on the battle of Almansa in the War of the Spanish Succession because it came from "the French News Writer," and one of Brydges's correspondents admitted a week or so later that he was "still at the Mercy of the French Relations, which make our defeat as big as ever any was."[66] Political leanings could make news unreliable. John Perceval's cousin wittily informed him, "I think I may venture to give you one Item in knowing the truth of news,—which is that whenever any Whigish news of carrying any thing in the Lords or Commons you may conclude it untrue or very much suspect it."[67] News from the other side of the aisle was equally problematic. George Berkeley, after sending Perceval some "Tory News," admitted, "the truth is I hear little news at present to be depended on."[68] Nefarious souls distorted news for profit and both nations and political groups swung it to complement their actions or policies. Such a news world was not for the faint of heart.

Some thrilled at the uncertainty of this world of news. As William Slauter has pointed out, this was a society swimming in speculation and ready to apply that spirit to news.[69] Gambling was a common pastime of the elite whether with cards, on horse races, or through stock speculation. Thus uncertainty and the embrace of risk and chance was part of everyday life for these letter writers. News could easily slip into this world of speculation. News writers of all sorts suspected individuals of manipulating the news to manage stock prices, and James Brydges exchanged war news with one correspondent so they could lay wagers on the War of the Spanish Succession.[70] Some readers, such as William Byrd II and Brydges, took this new news world in stride; others did not.

A correspondent of Brydges felt overwhelmed. He complained that he heard "the sound of News, News on Everyside, but seldom knows whence it comes or what impress it bears." He saw "things at a Distance and but very darkly, unless sett of by such a light as you give to them."[71] This correspondent had no problem getting news, but relying on it was another matter. He disliked that his information had no named "impress." What he and many others wanted was a story from a known and trusted source, ideally an eyewitness.[72] While these problems plagued the distribution of oral news, newspaper news exacerbated the problem. Most newspaper reports were anonymous or possessed lengthy trails of authority.[73] Editors did often cite the news source from which they gathered their news. The first story in the *Newcastle Courant* of 1 August 1724 was from the *Evening Post* of 23 July, and later stories came from newsletters like "Mr. W-'s Letter."[74] The *Evening Post* of

7–9 July 1724 had news from the *Hague Courant*, and that news came from "private Letters."[75] For all these reference points and chains of authority, the actual source of the news remained unclear. Readers had no idea whose private letters the *Hague Courant* had access to and no knowledge of who "Mr. W-" received his news from, or even who he was. This was the news world that bothered Brydges's correspondent. Its news was anonymous and thus untrustworthy. To sooth his worry he turned to Brydges, who brought light to the darkness. However, why his letters shone so bright remains in shadow.

News in letters was no more trustworthy than news in any other form. As the previous section illustrated, letters and newspapers usually carried the same news, and all of them could carry false news. No news form was safe. One Englishman declared oral news "inconstant and apt to err."[76] John Perceval took Matthew Buchanan to task for sending incorrect information in his letter, and another of his correspondents had to apologize for sending false news.[77] Newsletters were just as likely to slip up. A correspondent of Hans Sloane would not believe a report in his newsletter until Sloane, or "some other good Hand," confirmed it because he had "never given any great credit to the news Letter since it told us that the King sent for Col. Ludlow out of Switzerland."[78] These correspondents did not trust newspapers either. William Byrd II informed a correspondent that "We had a sad account of you here, but twas in print, and therefore by the grace of God, may be an untruth."[79] Perceval preferred epistolary news to printed news from Ireland.[80] None of this had changed by 1757 when Peter Collinson warned his correspondent in New York that his news was the "Newspaper view so can't be Depended on."[81] Newspapers often deserved such declarations of distrust. An acquaintance of Perceval's son congratulated him on a post he did not possess; as Perceval the younger noted, "This ridiculous report was occasioned by a foolish paragraph in the papers."[82]

Newsreaders knew they had to check and double-check news, to organize and confirm it. This was not easy. A correspondent sent James Brydges an "abundance of Intelligence," but he did not know "how you will reduce them to any coherency," and another wrote him that he could not "draw any solid conclusions & consequences from it, till it has been a little more bandy'd about."[83] The diversity of reports even flummoxed editors. The *Evening Post* reported, "They write from Petersburg, that their Accounts from Persia so often contradict each other, that People can credit none."[84] Besides a suspect few, most Britons involved in the world of news, whether they were letter writers or newspaper editors, tried to spread trustworthy news. They corrected themselves when they made mistakes. Letter writers admitted when news they had sent proved false. John Perceval's correspondent apologized that "My News to you touching the Marquis DeScans murder in Spain has proved false."[85] Newsletters corrected newspapers and newspapers admitted their own mistakes.[86] Newsreaders did not expect news itself to be truthful; it was what individuals did with it that made it so.

The British thought news in letters was the most trustworthy due to the personal and interactive nature of letters. John Perceval assured a correspondent, "I don't write you this from the Publick prints, but private letters which may be depended on."[87] This was not because the news they held was different. Usually they all held the same news, and often epistolary news had the disability of being stale. Many correspondents knew they sent old news in their letters. Perceval's cousin lamented the fact that he "had writ my Thursdays letter before I heard of the debate that happen'd in the House of Lords that day and therefore probably tel you old news in mentioning it."[88] But still he added it to his letter. Correspondents valued such news because their epistolary friends would never intentionally send false news. The foundation of a correspondence was the trust between the writers. A writer who consciously sent false news was not treating his correspondent like a friend or even a good business connection. The British corresponded with those they trusted and thus they expected their news to be relatively safe. Correspondents could also search out more direct reports. Letter writers had the ability to turn to correspondents in different locations when they wanted specific intelligence. John Perceval was constantly asking his estate agents in Ireland for information and, on the other side of the continent, he had friends in Rome confirm news for him.[89] Thus, correspondents could come closer to receiving an eyewitness report, but most important, letters and the networks they formed gave the British a place to filter, bandy about, and evaluate their news.

In their letters writers could comment on the quality of news and limit its distribution. Some news was only supposed to go to certain hands at certain times. John Perceval, after deriding the news he had, gave permission to his cousin to spread it.[90] His need to give permission insinuates that he could have halted its circulation. In fact, a correspondent of Edward Southwell's warned him, of another piece of news, not to "speak of it, till you hear further."[91] Neither of these reports was especially sensitive. They dealt with an outbreak of the plague in France and the possible elevation of individuals to specific government positions. These writers cautioned their correspondents because they did not want to spread false news. They wanted to slow its distribution and stop rumors from spreading. While in England William Byrd II told his brother-in-law in Virginia to avoid embracing any news stories until he had written and confirmed them.[92] Sometimes, instead of a warning, writers assured their correspondents of a piece of news by stating, "Tis credibly reported."[93] Writers could send on such news with more confidence.

But how did news become credible? The medium did not assure truth; some preferred letters, but not all. Most Britons longed for an eyewitness report, but those were hard to find, especially as their interests grew to encompass a greater area of the globe. Instead of basing trust on the news source, the British built it on the processing of that piece of news. A report became credible when multiple hands confirmed it.[94] Many news reports included some version of the phrase "confirmed from all hands."[95] Most correspondents believed that the accumulation of evidence would lead to a credible finding. Thus, determining the truth of news was different from determining truth in scientific experiments. As Steven Shapin has pointed out, those enmeshed in scientific networks longed for eyewitness accounts, but they relied more on their faith in an individual who embraced a code of conduct, not on the accumulation of evidence.[96] But newsreaders could not depend on an individual or an accepted code of conduct since their information did not originate from an experiment conducted by known acquaintances, but came from more distanced and anonymous sources.

However, letters were ideal places to evaluate news. John Perceval's brother compared news from several sources before reporting back on the battle of Almansa. He informed him that "the Paris letter says we had 5,000 kill'd, & 13 or 14 Regiments taken without fighting . . . but this coming only from the French News Writer we are in hopes to hear a more favourable account: Some private letters say we kept the Field."[97] Perceval's brother compared French reports to English accounts and information from news writers with that from private correspondents. He wanted to send on credible news, but at this point he did not possess enough information to do so. Still, to keep his brother up to date he sent it anyway; if he had waited for all the reports to come in the news would be stale and of little use to his brother. Usually letter writers sent on all the probable reports they received and allowed their correspondents to judge their own news by comparing them to other reports they received. They sent news to give their correspondents the tools with which to be dependably informed, not because they thought they were unaware of the occurrence. John Perceval's brother sent him all the news he had even when he knew his brother's news was probably more credible. He knew his brother liked to compare them and "see how they agree."[98] Some of these accounts came from newspapers and some from newsletters, but letters were places where all these reports came together; where writers evaluated them and sent them on their way, perhaps with the comment "all hands agree."

Not all news providers were equal, however. Many correspondents hired news writers to send them the latest news, and other correspondents were simply "better hands." Many writers assumed their correspondents received news from those better informed. Brydges's correspondent who had news bombarding him from every side obviously saw Brydges as a better hand. Many elements could have made Brydges a good news provider. He had a high social status and was often in situations that allowed him access to more news. Members of the aristocracy often had a hand in politics, they could afford newsletters, and they often lived in London, the center of news. One of John Perceval's friends thought he would have better news because as a baronet and nephew of an official he seemed destined to have a place in government and plenty of news. As he said, "Shou'd I go about to tell you all the news & Politicks I hear in every Coffee house in this nice juncture, I shou'd Swell to a larger letter than my father sent me 'tother day after paying my debts. But I know you have all those things from better hands."[99] In fact, it was often through members of the gentry and peerage, especially those serving as lord lieutenants or justices of the peace, that the government received much of its information about English occurrences outside of London, and in exchange these men usually received government sanctioned newsletters about happenings in London.[100] Thus, location mattered as well. One of the reasons Brydges's correspondent struggled was his place in the country. Those in London had access to better accounts of governmental and social happenings and they were near the docks where foreign news came ashore. Rarely, however, did social status or location alone make a correspondent a better hand.

Some writers simply never steered their correspondents wrong. When a friend informed James Brydges of the surrender of Barcelona, he told him, "this you may [be] as easie in as if you had it from the french kings own hand. My friend having this day confirmed it: and he never misinformed me."[101] Reliability made this correspondent a better hand, but his ability appears unrelated to his location or status. When giving Brydges the news about Barcelona his correspondent compared it to getting the news from the "french kings own hand." News from Louis XIV's pen was the most trusted source for this news, but Louis XIV was not at the siege of Barcelona; he was not an eyewitness. What the king did have was a large, trustworthy news network. Eyewitnesses sent him reports and he saw the event from many angles. He had a dense and highly functional epistolary network. It was such networks that provided those interested in news with trustworthy information. This is why writer after writer continued to send news when they knew their correspondent received information from better hands. By sending news they helped their correspondents gather reports. They might not be a "better hand," but their information could make their correspondent one. Better hands sent better news, but to truly have a trustworthy piece of news correspondents had to listen to all reports sent. It was the network that mattered.

The British of the late seventeenth and early eighteenth centuries knew news was an elusive creature, unbounded by the lines drawn by mediums. They passed on oral news through letters, printed epistolary news, and sent printed news back through oral and epistolary channels. These men and women were familiar with all these threads; they knew how the system worked and who could be trusted to send solid news. They needed all these sources and a trusted epistolary network to get a sense of their world because, while this was a fluid world of news, it was not a very trustworthy one. All forms of news could come under suspicion, in part because all forms were involved in the same project: to get news to readers as quickly as possible. The British depended on gathering multiple reports and comparing them until they could safely say the news was confirmed. A sense of unease runs through their constant news gathering. They hoped for reports from those directly connected to the event, correspondents with dense informational webs, or personal connections, but such correspondents were rare. Usually it was their own network they had to trust. Attitudes toward the newspaper were similar to attitudes toward the postal system: both made connecting with others and knowing about the world easier, but they were less controllable and less discerning. Using epistolary networks allowed letter writers to regain some control, but the process of collecting and evaluating was not the same for those in the distant corners of the British world.

"Out of the Latitude of News"

On 16 May 1719 William Byrd II interrupted his busy London routine to write a letter to his friend and brother-in-law John Custis in Virginia. Writing letters to Virginia was not an unusual occurrence for Byrd. Already that month he had composed six and he would write at least another five before June arrived.[102] The main purpose of this letter was to stop the rumors running rampant in Virginia about the replacement of Virginian councilors and his inability to present an address to the king. As he told Custis, "suspend your Belief of such idle storys for the future, til you hear from me, because you will find by these 2 instances, that your Palace news wants confirmation."[103] But getting London news and its confirmation was not easy from Virginia. William Parks did not peel the *Virginia Gazette* off his printing press until 1736 and even the news included in that publication had to cross the Atlantic and thus remained months behind. After William Byrd had returned to Virginia, he had to admit to a correspondent that at his plantation of Westover he was "quite out of the latitude of news."[104]

While those in the colonies felt their distance from metropolitan news the most keenly, once one moved away from London, the epicenter of printing, sociability, trade, and news, information from the center became increasingly scarce. John Perceval learned of a death in the family when he was in Bath through a newspaper and had to apologize that "My Distance from London makes me longer unacquainted with what passes than others."[105] But Perceval penned his letter only twenty days after the passing of this relative. A few days earlier, he had written to George Berkeley in Rhode Island to tell him of the death of a mutual friend.[106] This friend had died two months previously and Berkeley did not receive the news until almost a year after the dire event. Obviously Perceval did not feel the same pressing need to share this news and it circulated much more slowly.

That European news came slowly to the colonies is not a surprise, but it is only the beginning of the story.[107] How news filtered into William Byrd II's diary, kept between August 1739 and August 1741, provides a glimpse into his news world and the role the letter held within it. There are two main ways that news surfaces. First, he often simply noted when he read news and, second, he mentioned when visitors brought no news. He rarely elaborated on the content of the news he read. Only twice over the course of two years did he actually record exactly what news he had received: on 29 August 1739 he recorded, "Tom Short brought word from town that we should have a war and that it was proclaimed in England" and on 8 November 1740 he noted that "In the evening came news from England that poor John Grymes was dead."[108] Usually, however, due to the nature of the diary, which was a recording of his everyday actions rather than a news diary, he glossed over the content of his news. Still, even these muted references show the way news filtered into his life in Virginia.

What is clear is that he strained to hear news when he resided at Westover. Ten times in his diary he referred to the failure of visitors to bring news. These failed messengers came in all shapes and sizes. Twice it was his own people, either servants or slaves, who returned from Williamsburg empty-handed, and on four other occasions it was neighbors like Daniel Custis who failed to bring news. Byrd had used his own men to actively search out news and his disappointment is palatable when he recorded that "After dinner my man came from Williamsburg but no news."[109] Why he had sent the man in the first place or what he had accomplished is left unsaid and uncelebrated; it was the lack of news that stung. The same mix of hope and disappointment colors his notes about visitors. The coming of neighbors and friends often brightened Byrd's days at Westover and in his diary he kept careful track of who came and what they did together. At times, he recorded if they brought news. On a blustery January day in 1741 Byrd's delight at the arrival of Daniel Custis dimmed for he "could tell us no news but that his father was better."[110] He often looked to the Randolphs, prominent friends and mobile Virginians, for news, but in his diary he notes three occasions in which they disappointed him.[111] Both Isham and Edward Randolph were ship captains, and thus his hope that they would bring news was not unfounded. However, time after time Byrd lists the coming of a visitor only to qualify it with some version of the fatal "but brought no news."[112]

Yet the number of times Byrd recorded reading news in his diary far outnumbered the times he lamented the lack of it. Between 1739 and 1741 he referenced reading news thirty-seven times, sometimes twice or three times a day. The reading of news was part of his routine. Along with playing billiards and cards, writing letters, and settling accounts, Byrd read news before dinner. On rare occasions he read it after dinner or even as an intellectual nightcap. What this news was or how he got it remains unclear. While Byrd is quite open about what he ate for dinner, he rarely records where he got his news, what kind of news it was, or what form it took. One is left with conjectures. Sometimes his reading took place around the same time a number of visitors had come to share a meal. On 24 February 1740 a friend and a captain of a man of war dined with Byrd and stayed until the morning of the 26th. After their departure Byrd settled in and "read news till one when the Secretary and his lady came to dine with us and I ate boiled rabbit."[113] Did these visitors supply the news he perused? Perhaps. However, there are plenty of examples of news reading taking place when he dined alone and had noted no visitors for days. On another occasion he noted, "After dinner I had letters from Williamsburg and read the news."[114] Did the letters from Williamsburg hold news or come with newsletters or newspapers enclosed? Perhaps. His reading of news appears to correspond with the time that ships would arrive from England. With only one exception, he settled down to read news between February and August, which corresponds with the time when ships from England sailed into Chesapeake Bay.[115] Was he dependent on these ships for his European news? Almost certainly. That Byrd read news is certain, but what he read and where he got it remains mostly a mystery.

On a few rare occasions exactly how Byrd got his news and what form it took surface. At Westover he could not visit the coffeehouses that lay thick on the ground in London and were even sprouting up in Williamsburg and he could not visit the bustling docks; instead, he listened for the step of visitors bearing the latest news. One can picture Tom Short bursting into Westover, perhaps breathless, to share the "word from town that we should have a war."[116] However, Byrd's constant reading of news gestures to nonverbal forms as well. Some of his news did come from letters. On 23 January 1741 he noted, "I had letters from England but no news," and even more interestingly in February of that year he mentioned, "I had a letter full of news from Parks at Williamsburg, which I read."[117] Letters from England were indubitably a source, but he also seemingly received a newsletter from William Parks, the editor of the *Virginia Gazette*. So, like his compatriots in England, he found personal letters and newsletters familiar forums for news. He also received newspapers. Twice in the space of two months, Mr. Dering, a dancing master from Williamsburg, brought Byrd newspapers. In March he brought "a Gazette" and in April he carried with him "the newspapers."[118] The gazette is most probably the *Virginia Gazette*, but the use of the plural in the second case suggests that his access reached beyond the local paper. However, the most interesting aspect of these deliveries is Byrd's reaction to these papers. In March he wrote of Dering, "He brought a Gazette without news," and on the second occasion he recorded that "Mr. Dering brought the newspapers, with nothing in them."[119] He received the papers, but he did not find them useful. In Byrd's eyes the information within their folds did not deserve the name of news. This suggests that he was not dependent on the newspaper, but received most of his news through oral and epistolary channels.

However, getting European news through those channels was a complex process for colonists. While all Britons were dependent on shipping routes for their news, ships did not cross the Atlantic with the same frequency with which they crossed the Channel or the Irish Sea. Colonists were dependent on the fleet in a way Britons living in England, Scotland, or even Ireland were not. One of the reasons Byrd looked to Isham and Edward Randolph for news was that they were merchants who crossed the ocean with frequency. When in Williamsburg the arrival of a ship's captain after dinner caused some excitement until it was revealed he "brought no news."[120] William Byrd II listened as carefully for the docking of ships as he did the footsteps of visitors. In 1735 he wrote to Sir John Randolph, "We are told there is a Bristol ship arrivd in York River, if she brings any news, be so good as to communicate it to your Country Friends."[121] Residing in Williamsburg made Randolph a good informant, and this was not the only time Byrd wrote him asking for "any news either Forreign or Domestick."[122] Byrd also used ships to spread and confirm his own news. As he told one correspondent, "What I tell you will come confirmed by all the latter ships, else I shoud despair of being believed."[123] For these colonists "latter ships," not just better hands, confirmed news. The Byrds, both father and son, had a deep knowledge of these shipping routes and the implications they had for the flow of news. Byrd the elder was sure to send a report of a plot against King William to his correspondent in Bermuda, but he did not enlarge on the report since he knew it was "almost assured that you have letter of a latter date from England, then wee."[124] He used his maritime knowledge for his own benefit as well, for in the same letter he asked his correspondent for news since Virginians "possibly may have certain news round your way sooner than directly from England" because Byrd could not expect any ships in Virginia before Christmas. The Byrds felt their dependence on shipping routes more strongly than those in the British Isles and they knew how to manage those routes to get as much news as possible.

They felt the lack of news keenly, though. Byrd the elder sighed to a correspondent, "We have little news, here having received no certain advice from England since last years fleet."[125] At times their lack of news forced on them a sense of resignation. In 1688, when the fate of the three kingdoms and the colonies was uncertain, William Byrd I could only pray and write to his factors in London: "We are in great expectation to hear of affairs out of England, God in mercy send all for the best."[126] The slow crossing of news also produced gaps of knowledge about their personal networks. Correspondents and loved ones could be married, promoted, or dead long before they heard of it. Byrd the younger found the silver lining to even this conundrum. "One advantage in being at so great a distance," he informed one formerly ill correspondent, "is that the concern I should have for your indisposition, is prevented by the news of your being well again."[127] However, he had to be crafty to extract this information. While he had received two letters from this correspondent by that year's fleet, neither epistle mentioned his illness; that information he had to ferret out from others. But the two letters were at least proof that his correspondent still lived when he penned the letters. Silences were dangerous for they could mark the end of a necessary correspondence. Their distance from the epicenter of news bred in the Byrds a sense of anxiety about the world so far away and yet so integral to their own lives. At times they made their peace with it, but on other occasions anxiety and frustration fairly oozes from their letters.

This sense of resignation and indignation about news also resulted from the way those in the colonies got their news. As Byrd's diary illustrated, European news came in spurts. Sometimes a visitor would bring it, sometimes letters, but it all came by ship and usually in bulk. As his father declared to a brother-in-law in England in 1690, "We are here att the end of the world, & Europe may bee turned topsy turvy ere wee can hear a word of itt; but when news comes wee have itt by whole sale, very often much more than truth."[128] The lack of news frustrated the elder Byrd, but its delivery "whole sale" did as well. When the ships arrived, news came in bulk: the captain and the crew would be full of news and newspapers might arrive along with letters. However, this "whole sale" news, in Byrd's eyes, was rarely trustworthy. He, like his compatriots in Britain, wished for letters to help him separate the wheat from the chaff. In fact, he finished this complaint by stating to his brother-in-law, "therefore I beg the favor to hear from you as frequently as may be."[129] Letters might arrive as infrequently as newspapers but they often provided more commentary and guidance on the news.

On the surface, colonists had the same tools as their correspondents back in the metropole to filter and judge their news. They received letters, listened to oral networks, and looked to the newspaper for news. Their correspondents in Great Britain expected them to juggle multiple forms just as they themselves did. Perceval wrote to William Byrd II, "The News papers which relate the Smallest trifles, may have informed you that I am in parliament."[130] He assumed that even in Virginia Byrd would have access to the same news. At times, colonists did turn to the papers. In Rhode Island, George Berkeley found that he had to rely on the newspaper for news both foreign and domestic, even if the quality of the publication was not quite up to his standards. He found in "the monthly Register (which with us Supplies the place of all other Newspapers)" information about Perceval's involvement in the reform of the Fleet Prison and was sure to congratulate his friend on his actions.[131] Berkeley was still dependent on the "public papers" a year later when he expressed concern in a letter about an account he had read of the death of Perceval's cousin.[132] Newport, Rhode Island, was not as awash with newspapers as London was at the time, but colonists could look to them for news and found that newspaper news could travel more quickly and regularly than that in letters.[133] In fact, Perceval had already written to Berkeley about his cousin's death two month before his query, but he had not received the letter yet.[134] Ships did ferry newspapers along with goods and letters and many a colonist received their news through them. But while colonists possessed the same tools, they did not have the same amount of news or at least the same amount of "foreign" news. Their news channels might be filled with chatter about recent Indian attacks or the market for tobacco, but the noise produced by Londoners and in the capitals of continental Europe was usually nothing more than a faint whisper. Their connections across the ocean were more sparse and less functional, not unlike their personal networks. Since events in Europe greatly affected their own lives, this silence could be nerve wracking.

William Byrd II found his ignorance of European affairs especially trying when war loomed. The year 1729 found him fairly itching for news. Great Britain and Spain had declared a truce the year before, leaving the possibility for war open until the Treaty of Seville was signed in the fall of 1729 (and even then relations between the two countries remained strained and burst into further conflict in 1739). Byrd received pieces of news relating to the state of affairs. He had copies of the king's speech and the addresses of the Houses of Parliament, which seemed to "sound a charge for war," but his news left the final determination unsaid. Byrd found this highly unsatisfying and in two letters to two different correspondents written a month apart he complained, "we are ignorant whether it be war or peace."[135] This ignorance plagued him because he felt that war should be declared for Britain's own good and because such a war could easily affect colonial life. When war had been declared in 1727, Byrd had also lacked "publick advice of war," but noted that Virginians kept sending their ships forth hoping that "should they meet with an enemy, he will be no very formidable one."[136]

Yet such a war also allowed him to express his opinions about American affairs to his correspondents in England. He filled the letter of 1727 with his ideas about the need to take St. Augustine from the Spanish. The acquisition of this territory he felt would help by "removing that grievance to our trade, and enlarging the British Empire on the continent, which would then extend from Nova-Scotia, to the Gulph of Florida without interruption, and besides open to us a trade with the Florida Indians."[137] While the British failed to follow this advice in the 1720s, Byrd was equally in favor of the British siege of St. Augustine in 1740. Byrd longed for news from Britain because it helped keep his personal networks taut, allowed him to protect his tobacco, and gave him an excuse to enlarge on American affairs. Wars in Europe had colonial dimensions, meaning that American views mattered. In fact, Byrd ended his views on St. Augustine in his letter of 1727 by asking forgiveness "for saying so much upon our American affairs, but as they relate nearly to the good of Great Britain, your Lordship has an intrest in them."[138]

To a degree, his correspondent agreed with him. He recorded this letter in his letter book and summarized it stating "Observations upon the present political state of Europe and the West Indies."[139] While all newsreaders desired news from London, they also increasingly wanted to hear what was being talked of in other locations, including colonial locations. Such a desire fit right into epistolary practices. When news was offered in a letter there was a deep-seated sense that local news should be given in exchange. When John Perceval was traveling through the Netherlands on his way to Paris, he received a letter from an English correspondent who promised that if Perceval would "tell me some French news" he would "pay you as well as I can with English."[140] A few years later, Perceval declared from Bath to another acquaintance that "In return for the obligation you have laid upon me by the news you sent me from Town, I am obliged to let you know what passes here however trifling are the occurances."[141] News given called for news in return. And colonial news was becoming as valued, if not more, than trifles from Bath.

"Talk of the Town"

These writers wanted to hear the murmurs of noise from other places; they wanted to know what stirred beyond their own shores. Furthermore, they wanted to know not just what had happened, but what was talked about. Writers often corralled the cacophony of news stories into a single descriptive term: the talk. As Edward Southwell's correspondent in London told him, "All the talk here is war."[142] Newspapers too reflected this tendency. The *Boston News-Letter* reported, "Nothing is more talkt of at present than the

Cruel Execution of the horrid Decree against the Protestants of Thorn."[143] The Boston paper wished to inform its readers of the occurrences in Thorn (now Toruń), Poland (see below), but it also wanted them to know what Londoners were talking about. Sometimes letter writers qualified the type of talk: a correspondent of James Brydges referred to "The Publick talk" and Cassandra Willoughby asked after of "ye talk of Monmouthshire."[144] Most strikingly, correspondents reported on "the talk of the town" or "town talk."[145] For these readers knowing what was talked of among their peers was as important as knowing what was occurring in the world around them. While following the movements of troops or the state of the Congress of Cambray mattered on a national and personal scale; the exchange of news, especially in letters, also simply let those at a distance into the story. Knowing the talk at the center of the British world could pull correspondents into that realm and allow them to belong. Also, increasingly correspondents wanted and needed to know not just the talk enlivening the center, but the talk that echoed from the peripheries.

Talk and access to conversation mattered to these letter writers. During the late seventeenth and early eighteenth centuries the British spent a lot of time in groups discussing worldwide happenings and those close to home. They did so at home, in coffeehouses, and in the street.[146] The waning years of the seventeenth century found James Brydges in London, where, if he was not conversing with acquaintances at Tom's Coffeehouse, he was talking with them in their houses or his own.[147] On a March day in 1697 he met two acquaintances with whom he "talkt of severall matters," before leaving for the house of another friend, where their "discourse was chiefly concerning ye popish plot." When he finished this visit he proceeded to the abode of a third connection where they spoke "chiefly of Dr. Chamberlain's bank."[148] About twenty-five years later John Perceval participated in a similar social world in Bath. He remarked to his correspondent, "If we have any wisdom 'tis employ'd in commenting the news papers, & our wit in rayling at the Plot & the High powers who invented it."[149] He does not say where this commenting took place, but it obviously happened within a group of friends, and by providing his correspondent with Bath news he allowed him to join in their "rayling." It is the railing, the sense of social exchange, that was important, not the reality of the plot. By 1740 William Byrd II could do the same when he visited Williamsburg. During one visit he walked to a coffeehouse after dinner and when he finished reading the news and conducting business he wandered over to Lady Randolph's for tea and "talked with the girls."[150] This was a society that valued sociability and talk and thus knowing the talk of the town was an important social asset.

However, participating in such talk was easier for some. Williamsburg had not long possessed a coffeehouse and at times the houses of friends were distantly located and hard to visit. While Cassandra Brydges might have known the "talk of Monmouthshire," usually it was the "talk of the town" correspondents wanted, not the talk of the county. The town could mean Dublin or Bath, but usually it meant London. London coffeehouses, London docks, London assemblies, London drawing rooms, and Parliament in London were locations where conversation rolled around and increased in noise and clamor as it went. It was this talk correspondents often attempted to distill and inject into a letter. On one London day, John Perceval went to the Court of Requests and numerous coffeehouses simply to find news for his cousin.[151] For those at a distance letters served as virtual coffeehouses. Through them letter writers could discuss events in much the same way as they would in coffeehouses. With greater mobility many members of the British elite found that they had to keep up with "the talk of the town" from a distance. Both letters and newspapers allowed them to piece together what information they needed to know to participate in society's wider conversation.

The way information regarding the execution of a number of Protestants in Poland, a event known as the "Tumult of Thorn," wove its way through letters, newsletters, and newspapers illustrates how correspondents exchanged such talk. This event surfaced in all forms of news and was certainly the talk of the town, as well as the talk of Europe. As previously noted, the *Boston Newsletter* reported that this event was much talked of in London and the newsletter received by John Perceval stated that "This affair is become ye Grand subject of Discourse."[152] Obviously, it was for John Perceval and one of his correspondents who discussed the event in three letters and it surfaced multiple times in his newsletter and in newspapers such as the *Boston Newsletter*, the *Newcastle Courant*, and the *Evening Post*. These sources often repeated each other and in fact the newsletter often made its way into the *Newcastle Courant* verbatim.

The event was incendiary enough to kindle such interest. Thorn (now Torún) was the Lutheran center of Catholic Poland and a site of smoldering religious tension. Between 16 and 17 July 1724 conflict flared up once again as a Catholic procession sparked a fight between Jesuit students and Protestant citizens. The squabble turned into a riot that led to the desecration of the

Sacred Host and a picture of the Virgin Mary during a raid on the Jesuit college. The royal court sentenced ten Protestants, including the mayor of the town, to death, and this caused an uproar in the Protestant countries of Europe.[153]

On one level all the different forms of news were simply looking to inform their readers about the incident and its progression. This was one reason that John Perceval included it in a letter to his friend Captain Worth in Brussels. In his letter of 24 December John Perceval was sure to inform Worth that the king of Prussia was marching troops toward Thorn.[154] While he did not reveal the fact to Worth, he probably had this information from his newsletter of 22 December, which informed him: "they have heard that the King of Prussia's Forces were actually Marching towards Polish Prussia."[155] However he could also have read the same information in the *Evening Post* of 22 December 1724.[156] Perceval prefaced this news in his letter by stating "We hear." By adding the plural "we" he gestures to the fact that this was new public news that had the city abuzz. This information kept Worth up to date on the issue and allowed him to participate in London talk.

Perceval's letter moved beyond the facts of the event, however, as he proceeded to expound on the horror with which he viewed the occurrence. In this letter he included news not just to inform, but also to converse. He finished a long paragraph on the affair by declaring, "Surely Mr. Worth, this is not the Action or Principle of Christians, but rather of Turks and Infidels, or Savage beasts." But at the end of his letter he takes a deep breath and excuses himself stating, "If I thought this freedom disagreeable to you I would not venture to write in this manner, but I know you so good natured a Man as not to approve what has been done."[157] While the exchange of news possessed an established place in the letters between these two correspondents, Perceval rarely composed letter-long expositions on the news exchanged—usually he stuck to brief notes—but as a fervent Protestant this event moved him deeply. He was also right to ask his correspondent to excuse his ardent prose, for Captain Worth was an Irish Catholic living in Brussels and serving under the emperor there.[158] Thus, Perceval wanted to make sure he did not read the letter as evidence of "a cruel persecuting Spirit," but he did think it was a topic that would speak to Worth due to his religious background and military status. In his response Worth assured Perceval that he too found the event appalling and then ended his letter with a succinct summary of the talk of Brussels.[159] Letters could be places where correspondents filled in news gaps, but they were also places to discuss the events as they would during a visit or in the coffeehouse. In doing so they allowed the correspondent to participate in the larger conversation.

While colonists often strained to hear the news, which filled the capital so easily, the talk of the colonies was becoming increasingly important to those who lived far from colonial shores. Byrd the younger was not alone in assuming that his British correspondents would want to hear about American affairs. His father, years before, after complaining of his lack of news from England added, "About two moneths since the Indians assaulted some of our hunters in the night kild two dead & wounded severall others."[160] He knew that Lord Effingham, the nonresident governor of Virginia, would be interested in the continuing strains between the colonists and the local indigenous peoples. He also informed his factors, Perry and Lane, of occurrences in the Virginia Assembly and of the state of crops since both could affect their profits.[161] As the years passed colonial news increasingly came to matter, especially as European conflicts became global wars. During the Seven Years' War, Peter Collinson worriedly wrote a correspondent in New York: "Since the defeat of Bradock Wee have had no News from your Parts, neither by the Way of Virg. M'd, Pensv or New York &c, which makes our people very uneasie" and a few months later he sighed to another colonial correspondent, "We long to hear News from Crown Point & General Shirly."[162] As British imperial interests widened and became seen as more integral to the economic well-being of the nation, news from those corners of the world, especially when they were being threatened, became a desirable commodity. The talk of the colonies could become the talk of the town.

It was not just the greater national interest in the wider British world that fed this growing desire for news from places far away. Many Britons had personal connections or personal interests tied up in these locations and needed to know if news was stirring there. Perceval often asked his estate agents for news: he worried when he heard that arms had been seized in Cork and wanted to know the repercussions when the government recalled Wood's Patent to mint copper coins for Ireland.[163] He set up a regular correspondence with Marmaduke Coghill in Ireland for the exchange of political news when he himself was in London. He also looked to his cousins in Ireland for news, and when he was in Ireland his cousins looked to him for news from home.[164] News readers wanted information from places where upheavals took place, where news was stirring and made noise: events in Cork could damage Perceval's estates, rulings by the Virginia Assembly could affect trade with the colonies, and wars, wherever they might be, could upset trade and lead to further disruptions. These newsreaders listened for the noise news made around their locality, but they also strained to hear the murmurs of news from other locations because they knew that such muffled noises and muted stirrings could cause vibrations that would be felt throughout their wider network. There is a sense in these letters that the epicenter of news moved. At times a location could be quiet. As when John Perceval's brother assured him from Dublin, "All matters here are perfectly quiet, so much that we have not even any lies stirring, and of late our whole town discourse has run upon the affairs of private people."[165] However, letter writers always kept their ear to the ground to sense where news would stir next. Listening to your epistolary network was not unlike placing a hand on a railroad track to feel for the vibrations of an oncoming train. Many Britons had come to realize that the extent of the world they had to monitor had widened. Stirrings in Poland, China, or Virginia could make London shake.

∽

The newspaper created a new world of news, but letters helped control it. The printed form did not subsume all that came before it; rather it worked with other forms. The power of letters emanated from the informal personal networks they held together, and printed forms simply strengthened society's reliance on them. Just as *Philosophical Transactions* helped the Royal Society expand its network, newspapers allowed their readers to expand their knowledge of what occurred in distant places. But they did not put down their pens. Letters, and the social networks they supported, vetted their knowledge, made it useful, and allowed them to know about the world around them. For these correspondents, when news stirred, so did their letters.

Postscript

When Peter Collinson waxed poetic about his "speaking letters" to John Bartram, the American botanist, in 1762, the networks explored in this book were slipping into the hands of the next generation. Collinson, the youngest of the letter writers examined, died five years later in 1768. His last surviving letter was to the son of John Bartram.[1] The other voices that rang through this work had died at least ten years before 1762. Hans Sloane, the longest-lived correspondent, had breathed his last in 1753 at the old age of ninety-three. John Perceval passed away in 1748 and, oddly enough, William Byrd II and James Brydges, who had been born months apart in 1674, died within days of each other at seventy in 1744. Cassandra Brydges had died almost ten years previously in 1735 and Nicholas Blundell in 1737. Not only had this network of letter writers faded from view by 1762, but Collinson found himself in a very different British world from the one he had been born into in the waning years of the seventeenth century.

As Collinson sat writing to Bartram, the Treaty of Paris, which ended the Seven Years' War, was being negotiated. When it went into effect the British Empire would stretch from the West Indies through Florida to the great northern expanses of Canada. By this time, English merchants dominated the slave trade, and the East India Company had become a territorial power. This was a far cry from the empire that existed when Bartram's parents arrived in the Americas in the seventeenth century. England had altered as well. The population of London had risen from around 400,000 in 1650 to about 675,000 in 1750.[2] Parliament met regularly and the threat of a Jacobite rebellion and restoration had faded. Beyond London, cities such as Bath had emerged as social centers. Dublin was flourishing to the extent that one woman could exclaim that St. Stephen's Green "may be preferred justly to any square in London."[3] The centers and the peripheries of the British world were growing and becoming linked, and the networks that held them together were denser and had taken slightly different shapes. Collinson recognized these changes and declared to Bartram in his speaking letter: "See what a complete empire we have now got within ourselves."[4]

The offspring of many of these letter writers were still active in this complete empire. In 1762, William Byrd III had recently resettled himself and his family in Virginia, but the previous years had seen him fighting in the Seven Years' War and traveling the length and breadth of the British North American colonies, from South Carolina to Nova Scotia.[5] Interestingly, he served not only under George Washington but also under Henry Bouquet, whom Collinson mentioned in his 1762 letter as someone who might be able to find junior officers whose skill with the pencil could help in Collinson and Bartram's quest to bring "the Wonders of the World to Light."[6] While no letters survive between the Percevals and Byrds after William Byrd II's death, their sons' interests had strange echoes. While Byrd's son William would travel to Nova Scotia, John Perceval's son John had plans for it. He wanted to begin a quasi-feudal settlement on St. Johns Island (now Prince Edward Island) and was gathering plans for it in the early 1760s.[7] But differences between the two abound. Byrd's status would be worn away by money, familial, and imperial problems in the following years, ending in his suicide in 1777. While not beloved by his contemporaries, Perceval's star would rise. He celebrated the fulfillment of his father's wish to become an English peer in 1762. By the next year, he was First Lord of the Admiralty. Later, Port Egmont, in the Falkland Islands, came to bear his name and he was only chased out of office by his hatred of William Pitt the elder in 1766.[8] The vagaries of fate would change the course of the lives of many of the descendants of these correspondents. Sloane's daughter married Charles Cadogan and her son would become Earl Cadogan, although it would be the Sloane family property in Chelsea that brought the family wealth.[9] James Brydges's grandson, James, would be the third and last Duke of Chandos, and long before his death in 1789 the stately Cannons would be but a memory.[10] Nicholas Blundell had only one surviving daughter, but her son, Nicholas Peppard, would take the surname Blundell and Blundells would still be fervent Catholics and still reside at Crosby Hall at the beginning of the twentieth century.[11]

With the exception of John Perceval the younger, who actually became joint postmaster general in 1762 for a brief period, none of the letters of these descendants survive in mass like those of their forebears, although the postal system they had access to ran much more smoothly and was more profitable.[12] In 1688 the income of the Post Office was around £90,000; by 1764 it was over £225,000.[13] No momentous reforms were undertaken at the Post

Office during the eighteenth century, but the system did become more streamlined and more profitable under the care of men such as Ralph Allen, who ran the bye and cross posts, but in fact "was the medium through which the Post Office increased the services as the needs arose during the first half of the eighteenth century."[14] Allen oversaw the establishment of more post roads, cross posts and bye posts, introduced stamps for the bye and cross post letters, and checked franked letters, but it was not until the introduction of the mail coach in 1784 that way letters traveled altered. By the time Allen died in 1764, though, the postal system was part of the everyday life of most Britons. However, the "low-born" Allen's prosperity did not all stem from his postal endeavors.[15] He also used his access to the Bath stone on his estate to promote and profit from the rebuilding of Bath. Allen had managed to make a fortune by supporting two of the interlocking changes to occur in Britain during the late seventeenth and early eighteenth centuries: the rise of urban sociability and the need to communicate over a distance.

Indeed, during their lifetimes, Allen and all the letter writers examined here witnessed and participated in three overlapping changes. Besides benefiting from an expanded postal system, they all saw the nature of their social world alter, as urban sociability became a critical component of social identity, and as links to social (and political) power became navigated through geographically vast social networks that were usually centered in London. Furthermore, the nature of these networks began to alter as clubs and societies became a more engrained part of life and as business became more institutionalized or professionalized. They also saw the British world expand. The British continued to fight and travel across the English Channel and they increased their colonial holdings both in the Americas and beyond. When examining the world of the British elite through their letters, the way these changes played off and depended on each other surfaces. The changing social world allowed those on the periphery to interact with a center that was increasingly interested in them and the postal changes made communication between the two easier. All these ties, both new and old, came together to form vast networks of different sizes and shapes that made this world possible.

Relying on and studying the workings of the networks managed and navigated by the British elite highlights the importance of recognizing their geographic mobility. The period certainly saw the rise of "polite society" and the emergence of new social centers like Bath, and questions about the level of "openness" of this social world require examination, but so does mobility.[16] Scholars have not ignored the trips to and from London or the increasingly popular Grand Tour, but the main focus had been, for good reason, on how these individuals acted when together rather than on their shifting movements.[17] Debates over consumption and individual identity have pushed discussion literally indoors by focusing on what these individuals thought about their things and themselves.[18] All these these lines of inquiry are necessary to understand the lives of these individuals, but it is also important to look at the mobility implied by letters. When we do, the world of the British elite expands.

Letters bring in the voices of the geographic periphery. This work contains a flurry of Irish and colonial voices intermixed with those hailing from England; while it points to the obstacles faced by the mobile and distanced, it also pays tribute to their established place in polite society. While works on empire abound and the blossoming of Atlantic history has made transatlantic relationships a key area of study, investigations of the British Empire and of the American colonies have remained detached from mainstream British social history. This work has attempted to domesticate the empire and put it into discussion with what was occurring at home. This is what networks allow us to do. Here the colonies are but one place among many, an interesting and telling location it is true, but still only one among many. Looking at the shape of the British world in this manner allows it to emerge organically. Letters from Ireland mingled with letters from Somerset, Montpellier, and Pennsylvania. With this recognition this world begins to move: The letter writer in Montpellier could soon find himself in Paris or London and the complexion of the network he depended on would change. Acknowledging such movement keeps identity fluid and multiple. Colonists and Irishmen would often embrace their places of birth, but this did not keep them from being members of a wider network of acquaintances where their origins did not always play a defining role.

However, charting the origins and movements of letters reveals the borders of this British world and the consequences of living on its peripheries. The world of these letter writers was centered in England and more specifically in London whose social, economic, and political energy powered many of their networks. For those on the periphery connecting with this center mattered and was often an epistolary goal. But as the gaps within the postal system show, connecting was not always easy and postal links to the Continent ran more smoothly than those to the Atlantic colonies. But while many letter writers received epistles from continental connections, those links were rarely as strong as ties with those in England or the colonies. This world was cosmopolitan—these individuals flowed over national borders and cared more about the social value of an individual than their national origin—but each had a geographic or social center and for the British this was in London not Paris. The social longing for London and the networks embedded in it made an individual a member of the British world, and the increased need many in London had for colonial information created a place for colonists in the wider system. Colonial links with the center of the British world were more fragile than those emanating from Dublin or Bath, but writers recognized them and nurtured them. For these writers their social worlds consisted of overlapping, parallel, and intertwined networks. Some were local, some were not. Some were maintained through face-to-face interaction; some were not. Some were made of deeply enmeshed personal ties; some were born out of a shared interest. Location mattered, but it was only one factor out of many.

What these mobile Britons and their letters really reveal is the importance of networks. Letters held together the widening British world because they supplied a way to keep networks functioning at a distance. However, it pays to keep in mind that letters were not the only way individuals kept their social networks functioning. In the end, letters were necessary tools to extend face-to-face networks, but most saw them as a poor substitute. Recognizing letters as one networking tool among many frees us from an intense focus on the material letter and the links they alone nurtured. Some writers maintained a relationship solely through letters, but most did not. An epistolary correspondence usually complemented a physical relationship. Thus the language in letters mattered, but the way letters helped correspondents link into larger networks holds as much significance. Letters were meant to nurture whole networks, not only intense relationships between two people or an individual sense of self. Recognizing the networking function of letters provides us with a new way to see letters: they are less objects of personal and private meditation and more objects of larger social use.

These networks defined a place between private and public worlds and between traditional and modern societies. Scholars have long grappled with the emergence of the individual and the public sphere, both of which are pieces in the puzzle of modernization.[19] However, these letters reveal that correspondents were more interested in the space in-between the private and the public. It was this space, grounded by these different networks, that made their world turn. Certainly, on the margins of these sets of correspondence, ideas reflecting the growth of private and public worlds seep in. Some correspondents worried about printed letters, news distribution through letters helped create larger "imagined communities," individuals used the letter as a place of intimacy, but these are the edges. Letter writers preferred personal deliveries, circulated letters within trusted circles, and used epistolary connections to keep track of their world. Public institutions or public news were less trustworthy and less functional; it was within personal networks that power lay.

Concentrating on these personal networks brings together the whole social experience of these individuals. Historians have reasserted the importance of the family during this period and have complicated and redefined the nature of friendship, but looking at the society through their letters reveals how family, friends, social connections, employers, employees, and those within the same clubs and societies all worked together and depended on one another.[20] Understanding the interlocking and overlapping nature of these relationships shows the way this society functioned. Examining the subtle and practiced way networks worked helps us see why the personal was such a powerful space and why traditional forms of social maintenance remained such useful tools during this period of reconfiguration.

However, due to the geographic expansion and mobility of the individuals in this world, these networks needed to rely on forms of communication beyond the face-to-face. This is why letters mattered to the correspondents of the period. Other blossoming forms of communication, such as the newspaper, would tweak the workings of these webs, but it was letters that mattered most. Many shared Peter Collinson's glee when their letters lay spread out across their desks or tables pulsating with life and voice. But letters also show the strains of this networking world. The personal nature of these networks meant that outsiders rarely breached their walls. Birth, shared interests, and connections allowed entrance. Furthermore, the nature of networks altered. Links with those with similar interests were becoming tied to institutions and other networks were becoming more professionalized. These letters and these connections were different and left many a correspondent unsettled.

Letters also lay bare the anxiety caused by communication at a distance. For a society used to communicating in person, the inability to reaffirm a connection or monitor one with a visit was disconcerting. Laments about silence fill these epistles for a lull in letters could mean many things: a discarded connection, a sickness, or even a death. Such a loss snipped away at the power of an individual's network and too many cut ties would leave one adrift. Letters haunted the sleep of correspondents. A friend wrote to Hans Sloane that he had dreamt that "my Lady Dutchesse was very angry with me for not writing to her, and I know not whether it be fit to trouble her Grace with a Letter or not."[21] James Brydges recorded a dream in his journal where he received an answer to a letter that "was writ in white characters upon black paper & folded up, wch open'd, was in ye shape of a coffin, I thought it did not satisfy me, upon wch he went to write me another, but before he had write it, I lost him & could not find him Wakt."[22] Letters did not always lead to sweet dreams.

Epistolary networks held the widening British world together and studying them reveals their weaknesses as well as their strengths. Atlantic ties might be more long lasting than those with the Continent and many of them proved functional, but they did sit on the periphery of the British world and its postal system. Atlantic correspondents were quite savvy at sending their letters, and like their more centrally located correspondents they saw the value in turning to more informal means of delivery, but the lack of a solid infrastructure of exchange, and the basic reality of distance, was wearing. Personal networks ran this world: while those three thousand miles away could become entangled in them through letters, their links were always more fragile. The lack of government support for a transatlantic postal system allowed political ties to be cut more easily in the revolutionary years to come.[23] However, it is arguable that more personal networks remained intact as long as London remained the center of activity. In fact, in his last surviving letter, Peter Collinson was in search of a patron for John Bartram's son William, which he found in the Englishmen John Fothergill. This relationship would last until Fothergill's death in 1780 in the midst of the American Revolution.[24] On the other hand, one of the reasons suggested for the suicide of William Byrd III, besides his staggering debts, is the fashion in which the outbreak of hostilities between America and Britain strained his loyalties.[25] His widow, whose ties were suspected as well, was sure to let Thomas Jefferson know that the center of her world was not across the ocean, but in America. She wrote in 1781, "What am I but an American? All my friends and connexions are in America; my whole property is here—could I wish ill to everything I have an interest in?"[26] However, for the colonists examined here, their friends, connections, and interests were as often in England as they were in the Americas. All these correspondents constructed their sense of belonging from their "friends and connexions," or, one could say, from their social networks.

Letters were a way for the members of the British elite to keep their world turning. Through their epistles and the networks they called into action, letter writers called in favors, prompted help, received posts, and made news truthful. In fact, only a few days before he died, John Perceval, by then the first Earl of Egmont, was looking out for his wider network and using letters to do so. By this time he was too feeble to wait on Lord Harrington, the lord lieutenant of Ireland, or even to pick up his pen, for which he apologized, but he still managed to produce a letter. It was a letter that dealt with another death—that of his brother and constant correspondent Philip Perceval. However, it was not a letter lamenting his passing, but rather one that looked to fill his place in the family network. Perceval wanted Harrington to make sure that the post left empty on his brother's death stayed in the family and suggested that his second grandson, Cecil Parker Perceval, would be a likely candidate.[27]

Once death had stopped Perceval's epistolary machinations three days later on 1 May 1748, letters poured in lamenting his death and attempting to transfer ties from father to son. Twelve days after his death, a connection wrote with condolences and a hope that he could continue under the awning of Perceval patronage and protection.[28] The next day, George Berkeley, Perceval's friend of forty years and now bishop of Cloyne, sent his condolences and in his notebook the second earl made a note to reply.[29] By 16 May his sister's widower joined the newly minted earl in grief and thanked him for the exact account he had sent.[30] On the same day, Perceval's Irish land agent, Richard Purcell, added his condolences, thanked him for continuing him on as steward, and sent him accounts detailing the state of his lands.[31] About ten days later, a letter arrived from the warden at Lohort Castle in Ireland, a Perceval family possession, full of excuses for his tardy condolences. He opened by complaining that Purcell never informed him of the death, causing him to learn it from the "publick prints," but he closed with laments on the loss and the news that Perceval's passing was the talk of the town.[32] These employees, friends, and relatives were expressing their grief, but they were also using their letters to spin new threads for their networks and placing the son where the father once sat. One can imagine the new earl sitting at his desk surrounded by these letters; all of them speaking to him of the past, present, and future of the network that supported them all. Like Collinson, the young Perceval knew, as did his correspondents, that their place in the wider British world depended on the webs their pens helped them weave. When letters spoke, they listened.

Notes

Abbreviations

BL	British Library, London
Bod	Bodleian Library, Oxford
HEH	Huntington Library, San Marino, California
LMA	London Metropolitan Archives, London
LRO	Lancashire Record Office, Preston, UK
LS	Linnaean Society, London
NA	National Archives, Kew, UK
RSF	Religious Society of Friends in Britain Library, London
SRO	Shakespeare Birthplace Trust Record Office, Stratford-upon-Avon
VHS	Virginia Historical Society, Richmond, Virginia

Introduction

1. Alan Armstrong, ed., *"Forget not Mee & My Garden . . .": Selected Letters, 1725–1768, of Peter Collinson, F.R.S.* (Philadelphia: American Philosophical Society, 2002), 244.

2. John Hawkins, *The ENGLISH School-Master Compleated* (London, 1692), 24.

3. For neighborliness, see Keith Wrightson, *English Society, 1580–1680* (New Brunswick, N.J.: Rutgers University Press, 1982), 51–57.

4. Robert Coverte, *A True and Almost Incredible Report of an Englishman, that being cast away in the good ship called the Assention in Cambaya the farthest part of the East Indies) travelled by land through many unknowne kingdomes, and great cities* (London, 1612), 9; Richard Head, *The English rogue described, in the life of Meriton Latroon, a witty extravagant* (London, 1666), 236.

5. Head, 236.

6. Robert Baron, *An apologie for Paris for rejecting of Juno and Pallas, and presenting of Ate's golden ball to Venus with a discussion of the reasons that might induce him to favour either of the three* (London, 1649), 83.

7. Richard Blackmore, *A Treatise of Consumptions*, 2nd ed. (London, 1725), 19.

8. For a summary of the origins of the word "network" and its relative usefulness as a historical concept, see David Hancock, "The Trouble with Networks: Managing the

Scots' Early Modern Madeira Trade," *Business History Review* 79, 3 (Autumn 2005): 470–73.

9. John Perceval to Mr. Smallbrooke, 26 September 1708, BL Add. MS 47025, f. 99.

10. Marion Tinling, ed., *The Correspondence of the Three William Byrds of Westover, Virginia, 1684–1776* (Charlottesville: University Press of Virginia, 1977), 1: 8, 11, 12, 13, 18, 19, 20, 22, 23, 24, 31, 39, 43, 64, 79, 87, 91.

11. John Boyle to Herbert Bowen, 25 January 1753, Bod MS Eng misc. d. 97, 26v.

12. Joshua Slatt to Peter Collinson, 20 September 1763, BL Add. MS 28727, f. 98v.

13. J. A. Barnes, "Class and Committees in a Norwegian Island Parish," *Human Relations* 7, 1 (1954): 43.

14. Alan MacFarlane, "History, Anthropology and the Study of Communities," *Social History* 2, 5 (May 1977): 631–32; Alexandra Shepard and Phil Withington, "Introduction: Communities in Early Modern England," in *Communities in Early Modern England*, ed. Alexandra Shepard and Phil Withington (Manchester: Manchester University Press, 2000), 1–9; Naomi Tadmor, *Family and Friends in Eighteenth-Century England* (Cambridge: Cambridge University Press, 2001), 103–271; Wrightson, *English Society*, 51–57.

15. Raymond Williams, *Keywords: A Vocabulary of Culture and Society* (New York: Oxford University Press, 1985), 23.

16. Hancock, "The Trouble with Networks," 469.

17. Hancock, "The Trouble with Networks," 471.

18. MacFarlane, 637–52.

19. J. Clyde Mitchell, *Social Networks in Urban Situations* (Manchester: University of Manchester Press, 1969), 1.

20. Keith Wrightson and David Levine, *Poverty and Piety in an English Village: Terling, 1525–1700*, 2nd ed. (Oxford: Clarendon, 1995), or, for the American strand, John Demos, *A Little Commonwealth: Family Life in Plymouth Colony* (Oxford: Oxford University Press, 1970), and Darrett B. Rutman and Anita H. Rutman, *A Place in Time: Middlesex County, Virginia, 1650–1750* (New York: Norton, 1984).

21. Ilana Krausman Ben-Amos, *The Culture of Giving: Informal Support and Gift-Exchange in Early Modern England* (Cambridge: Cambridge University Press, 2008), 45; David Cressy, "Kinship and Kin Interaction in Early Modern England," *Past and Present* 113 (November 1986): 38–69; Keith Wrightson, "Kinship in an English Village: Terling, Essex 1550–1700," in *Land, Kinship and Life-Cycle*, ed. Richard M. Smith (Cambridge: Cambridge University Press, 1984), 315, 323.

22. For criticism of this local focus, see Cressy, 43–44; MacFarlane, 647; Wrightson, "Kinship in an English Village," 313–32; Wrightson and Levine, 188, 193, 195–96.

23. For example, see Tadmor, 103–66; Wrightson, *English Society*, 17–38.

24. Margaret Sena, "William Blundell and Networks of Catholic Dissent in Post-Reformation England," in *Communities in Early Modern England*, ed. Shepard and Withington, 38–75; Rosalind J. Beiler, "Dissenting Religious Communication Networks and European Migration, 1660–1710," in *Soundings in Atlantic History: Latent Structures and Intellectual Currents, 1500–1830*, ed. Bernard Bailyn and Patricia L. Denault (Cambridge,

Mass.: Harvard University Press, 2009), 210–36. For the tendencies of proselytizing zeal to form diasporas see Beiler, 221–36; Frederick Tolles, *Quakers and the Atlantic Culture* (New York: Macmillan, 1960); Rebecca Larson, *Daughters of Light: Quaker Women Preaching and Prophesying in the Colonies and Abroad* (New York: Knopf, 1999).

25. For interest in the social processes of knowledge creation, see Steven Shapin and Simon Schaffer, *Leviathan and the Air-Pump: Hobbes, Boyle, and the Experimental Life* (Princeton, N.J.: Princeton University Press, 1985); Steven Shapin, *A Social History of Truth: Civility and Science in Seventeenth-Century England* (Chicago: University of Chicago Press, 1994). For a similar focus on the republic of letters, see Dena Goodman, *The Republic of Letters: A Cultural History of the French Enlightenment* (Ithaca, N.Y.: Cornell University Press, 1994); Anne Goldgar, *Impolite Learning: Conduct and Community in the Republic of Letters, 1680–1750* (New Haven, Conn.: Yale University Press, 1995); L. W. B. Brockliss, *Calvet's Web: Enlightenment and the Republic of Letters in Eighteenth-Century France* (Oxford: Oxford University Press, 2002). For actor-network theory, see Bruno Latour, *Science in Action: How to Follow Scientists and Engineers Through Society* (Cambridge, Mass.: Harvard University Press, 1987); Bruno Latour, *Reassembling the Social: An Introduction to Actor-Network Theory* (Oxford: Oxford University Press, 2005); Michel Callon, "Some Elements of a Sociology of Translation: Domestication of the Scallops and the Fishermen of St Brieuc Bay," in *Power, Action and Belief: A New Sociology of Knowledge*, ed. John Law (London: Routledge and Kegan Paul, 1986), 196–233; John Law and John Hassard, eds., *Actor Network Theory and After* (Oxford: Blackwell, 1999).

26. Especially good in this regard is David S. Lux and Harold J. Cook, "Closed Circles or Open Networks?: Communicating at a Distance During the Scientific Revolution," *History of Science* 36, 2 (June 1998): 179–211.

27. For the fragility of such networks, see Brockliss, 79. For the importance of distant correspondents or travel, see Lux and Cook, 181; E. C. Spary, *Utopia's Garden: French Natural History from Old Regime to Revolution* (Chicago: University of Chicago Press, 2000), 68–69; Brockliss, 70–73.

28. For this point, see Bernard Bailyn, "Reflections on Some Major Themes," in *Soundings in Atlantic History*, ed. Bailyn and Denault, 2–3.

29. David Hancock, "The Triumphs of Mercury: Connection and Control in the Emerging Atlantic Economy," in *Soundings in Atlantic History*, ed. Bailyn and Denault, 112; R. Darrell Meadows, "Engineering Exile: Social Networks and the French Atlantic Community, 1789–1809," *French Historical Studies* 23, 1 (Winter 2000): 6.

30. Bernard Bailyn, *Atlantic History: Concept and Contours* (Cambridge, Mass.: Harvard University Press, 2005), 100; Horst Pietschmann, "Introduction: Atlantic History—History Between European History and Global History," in *Atlantic History: History of the Atlantic System, 1580–1830*, ed. Horst Pietschmann (Göttingen: Vandenhoeck and Ruprecht, 2002), 40.

31. John S. MacDonald and Leatrice D. MacDonald, "Chain Migration: Ethnic Neighborhood Formation and Social Networks," *Milbank Memorial Fund Quarterly* 42, 1 (January 1964): 82–97; Meadows, 67–102.

32. See Toby L. Ditz, "Shipwrecked; or, Masculinity Imperiled: Mercantile Representations of Failure in Eighteenth-Century Philadelphia," *Journal of American History* 81, 1 (1994): 51–80; Hancock, "The Trouble with Networks."

33. Hancock, "The Triumphs of Mercury," 119.

34. For a discussion about the need to look beyond the Atlantic, see the articles by Alison Games, Philip Stern, Paul W. Mapp, and Peter A. Coclanis, *William and Mary Quarterly* 3rd ser. 63, 4 (October 2006): 675–742.

35. For social polarization, see Margaret Spufford and Motoyasu Takahashi, "Families, Will Witnesses, and Economic Structure in the Fens and on the Chalk: Sixteenth and Seventeenth Century Willingham and Chippenham," *Albion* 28, 3 (Autumn 1996): 379–414. For political upheaval, see Linda Levy Peck, *Court Patronage and Corruption in Early Stuart England* (Boston: Unwin Hyman, 1990), 76–105.

36. Peck, 47–71.

37. Ben-Amos, esp. 309–75; Craig Muldrew, "From a 'Light Cloak' to an 'Iron Cage': Historical Changes in the Relation Between Community and Individualism," in *Communities in Early Modern England*, ed. Shepard and Withington, 156–77; Wrightson and Levine, 142–72.

38. Peter Borsay, *The English Urban Renaissance: Culture and Society in the Provincial Town, 1660–1770* (Oxford: Clarendon, 1989), 28–37, 225–56; Penelope Corfield, *The Impact of English Towns, 1700–1800* (Oxford: Oxford University Press, 1982), 66; James Rosenheim, *The Emergence of a Ruling Order: English Landed Society, 1650–1750* (London: Longman, 1998), 89–146, 215–52.

39. Claire Brant, *Eighteenth-Century Letters and British Culture* (New York: Palgrave Macmillan, 2006), 169; Rebecca Earle, "Introduction: Letters, Writers and the Historian," in *Epistolary Selves: Letters and Letter-Writers, 1600–1945*, ed. Rebecca Earle (Aldershot: Ashgate, 1999), 2–4; Toon Van Houdt, Jan Papy, Gilbert Tournoy, and Constant Matheeussen, eds., *Self-Presentation and Social Identification: The Rhetoric and Pragmatics of Letter Writing in Early Modern Times* (Leuven: Leuven University Press, 2002); James How, *Epistolary Spaces: English Letter Writing from the Foundation of the Post to Richardson's* Clarissa (Aldershot: Ashgate, 2003), 5; Bruce Redford, *The Converse of the Pen: Acts of Intimacy in the Eighteenth-Century Familiar Letter* (Chicago: University of Chicago Press, 1986); Ian Watt, *The Rise of the Novel* (Berkeley: University of California Press, 1957), 190–96.

40. Konstantin Dierks, *In My Power: Letter Writing and Communications in Early America* (Philadelphia: University of Pennsylvania Press, 2009), 9–99, 141–88; Susan Whyman, *The Pen and the People: English Letter Writers, 1660–1800* (Oxford: Oxford University Press, 2009), 75–157.

41. Sarah M. S. Pearsall, *Atlantic Families: Lives and Letters in the Later Eighteenth Century* (Oxford: Oxford University Press, 2008), esp. 26–55; Dierks, 9–51, 100–140; Eve Tavor Bannet, *Empire of Letters: Letter Manuals and Transatlantic Correspondence, 1680–1820* (Cambridge: Cambridge University Press, 2005), 105–222; Ian K. Steele, *The English Atlantic, 1675–1740: An Exploration of Communication and Community* (New York: Oxford University Press, 1986).

42. For invocations of the networking possibilities of letters, see Bannet, x, 38; James Daybell, *Women Letter Writers in Tudor England* (Oxford: Oxford University Press, 2006), 1, 41; Dierks, 161–63; Whyman, 33; Pearsall, 15; Ylva Hasselberg, "Letters, Social Networks and the Embedded Economy in Sweden," in *Epistolary Selves*, ed. Earle, 95–107.

43. Daybell, 200–228; Pearsall, 145–239; Dierks, 52–99; Whyman, 95–96, 114–54.

44. Daniel Lerner, *The Passing of Traditional Society: Modernizing the Middle East* (Glencoe, Ill: Free Press, 1958), 64; Edward Shils, *Political Development in the New States* ('s-Gravenhage: Mouton, 1962), 31–38.

45. Peter Lake and Steven Pincus, "Rethinking the Public Sphere in Early Modern England," *Journal of British Studies* 45, 2 (April 2006): 270–92; Bronwen Wilson and Paul Yachnin, eds., *Making Publics in Early Modern Europe: People, Things, Forms of Knowledge* (New York: Routledge, 2010), 1–9.

46. BL Add. MSS 47025–47033.

47. BL Add. MS 47025, f. 71v.

48. BL Add. MS 47073.

49. BL Add. MSS 46964–46999.

50. VHS Mss5:2 B9965: 1.

51. Louis B. Wright and Marion Tinling, eds., *The Secret Diary of William Byrd of Westover, 1709–1712* (Richmond: Dietz Press, 1941); Louis B. Wright and Marion Tinling, *The London Diary (1717–1721) and Other Writings* (New York: Oxford University Press, 1958); Maude H. Woodfin, ed., *Another Secret Diary of William Byrd of Westover, 1739–1741* (Richmond, Va.: Dietz Press, 1942).

52. These early letter books are found at the University of North Carolina, Chapel Hill, and the Huntington Library, San Marino.

53. VHS Mss5:2 B9966: 1–6.

54. Tinling, *The Correspondence of the Three William Byrds*, 2 vols.

55. BL Sloane MSS 4036–4069.

56. BL Add. MSS 28726–28727; LS Mss 323a–b.

57. Tinling, 1: 423–29.

58. HEH ST 57: 1–57.

59. HEH ST 58: 1–14.

60. HEH ST 26: 1–2.

61. Daniel Defoe, *Curious and diverting journies, Thro' the whole island of Great-Britain* (London, 1734), 252, Eighteenth Century Collections Online, Gale.

62. Rosemary O'Day, ed., *Cassandra Brydges, Duchess of Chandos, 1670–1735: Life and Letters* (Woodbridge: Boydell, 2007).

63. SRO DR 18/20/21/2.

64. HEH STB, Box 2, vol. 1. The original is held at the North London Collegiate School. For more on the history of this letter book, see O'Day, 8–9.

65. Nicholas Blundell, *The Great Diurnal of Nicholas Blundell*, ed. J. J. Bagley, 3 vols., Record Society of Lancashire and Cheshire (Liverpool: C. Tinling, 1968–1972); Letter book of Nicholas Blundell, LRO DDBL acc 6121.

66. HEH Hastings Correspondence, Box 5–29.

67. Blundell, 156; Peter Collinson to Thomas Story, 18 October 1729, RSF Ms 340/pg 668.

Chapter 1. The Perils of the Post Office

1. "Ye last night I received a letter from your honor by Darby post and this morninge I received two other letters one yt came by ye carrier and one yt came by Mr. Strong of Sutton." John Davys to Lucy Hastings, Countess of Huntingdon, 17 February 1661/2, HEH, Hastings Correspondence, Box 23, HA 2006.

2. The first postmark to surface in the Hastings correspondence appeared in 1661. Matthew Anderton to Henry Hastings, 15 May 1661, HEH, Hastings Correspondence, Box 22, HA 1174.

3. Howard Robinson, *The British Post Office: A History* (Princeton, N.J.: Princeton University Press, 1948), 3–112; Susan Whyman, *The Pen and the People: English Letter Writers, 1660–1800* (Oxford: Oxford University Press, 2009), 46–71; Howard Robinson, *Carrying the British Mails Overseas* (London: Allen and Unwin, 1964), 29–39, 40–46; Ian Steele, *The English Atlantic, 1675–1740: An Exploration of Communication and Community* (New York: Oxford University Press, 1986), 168–88.

4. Philip Beale, *A History of the Post in England from the Romans to the Stuarts* (Aldershot: Ashgate, 1998); Robinson, *The British Post Office*; Christopher Browne, *Getting the Message: The Story of the British Post Office* (Phoenix Mill, Far Thrupp Stroud, Gloucester: Alan Sutton, 1993). For the later seventeenth century and the eighteenth century see Peter Fraser, *The Intelligence of the Secretaries of State and Their Monopoly of Licensed News, 1660–1688* (Cambridge: Cambridge University Press, 1956); Kenneth Ellis, *The Post Office in the Eighteenth Century: A Study in Administrative History* (Oxford: Oxford University Press, 1958); Steven Pincus, *1688: The First Modern Revolution* (New Haven, Conn.: Yale University Press, 2009), 68–74.

5. Also see Whyman, *The Pen and the People*, 58–65.

6. Robinson, *The British Post Office*, 27–33.

7. Whyman, *The Pen and the People*, 48–49.

8. Whyman, *The Pen and the People*, 219.

9. James How, *Epistolary Spaces: English Letter Writing from the Foundation of the Post to Richardson's* Clarissa (Aldershot: Ashgate, 2003), 4.

10. Jürgen Habermas, *The Structural Transformation of the Public Sphere*, trans. Thomas Burger with Fredrick Lawrence (Cambridge, Mass.: MIT Press, 1989), 16.

11. Konstantin Dierks, *In My Power: Letter Writing and Communications in Early America* (Philadelphia: University of Pennsylvania Press, 2009), 189–225.

12. Ellis, 7–8. Declared Accounts of Post Office, NA E 351 / 2758, 2782.

13. HEH, Hastings Correspondence, Boxes 70–71. For this number the surviving postmarks were counted, but many letters were probably sent by the post whose postmarks were lost.

14. Nicholas Blundell, *The Great Diurnal of Nicholas Blundell*, ed. J. J. Bagley, vol. 1, *1702–1711*, Record Society of Lancashire and Cheshire (Liverpool: C. Tinling, 1968), 25.

15. Richard Smallbrooke to John Perceval, 11 November 1708, BL Add. MS 47025, f. 102v.

16. Whyman, *The Pen and the People*, 64.

17. Michael Warner makes this point about print technology, but it can be extended to the epistolary world. Michael Warner, *The Letters of the Republic: Publication and the Public Sphere in Eighteenth-Century America* (Cambridge, Mass.: Harvard University Press, 1990), ix.

18. See Whyman, *Pen and the People*, 49–50; Eve Tavor Bannet, *Empire of Letters: Letter Manuals and Transatlantic Correspondence, 1680–1820* (Cambridge: Cambridge University Press, 2005), 225–315; Fraser, 20–28; Peter Marshall, *Intelligence and Espionage in the Reign of Charles II, 1660–1685* (Cambridge: Cambridge University Press, 1994), 78–95.

19. Whyman, *The Pen and the People*, 61–64; Robinson, *The British Post Office*, 59–62, 64–67.

20. An act passed in 1711 required that postmasters have a warrant to open letters. Between 1712 and 1778, ninety warrants were issued for the opening of letters—and one warrant could open the letters of multiple people. Ellis, 72; Robinson, *British Post Office*, 119–25; Gary Schneider, *The Culture of Epistolarity: Vernacular Letters and Letter Writing in Early Modern England, 1500–1700* (Newark: University of Delaware Press, 2005), 75, 100–101; Fraser, 20–25.

21. Lord Castlecomer to John Perceval, 10 April 1713, BL Add. MS 47027, f. 25.

22. Philip Parker to John Perceval, 1 January 1711/2, BL Add. MS 47026, f. 103.

23. Whyman, *Pen and the People*, 68–71.

24. William King to John Boyle, 25 March 1740, Bod MS Eng. Hist d. 103, f. 12.

25. William King to John Boyle, 24 June 1745, Bod MS Eng. Hist d. 103, f. 90v; William Cole to Edward Southwell, 17 October 1692, BL Add. MS 18598, f. 117v.

26. John Perceval to Berkeley Taylor, 6 July 1727, BL Add. MS 46978, f. 66.

27. James Brydges to Col. Worsley, 12 November 1724, HEH ST 57: 24, f. 342; John Perceval to William Taylor, 4 October 1741, BL Add. MS 46992, f. 36; Daniel Dering to John Perceval, 19 February 1722/3, BL Add. MS 47029, f. 153.

28. Berkeley Taylor to John Perceval, 27 December 1714, BL Add. MS 46966, f. 6.

29. William Dockwra, *The Practical Method of the Penny Post* (London, 1681).

30. Robinson, *British Post Office*, 55.

31. Nicholas Blundell to Mr. Boucher, 8 January 1705/6, LRO DDBL acc 6121, f. 46.

32. Whyman, *Pen and the People*, 55–57. For John Perceval's delight at the establishment of a cross post between Chester and Bath, see John Perceval to Berkeley Taylor, 15 December 1722, BL Add. MS 46973, f. 95v.

33. John Perceval to George Berkeley, 11 December 1716, BL Add. MS 47028, f. 174; Cassandra Brydges to Lady Thomas Willoughby, 7 January 1719, HEH STB Box 2:1, f. 34.

34. Lady Petre to Peter Collinson, 22 May 1748, BL Add. MS 28727, f. 11.

35. Ferdinand Mendes to Hans Sloane, 15 September 1721, BL Sloane MS 4046, f. 132.

36. Henry Newman to John Perceval, 4 November 1723, BL Add. MS 47030, f. 32–32v.

37. Letters sent within London cost only one penny prepaid; when they were sent to country districts like Charlton an extra penny was charged. Robinson, *The British Post Office*, 72.

38. Dockwra, 2.

39. For the workings of the Penny Post, see Robinson, *British Post Office*, 69–76.

40. One more penny was charged for the letter to be delivered to the receiver outside the city. Dockwra, 3.

41. John Perceval to Henry Newman, 6 November 1723, BL Add. MS 47030, f. 33–33v. Since John Perceval copied Newman's letter into his letter book, it is not certain if he actually sent it by the Penny Post, but Perceval mentions the Penny Post in his response so the likelihood is high.

42. Henry Newman to John Perceval, 6 November 1723, BL Add. MS 47030, f. 34.

43. Robinson, *The British Post Office*, 93.

44. Thomas Brett to James Gadderar, 13 August 1726, Bod MSS.Eng.th.c.40, f. 66.

45. For letters sent to Scotland by the post, see Charles Preston to Hans Sloane, 25 May 1699, BL Sloane MS 4037, f. 272; Patrick Blair to Hans Sloane, 5 August 1709, BL Sloane MS 4042, f. 28.

46. Berkeley Taylor to John Perceval, 9 December 1720, BL Add. MS 46971, f. 111.

47. Richard Purcell to John Perceval, 13 December 1743, BL Add. MS 46994, f. 80.

48. For Perceval's last letter, see John Perceval to Berkeley Taylor, 26 November 1720, BL Add. MS 46971, f. 108.

49. There were two packet services to Ireland, one from Holyhead to Dublin and another from Milford Haven to Waterford. The northerly route was more popular, but it is possible Perceval used the southern route as well. Robinson, *The British Post Office*, 176–77.

50. Robinson, *The British Post Office*, 91.

51. John Perceval to Berkeley Taylor, 28 October 1721, BL Add. MS 46972, f. 111.

52. William Taylor to John Perceval, 8 November 1735, BL Add. MS 46986, f. 98v. There was a problem with franking, especially in Ireland for by 1718 it was thought that five times more letters were franked than posted. Robinson, *British Post Office*, 114–16.

53. A letter to Dublin would have cost 6d and since Kinsale is 171 miles from Dublin this meant an extra 4d charge (if Kinsale had been within forty miles of Dublin it would have been a 2d charge). T. Goodman, *The experienc'd secretary, or, Citizen and country-man's companion* (London, 1699), 77–78; Robinson, *The British Post Office*, 96–97. Richard Purcell verified this price. Richard Purcell to John Perceval, 28 December 1739, BL Add. MS 46990, f. 132.

54. John Perceval to Berkeley Taylor, 29 November 1720, BL Add. MS 46971, f. 109.

55. John Perceval to Berkeley Taylor, 28 December 1720, BL Add. MS 46971, f. 117.

56. John Perceval to Berkeley Taylor, 14 April 1716, BL Add. MS 46967, f. 49v.

57. For directions to deliver letters to his Pall Mall residence, see John Perceval to Berkeley Taylor, 6 June 1718, BL Add. MS 46969, f. 61.

58. Lord Richmond to Peter Collinson, 17 May 1764, BL Add. MS 28727, f. 103.

59. Lord Petre to Peter Collinson, 1 February 1738/9, BL Add. MS 28726, f. 64.

60. Major Charles Percival to John Perceval, 23 May 1708, BL Add. MS 47025, f. 88.

61. John Perceval to Lady Rook, 11 November 1709, BL Add. MS 47025, f. 140.

62. Alice Spencer, Countess of Derby, to George Hastings, fourth Earl of Huntington, 30 December 1600, HEH Hastings Correspondence, Box 5, HA 2505.

63. William Gardiner to Theophilus Hastings, ninth Earl of Huntington, 4 July 1734, HEH Hasting Correspondence, Box 75, HA 3362.

64. Tim Cockleshell to Hans Sloane, 25 April 1713, BL Sloane MS 4043, f. 144.

65. Dockwra, 2.

66. John Perceval to Berkeley Taylor, 24 October 1720, BL Add. MS 46971, f. 97.

67. Cassandra Willoughby to Mrs. North, no date, SRO DR 18/20/21/2.

68. John Ray to Hans Sloane, 21 August 1700, BL Sloane MS 4038, f. 53.

69. Thomas Rice to John Perceval, 16 October 1703, BL Add. MS 47025, f. 62.

70. William Fisher to John Perceval, 22 November 1717, BL Add. MS 46968, f. 165.

71. See the end of the letter book of Nicholas Blundell, LRO DDBL acc 6121. R.A. Roberts, ed., *Historical Manuscripts Commission: Manuscripts of the Earl of Egmont. Diary of the First Earl of Egmont (Viscount Percival)*, vol. 3, *1739–1747* (London: HMSO, 1923), 319.

72. See Dr. Cockburn to John Perceval, 16 May 1709, BL Add. MS 47025, f. 120v; Dorothea Taylor to John Perceval, 10 March 1746/7, BL Add. MS 46998, f. 29; John Barry to John Perceval, 29 September 1736, BL Add. MS 46987, f. 97; Francis Clerke to John Perceval, 9 October 1730, BL Add. MS 47032, f. 230.

73. Lord Richmond to Peter Collinson, 6 March 1747/8, BL Add. MS 28727, f. 6v.

74. Thomas Brett to [Revd. Gordon], 1 September 1731, Bod MSS.Eng.th.c.53, f. 25.

75. James Cuninghame to Hans Sloane, 6 March 1702/3, BL Sloane MS 4039, f. 85v.

76. George Berkeley to John Perceval, 3 September 1728, BL Add. MS 47032, f. 82.

77. John Perceval to Berkeley Taylor, 31 July 1725, BL Add. MS 46976, f. 77.

78. John Perceval to Philip Percival, 19 September 1725, BL Add. MS 47031, f. 4.

79. Matthew Buchanan to John Perceval, 17 August 1711, BL Add. MS 47026, f. 74v.

80. John Perceval to Daniel Dering, 1 July 1718, BL Add. MS 47028, f. 236v; John Perceval to Philip Perceval, 1 July 1718, BL Add. MS 47028, f. 237.

81. Robinson, *Carrying British Mails Overseas*, 27–29.

82. For information of the Dutch postal system, see Peter C. Sutton, Lisa Vergara, et al., *Love Letters: Dutch Genre Paintings in the Age of Vermeer* (London: Francis Lincoln, 2003), 28–31. Also see J. C. Overvoode, *Geschiedenis van het Postwezen in Nederlanden voor 1795* (Leiden, 1902).

83. For complaints about the postal system of the Holy Roman Empire see Robinson, *Carrying British Mails Overseas*, 26. For more on continental posts, see Christina Borreguero Beltrán, "Philip of Spain: The Spider's Web of News and Information," in *The Dissemination of News and the Emergence of Contemporaneity in Early Modern Europe*, ed. Brendan Dooley (Burlington, Vt.: Ashgate, 2010), 23–49; Wolfgang Behringer, *Thurn und Taxis: Die Geschichte ihrer Post und ihrer Unternehmen* (München: Piper, 1990).

84. John Perceval to Daniel Dering, 17 June 1718, BL Add. MS 47028, f. 232v.

85. John Perceval to Henry Cairns and Hugh Mitchell, 27 June 1718, BL Add. MS 47028, f. 235.

86. John Perceval to Daniel Dering, 1 July 1718, BL Add. MS 47028, f. 236v; John Perceval to Daniel Dering, 8 July 1718, BL Add. MS 47028, f. 239–239v; Daniel Dering to John Perceval, 7 August 1718, BL Add. MS 47028, f. 245v.

87. John Perceval to Berkeley Taylor, 9 September 1718, BL Add. MS 46969, f. 74.

88. Edmund Drummer established a packet service to the West Indies in 1702, but it lasted only until 1711. There was a short-lived attempt to set up service to New York in 1709, which petered out by 1711 or 1712. Robinson, *Carrying British Mail Overseas*, 35–38; Steele, 168–88; Dierks, 38–48.

89. George Berkeley had Perceval send his letters through Thomas Corbett at the Admiralty Office. George Berkeley to John Perceval, 3 September 1728, BL Add. MS 47032, f. 82.

90. Steele, 119–20.

91. Henry Newman to John Perceval, 25 September 1729, BL Add. MS 47032 f. 140.

92. In 1718 Edward Southwell informed Perceval that "I did propose Bird and I should have gone but he is not just now in town." Edward Southwell to John Perceval, 31 July 1718, BL Add. MS 47028, f. 244.

93. Byrd often notes that he sent his letters by merchant ships, but how those letters got from Westover to the ship is bit unclear. He does mention writing a letter while a captain's ship "rides over against my house." However, this is the only mention of such an event. He did, however, dine with many a ship's captain and it is probable that he delivered his letters to them at that time. Marion Tinling, ed., *The Correspondence of the Three William Byrds of Westover, Virginia, 1684–1776* (Charlottesville: University Press of Virginia, 1977), 2: 554.

94. For the intercolonial post, see William Smith, *The History of the Post Office in British North America, 1639–1870* (Cambridge: Cambridge University Press, 1920), 1–73, and Dierks, 38–48, 131, 189–206.

95. Tinling, 1: 52–59.

96. Byrd wrote most of his letters to England during the summer, especially June and July. He sent out some as early as February and some as late as October, but October was rare. Winter passages were rough, so Byrd only sent letters after August if a ship was late loading or if the ships had changed their patterns due to war. (In 1740 he sent forth a slew of letters in September and even one in October because the War of Jenkin's Ear has changed shipping patterns). Tinling, 2: 568; Steele, 292.

97. Nicholas Blundell to Richard Blundell, 2 April 1705, LRO DDBL acc 6121, f. 31.

98. William Byrd II to Anne Taylor Otway, 30 June 1736, VHS Mss5:2 B9966:3, f. 47.

99. William Byrd II to Anne Taylor Otway, 30 June 1736, VHS Mss5:2 B9966:3, f. 47–48.

100. Tinling, 2: 520.

101. Tinling, 2: 525.

102. William Byrd II to M. Perry, [July 1728], VHS Mss5:2 B9966:1, f. 17.

103. In fact, he sent his duplicates by Henry Newman's packet for the Society for Promoting Christian Knowledge. John Perceval to George Berkeley, 25 April 1729 and 20 September 1729, BL Add. MS 47032, f. 111, 138.

104. John Perceval to William Byrd II, 3 December 1729, BL Add. MS 47032, f. 145.

105. Perceval noted in his letter book that he received Byrd's letter of 20 August 1730 on 25 October 1730, but he did not respond until 28 December 1730. William Byrd to John Perceval, 20 August 1730, BL Add. MS 47032, f. 209v–210v; John Perceval to William Byrd, 28 December 1730, BL Add. MS 47032, f. 260–62.

106. George Berkeley to John Perceval, 29 March 1730, BL Add. MS 47032, f. 167.

107. William Byrd II to John Perceval, 10 June 1729, BL Add. MS 47032, f. 118v.

108. For sending letters to North America by delivery to a coffeehouse, see Blundell, 1: 37, and Patrick Gordon to Hans Sloane, 27 April 1702, BL Sloane MS 4038, f. 330.

109. Unknown to Thomas Brett, 17 September 1724, Bod MS.Eng.th.c.28, f. 320v.

110. William Wogan to Edward Southwell, 10 January 1716/7, BL Add. MS 37674, f. 63.

111. Berkeley Taylor to John Perceval, 16 December 1711, BL Add. MS 46964B, f. 136; John Perceval to William Taylor, 28 September 1727, BL Add. MS 46978, f. 79.

112. George Berkeley to John Perceval, 20 July 1730, BL Add. MS 47032, f. 204v.

113. John Perceval to George Berkeley, 23 December 1730, BL Add. MS 47032, f. 256v.

114. George Berkeley to John Perceval, 20 July 1730, BL Add. MS 47032, f. 204v.

115. William Percival to John Perceval, 4 August 1715, BL Add. MS 47028, f. 50v.

116. For the delivery of letters during the Tudor period, see James Daybell, *Women Letter Writers in Tudor England* (Oxford: Oxford University Press, 2006), 128–33.

117. Norman Davis, ed., *Paston Letters and Papers of the Fifteenth Century, Part 1* (Oxford: Oxford University Press, 2004), 139, 205.

118. Robinson, *The British Post Office*, 68; Daybell, 128–33; Schneider, 76–90; Bannet, 13; Whyman, *The Pen and the People*, 64–65.

119. John Eliot to Philip Eliot, 17 November 1757, LMA Acc 1017/956, f. 6; John Eliot to William Shallcross, 4 May 1765, LMA Acc 1017/953, f. 10v; John Eliot to John Trehawke, 22 June 1765, LMA Acc 1017/953, f. 12.

120. John Eliot to John Trehawke, 22 June 1765, LMA Acc 1017/953, f. 12.

121. Peter Collinson to Karl Linnaeus, 13 May 1739, BL Add. MS 28545, f. 140; Peter Collinson to Karl Linnaeus, 3 April 1741, LS Linnaeus Correspondence, Vol. XVII, Supplement, f. 4; Alan Armstrong, ed., *"Forget not Mee & My Garden . . .": Selected Letters, 1725–1768, of Peter Collinson, F.R.S.* (Philadelphia: American Philosophical Society, 2002), 174.

122. John Chamberlayne to Hans Sloane, 4 August 1719, BL Sloane MS 4045, f. 229.

123. Mr. Posford from William Byrd II, [1736], VHS Mss5:2 B9966:3, f. 71.

124. See Journal of James Brydges, 11 September and 2 December 1698, HEH ST 26: 1.

125. William Byrd II to Mrs. Pitt, 6 January 1736, VHS Mss5:2 B9966:3, f. 32.

126. Richard Boulton to Hans Sloane, 1 September [no year], BL Sloane MS 4058, f. 55.

127. William Taylor to John Perceval, 5 July 1737, BL Add. MS 46988, f. 101; Rogers Holland to John Perceval, 15 March 1729/30, BL Add. MS 47032, f. 165–165v.

128. James Bobert to Hans Sloane, 17 December 1685, BL Sloane MS 4036, f. 18.

129. John Boyle to Thomas Birch, 1 February 1747, BL Add. MS 4303, f. 140; John Boyle to Thomas Birch, 12 March 1747, BL Add. MS 4303, f. 141.

130. T. Molyneux to Hans Sloane, 7 August 1707, BL Sloane MS 4041, f. 10.

131. Daybell, 133; Schneider, 22, 61, 81.

132. John Perceval to Robert Southwell, 18 April 1699, BL Add. MS 47025, f. 16v.

133. For example, see James Brydges to Mr. Marye, 20 December 1724, HEH ST 57: 25, f. 82; James Brydges to Mr. Pearce, 11 April 1707, HEH ST 57: 1, f. 93.

134. Cassandra Brydges to Mrs. Dunbar, 1 October 1725, HEH STB Box 2: 1, f. 117.

135. Mary Crofts to John Perceval, 15 November 1740, BL Add. MS 46991, f. 52.

136. John Perceval to Richard Purcell, 6 March 1745/6, BL Add. MS 46997, f. 13; John Perceval to William Taylor, 2 December 1740, BL Add. MS 46991, f. 56.

137. Journal of James Brydges, 12 June 1699, HEH ST 26: 1; Philip Eliot to John Eliot, 17 November 1757, LMA Acc 1017/978; Arthur Charlett to Hans Sloane, 5 March 1704/5, BL Sloane MS 4040, f. 12.

138. Schneider, 22–27, 67–73; Daybell, 46, 86–90, 141–43.

139. John Perceval to Sir Edmond Bacon, 15 September 1722, BL Add. MS 47029, f. 133v.

140. John Perceval to Philip Percival, 8 April 1714, BL Add. MS 47027, f. 91v.

141. See John Boyle to Thomas Birch, 1 February 1747, BL Add. MS 4303, f. 139; John Boyle to Thomas Birch, 19 October 1747, BL Add. MS 4303, f. 130v.

142. Daniel Dering to John Perceval, 25 July 1728, BL Add. MS 47032, f. 76.

143. Elizabeth and William Petty to Robert Southwell, 12 July 1684, BL Add. MS 73855, f. 20.

144. P. Williams and Lady Petre to Peter Collinson, 11 January 1752, BL Add. MS 28727, f. 25.

145. "I'me obliged to you for your last letter tho it was but 2 or 3 lines at the bottom of Mr. Clerkes." William Percival to John Perceval, 14 February 1706/7, BL Add. MS 47025, f. 71.

146. Daniel Dering to John Perceval, 13 January 1725/6, BL Add. MS 47031, f. 76. Also see Daniel Dering to John Perceval, 31 January 1725/6, BL Add. MS 47031, f. 90v–92v.

147. For example, see Lord Tullamore to John Perceval, 21 January 1715/6, BL Add. MS 47028, f. 122.

148. Daniel Dering to John Perceval, 5 March 1722/3, BL Add. MS 47029, f. 158; Daniel Dering to John Perceval, 16 December 1729, BL Add. MS 47032, f. 150.

149. Lady Rook to John Perceval, 24 June [1724], BL Add. MS 47030, f. 70.

150. See James Brydges to Mr. Grosvenour, 20 November 1724, HEH ST 57: 25, f. 29; E. M. da Costa to Peter Collinson, 29 June 1759, BL Add. MS 28536, f. 69.

151. Peter Collinson to Hans Sloane, 4 July 1738, BL Sloane MS 4054, f. 62.

152. Peter Collinson to Hans Sloane, Wednesday [1740], BL Sloane MS 1968, f. 97.

153. Hans Sloane to Peter Collinson, no date, BL Sloane MS 4069, f. 48v.

154. See John Perceval to Berkeley Taylor, 25 September 1716, BL Add. MS 46967, f. 90v.

155. William Taylor to John Perceval, 15 May 1738, BL Add. MS 46989, f. 83.

156. See John Ray to Hans Sloane, 14 August 1700, BL Sloane MS 4038, f. 49.

157. Ralph Thoresby to Hans Sloane, 6 December 1701, BL Sloane MS 4038, f. 272.

158. Anne Goldgar, *Impolite Learning: Conduct and Community in the Republic of Letters, 1680–1750* (New Haven, Conn.: Yale University Press, 1995), 13–52, 116–68, 223–42.

159. Schneider, 91–108.

160. Blundell, 1: 68.

161. James Brydges to Mr. Peters, 28 April 1724, HEH ST 57: 24, f. 57; James Brydges to Mr. Pescod, 7 August 1724, HEH ST 57: 24, f. 196.

162. James Brydges to Mr. Pescod, 21 August 1724, HEH ST 57: 24, f. 207.

163. Schneider, 233–35. The most obvious notable exception is the correspondence of Charles I, printed in 1645 as *The King's Cabinet Opened.*

164. Maynard Mack, *Alexander Pope: A Life* (New York: Norton, 1985), 652–58; Mark Rose, *Authors and Owners: The Invention of Copyright* (Cambridge, Mass.: Harvard University Press, 1993), 58–66.

165. John Boyle to Jonathan Swift, 18 March 1736/7, BL Add. MS 4806, f. 189.

166. John Boyle to Alexander Pope, no date, BL Add. MS 4806, f. 189.

167. Warner, 35.

168. Sarah M. S. Pearsall, *Atlantic Families: Lives and Letters in the Later Eighteenth Century* (Oxford: Oxford University Press, 2008), 15–16; Clare Brant, *Eighteenth-Century Letters and British Culture* (New York: Palgrave Macmillan, 2006), 5.

Chapter 2. Mapping the Epistolary World

1. Henry Roby to John Perceval, 23 May 1697, BL Add. MS 47025, f. 2v–3.

2. Eve Tavor Bannet, *Empire of Letters: Letter Manuals and Transatlantic Correspondence, 1680–1820* (Cambridge: Cambridge University Press, 2005), 29; James Daybell, *Women Letter Writers in Tudor England* (Oxford: Oxford University Press, 2006), 163; Clare Brant, *Eighteenth-Century Letters and British Culture* (New York: Palgrave Macmillan, 2006), 1; Konstantin Dierks, *In My Power: Letter Writing and Communication in Early America* (Philadelphia: University of Pennsylvania Press, 2009), 2–3, 100–140; Sarah Pearsall, *Atlantic Families: Lives and Letters in the Later Eighteenth Century* (Oxford: Oxford University Press, 2008), 5; Susan Whyman, *The Pen and the People: English Letter Writers, 1660–1800* (Oxford: Oxford University Press, 2009), 13.

3. For the importance of mobility, see Alison Games, *The Web of Empire: English Cosmopolitans in an Age of Expansion, 1560–1660* (Oxford: Oxford University Press, 2008).

4. The need to look beyond artificial boundaries was emphasized in a 2006 forum in the *William and Mary Quarterly*. See Alison Games, "Beyond the Atlantic: English Globetrotters and Transoceanic Connections"; Philip J. Stern, "British Asia and British Atlantic: Comparisons and Connections"; Paul W. Mapp, "Atlantic History from Imperial, Continental, and Pacific Perspectives"; Peter A. Coclanis, "Atlantic World or Atlantic/World?" *William and Mary Quarterly* 3rd ser. 63, 4 (October 2006): 675–742.

5. These maps are made from the places noted on all the surviving letters of Nicholas Blundell, Cassandra Brydges, William Byrd I and II, Peter Collinson, John Eliot, and John Perceval, and selected letters of Charles and John Boyle, James Brydges, Hans Sloane, and Edward Southwell. The number of letters mapped was 8,908.

6. These calculations are based on the cities listed in Jan De Vries, *Economy of Europe in an Age of Crisis, 1600–1750* (Cambridge: Cambridge University Press, 1976), 150.

7. De Vries, 154–55. De Vries uses the twentieth-century term Randstad to designate the cities of Amsterdam, Haarlem, Leiden, The Hague, Delft, and Rotterdam.

8. James Rosenheim, *The Emergence of a Ruling Order: English Landed Society, 1650–1750* (London: Longman, 1998), 216.

9. Penelope Corfield, *The Impact of English Towns, 1700–1800* (Oxford: Oxford University Press, 1982), 66; Peter Borsay, *The English Urban Renaissance: Culture and Society in the Provincial Town, 1660–1770* (Oxford: Clarendon, 1989), 20; Keith Wrightson, *Earthly Necessities: Economic Lives in Early Modern Britain* (New Haven, Conn.: Yale University Press, 2000), 227–48.

10. Borsay, 31.

11. De Vries, 151; S. J. Connolly, *Religion, Law and Power: The Making of Protestant Ireland, 1660–1760* (Oxford: Clarendon, 1992), 44; Peter Clark, *British Clubs and Societies, 1580–1800: The Origins of an Associational World* (Oxford: Clarendon, 2000), 143–46; Borsay, 8; Wrightson, 236, 240.

12. William Byrd II to Jane Pratt Taylor, 10 October 1735, VHS Mss5:2 B9966:3, f. 24.

13. E. Smith to Hans Sloane, 19 November 1707, BL Sloane MS 4041, f. 70.

14. Carl B. Estabrook, *Urbane and Rustic England: Cultural Ties and Social Spheres in the Provinces, 1660–1780* (Manchester: Manchester University Press, 1998), 9, 193.

15. Thomas Knatchbull to John Perceval, June 1700, BL Add. MS 47025, f. 29; Henry Roby to John Perceval, 19 May 1697, BL Add. MS 47025, f. 2.

16. Philip Percival to John Perceval, 18 June 1717, BL Add. MS 47028, f. 193; Unknown to Hans Sloane, 23 June 1699, BL Sloane MS 4037, f. 291.

17. John Boyle to Thomas Birch, 23 February 1746/7, BL Add. MS 4303, f. 120.

18. John Boyle to Jonathan Swift, 15 March 1736/7, BL Add. MS 4806, f. 187.

19. John Perceval to Digby Cotes, 18 September 1701, BL Add. MS 47025, f. 54v–55v.

20. John Boyle to Jonathan Swift, 15 March 1736/7, BL Add 4806, f. 187.

21. Patrick Blair to Hans Sloane, 30 November 1708, BL Sloane MS 4041, f. 251; Patrick Blair to Hans Sloane, 29 July 1712, BL Sloane MS 4043, f. 64v.

22. Alan Armstrong, ed., *"Forget not Mee & My Garden . . .": Selected Letters, 1725–1768, of Peter Collinson, F.R.S.* (Philadelphia: American Philosophical Society, 2002), 114.

23. John Perceval to Daniel Dering, 6 October 1725, BL Add. MS 47031, f. 15v.

24. D. R. Hainsworth, *Stewards, Lords and People: The Estate Steward and His World in Later Stuart England* (Cambridge: Cambridge University Press, 1992), 13; Peter Roebuck, "Absentee Landownership in the Late Seventeenth and Early Eighteenth Centuries: A Neglected Factor in English Agrarian History," *Agricultural History Review* 21 (1973): 1–21; Rosenheim, 47–88; Felicity Heal, *Hospitality in Early Modern England* (Oxford: Oxford University Press, 1990), 119–21; Toby Barnard, *A New Anatomy of Ireland: The Irish Protestants, 1649–1770* (New Haven, Conn.: Yale University Press, 2003), 29, 32–33, 208.

25. John Boyle to Thomas Birch, 13 October 1742, BL Add. MS 4303, f. 112.

26. For an extended rant on the subject, see John Perceval to Philip Perceval, 29 November 1729, BL Add. MS 47032, f. 143v–144v.

27. Gary Nash, *The Urban Crucible: The Northern Seaports and the Origins of the American Revolution*, abridged ed. (Cambridge, Mass.: Harvard University Press, 1986), 33.

28. Marion Tinling, ed., *The Correspondence of the Three William Byrds of Westover, Virginia, 1684–1776*, (Charlottesville: University Press of Virginia, 1977), 1: 208.

29. George Berkeley to John Perceval, 29 March 1730, BL Add. MS 47032, f. 167.

30. Tinling, 2: 461.

31. Richard D. Brown, *Knowledge Is Power: The Diffusion of Information in Early America, 1700–1865* (New York: Oxford University Press, 1989), 42–64.

32. Tinling, 2: 461.

33. Tinling, 1: 355.

34. William King to John Boyle, 5 July 1741, Bod MS Eng Hist d. 103, f. 25.

35. Antonello Gerbi, *The Dispute of the New World: The History of a Polemic, 1750–1900*, trans. Jeremy Moyle (Pittsburgh: University of Pittsburgh Press, 1973), 61, 14; Don Cameron Allen, *The Legend of Noah* (Urbana: University of Illinois Press, 1949); Paolo Rossi, *The Dark Abyss of Time*, trans. Lydia G. Cochrane (Chicago: University of Chicago Press, 1984).

36. Armstrong, 236.

37. Tinling, 1: 357.

38. Tinling, 357. In fact, Byrd called his lands along the Roanoke River "Eden." Tinling, 1: 198.

39. Byrd certainly does not ignore the work of slaves. He simply insists that their labor is less than that undertaken by English tenants. Tinling, 1: 358.

40. George Berkeley to John Perceval, 1 March 1709/10, BL Add. MS 47026, f. 3v.

41. John Perceval to George Berkeley, 23 December 1730, BL Add. MS 47032, f. 256v.

42. John Perceval to William Byrd II, 15 October 1720, BL Add. MS 47029, f. 40.

43. John Perceval to Coghill, 6 February 1730/1, BL MS Add. 47033, f. 19–19v.

44. Michael J. Braddick, *State Formation in Early Modern England, c. 1550–1700* (Cambridge: Cambridge University Press, 2000), 340–419.

45. Susan Whyman notes the same phenomena for her letter writers. Whyman, 13.

46. For Perceval's interest in Bermuda, see letters between him and George Berkeley in BL Add. MS 47030.

47. Cassandra Brydges to the Countess of Coventry, 19 October 1734, HEH STB Box 2:1, f. 249.

48. Hans Sloane, *A Voyage to the Islands Madera, Barbados, Nieves, S. Christophers and Jamaica, with the Natural History of the Herbs and Trees, Four-footed Beasts, Fishes, Birds, Insects, Reptiles, &c. Of the last of those ISLANDS* (London, 1707); LS Mss 323 a, f.106–11; Margaret Beck Pritchard and Virginia Lascara Sites, *William Byrd II and His Lost History: Engravings of the Americas* (Williamsburg, Va.: Colonial Williamsburg Foundation, 1993), 102.

49. William Byrd II to John Perceval, 12 July 1736, VHS Mss5:2 B9966:3, f. 50.

50. William Byrd II to John Perceval, 10 June 1729, BL Add. MS 47032, f. 117–117v.

51. Peter Fontaine to John Perceval, 4 April 1721, BL Add. MS 47029, f. 63.

52. Tinling, 1: 246, 326.

53. William Byrd II to Charles Boyle, 6 March 1719, VHS ViH Mss10: no.130, f. 3 (microfilm).

54. William Byrd II to Jane Pratt Taylor, 28 July 1728, VHS Mss5:2 B9966:1, f. 23–24.

55. William Byrd II to [Hans Sloane], 10 April 1741, VHS Mss5:2 B9966:6, f. 27.

56. John Eliot to Richard How, Jr., undated, LMA Acc 1017/956, f. 32–32v.

57. Jeremy Black, *The British Abroad: The Grand Tour in the Eighteenth Century* (New York: St. Martin's, 1992), 7–8, 221–22.

58. Armstrong, 182.

59. Mark R. Wenger, ed., *The English Travels of Sir John Percival and William Byrd II: The Percival Diary of 1701* (Columbia: University of Missouri Press, 1989), 165.

60. George Berkeley to John Perceval, 1 May 1714, BL Add. MS 47027, f. 103v.

61. John Perceval to Daniel Dering, 21 August 1725, BL Add. MS 47030, f. 150v. In the indexes of both his journals kept during his trips to the Continent Perceval has a category for superstition. BL Add. MS 47059, f. 18, 162.

62. Christopher Hibbert, *The Grand Tour* (New York: Putnam's, 1969), 20.

63. See Mr. Gibb to John Perceval, 3 December 1707, BL Add. MS 47025, f. 81v–82.

64. See John Perceval to Daniel Dering, 29 December 1725, BL Add. MS 47031, f. 67.

65. For Perceval's European journals, see BL Add. MS 47059.

66. John Perceval to Edward Southwell, 22 January 1725/6, BL Add. MS f. 84–84v.

67. John Perceval to Anne Whorwood, 15 January 1706/7, BL Add. MS 47025, f. 66.

68. Mr. Gordon to Hans Sloane, 23 June 1701, BL Sloane 4038, f. 178; George Rooke to James Brydges, 13 April 1703, HEH ST 58: 1, f. 31; John Barrett to John Perceval, 24 November 1723, BL Add. MS 47030, f. 39; John Barrett to John Perceval, 2 December 1723, BL Add. MS 47030, f. 42v.

69. John Perceval II to Catherine Perceval, 1 May 1731, BL Add. MS 47033, f. 89v–90; William Taylor to John Perceval, 31 December 1729, BL Add. MS 46980, f. 131;

William Taylor to John Perceval, 17 June 1730, BL Add. MS 46981, f. 31; William Taylor to John Perceval, 21 April 1735, BL Add. MS 46986, f. 35.

70. Marmaduke Penwell to John Perceval, 30 November 1722, BL Add. MS 47029, f. 155.

71. James Cuninghame to Hans Sloane, 29 July 1700, BL Sloane MS 4038, f. 35.

72. Daniel Dering to John Perceval, 2 June 1730, BL Add. MS 47032, f. 194.

73. See Velters Cornwall to John Perceval, Mockas Court, 15 November 1730, BL Add. MS 47032, f. 239; Velters Cornwell to John Perceval, London, 12 May 1730, BL Add. MS 47032, f. 182.

74. Philip Parker to John Perceval, London, 12 May 1730; Calais, 25 May 1730; Spa, 25 July, 1730; Leyden, 9 September 1730; Rochester, 12 October 1730; BL Add. MS 47032, f. 181v, 191v, 205, 217, 230v–231.

75. Velters Cornwall to John Perceval, 12 May 1730, BL Add. MS 47032, f. 182; Velters Cornwell to John Perceval, 19 May 1730, BL Add. MS 47032, f. 185–185v; John Perceval II to John Perceval I, 20 May 1730, BL Add. MS 47032, f. 186v–187; John Perceval to Velters Cornwall, 24 May 1730, BL Add. MS 47032, f. 189v–190; John Perceval to Edward Southwell, 22 January 1725/6, BL Add. MS 47031, f. 84–84b; John Perceval to Daniel Dering, 16 April 1726, BL Add. MS 47031, f. 147.

76. Nicholas Blundell, *The Great Diurnal of Nicholas Blundell*, ed. J. J. Bagley, 3 vols., Record Society of Lancashire and Cheshire (Liverpool: C. Tinling, 1968–1972); Letter book of Nicholas Blundell, LRO DDBL acc 6121.

77. R. A. Roberts, ed., *Historical Manuscripts Commission: Manuscripts of the Earl of Egmont. Diary of the First Earl of Egmont (Viscount Percival)*, 3 vols. (London: HMSO, 1920–1923).

78. For Perceval's personal correspondence, see BL Add. MS 47025–47032. For his estate correspondence, see BL Add. MS 46964a–46999.

79. Louis B. Wright and Marion Tinling, eds., *The Secret Diary of William Byrd of Westover, 1709–1712* (Richmond: Dietz Press, 1941); Louis B. Wright and Marion Tinling, *The London Diary (1717–1721) and Other Writings* (New York: Oxford University Press, 1958); Maude H. Woodfin, ed., *Another Secret Diary of William Byrd of Westover, 1739–1741* (Richmond: Dietz Press, 1942). For his letter books that cover the period 1728–40, see VHS Mss5:2 B9966:1–6.

80. Wright and Tinling, *London Diary*, 412–13.

81. Nicholas Blundell, *The Great Diurnal of Nicholas Blundell*, ed. J. J. Bagley, vol. 1, *1702–1711*, Record Society of Lancashire and Cheshire (Liverpool: C. Tinling, 1968–1972), 1: 13.

82. Woodfin, 61.

83. Roberts, ed., *Historical Manuscripts Commission*, vol. 3, *1739–1747* (London: HMSO, 1923), 130.

84. Margaret Blundell, *Blundell's Diary and Letter Book, 1702–1728* (Liverpool: Liverpool University Press, 1952); John Bossy, *The English Catholic Community, 1570–1850* (New York: Oxford University Press, 1976), 94–95; Margaret Sena, "William Blundell and the Networks of Catholic Dissent in Post-Reformation England," in *Communities in Early*

Modern England, ed. Alexandra Shepard and Phil Withington (Manchester: Manchester University Press, 2000), 54–75.

85. Heal, 91–140.

86. Blundell, 1: 79.

87. John Perceval to Uncle Charles Dering, 16 September 1718, BL Add. MS 47028, f. 251.

88. He dined or visited with six out of seventeen correspondents.

89. Perceval dined or visited with twenty-four of his sixty-five correspondents and Byrd with two of his twenty-three correspondents.

90. Nicholas Blundell to Richard Boucher, 5 May 1705, 23 July 1705, 18 September 1705, 25 September 1705, LRO DDBL acc 6121; Nicholas Blundell to John Hurst, 24 July 1705, LRO DDBL acc 6121.

91. Nicholas Blundell to Thomas Howet, 27 February 1705, LRO DDBL acc 6121; Blundell, 1: 96, 98, 99, 100.

92. Blundell, 1: 84, 81.

93. Velters Cornwall to John Perceval, 22 February 1729/30, BL Add. MS 47032, f. 161.

94. Roberts, ed., *Historical Manuscripts Commission*, vol. 1, *1730–1733* (London: HMSO, 1920), 55, 77.

95. BL Sloane MS 4058, f. 144, 191, 151.

96. Woodfin, 32, 45, 54; Tinling, 2: 572.

97. Woodfin, 57, 62, 64, 75, 96, 106; Tinling, 2: 543.

98. Woodfin, 28, 40, 46, 53, 81.

99. Woodfin, 60, 63.

100. For the texture of Virginia life, see Darrett B. Rutman and Anita H. Rutman, *A Place in Time: Middlesex County, Virginia, 1650–1750* (New York: Norton, 1984), and Rhys Isaac, *The Transformation of Virginia, 1740–1790* (Chapel Hill: University of North Carolina Press, 1982).

101. Wright and Tinling, *London Diary*, 250.

102. William Byrd to Charles Wager, 26 May 1740, [6 September 1740], VHS Mss5:2 B9966:5, f. 21, 39; William Byrd II to Edward Southwell II, 12 May 1740, VHS Mss5:2 B9966:6, f. 1; William Byrd to John Perceval, 27 October 1740, VHS Mss5:2 B9966:6, f. 12.

103. William Byrd II to Charles Wager, 26 May 1740, VHS Mss5:2 B9966:5, f. 22.

104. William Byrd II to Charles Wager, [6 September 1740], VHS Mss5:2 B9966:5, f. 39.

105. William Byrd II to Francis Otway, 15 September 1740, VHS Mss5:2 B9966:6, f. 4–5; William Byrd II to Jane Pratt Taylor, 17 September 1740, VHS Mss5:2 B9966:6, f. 6–8; William Byrd II to Anne Taylor Otway, 20 September 1740, VHS Mss5:2 B9966:6, f. 8.

106. For example, see Tinling, 2: 566–67, 587–93, 596.

107. Tinling, 2: 587.

108. William Byrd II to John Hanbury, 10 July 1740, VHS Mss5:2 B9966:5, f. 27; William Byrd II to Thomas Chamberlayne, 5 September 1740, VHS Mss5:2 B9966:5, f. 30; William Byrd II to Christopher Smith, 12 July 1740, VHS Mss5:2 B9966:5, f. 29.

109. For example, Captain Thomas Bolling came and dined with Byrd eleven times in 1740. Woodfin, 79, 81, 91, 93, 94, 101, 103.

110. William Byrd II to Christopher Smith, 12 July 1740, VHS Mss5:2 B9966:5, f. 29.

111. For the two letters dealing with his courtship of Mary Smith, see Tinling, 1: 311, 313; for the three letters dealing with the commissioners of trade and plantations, see Tinling, 1: 314, 316, 320; for the ten letters to and from John Custis, see Tinling 1: 290–91, 292–94, 296–300, 305–8, 315, 317–20, 322–24; for the four letters to Philip Ludwell, see Tinling, 1: 300–305, 308–11.

112. Tinling, 1: 291, 294, 306, 319.

113. Tinling, 1: 297.

114. Tinling, 1: 290, 298, 307, 315, 320.

115. Rosenheim, 47–88; Barnard, 29, 32–33, 208. Susan Dwyer Amussen, *Caribbean Exchanges: Slavery and the Transformation of English Society, 1640–1700* (Chapel Hill: University of North Carolina Press, 2007), 177–79.

116. Forty-one of Perceval's 218 letters came from Ireland in 1730.

117. For references to dining with Taylor, see Roberts, 1: 6, 16, 32, 60. For visits, see Roberts, 1: 2, 9, 32, 34, 55, 76, 92, 94, 96.

118. William Taylor to John Perceval, 16 May 1730, BL Add. MS 46981, f. 28.

119. For letters with Coghill in 1730, see Marmaduke Coghill to John Perceval, 27 January 1729/30, 14 February 1729/30, 5 March 1729/30, 8 April, 23 April, 16 May 1730, BL Add. MS 47032, f. 158v, 159v–160, 162–64, 168v, 170–71, 184–184v; John Perceval to Marmaduke Coghill, 17 March 1729/30, 6 May 1730, BL Add. MS 47032, f. 165v–166, 178–179v.

120. Roberts, 1: 6, 24; John Perceval to Marmaduke Coghill, 6 May 1730, BL Add. MS 47032, f. 178v.

121. Forty-nine of Perceval's 218 letters came from London in 1730.

122. Roberts, 1: 118–21.

123. Nine of John Perceval's 282 letters between 10 January 1709 and 31 December 1712 came from the same locations that he resided in at the time. See BL Add. MS 46964b, 47026.

124. Five of John Perceval's 218 letters from 1730 came from the same locations he resided in at the time. See BL Add. MS 47032 and BL Add. MS 46981.

125. Tinling, 2: 489.

126. Only one letter sent to Edward Southwell the younger survives and no mention of him is made later. Tinling, 2: 560.

127. Tinling, 2: 592.

128. Nicholas Blundell to John Gelibrond, 11 September 1705, LRO DDBL acc 6121, f. 40; Nicholas Blundell to Henry Eyre, 2 October 1705, LRO DDBL acc 6121, f. 42;

Nicholas Blundell to Mr. Cole, 23 March 1705, 18 September 1705, LRO DDBL acc 6121, f. 31, 41.

129. He noted dining with John Gelibrond on 9 March 1705 and with his Cozen Eyre on 29 June 1705. He just refers to his "Cozen Eyre" in this entry, so this could be his cousin John Eyre, but he did dine with Henry Eyre on 2 June 1703. Blundell, 1: 80, 88.

130. Nicholas Blundell to Sister Margaret Blundell, 26 August 1705, LRO DDBL acc 6121, f. 37. He noted writing this letter in his diary. Blundell, 1: 91.

131. Nicholas Blundell to Mary Blundell, 1 and 5 March 1707, LRO DDBL acc 6121, f. 57; Nicholas Blundell to Mary Blundell, 3 May and 12 July 1707, LRO DDBL acc 6121, f. 64.

132. Nicholas Blundell to Mary Blundell, 24 January 1707, LRO DDBL acc 6121, f. 54.

133. Nicholas Blundell to Mary Blundell, 17 October 1707, LRO DDBL acc 6121, f. 67; Nicholas Blundell to Ailes Blundell, 2 March 1708/9, LRO DDBL acc 6121, f. 82.

134. Nicholas Blundell to Richard Blundell, 23 September 1702, LRO DDBL acc 6121, f. 6.

135. Nicholas Blundell to Richard Blundell, 23 September 1702, LRO DDBL acc 6121, f. 6–7.

136. Nicholas Blundell to Richard Blundell, 26 January 1702/3, LRO DDBL acc 6121, f. 11.

137. Nicholas Blundell to Richard Blundell, 2 September 1704, 16 December 1704, 2 April 1705, LRO DDBL acc 6121, f. 22–24, 28, 31–32.

138. Nicholas Blundell to Richard Blundell, 2 September 1704, LRO DDBL acc 6121, f. 25; Nicholas Blundell to Richard Blundell, 2 April 1705, LRO DDBL acc 6121, f. 32.

139. John Perceval to George Berkeley, 9 July 1730, BL Add. MS 47032, f. 203v–204, and 23 December 1730, BL Add. MS 47032, f. 256v–258; George Berkeley to John Perceval, 20 July 1730, BL Add. MS 47032, f. 204–5.

140. John Perceval to William Byrd II, 28 December 1730, BL Add. MS 47032, f. 260–62.

Chapter 3. Networking in the Epistolary World

1. Marion Tinling, ed., *The Correspondence of the Three William Byrds of Westover, Virginia, 1684–1776*, (Charlottesville: University Press of Virginia, 1977), 1: 16–21, 32–37, 52–59.

2. Tinling, 1: 52, 53, 54–55, 55–56, 56–57.

3. Tinling, 1: 52–53, 54, 57–59.

4. Most scholars of letters note that letters formed networks: Eve Tavor Bannet, *Empire of Letters: Letter Manuals and Transatlantic Correspondence, 1680–1820* (Cambridge: Cambridge University Press, 2005), x, 38; James Daybell, *Women Letter Writers in Tudor England* (Oxford: Oxford University Press, 2006), 1, 41; Konstantin Dierks, *In My Power:*

Letter Writing and Communication in Early America (Philadelphia: University of Pennsylvania Press, 2009), 161–63; Susan Whyman, *The Pen and the People: English Letter Writers, 1660–1800* (Oxford: Oxford University Press, 2009), 33.

5. All the networks produced in this book were made using UCINET and Netdraw. S. P. Borgatti, M. G. Everett, and L. C. Freeman, *Ucinet for Windows: Software for Social Network Analysis* (Cambridge, Mass.: Analytic Technologies, 2002), and S. P. Borgatti, *NetDraw Software for Network Visualization* (Lexington, Ky.: Analytic Technologies, 2002). The number of letters determined the time frame mapped for each correspondent, so while the number of years might vary from figure to figure, the number of letters does not.

6. In social network analysis such connections are known as first and second order connections. Stanley Wasserman and Katherine Faust, *Social Network Analysis* (Cambridge: Cambridge University Press, 1994), 34.

7. Philip Perceval to John Perceval, 24 February 1724/5, BL Add. MS 47030, f. 136v.

8. Naomi Tadmor, *Friends and Family in Eighteenth-Century England* (Cambridge: Cambridge University Press, 2001), 103–66.

9. For an examination of kinship links using social network analysis, see Robert Morrissey, "Kaskaskia Social Network: Kinship and Assimilation in the French-Illinois Borderlands, 1695–1735," *William and Mary Quarterly* 3rd ser. 70, 1 (2013): 103–46.

10. Philip Perceval to John Perceval, 24 February 1724/5, BL Add. MS 47030, f. 137.

11. William Byrd I exchanged six letters with his brother Thomas Byrd, one his sister Sarah Robinson, one with his sister Grace Richards, and one with his brother-in-law Mr. Richards. He exchanged nine letters with his father-in-law Warham Horsmanden, seven with his brother-in-law Daniel Horsmanden, and seven with his brother-in-law Nordest Rand.

12. For his attempt to foster a relationship between his son and nephew, see William Byrd II to Francis Otway, Jr., 16 February 1740, VHS Mss5:2 B9966:6, f. 22.

13. Joan Johnson, *Princely Chandos: James Brydges, 1674–1744* (Gloucester: Sutton, 1984), 87, 91.

14. Tinling, 1: 32, 35.

15. Tadmor, 1–17; Keith Wrightson, "Mutualities and Obligations: Changing Social Relationships in Early Modern England," *Proceedings of the British Academy* 139 (2006): 160–61.

16. Ilana Krausman Ben-Amos, *The Culture of Giving: Informal Support and Gift-Exchange in Early Modern England* (Cambridge: Cambridge University Press, 2008), 45–47; Wrightson, "Mutualities and Obligations," 159–61.

17. Ben-Amos, 47.

18. Susan Whyman, *Sociability and Power in Late-Stuart England* (Oxford: Oxford University Press, 1999), 23–33.

19. Sarah Pearsall, *Atlantic Families: Lives and Letters in the Later Eighteenth Century* (Oxford: Oxford University Press, 2008), 7.

20. Nicholas Blundell to Henry Eyre, 2 October 1705, LRO DDBL acc 6121, f. 42; Nicholas Blundell to Dorothy Blundell, 4 January 1705/6, LRO DDBL acc 6121, f. 45;

William Perceval to John Perceval, 1 June 1710, BL Add. MS 47026, f. 16; Edward Southwell to John Perceval, 1 July 1710, BL Add. MS 47026, f. 18v; Charles Dering to John Perceval, 6 July 1710, BL Add. MS 47026, f. 19–19v; Mary Knatchbull to John Perceval, 25 June 1710, BL Add. MS 47026, f. 20v; George Berkeley to John Perceval, 29 June 1710, BL Add. MS 47026, f. 20v–21.

21. John Perceval to Edward Southwell, 10 July 1708, BL Add. MS 47025, f. 90.

22. Charles Dering to John Perceval, 21 December 1717, BL Add. MS 47028, f. 215v.

23. R. A. Roberts, ed., *Historical Manuscripts Commission: Manuscripts of the Earl of Egmont. Diary of Viscount Percival, Afterwards First Earl of Egmont*, vol. 1, *1730–1733* (London: HMSO, 1920), 104.

24. Roberts, 1: 104.

25. Philip Perceval to John Perceval, 24 February 1724/5, BL Add. MS 47030, f. 135; John Perceval to Philip Perceval, 25 September 1727, BL Add. MS 47032, f. 48.

26. John Perceval to Edward Southwell, 10 July 1708, BL Add. MS 47025, f. 90.

27. Philip Perceval to John Perceval, 11 March 1710, BL Add. MS 47026, f. 8; Philip Perceval to John Perceval, 5 July 1712, BL Add. MS 47026, f. 72–72v.

28. Daniel Dering to John Perceval, 27 May 1712, BL Add. MS 47026, f. 123–24.

29. John Perceval to Philip Perceval, 18 October 1716, BL Add. MS 47028, f. 166.

30. Philip Perceval to John Perceval, 2 February 1716/7, BL Add. MS 47028, f. 180.

31. See letters about John Turner in LMA Acc 1017/954–5, 957.

32. Johnson, 91.

33. John Perceval to Philip Perceval, 2 March 1709/10, BL Add. MS 47026, f. 5v–7.

34. John Perceval to William Perceval, 24 March 1710, BL Add. MS 47026, f. 9v–10; William Perceval to John Perceval, 1 July 1710, BL MS Add. 47026, f. 18.

35. Helena le Grand to John Perceval, 25 November 1711, BL Add. MS 47026 f. 94v–95

36. Helena le Grand to John Perceval, 11 December 1711, BL Add. MS 47026, f. 95v–96.

37. Susan Whyman, "Gentle Companions: Single Women and Their Letters in Late Stuart England," in *Early Modern Women's Letter Writing, 1540–1700*, ed. James Daybell (New York: Palgrave, 2001), 177–93.

38. Mary Knatchbull to John Perceval, 3 September 1710, 11 March 1710/11, BL Add. MS 47026, f. 27, 61.

39. William Perceval to John Perceval, 15 January 1710/11, BL Add. MS 47026, f. 54–55.

40. Charles Dering to John Perceval, 6 July 1710, BL Add. MS 47026, f. 19; Helena le Grand to John Perceval, 5 February 1711/12, BL Add. MS 47026, f. 112.

41. John Perceval to Philip Perceval, 2 March 1709/10, BL Add. MS 47026, f. 6v; Mary Knatchbull to John Perceval, 25 June 1710, BL Add. MS 47026, f. 20v; Helena le Grand to John Perceval, 25 November 1711, 11 December 1711, BL Add. MS 47026, f. 95–95v; Philip Parker to John Perceval, 1 January 1711/12, BL Add. MS 47026, f. 103.

42. Pearsall, 7, 26–28.

43. Philip Perceval to John Perceval, 24 February 1724/5, BL Add. MS 47030, f. 135; John Perceval to Catherine Rook, 2 July 1724, BL Add. MS 47030, f. 71.

44. Nicholas Blundell to Richard Blundell, 2 September 1704, LRO DDBL acc 6121, f. 24.

45. Tinling, 1: 384; Tinling, 2: 566.

46. Nicholas Blundell to Richard Blundell, 26 January 1702/3, LRO DDBL acc 6121, f. 11; Nicholas Blundell to Captain Brown, 26 January 1702/3, LRO DDBL acc 6121, f. 10.

47. Nicholas Blundell, *The Great Diurnal of Nicholas Blundell*, ed. J. J. Bagley, vol. 1, *1702–1711*, Record Society of Lancashire and Cheshire (Liverpool: C. Tinling, 1968), 93.

48. Tinling, 2: 606.

49. Louis B. Wright and Marion Tinling, eds., *The London Diary (1717–1721) and Other Writings* (New York: Oxford University Press, 1958), 345–48.

50. Tinling, 2: 475.

51. Philip Perceval to John Perceval, 2 February 1716/7, BL Add. MS 47028, f. 180.

52. Cassandra Brydges to Cousin Robinson, 4 December 1722, HEH STB Box 2: 1, f. 66.

53. BL Add. MS 47025, 110v.

54. John Perceval exchanged 120 letters with George Berkeley.

55. George Berkeley to John Perceval, 1 March 1709/10, BL Add. MS 47026, f. 5; George Berkeley to John Perceval, 3 June 1711, BL Add. MS 47026, f. 69–69v.

56. George Berkeley to John Perceval, 17 May 1712, BL Add. MS 47026, f. 120–21v; George Berkeley to John Perceval, 18 August 1712, BL Add. MS 47026, f. 127–28.

57. George Berkeley to John Perceval, 18 August 1712, BL Add. MS 47026, f. 128.

58. Tinling, 1: 330, 365.

59. Tinling, 2: 568; Tinling, 1: 403.

60. Tinling, 1: 364.

61. Tinling, 2: 596.

62. Tinling, 1: 402–5, 435–37; Tinling, 2: 487–89, 525–27.

63. See Helena le Grand to John Perceval, 17 January 1706/7, BL Add. MS 47025, f. 67; Edward Southwell to John Perceval, 31 July 1718, BL Add. MS 47028, f. 244.

64. Tinling, 1: 438–41.

65. Ambrose Godfrey to Hans Sloane, 7 July 1724, BL Sloane MS 4047, f. 197.

66. Donald I. Warren, *Helping Networks: How People Cope with Problems in the Urban Community* (South Bend, Ind.: University of Notre Dame Press, 1981). For use by historians, see Ben-Amos, 45–81; Robert Jütte, *Poverty and Deviance in Early Modern Europe* (Cambridge: Cambridge University Press, 1994), 83–86.

67. Ambrose Godfrey to Hans Sloane, 8 July 1721, BL Sloane MS 4046, f. 93–94; Ambrose Godfrey to Hans Sloane, 7 July 1724, BL Sloane MS 4047, f. 197; Ambrose Godfrey to Hans Sloane, 14 October 1724, BL Sloane MS, f. 274; Ambrose Godfrey to Hans Sloane, 26 April 1725, BL Sloane MS 4047, f. 340; Ambrose Godfrey to Hans Sloane, 29 October 1725, BL Sloane MS 4048, f. 78.

68. Ambrose Godfrey to Hans Sloane, 7 July 1724, BL Sloane MS 4047, f. 197.

69. Wrightson, "Mutualities and Obligations," 192.

70. Ben-Amos, 47–79.

71. Ben-Amos, 71; Lewis Namier, *The Structure of Politics at the Accession of George III* (London: Macmillan, 1929); Harold Perkin, *The Origins of Modern English Society, 1780–1880* (London: Routledge and Kegan Paul, 1969), 39, 44, 49; Whyman, *Sociability and Power*, 18; Keith Wrightson, *English Society, 1580–1680* (New Brunswick, N.J.: Rutgers University Press, 1982), 57–61.

72. Linda Levy Peck, *Court Patronage and Corruption* (Boston: Unwin Hyman, 1990), 106–33; Michael Braddick, *State Formation in Early Modern England, c. 1550–1700* (Cambridge: Cambridge University Press, 2000), 87–90, 170–71.

73. Daniel Webber to John Perceval, 12 November 1711, BL Add. MS 47026, f. 90–92v.

74. Thomas Hodder to John Perceval, 5 October 1711, 30 October 1711, 21 November 1711, BL Add. MS 47026, f. 80b, 85v–88, 93–93v; John Perceval to Thomas Hodder, 3 November 1711, BL Add. MS 47026, f. 88v–90; Thomas Hodder to John Perceval, 15 January 1712/13, 26 November 1713, BL Add. MS 47027, f. 4v–7b, 55v–57; John Perceval to Thomas Hodder, no dates, BL Add. MS 47027, f. 7v–8b, 57–58.

75. Hanna Wills to John Perceval, 6 June 1710, BL Add. MS 46964b, f. 23; William Crofts to John Perceval, 27 August 1711, BL Add. MS 46964b, f. 101; William Davenport to John Perceval, 28 June 1711, BL Add. MS 46964b, f. 90.

76. David Roberts, ed., *Lord Chesterfield's Letters* (Oxford: Oxford University Press, 1992), 207.

77. Hans Hamilton to Edward Southwell, 23 December 1703, BL Add. MS 60582, f. 25v.

78. Tinling, 2: 485.

79. Cassandra Brydges to Cousin Robinson, January 1721, HEH STB, Box 2: 1. Rosemary O'Day notes Cassandra's importance as a giver of patronage. Rosemary O'Day, ed., *Cassandra Brydges, Duchess of Chandos, 1670–1734: Life and Letters* (Woodbridge: Boydell, 2007), 13, 57–61.

80. James Brydges to Mrs. Hartstongue, 5 October 1724, HEH ST 57: 24, f. 273.

81. Robert Southwell to John Perceval, Oct 1702, BL Add. MS 47025, f. 67.

82. Berkeley Taylor to John Perceval, 12 July 1713, BL Add. MS 46965, f. 146.

83. For Irish elections, see T. C. Barnard, "Considering the Inconsiderable: Electors, Patrons and Irish Elections, 1659–1761," in *The Irish Parliament in the Eighteenth Century: The Long Apprenticeship*, ed. D. W. Hayton (Edinburgh: Edinburgh University Press, 2001), 107–27.

84. Emmanuel Moore to John Perceval, 22 November 1710, BL Add. MS 47026, f. 40v; Henry Maule to John Perceval, 25 November 1710, BL Add. MS 46964b, f. 49; Viscount Doneraile to John Perceval, 25 November 1710, BL Add. MS 47026, f. 40v–41.

85. Christopher Crofts to John Perceval, 28 November 1710, BL Add. MS 46964b, f. 51; Francis Bernard to John Perceval, 30 November 1710, BL Add. MS 47026, f. 42–42v.

86. Philip Crofts to John Perceval, 9 December 1710, BL Add. MS 47026, f. 42v–43v.

87. For Moore's letters regarding elections, see Emmanuel Moore to John Perceval, 22 November 1710, 18 December 1711, 18 January 1711/12, 7 February 1711/12, BL Add. MS 47026, f. 40b, 96b, 107–107b, 112v–113; Emmanuel Moore to John Perceval, 17 February 1713/14, 18 August 1714, BL Add. MS 47027, f. 74–74b, 159v–161. For the other letters, see John Perceval to Emmanuel Moore, 15 May 1708, BL Add. MS 47025, f. 89; Emmanuel Moore to John Perceval, 9 January 1713/14, BL Add. MS 47027, f. 66–67v; Emmanuel Moore to John Perceval, 6 March 1727/8, 27 July 1728, BL Add. MS 46979, f. 33, 73; John Perceval to Emmanuel Moore, 31 July 1728, BL Add. MS 46979, f. 75.

88. For letters involving elections, see Francis Bernard to John Perceval, 2 August 1709, BL Add. MS 47025, f. 130; Francis Bernard to John Perceval, 30 November 1710, BL Add. MS 47026, f. 42–42v; Francis Bernard to John Perceval, 31 August 1714, BL Add. MS 47027, f. 166–167v; Francis Bernard to John Perceval, 5 March 1714, BL Add. MS 47028, f. 12. For other letters, see Francis Bernard to John Perceval, 19 September 1729, BL Add. MS 46980, f. 99; John Perceval to Francis Bernard, 4 October 1729, BL Add. MS 46980, f. 112.

89. Henry Peck to Edward Southwell, 4 March 1704/5, BL Add. MS 21137, f. 82.

90. See Henry Trench to John Perceval, 26 November 1708, 25 January 1708/9, BL Add. MS 47025, f. 104, 112v; Henry Trench to John Perceval, 12 March 1710, 18 March 1710, BL Add. MS 47026, f. 8–8b, 8v–9.

91. Perceval added an annotation on Trench's death near his letter to Mr. Gouge. John Perceval to Mr. Gouge, 17 October 1707, BL Add. MS 47025, f. 80.

92. Matthew Buchanan to John Perceval, 31 January 1710/11, BL Add. MS 47026, f. 57–57v.

93. Matthew Buchanan to John Perceval, 17 August 1711, BL Add. MS 47026, f. 73v–75.

94. Matthew Buchanan to John Perceval, 13 September 1711, BL Add. MS 47026, f. 78v–77v.

95. Matthew Buchanan to John Perceval, 19 October 1711, BL Add. MS 47026, f. 81–82v.

96. Matthew Buchanan to John Perceval, 4 January 1711/12, BL Add. MS 47026, f. 104v–105.

97. Matthew Buchanan to John Perceval, 27 September 1712, BL Add. MS 47026, f. 128v–129.

98. John Perceval to Matthew Buchanan, 13 May 1721, BL Add. MS 47029, f. 60.

99. Matthew Buchanan to John Perceval, 22 November 1726, BL Add. MS 47031, f. 207v–209v.

100. Margaret Buchanan to John Perceval, 13 June 1730, BL Add. MS 47032, f. 200.

101. Although in the margin, next to Margaret Buchanan's last letter, he notes that he answered it. BL Add. MS 47032, f. 200. In the margin of his letter book Perceval wrote of Buchanan: "a justice of Peace in Ireland a religious man and zealous against Popery, but falling into unavoidable debts he dy'd a begger, leaving a widow & many children." BL Add. MS 47025, f. 91v.

102. John Perceval to [Matthew Buchanan], 14 March 1710/11, BL Add. MS 47026, f. 61v; John Perceval to Matthew Buchanan, 11 May 1711, BL Add. MS 47026, f. 68v; Bishop of Clogher to John Perceval, 11 October 1712, BL Add. MS 47026, f. 129–129v.

103. John Perceval to Margaret Buchanan, 30 October 1711, BL Add. MS 47026, f. 84v–85.

104. Matthew Buchanan to John Perceval, 17 August 1711, BL Add. MS 47026, f. 75; Matthew Buchanan to John Perceval, 24 October 1711, BL Add. MS 47026, f. 82v.

105. Matthew Buchanan to John Perceval, 31 January 1710/11, BL Add. MS 47026, f. 57.

106. Matthew Buchanan to John Perceval, 22 November 1726, BL Add. MS 47031, f. 208v.

107. Matthew Buchanan to John Perceval, 17 August 1711, BL Add. MS 47026, f. 74; Matthew Buchanan to John Perceval, 22 November 1726, BL Add. MS 47031, f. 208v; Alexander Cairnes to John Perceval, 15 September 1729, BL Add. MS 47032, f. 137v.

108. Mark S. Granovetter, "The Strength of Weak Ties," *Journal of Sociology* 78 (1973): 1369–80.

109. For the redefinition of the public realm and its affect on women, see Mary Beth Norton, *Separated by Their Sex: Women in Public and Private in the Colonial Atlantic World* (Ithaca, N.Y.: Cornell University Press, 2011).

110. Dierks, 1–3, 52–99, 141–88, 235–79. For the growth of the middle class, see P. Earle, *The Making of the English Middle Class: Business, Society and Family Life in London, 1660–1730* (London: Methuen, 1989); Peter Langford, *A Polite and Commercial People: England 1727–1783* (Oxford: Oxford University Press, 1989); Peter Borsay, *The English Urban Renaissance: Culture and Society in the Provincial Town, 1660–1770* (Oxford: Clarendon, 1989).

111. Blundell, 1: 206, 279.

112. Susan Whyman examines the letters of many writers from the laboring classes, but mostly from the later eighteenth century. Whyman, *The Pen and the People*, 75–111.

113. E. P. Thompson, *Customs in Common* (New York: New Press, 1993), 42, 45–46, 57.

114. Francis Leicester to John Perceval, 16 September 1746, BL Add. MS 46997, f. 75–75v. For the use of language in petitions, see Susan Broomhall, "'Burdened with Small Children': Women Defining Poverty in Sixteenth Century Tours," in *Women's Letters Across Europe, 1400–1700*, ed. Jane Couchman and Ann Crabb (Aldershot: Ashgate, 2005), 223–37; Daybell, *Women Letter-Writers in Tudor England*, 250–57.

115. Wrightson, *English Society*, 58–61.

116. Thomas Sokoll argues that the reason British petitions, unlike Prussian petitions, have this mixture of forms is that the British were more familiar with letter writing than the Prussians. Thomas Sokoll, ed., *Essex Pauper Letters, 1731–1837*, Records of Social and Economic History New Series 30 (Oxford: Oxford University Press, 2001), 57, 60.

117. John Anster to John Perceval, 10 November 1731, BL Add. MS 46982, f. 84.

118. Oliver Williams to John Perceval, 13 February 1729/30, 18 September 1730, BL Add. MS 46981, f. 14, 43.

119. Oliver Williams to John Perceval, 18 September 1730, BL Add. MS 46981, f. 43.

120. John Perceval to William Taylor, 11 November 1730, BL Add. MS 46981, f. 68.

121. John Perceval to Berkeley Taylor, 6 July 1727, BL Add. MS 46978, f. 66v.

122. William Byrd II to John Boyle, 2 February 1726/7, VHS Mss10:130, f. 44; William King to John Boyle, 15 January 1739/40, Bod MS Eng. Hist d. 103, f. 10.

123. James Daybell, "Privacy and the Social Practice of Reading Women's Letters," in *Women's Letters Across Europe, 1400–1700*, ed. Couchman and Crabb, 148.

124. Rosemary O'Day, *Education and Society 1500–1800* (London: Longman, 1982), 194–95.

125. For some limits, see Whyman, *The Pen and the People*, 32.

126. John Perceval I to John Perceval II, 6 June 1730, BL Add. MS 47032, f. 196v.

127. In Blundell's diary between 1702 and 1711 his wife is mentioned writing letters ten times. On 23 December 1705 Blundell rewrote a letter for her; on 22 October 1710 he mentions helping her write some letters. Blundell, 1: 72, 75, 99, 125, 146, 150, 151, 194, 202, 215, 269.

128. Susan Amussen, *An Ordered Society: Gender and Class in Early Modern England* (Oxford: Blackwell, 1988); Leonore Davidoff and Catherine Hall, *Family Fortunes: Men and Women of the English Middle Class, 1780–1850* (Chicago: University of Chicago Press, 1987); Robert Shoemaker, *Gender in English Society, 1650–1850: The Emergence of Separate Spheres?* (London: Longman, 1998); Lawrence Stone, *The Family, Sex, and Marriage* (New York: Harper and Row, 1977). For a critique of the idea of separate spheres, see Amanda Vickery, *The Gentleman's Daughter* (New Haven, Conn.: Yale University Press, 1998), 1–8.

129. Dena Goodman, *Becoming a Woman in the Age of Letters* (Ithaca, N.Y.: Cornell University Press, 2009), 1–14.

130. Norton, 76–104.

131. For this approach, see Clare Brant, *Eighteenth-Century Letters and British Culture* (New York: Palgrave Macmillan, 2006); Amanda Gilroy and W. M. Verhoeven, eds., *Epistolary Histories: Letters, Fiction, Culture* (Charlottesville: University Press of Virginia, 2000); James How, *Epistolary Spaces: English Letter Writing from the Foundation of the Post Office to Richardson's* Clarissa (Aldershot: Ashgate, 2003); Caroline Bland and Maire Cross, "Gender Politics: Breathing New Life into Old Letters," and Anne-Francoise Gilbert, "Deconstructing Gender: Henriette's Correspondence with Rousseau," in *Gender and Politics in the Age of Letter Writing, 1750–2000*, ed. Caroline Bland and Maire Cross (Aldershot: Ashgate, 2004); Daybell, *Women Letter-Writers in Tudor England*, 167–74; Whyman, *The Pen and the People*, 161–217; Whyman, "Gentle Companions," 177–93.

132. Duchess of Marlborough to Lady Egmont, undated, BL Add. MS 47012B, f. 8.

133. Duchess of Marlborough to the Duke of Somerset, 6 July 1736, BL Add. MS 47012B, f. 10.

134. John Perceval II to Lady Burlington, undated, BL Add. MS 47012B, f. 12; John Perceval II to Duchess of Marlborough, 19 July 1736, BL Add. MS 47012B, f. 12v.

135. Duchess of Marlborough to Mrs. Southwell, 5 September 1736, BL Add. MS 47012B, f. 13.

136. Also see Laura Gowing, "The Politics of Women's Friendship in Early Modern England," in *Love, Friendship and Faith in Europe, 1300–1800*, ed. Laura Gowing, Michael Hunter, and Miri Rubin (Houndsmills: Palgrave Macmillan, 2005), 138.

137. John Perceval to Charles Dering, 8 January 1715/6, BL Add. MS 47028, f. 118–118v.

138. Lady Burlington to the Duchess of Marlborough, 6 July [1736], BL Add. MS 47012B, f. 11; Duchess of Marlborough to Lady Egmont, undated, BL Add. MS 47012B, f. 8.

Chapter 4. Nurturing the Epistolary World

1. Unfinished autobiography by Sir John Perceval, BL Add. MS 47072, f. 103v.

2. Lorenzo Magnolfi to John Perceval, 22 November 1707, BL Add. MS 47025, f. 81–81v.

3. John Perceval to Lorenzo Magnolfi, 5 July 1708, BL Add. MS 47025, f. 89v; Lorenzo Magnolfi to John Perceval, 12 June 1708, BL Add. MS 47025, f. 90v.

4. Lorenzo Magnolfi to John Perceval, 12 June 1708, BL Add. MS 47025, f. 90v.

5. Lorenzo Magnolfi to John Perceval, 19 August 1708, BL Add. MS 47025, f. 94.

6. Cosimo III de'Medici, Grand Duke of Tuscany, to John Perceval, 18 December 1708, BL Add. MS 47025, f. 109; Lorenzo Magnolfi to John Perceval, 26 November 1709, BL Add. MS 47025, f. 142.

7. John Perceval to Lorenzo Magnolfi, 9 February 1708/9, BL Add. MS 47025, f. 114.

8. For scholarship on the tone of letters, see James Daybell, *Women Letter Writers in Tudor England* (Oxford: Oxford University Press, 2006), 226–27; Gary Schneider, *The Culture of Epistolarity: Vernacular Letters and Letter Writing in Early Modern England, 1500–1700* (Newark: University of Delaware Press, 2005), 41–43; Susan Whyman, *The Pen and the People: English Letter Writers, 1660–1800* (Oxford: Oxford University Press, 2009), 12, 22, 215; Eve Tavor Bannet, *Empire of Letters: Letter Manuals and Transatlantic Correspondence, 1680–1820* (Cambridge: Cambridge University Press, 2005), xiii, 43–46; Konstantin Dierks, *In My Power: Letter Writing and Communications in Early America* (Philadelphia: University of Pennsylvania Press, 2009), 144–50; Sarah Pearsall, *Atlantic Families: Lives and Letters in the Later Eighteenth Century* (Oxford: Oxford University Press, 2008), 80–110.

9. Whyman, *The Pen and the People*, 12.

10. These changes can be viewed through an examination of the correspondence of the earls of Huntingdon from 1600 to 1670. HEH Hastings Correspondence, Boxes 5–31.

11. Digby Cotes to John Perceval, 25 November 1702, BL Add. MS 47025, f. 59.

12. T. Goodman, *The experienc'd secretary, or, Citizen and country-man's companion* (London, 1699), 58.

13. Samuel Willes to Theophilus Hastings, 30 March 1670, HEH Hastings Correspondence, Box 28, HA 13321.

14. W.P., *A Flying Post* (London, 1678), no pagination.

15. Peter Borsay, *The English Urban Renaissance: Culture and Society in the Provincial Town, 1660–1770* (Oxford: Clarendon, 1989), 267–83; Lawrence Klein, *Shaftsbury and the Culture of Politeness: Moral Discourse and Cultural Politics in Early Eighteenth Century England* (Cambridge: Cambridge University Press, 1994), 3–10, 176–92; James M. Rosenheim, *The Emergence of a Ruling Order: English Landed Society, 1650–1750* (London: Longman, 1998), 226–27.

16. T. Hastings to Elizabeth Hastings, 24 April 1656, HEH Hastings Correspondence, Box 20, HA 5863.

17. John Perceval II to John Perceval I, undated, BL Add. MS 47028, f. 248v; Catherine Perceval II to John Perceval I, undated, BL Add. MS 47028, f. 248v.

18. Pearsall, 80–110.

19. Anna Bryson, *From Courtesy to Civility: Changing Codes of Conduct in Early Modern England* (Oxford: Oxford University Press, 1998).

20. Klein, 4.

21. Henry Care, *The Female Secretary* (London, 1671), 145.

22. George Saintsbury, *A Letterbook* (London: G. Bell and Sons, 1922), 21.

23. Borsay, 226; Penelope Corfield, "The Rivals: Landed and Other Gentleman," in *Land and Society in Britain, 1700–1914*, ed. Negley Harte and Roland Quinault (Manchester: Manchester University Press, 1996), 8–9; Paul Langford, *A Polite and Commercial People: England, 1727–1783* (Oxford: Oxford University Press, 1989), 66; G. E. Mingay, *Landed Society in the Eighteenth Century* (London: Routledge and Kegan Paul, 1963), 26; L. Stone and J. Stone, *An Open Elite? England 1540–1880* (Oxford: Clarendon, 1984), 412; Susan Whyman, *Sociability and Power in Late-Stuart England* (Oxford: Oxford University Press, 1999), 87.

24. Lawrence Klein, *Shaftsbury and the Culture of Politeness* (Cambridge: Cambridge University Press, 1994). Also see Edward Hundert, *The Enlightenment's Fable: Bernard Mandeville and the Discovery of Society* (Cambridge: Cambridge University Press, 1994), 116–74; Corfield, 17.

25. Peter Collinson to Thomas Story, 4 August 1729, RSF Ms 337/33.

26. Care, 139–40.

27. Daybell, 226–27; Schneider, 41–43; Whyman, *The Pen and the People*, 12, 22, 215; Bannet, xiii, 43–46; Dierks, 144–50; Pearsall, 80–110.

28. Nicole Eustace, "'The Cornerstone of a Copious Work': Love and Power in Eighteenth Century Courtship," *Journal of Social History* 34, 3 (Spring 2001): 517–46; Pearsall, 80–110.

29. See also David S. Lux and Harold J. Cook, "Closed Circles or Open Networks?: Communicating at a Distance During the Scientific Revolution," *History of Science* 36, 2 (June 1998): 188–90.

30. Schneider, 30–32, 114–15.

31. William Byrd II to Jane Pratt Taylor, 28 July 1728, VHS Mss 5:2 B9966:1, f. 23.

32. William Byrd II to Jane Pratt Taylor, 28 July 1728, VHS Mss 5:2 B9966:1, f. 23.

33. Janet Gurkin Altman, "The 'Triple Register': Introduction to Temporal Complexity in the Letter-Novel," *L'Esprit Créateur* 17 (1977): 309.

34. J. Drummond to James Brydges, 4 December 1705, HEH ST 58: 1, f. 52v; John Boyle to Alexander Pope, undated, BL Add. MS 4806, f. 189v.

35. For discussions of hand kissing, see Susan Whyman, "'Paper Visits': The Post-Restoration Letter as Seen Through the Verney Family Archive," in *Epistolary Selves: Letters and Letter-Writers, 1600–1945*, ed. Rebecca Earle (Aldershot: Ashgate, 1999), 35; Schneider, 116–17; Pearsall, 100. M. Percival to Lady Perceval, 22 July 1718, BL Add. MS 47028, f. 240v.

36. Marion Tinling, ed., *The Correspondence of the Three William Byrds of Westover, Virginia, 1684–1776* (Charlottesville: University Press of Virginia, 1977), 2: 530–31.

37. L. Clayton to John Perceval, 28 December 1711, BL Add. MS 47026, f. 98.

38. Peter Collinson to Mary Collinson, 27 July [no year], BL Add. MS 28558, f. 38.

39. Joan Wildeblood and Peter Brison, *The Polite World: A Guide to English Manners and Deportment from the Thirteenth to the Nineteenth Century* (Oxford: Oxford University Press, 1965), 198.

40. Daybell, 108–13; Schneider, 121, 156–60; Bannet, 42.

41. Francis Nivelon, *The Rudiments of Genteel Behavior* ([London?], 1737); Wildeblood and Brison, 225–27.

42. Peter Collinson to Mary Collinson, 27 July [no year], BL Add. MS 28558, f. 38.

43. For blushes, see Schneider, 132–40.

44. Care, 139.

45. Bannet, 48.

46. Bannet, 44.

47. Bruce Redford, *The Converse of the Pen: Acts of Intimacy in the Eighteenth-Century Familiar Letter* (Chicago: University of Chicago Press, 1986), 2; Clare Brant, *Eighteenth-Century Letters and British Culture* (New York: Palgrave Macmillan, 2006), 21–22; Schneider, 16, 110; Bannet, 44–46; Pearsall, 67–68; Dierks, 160.

48. Lord Jersey to Peter Collinson, 3 October [no year], BL Add. MS 28727, f. 134v; William King to John Boyle, 20 May 1741, Bod MS Eng. Hist d. 103, f. 22v.

49. Frank William Sharpe to Peter Collinson, undated, BL Add. MS 28727, f. 150.

50. John Boyle to Thomas Birch, 26 May 1747, BL Add. MS 4303, f. 125v.

51. Tinling, 2: 518.

52. For further a discussion, see Bannet, 61.

53. W.P., *A Flying Post*, no pagination.

54. Lord Richmond to Peter Collinson, 20 July 1742, BL Add. MS 28726, f. 120; Peter Collinson to E. M. da Costa, 18 December 1750, BL Add. MS 28536, f. 62.

55. E. M. da Costa to Peter Collinson, 17 July 1747, BL Add. MS 28536, f. 57.

56. For this example, see Whyman, "Paper Visits," 24.

57. William King to John Boyle, 5 July 1741, Bod MS Eng. Hist d. 103, f. 25.

58. For reciprocity and letters, see Dena Goodman, *The Republic of Letters: A Cultural History of the French Enlightenment* (Ithaca, N.Y.: Cornell University Press, 1994), 18; Ylva Hasselberg, "Letters, Social Networks and the Embedded Economy in Sweden," in *Epistolary Selves*, ed. Earle, 95–107; Whyman, "Paper Visits," 15–36; Henk J. M. Nellen,

"In Strict Confidence: Grotius' Correspondence with His Socinian Friends," in *Self-Presentation and Social Identification: The Rhetoric and Pragmatics of Letter Writing in Early Modern Times,* ed. Toon Van Houdt, Jan Papy, Gilbert Tournoy, and Constant Matheeussen (Leuven: Leuven University Press, 2002), 227–45.

59. Also see Sharon Kettering, "Gift-Giving and Patronage in Early Modern France," *French History* 2 (1988): 142–43.

60. Alan Armstrong, ed., *"Forget not Mee & My Garden . . .": Selected Letters, 1725–1768, of Peter Collinson, F.R.S.* (Philadelphia: American Philosophical Society, 2002), 151; Daniel Dering to John Perceval, 31 July 1728, BL Add. MS 47032, f. 78; James Brydges to Mr. Drummond, 26 September 1724, HEH ST 57: 24, f. 254; Lord Petre to Peter Collinson, 2 August 1736, BL Add. MS 28726, f. 7.

61. Cadwallader Vaughan to T. Hastings, 27 June 1671, HEH Hastings Correspondence, Box 29, HA 12954.

62. Daybell, 161–62; Pearsall, 112–26; Schneider, 61–63.

63. C. Dering to John Perceval, 20 February 1719/20, BL Add. MS 47029, f. 18v; Archbishop of Dublin to John Perceval, 23 February 1719/20, BL Add. MS 47029, f. 19.

64. Helena le Grand to John Perceval, 6 February 1706/7, BL Add. MS 47025, f. 69v.

65. Armstrong, 36.

66. Daybell, 162.

67. Peter du Moulin to Lucy Hastings, 23 September 1654, HEH Hasting Correspondence, Box 19, HA 9465.

68. Craig Muldrew, *The Economy of Obligation* (New York: St. Martin's, 1998), 2–4, 123–48; Pearsall, 112–33. Also see Margot Finn, *The Character of Credit: Personal Debt in English Culture, 1740–1914* (Cambridge: Cambridge University Press, 2003).

69. Armstrong, 183.

70. Marcel Mauss, *The Gift: Forms and Functions of Exchange in Archaic Societies,* trans. Ian Cunnison (New York: Norton, 1967). Other works on gift giving include Marshal Sahlins, *Stone Age Economies* (Chicago: Aldine, 1972); Annette B. Weiner, *Women of Value, Men of Renown: New Perspectives in Trobriand Exchange* (Austin: University of Texas Press, 1976); C. A. Gregory, *Gifts and Commodities* (London: Academic Press, 1982); Karl Polanyi, *The Great Transformation* (Boston: Beacon Press, 1957); Georges Duby, *The Early Growth of the European Economy,* trans. Howard B. Clarke (Ithaca, N.Y.: Cornell University Press, 1974); Kettering, "Gift-Giving and Patronage in Early Modern France"; Natalie Zemon Davis, *The Gift in Sixteenth-Century France* (Madison: University of Wisconsin Press, 2000); Ilana Krausman Ben-Amos, *The Culture of Giving: Informal Support and Gift-Exchange in Early Modern England* (Cambridge: Cambridge University Press, 2008); Felicity Heal, "Food Gifts, the Household and the Politics of Exchange in Early Modern England," *Past and Present* 199 (May 2008): 41–70.

71. Ben-Amos, 8–9.

72. Davis, 34–36; Heal, 41–70.

73. For news as a gift, see Goodman, "Republic of Letters," 117; Daybell, 164–65; David Randall, "Joseph Mead, Novellante: News, Sociability, and Credibility in Early

Stuart England," *Journal of British Studies* 45, 2 (April 2006): 298–99. Also see John Boyle to Lord Strafford, 18 March 1732/3, BL Add. 31142, f. 69.

74. William Wogan to John Perceval, 30 April 1713, BL Add. MS 47027, f. 30v; Philip Perceval to John Perceval, 9 November 1723, BL Add. MS 47030, f. 35.

75. Alan McKenzie, ed., *Sent as a Gift: 8 Correspondences from the Eighteenth Century* (Athens: University of Georgia Press, 1993); Goodman, "Republic of Letters," 117; Daybell, 159–65; Schneider, 27.

76. Daybell, 164.

77. Christiana Hastings to T. Hastings, [1665], HEH Hastings Correspondence, Box 25, HA 4678.

78. Peter Collinson to Gov. Morris, 10 July 1743, LS Mss 323 a, f. 151.

79. Schneider, 111.

80. Eustace, "The Cornerstone of a Copious Work," 525; Kettering, 140.

81. Davis, 42; Kettering, 131; Whyman, *Sociability and Power*, 30–31.

82. Berkeley Taylor to John Perceval, 9 October 1719, BL Add. MS 46970, f. 103; Philip Perceval to John Perceval, 15 November 1727, BL Add. MS 47032, f. 51.

83. John Perceval to William Byrd II, 28 December 1730, BL Add. MS 47032, f. 261.

84. Lorenzo Magnolfi to John Perceval, 12 June 1708, BL Add. MS 47025, f. 90v.

85. William Perceval to John Perceval, 4 December 1729, BL Add. MS 47032, f. 147; William Perceval to John Perceval, 12 January 1730/31, BL Add. MS 47033, f. 3.

86. Margaret Beck Pritchard and Virginia Lascara Sites, *William Byrd II and His Lost History: Engravings of the Americas* (Williamsburg, Va.: Colonial Williamsburg Foundation, 1993), 102.

87. Tinling, 1: 61.

88. Nicholas Blundell to Richard Blundell, 23 September 1702, LRO DDBL acc 6121, f. 7; Nicholas Blundell to Richard Blundell, 2 September 1704, LRO DDBL acc 6121, f. 22.

89. Lord Petre to Peter Collinson, 9 May 1737, BL Add. MS 28726, f. 26v.

90. Cassandra Brydges to Mrs. Dunbar, 5 March 1723/4, HEH STB, Box 2, vol. 1, f. 89.

91. Armstrong, 36.

92. Armstrong, 37.

93. Davis, 65.

94. LS Mss 323b, f.195; Lord Richmond to Peter Collinson, 26 September 1762, BL Add. MS 28727, f. 88.

95. James Brydges to Capt Herring, 13 July 1724, HEH ST 57: 24, f. 144.

96. James Brydges to Capt Herring, 24 July 1724, HEH ST 57: 24, f. 164–65.

97. Edmund Ince to T. Hastings, 16 February 1668/9, HEH Hastings Correspondence, Box 27, HA 6971.

98. Emmanuel Moore to John Perceval, 6 March 1727/8, BL Add. MS 46979, f. 33.

99. Peter Collinson to Hans Sloane, undated, BL Sloane MS 4058, f. 170.

100. Mark Osteen, "Gift or Commodity?" in *The Question of the Gift: Essays Across Disciplines*, ed. Mark Osteen (London: Routledge, 2002), 229–47.

101. Kettering, 139.

102. James Brydges to Mr. Stratford, 24 September 1724, HEH ST 57: 24, f. 253.

103. James Brydges to Mr. Harper, 22 September 1724, HEH ST 57: 24, f. 249.

104. Lord Jersey to Peter Collinson, undated, BL Add. MS 28727, f. 140; Peter Collinson to Karl Linnaeus, 13 May 1739, BL Add. MS 28545, f. 140–140v.

105. Davis, 55–65.

106. Sarah Churchill, *The Private Correspondence of Sarah, Duchess of Marlborough* (London: Henry Colburn, 1838), 39.

107. James Brydges to Duchess of Marlborough, 17 September 1706, HEH ST 57: 1, f. 122.

108. William Perceval to John Perceval, 4 December 1729, BL Add. MS 47032, f. 146v–147; William Perceval to John Perceval, 12 January 1730/1, BL Add. MS 47033, f. 2v–3.

109. John Perceval to Philip Perceval, 11 June 1715, BL Add. MS 47028, f. 27v; Edward Southwell to John Perceval, 30 September 1707, BL Add. MS 47025, f. 78v.

110. Edward Southwell to John Perceval, 24 May 1709, BL Add. MS 47025, f. 121; Charles Dering to John Perceval, 11 September 1717, BL Add. MS 47028, f. 201.

111. Dierks, 57–58; Kettering, 135, 133; Whyman, *The Pen and the People*, 125; Whyman, "Paper Visits," 24.

112. John Joynes to T. Hastings, 11 March 1667/8, HEH Hastings Correspondence, Box 26, HA 7988.

113. W.P., *The flying post*, no pagination.

114. An inspection of the Hastings Correspondence from 1600 to 1660 shows the first service surfacing in 1605. On average about two services are noted per year. They peak quite strongly in the 1620s (36) and the 1650s (33). See HEH Hastings Correspondence, Boxes 5–31.

115. Wildeblood and Brison, 197.

116. Susan Brigden, *New Worlds, Lost Worlds: The Rule of the Tudors, 1485–1603* (New York: Penguin, 2000), 73–77.

117. John Joynes to T. Hastings, 11 March 1667/8, HEH Hastings Correspondence, Box 26, HA 7988.

118. John Joynes to T. Hastings, 11 March 1667/8, 18 November 1668, HEH Hastings Correspondence, Box 26, HA 7988, HA 7989; John Joynes to T. Hastings, 4 September 1669, 10 December 1669, HEH Hastings Correspondence, Box 27, HA 7990, HA 7991; John Joynes to T. Hastings, 20 September 1671, 9 November 1671, 15 November 1671, HEH Hastings Correspondence, Box 31, HA 7992, HA 7950, HA 7993.

119. Rosemary O'Day, ed., *Cassandra Brydges, Duchess of Chandos, 1670–1734: Life and Letters* (Woodbridge: Boydell, 2007), 14.

120. Edward Southwell to John Perceval, 24 May 1709, BL Add. MS 47025, f. 121; Charles Dering to John Perceval, 11 September 1717, BL Add. MS 47028, f. 201.

121. J. Palmer to John Perceval, 10 August 1706, BL Add. MS 47025, f. 66.

122. William Taylor to John Perceval, 7 October 1735, BL Add. MS 46986, f. 80.

123. James Brydges to William Brydges, 14 May 1694, HEH ST 57: 1, f. 12.

124. George Reid to Hans Sloane, 30 June 1690, BL Sloane MS 4036, f. 87.

125. Tinling, 1: 36.

126. James Brydges to A. Romswinkle, 25 April 1707, HEH ST 57: 1, f. 98; James Brydges to Mr. Drummond, 12 May 1707, HEH ST 57: 1, f. 111.

127. Daniel Dering to John Perceval, 25 June 1728, BL Add. MS 47032, f. 68.

128. Lady Rooke to John Perceval, 3 September 1729, BL Add. MS 47032, f. 135; B. Bourchier to Cassandra Willoughby, 22 May 1710, SRO, DR 1101/3.

129. Daniel Dering to John Perceval, 20 June 1728, BL Add. MS 47032, f. 64v.

130. Henry Newman to John Perceval, 30 March 1723, BL Add. MS 47030, f. 1v.

131. John Perceval to Robert Southwell, 18 December 1699, BL Add. MS 47025, f. 19v.

132. Lorenzo Magnolfi to John Perceval, 26 November 1709, BL Add. MS 47025, f. 142.

133. John Perceval to William Taylor, 25 January 1732/3, BL Add. MS 46984, f. 12; T. Medlycott to Edward Southwell, 22 July 1721, BL Add. MS 34778, f. 75v; John Perceval II to John Perceval I, 10 June 1727, BL Add. MS 47032, f. 17v.

134. William Wogan to Edward Southwell, 5 September 1710, BL Add. MS 37673, f. 107v.

135. William Byrd I mentioned toasts in eleven letters; James Brydges, duke of Chandos, noted toasting in six letters; in the correspondence of John Perceval toasts were mentioned twenty times; in the letters of Sir Hans Sloane they surfaced fifteen times; and the letters of Edward Southwell mentioned them ten times.

136. Peter Collinson to Cadwallader Colden, 24 June 1765, in Cadwallader Colden, *The Letters and Papers of Cadwallader Colden*, vol. 7 (New York: New-York Historical Society, 1923), 44.

137. Peter Clark, *The English Alehouse: A Social History, 1200–1830* (London: Longman, 1983), 212.

138. Peter Clark, *British Clubs and Societies, 1580–1800: The Origins of an Associational World* (Oxford: Clarendon, 2000), 163–64.

139. Clark, *The English Alehouse,* 212; Clark, *British Clubs and Societies*, 163–64, 226.

140. Uncle Dering to John Perceval, 17 March 1708/9, BL Add. MS 47025, f. 117v.

141. Tinling, 1: 208.

142. Daniel Dering to John Perceval, 13 October 1724, BL Add. MS 47030, f. 103.

143. Daniel Dering to John Perceval, 13 October 1724, BL Add. MS 47030, f. 103.

144. Mary Knatchbull to John Perceval, 25 June 1710, BL Add. MS 47026, f. 20v; Aunt Whorwood to John Perceval, 3 February 1727/8, BL Add. MS 47032, f. 57.

145. Daniel Dering to John Perceval, 18 July 1728, BL Add. MS 47032, f. 74.

146. Velters Cornwall to John Perceval, 28 May 1730, BL Add. MS 47032, f. 192.

147. Lorenzo Magnolfi to John Perceval, 12 June 1708, BL Add. MS 47025, f. 90.

148. Tinling, 1: 13, 19.

149. Nicholas Blundell to Henry Eyre, 19 September 1703, LRO DDBL acc 6121, f. 18.

Chapter 5. New Networks and Letters Less Familiar

1. John Perceval to William Taylor, 15 June 1734, BL Add. MS 46985, f. 23.

2. William Taylor to John Perceval, 25 June 1734, BL Add. MS 46985, f. 24.

3. John Perceval to William Taylor, 20 July 1734, BL Add. MS 46985, f. 27.

4. While many of Perceval's estate letter books have indexes, they are bound compilations of the original letters, not transcribed letters like those found in his personal letter books.

5. Mordechai Feingold, "Of Records and Grandeur: The Archive of the Royal Society," in *Archives of the Scientific Revolution*, ed. Michael Hunter (Woodbridge: Boydell, 1998), 176.

6. W. K. Lowther Clarke, *Eighteenth Century Piety* (London: SPCK, 1944), 37.

7. For merchant letters, see Toby Ditz, "Formative Ventures: 18th Century Commercial Letters and the Articulation of Experience," in *Epistolary Selves: Letters and Letter-Writers, 1600–1945*, ed. Rebecca Earle (Aldershot: Ashgate, 1999), 59–78; Toby L. Ditz, "Shipwrecked; or, Masculinity Imperiled: Mercantile Representations of Failure in Eighteenth-Century Philadelphia," *Journal of American History* 81, 1 (1994), 51–80; David Hancock, *Citizens of the World: London Merchants and the Integration of the British Atlantic Community, 1735–1785* (Cambridge: Cambridge University Press, 1995); David Hancock, "The Trouble with Networks: Managing the Scots' Early Modern Madeira Trade," *Business History Review* 79, 3 (Autumn 2005): 467–91; David Hancock, "The Triumphs of Mercury: Connection and Control in the Emerging Atlantic Economy," in *Soundings in Atlantic History: Latent Structures and Intellectual Currents, 1500–1830*, ed. Bernard Bailyn and Patricia L. Denault (Cambridge, Mass.: Harvard University Press, 2009), 112–40; Francesca Trivellato, *The Familiarity of Strangers: The Sephardic Diaspora, Livorno, and Cross-Cultural Trade in the Early Modern Period* (New Haven, Conn.: Yale University Press, 2009), 178–92. For works on estate agents and correspondence, see Peter Roebuck, "Absentee Landownership in the Late Seventeenth and Early Eighteenth Centuries: A Neglected Factor in English Agrarian History," *Agricultural History Review* 21 (1973): 1–21.

8. D. R. Hainsworth, *Stewards, Lords and People: The Estate Steward and His World in Later Stuart England* (Cambridge: Cambridge University Press, 1992), 14.

9. Toby Barnard, *A New Anatomy of Ireland: The Irish Protestants, 1649–1770* (New Haven, Conn.: Yale University Press, 2003), 29, 32–33, 208.

10. John Perceval to Philip Perceval, 29 November 1729, BL Add. MS 47032, f. 143v–144.

11. John Brewer, *The Sinews of Power: War, Money, and the English State, 1688–1783* (Cambridge, Mass.: Harvard University Press, 1988); James Rosenheim, *The Emergence of a Ruling Order: English Landed Society, 1650–1750* (London: Longman, 1998), 166–71.

12. Konstantin Dierks, *In My Power: Letter Writing and Communications in Early America* (Philadelphia: University of Pennsylvania Press, 2009), 12–23.

13. For the rise of the professions, see G. S. Holmes, *Augustan England: Professions, State, and Society 1680–1730* (London: Allen and Unwin, 1982); Penelope Corfield, *Power and the Professions in Britain 1700–1850* (London: Routledge, 1995).

14. John Perceval had four agents during his lifetime: William Taylor, Berkeley Taylor, another William Taylor, and Richard Purcell.

15. For the more open and free style, see Susan Whyman, *The Pen and the People: English Letter Writers, 1660–1800* (Oxford: Oxford University Press, 2009), 218; Sarah Pearsall, *Atlantic Families: Lives and Letters in the Later Eighteenth Century* (Oxford: Oxford University Press, 2008), 131. For changes in the way merchants used letters, see Dierks, 52–99.

16. Trivellato, 178–87.

17. I.W., *A Speedie Post* (London, 1629), 9.

18. T. Goodman, *The experienc'd secretary, or, Citizen and country-man's companion* (London, 1699), 67.

19. David Roberts, ed., *Lord Chesterfield's Letters* (Oxford: Oxford University Press, 1992), 244.

20. William Cooley to John Perceval II, 14 June 1745, BL Add. MS 47005A, f. 65.

21. John Perceval to Berkeley Taylor, 8 January 1715/6, BL Add. MS 46967, f. 1v.

22. William Taylor to John Perceval, 24 October 1732, BL Add. MS 46983, f. 92v.

23. James Brydges to Mr. Sweet, 14 March 1706/7, and James Brydges to Mr. Drummond, 14 March 1706/7, HEH ST 57: 1, f. 78.

24. Marion Tinling, ed., *The Correspondence of the Three William Byrds of Westover, Virginia, 1684–1776* (Charlottesville: University Press of Virginia, 1977), 1: 8.

25. Tinling, 1: 26.

26. Tinling, 1: 93.

27. Tinling, 1: 8, 28.

28. Tinling, 1: 63.

29. Tinling, 1: 30.

30. Richard Purcell to John Perceval, 25 February 1739/40, BL Add. MS 46991, f. 13.

31. John Perceval to William Taylor, 13 February 1744/5, BL Add. MS 46996, f. 31.

32. For problems with agents, see Barnard, 165–66; William Taylor to John Perceval, 6 July 1731, BL Add. MS 46982, f. 54.

33. Appendix, BL Add. MS 46997. This contrasts unfavorably with the recording of his father's death whom Perceval remembered as "formerly my steward, an upright gentleman." Appendix, BL Add. MS 46987.

34. Susan Dwyer Amussen, *Caribbean Exchanges: Slavery and the Transformation of English Society, 1640–1700* (Chapel Hill: University of North Carolina Press, 2007), 102–3.

35. Tinling, 1: 67.

36. John Perceval to William Taylor, 29 February 1727/8, BL Add. MS 46979, f. 31v.

37. John Perceval to Berkeley Taylor, 30 January 1717/8, BL Add. MS 46969, f. 2v.

38. John Perceval to William Taylor, 22 August 1736, BL Add. MS 46987, f. 62v–63. For a similar statement of trust, see John Perceval to Richard Purcell, 21 November 1745, BL Add. MS 46996, f. 113v.

39. See Will Freeman to John Perceval, 13 January 1729, BL Add. MS 46981, f. 6.

40. Richard Purcell to John Perceval, 14 May 1745, BL Add. MS 46996, f. 76v–77.

41. William Taylor to John Perceval, 14 November 1729, BL Add. MS 46980, f. 122.

42. Richard Purcell to John Perceval, 29 February 1747/8, BL Add. MS 46999, f. 29.

43. James Brydges to A. Romswinkle, 25 April 1707, HEH ST 57: 1, f. 98, and James Brydges to Mr. Drummond, 12 May 1707, HEH ST 57: 1, f. 111.

44. John Eliot to Schalckhauser Hugel and Jastram, 18 September 1756, LMA Acc 1017/950, f. 6v.

45. Dierks, 57–58; Hancock, "The Trouble with Networks," 479; Trivellato, 182.

46. Hancock, "The Trouble with Networks," 481; Pearsall, 162.

47. Tinling, 1: 351.

48. John Perceval to William Taylor, 3 July 1739, BL Add. MS 46990, f. 78.

49. John Perceval to Richard Purcell, 29 July 1738, BL Add. MS 46989, f. 105v.

50. James Brydges to Mr. Vincent, 20 September 1707, HEH ST 57: 1, f. 226.

51. James Brydges to Mr. Hallungius, 8 September 1707, HEH ST 57: 1, f. 222.

52. Tinling, 1: 115.

53. Tinling, 1: 155.

54. Tinling, 1: 8, 11, 31, 64, 87, 91.

55. Richard Purcell to John Perceval, 4 February 1747/8, BL Add. MS 46999, f. 23.

56. Tinling, 1: 56.

57. Hainsworth, 23–28.

58. John Perceval to William Taylor, 15 January 1736/7, BL Add. MS 46988, f. 4.

59. [no author], "A Book of Strangers," 1721, HEH Ch ST 59.

60. Tinling, 1: 67.

61. John Perceval to Richard Purcell, 11 February 1742/3, BL Add. MS 46994, f. 8v.

62. John Perceval to Richard Purcell, 29 March 1742/3, BL Add. MS 46994, f. 27.

63. Tinling, 1: 68.

64. Brewer, 245.

65. Joan Johnson, *Princely Chandos: James Brydges, 1674–1744* (Gloucester: Alan Sutton, 1984), 40.

66. Johnson, 40.

67. James Brydges to Mr. Sweet, 15 May 1707, HEH ST 57: 1, f. 124.

68. Lord Bolingbroke to Charles Boyle, 30 March 1711, Bod MS Eng. Letters e. 180, f. 97.

69. Brewer, 245.

70. James Brydges to Mr. Cardonnell, 30 June 1707, HEH ST 57: 1, f. 163.

71. Lord Bolingbroke to Charles Boyle, 25 September 1711, Bod MS Eng. Letters e. 4, f. 113.

72. Colin Brooks, "Interest, Patronage and Professionalism: John, 1st Baron Ashburnham, Hastings and the Revenue Services," *Southern History* 9 (1987): 51–70; Colin Brooks, "John, 1st Baron Ashburnham, and the State, c. 1688–1710," *Historical Research* 60, 141 (1987): 51–70.

73. G. E. Aylmer, "From Office-Holding to Civil Service: The Genesis of Modern Bureaucracy," *Transactions of the Royal Historical Society*, 5th ser., 30 (1980): 106.

74. Linda Colley, *Britons: Forging the Nation, 1707–1837* (New Haven, Conn.: Yale University Press, 1992); Jürgen Habermas, *The Structural Transformation of the Public*

Sphere, trans. Thomas Burger with the assistance of Fredrick Lawrence (Cambridge, Mass.: MIT Press, 1989).

75. Alexandra Shepard and Phil Withington, "Introduction: Communities in Early Modern England," in *Communities in Early Modern England*, ed. Alexandra Shepard and Phil Withington (Manchester: Manchester University Press, 2000), 11.

76. Bronwen Wilson and Paul Yachnin, "Introduction," in *Making Publics in Early Modern Europe: People, Things, Forms of Knowledge*, ed. Bronwen Wilson and Paul Yachnin (New York: Routledge, 2010), 1.

77. Craig Muldrew, "From a 'Light Cloak' to an 'Iron Cage': Historical Changes in the Relation Between Community and Individualism," in *Communities in Early Modern England*, ed. Shepard and Withington, 170.

78. Peter Clark, *British Clubs and Societies, 1580–1800: The Origins of an Associational World* (Oxford: Clarendon, 2000), 85.

79. Clark, 2.

80. Clark, 141–82. For distance and science, see David S. Lux and Harold J. Cook, "Closed Circles or Open Networks?: Communicating at a Distance During the Scientific Revolution," *History of Science* 36, 2 (June 1998): 196–203.

81. Clark, 69.

82. Clark, 449.

83. Perceval had become involved with the SPCK in 1710 at twenty-seven and became a member in 1720.

84. Leonard W. Cowie, *Henry Newman: An American in London, 1708–43* (London: SPCK, 1956), 21–52.

85. See BL Add. MS 46965–46971.

86. Peter Clark also found such intersections. Clark, 218, 448.

87. Clark, 64–66. For the reformation of manners, see Dudley Bahlman, *The Moral Revolution of 1688* (New Haven, Conn.: Yale University Press, 1957). For the transition from the "republic of letters" to a scientific and institutionally based society, see Robert H. Hatch, "Between Erudition and Science: The Archive and Correspondence of Ismael Boulliau," in *Archives of the Scientific Revolution*, ed. Hunter, 49–71.

88. For the best recent inspections of the establishment of the Royal Society, see Michael Hunter, *Establishing the New Science: The Experience of the Early Royal Society* (Woodbridge: Boydell, 1989); Michael Hunter, *Science and the Shape of Orthodoxy* (Woodbridge: Boydell, 1995), 120–34; James E. McClellan, *Science Reorganized: Scientific Societies in the Eighteenth Century* (New York: Columbia University Press, 1985). For a broader view of the world of science and its changes during this period, see David S. Lux, "The Reorganization of Science 1450–1700," in *Patronage and Institutions: Science, Technology, and Medicine at the European Court, 1500–1750*, ed. Bruce T. Moran (Rochester, N.Y.: Boydell, 1991), 185–94.

89. Hunter, *Science and the Shape of Orthodoxy*, 121–24.

90. H. P. Thompson, *Thomas Bray* (London: SPCK, 1954), 36–42; E. G. Rupp, *Religion in England, 1688–1791*(Oxford: Clarendon, 1986), 299.

91. Herbert Butterfield, *The Origins of Modern Science* (New York: Free Press, 1957), 31; Steven Shapin, *The Scientific Revolution* (Chicago: University of Chicago Press, 1996), 19–20.

92. Thomas Sprat, *History of the Royal Society*, ed. Jackson I. Cope and Harold Witmore Jones (St. Louis: Washington University Press, 1958), 383.

93. Alan Armstrong, ed., *"Forget not Mee & My Garden . . .": Selected Letters, 1725–1768, of Peter Collinson, F.R.S.* (Philadelphia: American Philosophical Society, 2002), 119.

94. R. Middleton Massey to Hans Sloane, 23 November 1717, BL Sloane MS 4045, f. 73.

95. Thompson, 13–26.

96. John Perceval was a member of both. Clark, 448.

97. Marie Boas Hall, *Promoting Experimental Learning: Experiment and the Royal Society, 1660–1727* (Cambridge: Cambridge University Press, 1991); Hunter, *Science and the Shape of Orthodoxy*, 120–34.

98. Michael Hunter, *The Royal Society and Its Fellows, 1660–1700: The Morphology of an Early Scientific Institution*, 2nd ed. (London: British Society for the History of Science, 1994), 27; McClellan, 158.

99. Hunter, *Science and the Shape of Orthodoxy*, 131; Feingold, 172, 176.

100. 26 October 1699, Notes by Chamberlayne and Newman on SPCK Business, Bod MS Rawl C 844, f. 6v.

101. 2 November 1699, Notes by Chamberlayne and Newman on SPCK Business, Bod MS Rawl C 844, f. 7–8.

102. 8 February 1699, 9 May 1700, Notes by Chamberlayne and Newman on SPCK Business, Bod MS Rawl C 844, f. 16, 25v; Henry Newman to Mr. Tomlinson, 28 January 1719/20, Cambridge University Library, Manuscripts Collection, SPCK MS D4/9, f. 26.

103. William Gibson, ed., *Religion and Society in England and Wales, 1689–1800* (London: Leicester University Press, 1998), 60–62. This selection in Gibson's anthology of documents is from M. Clement, *Correspondence and Minutes of the SPCK Relating to Wales, 1699–1740* (Cardiff: University of Wales Press, 1952).

104. Cowie, 35–36.

105. John Perceval to Henry Newman, 14 June 1724, BL Add. MS 47030, f. 69.

106. For example, see Henry Hoare to Henry Newman, 28 June 1711, Bod MS Rawl D 839, f. 72; Peter Lavigne to Henry Newman, 12 April 1710, Bod MS Rawl D 839, f. 89.

107. Clark, 65.

108. This network was created not from Sloane's official correspondence but that which he kept in his private hands and is held at the British Library.

109. Hunter, *Establishing the New Science*, 253.

110. 2 May, 28 March 1700, Notes by Chamberlayne and Newman on SPCK Business, Bod MS Rawl C 844, f. 25, 21.

111. Charles Kinnard to Hans Sloane, 10 October 1705, BL Sloane MS 4040, f. 77v.

112. Peter Collinson to E. M. da Costa, 18 December 1750, BL Add. MS 28536, f. 62; Nicholas Martin to Hans Sloane, 20 December 1717, BL Sloane MS 4045, f. 83; James

Yonge to Hans Sloane, 18 September 1716, BL Sloane MS 4044, f. 218; R. Middleton Massey to Hans Sloane, 23 November 1717, BL Sloane MS 4045, f. 73.

113. Steven Shapin, *A Social History of Truth: Civility and Science in Seventeenth-Century England* (Chicago: University of Chicago Press, 1994), 42.

114. John Perceval to Henry Newman, 6 November 1723, BL Add. MS 47030, f. 33v; Henry Newman to John Perceval, 1 December 1726, BL Add. MS 47031, f. 213.

115. Hunter, *The Royal Society and Its Fellows*, 14; John Chamberlayne to John Perceval, 15 June 1710, BL Add. MS 47026, f.16v.

116. Henry Newman to Zech Gee, 19 January 1719/20, Cambridge University Library, Manuscript Collection, SPCK MS D4/9.

117. Mr. Pitcarn to Hans Sloane, 29 September 1701, BL Sloane MS 4038, f. 247.

118. Ralph Thoresby to Hans Sloane, 29 May 1703, BL Sloane MS 4039, f. 136.

119. J. Burnet to Hans Sloane, no date, BL Sloane MS 4058, f. 83.

120. Ralph Thoresby to Hans Sloane, 23 May 1715, BL Sloane MS 4044, f. 48.

121. Abraham de la Pryme to Hans Sloane, 1 December 1701, BL Sloane MS 4038, f. 271.

122. John Perceval to Henry Newman, 2 March 1722/3, BL Add. MS 47029, f. 156; John Perceval to Henry Newman, 9 March 1722/3, BL Add. MS 47029, f. 161–161v; John Perceval to Henry Newman, 22 September 1725, BL Add. MS 47031, f. 12.

123. Henry Newman to John Perceval, 21 October 1725, BL Add. MS 47031, f. 23.

124. For information on the involvement of the SPCK with the African princes, see the letters recorded by John Perceval between December 1721 and December 1722 found in BL Add. MS 47029. For letters about and by John Barrett, the fake convert, see letters between 23 April 1722 and 23 March 1722/3, BL Add. MS 47029, and letters between 30 March 1723 and 25 August 1724, BL Add. MS 47030.

125. BL Add. MS 47029, f. 98.

126. Cowie, 40.

127. Geoffroy to Hans Sloane, 7 March 1699, BL Sloane MS 4037, f. 222; Lux and Cook, 196–98.

128. McClellan, 158, 180, 208–14, 216–20.

129. McClellan, 51, 155–57, 159–60, 161–62, 180.

130. 2 May 1700, Notes by Chamberlayne and Newman on SPCK Business, Bod MS Rawl C 844, f. 24v.

131. Clark, 453–54.

132. *Philosophical Transactions* went unprinted after Oldenburg's death until 1683, when it was revived, and it is still printed today. Hunter, *The Royal Society and Its Fellows*, 43–44.

133. Hunter, *Science and the Shape of Orthodoxy*, 130.

134. Anne Goldgar, *Impolite Learning: Conduct and Community in the Republic of Letters, 1680–1750* (New Haven, Conn.: Yale University Press, 1995), 54–114; McClellan, 53.

135. For other publications with similar consequences, see Natasha Glaisyer, "Readers, Correspondents and Communities: John Houghton's *A Collection for Improvement of*

Husbandry and Trade (1692–1703)," in *Communities in Early Modern England*, ed. Shepard and Withington, 235–51; Helen Barry, "An Early Coffee House Periodical and Its Readers: The *Athenian Mercury*, 1691–1697," *London Journal* 25, 1 (2000): 14–33.

136. Kevin Hayes, *The Library of William Byrd of Westover* (Madison, Wis.: Madison House, 1997), 152–55.

Chapter 6. Stirring News and the Role of the Letter

1. James Brydges to Mr. Hallungius, 25 July 1707, HEH ST 57: 1, f. 197; William Percival to John Perceval, 17 March 1710/11, BL Add. MS 47026, f. 62v; Philip Percival to John Perceval, 28 November 1730, BL Add. MS 47032, f. 241v.

2. Philip Percival to John Perceval, 22 September 1723, BL Add. MS 47030, f. 17; Philip Percival to John Perceval, 8 December 1723, BL Add. MS 47030, f. 44v.

3. James Morgan to James Brydges, 25 November 1700, HEH ST 58: 1, f. 16.

4. Edward Husband, *A briefe relation of some affaires and transactions, civill and military, both forraigne and domestique*, 9 October 1649, issue 2, 1.

5. For the emergence of the newspaper during the English Civil Wars see Joad Raymond, *The Invention of the Newspaper: English Newsbooks, 1641–1649* (Oxford: Clarendon Press, 1996), 81, 119–26; David Zaret, *Origins of Democratic Culture: Printing, Petitions, and the Public Sphere in Early-Modern England* (Princeton, N.J.: Princeton University Press, 2000).

6. Brendan Dooley, "Introduction," in *The Politics of Information in Early Modern Europe*, ed. Brendan Dooley and Sabrina A. Baron (London: Routledge, 2001), 3.

7. Laurence Hanson, *Government and the Press, 1695–1763* (Oxford: Oxford University Press, 1936); Peter Fraser, *The Intelligence of the Secretaries of State and Their Monopoly of Licensed News, 1660–1688* (Cambridge: Cambridge University Press, 1956); F. S. Siebert, *Freedom of the Press in England, 1476–1776* (Urbana: University of Illinois Press, 1952); Jason McElligott, "'A Couple of Hundred Squabbling Small Tradesmen'? Censorship, the Stationers' Company, and the State in Early Modern England," in *News Networks in Seventeenth-Century Britain and Europe*, ed. Joad Raymond (London: Routledge, 2006).

8. Raymond, *The Invention*, 115; C. John Sommerville, *The News Revolution in England: Cultural Dynamics of Daily Information* (Oxford: Oxford University Press, 1996), 4; Daniel Woolf, "News, History and the Construction of the Present in Early Modern England," in *Politics of Information*, ed. Dooley and Baron, 86–88. For a later period, see Benedict Anderson, *Imagined Communities: Reflections on the Origin and Spread of Nationalism*, rev. ed. (1983; London: Verso, 1991), 34–36.

9. Sabrina Baron, "The Guises of Dissemination in Early 17th C. England: News in Manuscript and Print," in *Politics of Information*, ed. Dooley and Baron, 51–56; Adam Fox, *Oral and Literate Culture in England, 1500–1700* (Oxford: Clarendon, 2000), 336; F. J. Levy, "How Information Spread Among the Gentry, 1550–1640," *Journal of British Studies* 21, 2 (Spring 1982): 22; Henry L. Snyder, "Newsletters in England, 1689–1715, with Special Reference to John Dyer—A Byway in the History of England," in *Newsletters to*

Newspapers: Eighteenth Century Journalism, ed. Donovan H. Bond and W. Reynolds McLeod (Morgantown: School of Journalism, West Virginia University, 1977); Sommerville, 43; Filippo de Vivo, "Paolo Sarpi and the Uses of Information in Seventeenth Century Venice," in *News Networks*, ed. Raymond, 41.

10. Robert Darnton, "An Early Information Society: News and the Media in Eighteenth-Century Paris," *American Historical Review* 105, 1 (February 2000): 1–35; Donald McKenzie, *Bibliography and the Sociology of Texts* (Cambridge: Cambridge University Press, 1999); William Slauter, "News and Diplomacy in the Age of the American Revolution" (Ph.D. dissertation, Princeton University, 2007), 11; Joad Raymond, ed., *News Networks in Seventeenth Century Britain and Europe* (London: Routledge, 2006).

11. For news in letters, see Eve Tavor Bannet, *Empire of Letters: Letter Manuals and Transatlantic Correspondence, 1688–1820* (Cambridge: Cambridge University Press, 2005), 12–13, 57; Clare Brant, *Eighteenth-Century Letters and British Culture* (New York: Palgrave Macmillan, 2006), 172–96; James Daybell, *Women Letter-Writers in Tudor England* (Oxford: Oxford University Press, 2006), 152–57, 165; Dena Goodman, *The Republic of Letters: A Cultural History of the French Enlightenment* (Ithaca, N.Y.: Cornell University Press, 1994), 117, 142; Levy, 21–22; David Randall, "Joseph Mead, Novellante: News, Sociability, and Credibility in Early Stuart England," *Journal of British Studies* 45, 2 (April 2006): 293–312; Gary Schneider, *The Culture of Epistolarity: Vernacular Letters and Letter Writing in Early Modern England, 1500–1700* (Newark: University of Delaware Press, 2005), 27, 145–74; Vivo, 37; Susan Whyman, *The Pen and the People: English Letter Writers, 1660–1800* (Oxford: Oxford University Press, 2009), 66–68.

12. Philip Perceval to John Perceval, 28 November 1730, BL Add. MS 47032, f. 241v.

13. Jürgen Habermas, *The Structural Transformation of the Public Sphere*, trans. Thomas Burger with the assistance of Fredrick Lawrence (Cambridge, Mass.: MIT Press, 1989), 20–22.

14. Norman Davis, ed., *Paston Letters and Papers of the Fifteenth Century* (Oxford: Oxford University Press, 2004), 28.

15. I.W., *A Speedie Post* (London, 1629); W.P., *A Flying Post* (London, 1678), 40.

16. Peter Collinson II to Peter Collinson I and Elizabeth Collinson, 29 August 1738, BL Add. MS 28726, f. 51.

17. James Brydges to Mr. Romwinkle, 9 May 1707, Hunt ST 57: 1, f. 107.

18. Philip Perceval to John Perceval, 20 September 1709, BL Add. MS 47025, f. 133.

19. Henry Hastings, fifth Earl of Huntington, to unknown, 6 November [1605], HEH Hastings Correspondence, Box 5, HA 5416; John Harington to Henry Hastings, fifth Earl of Huntingdon, 7 November 1605, HEH Hastings Correspondence, Box 5, HA 4582.

20. For early letters of news from Gervase Jaques to Theophilus Hastings, seventh earl of Huntingdon, see HEH Hastings Correspondence, Box 21, HA 7644, 7645, 7646. For the letter mentioning better hands, see Gervase Jaques to Theophilus Hastings, 25 April 1665, HEH Hastings Correspondence, Box 24, HA 7649.

21. Henry Muddiman to T. Hastings, 5 October 1669, HEH Hastings Correspondence, Box 27, HA 9599.

22. Henry Muddiman to T. Hastings, 8 November 1670, HEH Hastings Correspondence, Box 29, HA 9610.

23. Henry Newman to John Perceval, 17 January 1722/3, BL Add. MS 47029, f. 148; Philip Percival to John Perceval, 28 November 1730, BL Add. MS 47032, f. 241v; George Berkeley to John Perceval, 16 April 1713, BL Add. MS 47027, f. 25v.

24. George Berkeley to John Perceval, 16 April 1713, BL Add. MS 47027, f. 25v.

25. John Perceval to Lord Castlecomer, 16 June 1713, BL Add. MS 47027, f. 38v.

26. John Brewer, *The Sinews of Power: War, Money and the English State, 1688–1783* (Cambridge, Mass.: Harvard University Press), 230.

27. For example, see John Perceval to Lord Tullamore, 3 January 1715/6, BL Add. MS 47028, f. 115v.

28. John Perceval II to John Perceval I, 13 May 1730, BL Add. MS 47032, f. 181

29. Marion Tinling, ed., *The Correspondence of the Three William Byrds of Westover, Virginia, 1684–1776* (Charlottesville: University Press of Virginia, 1977), 1: 367.

30. An inspection of the *Boston News-Letter*, *Evening Post*, and *Newcastle Courant* for six months in 1724 and 1725 reveals that these were frequent news topics.

31. Edward Southwell to John Perceval, 7 April 1713, BL Add. MS 47027, f. 22; Velters Cornewall to John Perceval, 12 May 1730, BL Add. MS 47032, f. 182; John Perceval to Charles Dering, 4 July 1716, BL Add. MS 47028, f. 159v.

32. John Perceval to Charles Dering, 18 February 1717/8, BL Add. MS 47028, f. 226.

33. John Perceval II to John Perceval I, 13 May 1730, BL Add. MS 47032, f. 181.

34. John Perceval to William Byrd II, 3 December 1729, BL Add. MS 47032, f. 146v.

35. William Gould to Hans Sloane, 25 January 1680/1, BL Sloane MS 4036, f. 1v.

36. George Berkeley to John Perceval, 19 February 1713/4, BL Add. MS 47027, f. 76v.

37. George Berkeley to John Perceval, 17 November 1715, BL Add. MS 47028, f. 105.

38. Thomas Knatchbull to John Perceval, June 1700, BL Add. MS 47025, f. 29.

39. George Berkeley to John Perceval, 4 February 1714, BL Add. MS 47027, f. 71v.

40. John Perceval to George Berkeley, 8 April 1714, BL Add. MS 47027, f. 86v–87v.

41. Edward Southwell to John Perceval, 7 April 1713, BL Add. MS 47027, f. 22

42. Daniel Dering to John Perceval, 19 July 1715, BL Add. MS 47028, f. 41; George Berkeley to John Perceval, 17 November 1715, BL Add. MS 47028, f. 104v.

43. John Perceval to Robert Southwell, 14 December 1699, BL Add. MS 47025, f. 19.

44. George Berkeley to John Perceval, 28 July 1715, BL Add. MS 47028, f. 43v.

45. Tinling, 1: 367.

46. Daybell, 165; Schneider, 157.

47. John Perceval to Thomas Knatchbull, 11 March 1701/2, BL Add. MS 47025, f. 56.

48. Thomas Knatchbull to John Perceval, 2 November 1700, BL Add. MS 47025, f. 35.

49. William Percival to John Perceval, 17 March 1710/11, BL Add. MS 47026, f. 62v.

50. John Perceval to Matthew Buchanan, 13 May 1721, BL Add. MS 47029, f. 60.

51. Charles Dering to John Perceval, 11 April 1722, BL Add. MS 47029, f. 114.

52. Cassandra Brydges to Henry Brydges, [no date], HEH STB Box 2, vol. 1, f. 126.

53. Cassandra Brydges to Mr. Moore, 15 September 1735, SRO DR 1101/3.

54. Journal of James Brydges, 20 April 1698, HEH ST 26: 1.

55. John Anstis Garter to Hans Sloane, 24 March 1715/6, BL Sloane MS 4044, f. 145; Thomas Isted to Hans Sloane, 2 August 1722, BL Sloane MS 4046, f. 275.

56. For example, see John Perceval to Edward Southwell II, 29 July 1729, BL Add. MS 47032, f. 128.

57. Tinling, 2: 560.

58. Nicholas Blundell to Mary Blundell, 1 and 5 March 1706/7, LRO DDBL acc 6121, f. 57.

59. See James Waller to Edward Southwell, 22 May 1693, BL Add. MS 38147, f. 23; James Waller to Edward Southwell, 22 December 1693, BL Add. MS 38147, f. 56.

60. Brendan Dooley, *The Social History of Skepticism* (Baltimore: Johns Hopkins University Press, 1999); Martin Nevitt, "Ben Jonson and the Serial Publication of News," in *News Networks*, ed. Raymond, 53–55; David Randall, *Credibility in Elizabethan and Early Stuart Military News* (London: Pickering and Chatto, 2008); Randall, "Joseph Mead," 293–312; Schneider, 146–49.

61. R. Thayer, ed., *The Genuine Remains in Verse and Prose of Mr. Samuel Butler*, vol. 2 (London, 1759), 296.

62. Donald Bond, ed., *The Spectator* (Oxford: Clarendon, 1965), 5:137.

63. *Newcastle Courant*, 18 July 1724, issue 213, *Early English Newspapers* (microfilm) S 1460, 1022: 7–8.

64. William Byrd II to John Custis, 16 May 1719, VHS Mss1 L5114 a 22.

65. Egmont Newsletters, 13 August 1724, BL Add. MS 47078, f. 117v.

66. Philip Percival to John Perceval, 2 May 1707, BL Add. MS 47025, f. 72v; William Cadogan to James Brydges, 15 May 1707, HEH ST 58:1, f. 166.

67. Edward Southwell to John Perceval, 4 March 1711/2, BL Add. MS 47026, f. 115v.

68. George Berkeley to John Perceval, 6 July 1715, BL Add. MS 47028, f. 32–32v.

69. Slauter, 65–89.

70. William Cadogan to James Brydges, 15 May 1707, HEH ST 58: 1, f. 165.

71. James Morgan to James Brydges, 25 November 1700, HEH ST 58: 1, f. 16.

72. See Steven Shapin and Simon Schaffer, *Leviathan and the Air-Pump: Hobbes, Boyle, and the Experimental Life* (Princeton, N.J.: Princeton University Press, 1985), 55–65; Steven Shapin, *A Social History of Truth: Civility and Science in Seventeenth-Century England* (Chicago: University of Chicago Press, 1994), 42.

73. Randall, "Joseph Mead," 302–4.

74. *Newcastle Courant*, 1 August 1724, issue 214, *Early English Newspapers* (microfilm) S 1460, 1022: 1.

75. *Evening Post*, 7–9 July 1724, issue 2333, *Early English Newspapers* (microfilm) S 1460, 123:1.

76. Quoted in Keith Thomas, "Literacy in Early Modern England," in *The Written Word*, ed. Gerd Baumann (Oxford: Clarendon, 1986), 112.

77. John Perceval to Matthew Buchanan, 13 May 1721, BL Add. MS 47029, f. 60; Captain Worth to John Perceval, 20 September 1724, BL Add. MS 47030, f. 100v.

78. Peter Barwick to Hans Sloane, 11 January 1689/90, BL Sloane MS 4036, f. 66.

79. Tinling, 1: 232.

80. Daniel Dering to John Perceval, 1 July 1729, BL Add. MS 47032, f. 123.

81. Alan Armstrong, ed., *"Forget not Mee & My Garden . . .": Selected Letters, 1725–1768, of Peter Collinson, F.R.S.* (Philadelphia: American Philosophical Society, 2002), 204.

82. John Perceval II to Catherine Perceval, 17 October 1730, BL Add. MS 47032, f. 235.

83. George Rooke to James Brydges, 8 June 1703, HEH ST 58: 1, f. 34; James Morgan to James Brydges, 25 November 1700, HEH ST 58: 1, f. 17.

84. *Evening Post*, 18–21 July 1724, issue 2338, *Early English Newspapers* (microfilm) S 1460, 123:1.

85. Captain Worth to John Perceval, 20 September 1724, BL Add. MS 47030, f. 100v.

86. Egmont Newsletters, 24 October 1724, BL Add. MS 47078, f. 179v; *Evening Post*, 13–15 August 1724, issue 2349, *Early English Newspapers* (microfilm) S 1460, 123: 2; *Newcastle Courant*, 31 October 1724, issue 228, *Early English Newspapers* (microfilm) S 1460, 1022: 10.

87. John Perceval to Lord Tullamore, 3 January 1715/6, BL Add. MS 47028, f. 115v.

88. Daniel Dering to John Perceval, 23 March 1722/3, BL Add. MS 47029, f. 163–163v.

89. John Perceval to Berkeley Taylor, 30 April 1719, BL Add. MS 46970, f. 47b; Mr. Gouge to John Perceval, 18 June 1707, BL Add. MS 47025, f. 75v–76v.

90. John Perceval to Charles Dering, 21 September 1721, BL Add. MS 47029, f. 70v.

91. T. Medlycott to Edward Southwell, 12 May 1721, BL Add. MS 34778, f. 44–44v.

92. William Byrd II to John Custis, 16 May 1719, VHS Mss 1 L5114 a 22.

93. James Waller to Edward Southwell, 22 May 1693, BL Add. MS 38147, f. 23; James Waller to Edward Southwell, 22 December 1693, BL Add. MS 38147, f. 56.

94. Also see Randall, "Joseph Mead," 306–11.

95. William Cadogan to James Brydges, 21 September 1706, HEH ST 58: 1, f. 1; Charles Dering to John Perceval, 21 December 1717, BL Add. MS 47028, f. 215.

96. Shapin, 42.

97. Philip Percival to John Perceval, 2 May 1707, BL Add. MS 47025, f. 72v.

98. Philip Percival to John Perceval, 4 August 1707, BL Add. MS 47025, f. 77v.

99. Digby Cotes to John Perceval, 21 February 1700/01, BL Add. MS 47025, f. 39.

100. Alan Marshall, *Intelligence and Espionage in the Reign of Charles II, 1660–1685* (Cambridge: Cambridge University Press, 1994), 96–115.

101. John Drummond to James Brydges, 20 November 1705, HEH ST 58: 1, f. 47v.

102. Louis B. Wright and Marion Tinling, eds., *The London Diary (1717–1721) and Other Writings* (New York: Oxford University Press, 1958), 265–66, 269, 271–73.

103. William Byrd II to John Custis, 16 May 1719, VHS Mss 1 L5114 a 22.

104. Tinling, 2: 461.

105. John Perceval to William Percival, 28 December 1730, BL Add. MS 47032, f. 262.

106. John Perceval to George Berkeley, 23 December 1730, BL Add. MS 47032, f. 257v. The friend, Daniel Dering, died in Leiden on 13 September 1730.

107. For other considerations of the speed of colonial news, see Richard D. Brown, *Knowledge Is Power: The Diffusion of Information in Early America, 1700–1865* (New York: Oxford University Press, 1989), 42–64; Ian K. Steele, *The English Atlantic, 1675–1740: An Exploration of Communication and Community* (New York: Oxford University Press, 1986), 132–67, 213, 270.

108. Maude H. Woodfin, ed., *Another Secret Diary of William Byrd of Westover, 1739–1741 with Letters & Literary Exercises, 1696–1726*, trans. and collated Marion Tinling (Richmond, Va.: Dietz Press, 1942), 10, 109.

109. Woodfin, 49.

110. Woodfin, 126.

111. Woodfin, 14, 80, 120.

112. For example, see Woodfin, 61.

113. Woodfin, 42.

114. Woodfin, 159.

115. Between 1737 and 1738 most ships arrived in Virginia between February and July. Steele, 292.

116. Woodfin, 10.

117. Woodfin, 129, 135.

118. Woodfin, 144, 149.

119. Woodfin, 144, 149.

120. Woodfin, 61.

121. William Byrd II to John Randolph, 21 January 1735, VHS Mss5:2 B9966:3, f. 33.

122. William Byrd II to John Randolph, 23 June 1736, VHS Mss5:2 B9966:3, f. 45.

123. William Byrd II to Mr. Lamport, 23 August 1735, VHS Mss5:2 B9966:3, f. 18.

124. Tinling, 1: 146.

125. Tinling, 1: 145.

126. Tinling, 1: 97.

127. Tinling, 1: 429.

128. Tinling, 1: 136.

129. Tinling, 1: 136.

130. John Perceval to William Byrd II, 3 December 1729, BL Add. MS 47032, f. 145.

131. George Berkeley to John Perceval, 30 August 1729, BL Add. MS 47032, f. 132.

132. George Berkeley to John Perceval, 2 March 1730/31, BL Add. MS 47033, f. 32.

133. Newport did have a paper, the *Rhode Island Gazette*, between 1732 and 1733. Charles Clark, *The Public Prints: The Newspaper in Anglo-American Culture, 1665–1740* (New York: Oxford University Press, 1994), 268.

134. John Perceval to George Berkeley, 23 December 1730, BL Add. MS 47032, f. 257v.

135. Tinling, 1: 395; William Byrd II to unknown, 27 June 1729, VHS Mss5:2 B9966:2, f. 39.

136. Tinling 1: 362.

137. Tinling, 1: 364.

138. Tinling, 1: 364.

139. Tinling, 1: 365.

140. John Chamberlayne to John Perceval, 22 June 1718, BL Add. MS 47028, f. 234.

141. John Perceval to Mr. Forster, 17 January 1722/3, BL Add. MS 47029, f. 147.

142. William Wogan to Edward Southwell, 29 April 1712, BL Add. MS 37674, f. 43.

143. *Boston News-Letter*, 10–17 June 1725, issue 1116, *Early American Newspapers* (microfilm) An M382: 1.

144. A. Romswinckle to James Brydges, 10 May 1707, HEH ST 58: 1, f. 161; Cassandra Willoughby to the Marchioness of Worcester, undated, SRO DR 18/20/21/2.

145. Cassandra Brydges to Anne Coventry, Countess of Coventry, 7 June 1735, HEH STB Box 2: 1, f. 258; Daniel Dering to John Perceval, 30 June 1715, BL Add. MS 47028, f. 30; J. Roby to Edward Southwell, 26 June 1705, BL Add. MS 60582, f. 48.

146. Jürgen Habermas, *The Structural Transformation of the Public Sphere*, trans. Thomas Burger with the assistance of Fredrick Lawrence (Cambridge, Mass.: MIT Press, 1989), 32. Also see Brian Cowan, *The Social Life of Coffee: The Emergence of the British Coffeehouse* (New Haven, Conn.: Yale University Press, 2005); Lawrence E. Klein, "Coffeehouse Civility, 1660–1714: An Aspect of Post-Courtly Culture in England," *Huntington Library Quarterly* 59, 1 (1996): 30–51; Steven Pincus, "'Coffee Politicians Does Create': Coffeehouses and Restoration Political Culture," *Journal of Modern History* 67, 4 (December 1995): 807–34.

147. Journal of James Brydges, 7 April 1697; 22 June 1697, HEH ST 26:1.

148. Journal of James Brydges, 16 March 1697, HEH ST 26:1.

149. John Perceval to Mr. Forster, 17 January 1722/3, BL Add. MS 47029, f. 147v.

150. Woodfin, 75.

151. John Perceval to Thomas Knatchbull, 11 March 1701/2, BL Add. MS 47025, f. 56.

152. Egmont Newsletters, 22 December 1724, BL Add. MS 47078, f. 229v.

153. Wl. Konopczyński, "Early Saxon Period, 1697–1733," in *The Cambridge History of Poland, 1697–1935*, ed. W. F. Reddaway, J. H. Penson et al. (Cambridge: Cambridge University Press, 1951), 18, and J. Tazbir, "The Commonwealth in the Years of Crisis (1648–1696)," in *History of Poland*, ed. Aleksander Gieysztor, Stefan Kieniewicz et al. (Warsaw: PWN-Polish Scientific Publishers, 1968), 298–99.

154. John Perceval to Mr. Worth, 24 December 1724, BL Add. MS 47030, f. 121v–122v.

155. Egmont Newsletters, 22 December 1724, BL Add. MS 47078, f. 229.

156. *Evening Post*, 19–22 December 1724, issue 2404, *Early English Newspapers* (microfilm) S 1460, 123: 1.

157. John Perceval to Captain Worth, 24 December 1724, BL Add. MS 47030, f. 122–122v.

158. BL Add. MS 47059, f. 3, 17.

159. Captain Worth to John Perceval, 8 March 1724/5, BL Add. MS 47030, f. 139v–140.

160. Tinling, 1: 145.

161. Tinling, 1: 21.

162. Armstrong, 191, 193.

163. John Perceval to Berkeley Taylor, 30 April 1719, BL Add. MS 46970, f. 47v; John Perceval to Berkeley Taylor, 23 October 1725, BL Add. MS 46976, f. 86v.

164. Charles Dering to John Perceval, 3 January 1715/6, BL Add. MS 47028, f. 114–114v; Edward Southwell to John Perceval, 26 April 1709, BL Add. MS 47025, f. 119.

165. Philip Percival to John Perceval, 5 January 1719/20, BL Add. MS 47029, f. 1v.

Postscript

1. Alan Armstrong, ed., *"Forget not Mee & My Garden . . .": Selected Letters, 1725–1768, of Peter Collinson, F.R.S.* (Philadelphia: American Philosophical Society, 2002), 281–82.

2. E.A. Wrigley, "A Simple Model of London's Importance in Changing English Society and Economy, 1650–1750," *Past & Present* 37 (July 1967): 44.

3. Quoted in S. J. Connolly, *Religion, Law and Power: The Making of Protestant Ireland, 1660–1760* (Oxford: Clarendon, 1992), 44.

4. Armstrong, 245.

5. For the career of William Byrd III, see Marion Tinling, ed., *The Correspondence of the Three William Byrds of Westover, Virginia, 1684–1776* (Charlottesville: University Press of Virginia, 1977), 2: 606–9.

6. Armstrong, 245.

7. For John Perceval II's letters on this, see BL Add. MSS 47053–47054A.

8. For details on the life of the second earl, see Clive Wilkinson, "Perceval, John, Second Earl of Egmont (1711–1770)," *Oxford Dictionary of National Biography*, online ed., February 2014.

9. For Sloane's son-in-law, Charles Cadogan, see the entry for his elder brother, William, *Oxford Dictionary of National Biography*. James Falkner, "Cadogan, William, Earl Cadogan (1671/2–1726)," *Oxford Dictionary of National Biography*, online ed., Febrary 2014.

10. Cannons would be torn down between 1747 and 1748 to pay off the debts the family had accumulated. Joan Johnson, "Brydges, James, First Duke of Chandos (1674–1744)," *Oxford Dictionary of National Biography*, online ed., Febrary 2014.

11. John Burke, *A Genealogical and Heraldic Dictionary of the Landed Gentry of Great Britain and Ireland*, vol. 1 (London: Henry Colburn, 1847), 114. Francis Blundell, who died in 1936, helped push through the Roman Catholic Relief Act of 1926, which ended any laws pertaining to the restriction of Catholicism. Brian Whitlock Blundell, "Blundell,

Francis Nicholas Joseph (1880–1936)," *Oxford Dictionary of National Biography*, online ed., February 2014.

12. John Perceval, second earl of Egmont, did leave behind a number of letter books mostly detailing his estate and official business. See BL Add. MSS 47001A–47014B.

13. Howard Robinson, *The British Post Office: A History* (Princeton, N.J.: Princeton University Press, 1948), 109.

14. Robinson, 105.

15. Alexander Pope referred to Allen in a poem as "low born," although this was later changed to "humble." See Brenda J. Buchanan, "Allen, Ralph (*bap.* 1693, *d.* 1764)," *Oxford Dictionary of National Biography*, online ed., Febrary 2014.

16. See especially Peter Borsay, *The English Urban Renaissance* (Oxford: Clarendon Press, 1989); Lawrence Klein, *Shaftsbury and the Culture of Politeness* (Cambridge: Cambridge University Press, 1994); James Rosenheim, *The Emergence of a Ruling Order: English Landed Society, 1650–1750* (London: Longman, 1998); L. Stone and J. Stone, *An Open Elite? England 1540–1880* (Oxford: Clarendon, 1984), 3–5; Susan Whyman, *Sociability and Power in Late-Stuart England* (Oxford: Oxford University Press, 1999).

17. For scholars who have noted the importance of mobility, see Alison Games, *The Web of Empire: English Cosmopolitans in an Age of Expansion, 1560–1660* (Oxford: Oxford University Press, 2008); J. Paul Hunter, *Before Novels: The Cultural Contexts of Eighteenth-Century English Fiction* (New York: Norton, 1990), 77–79; Rosenheim, 255. For the Grand Tour, see Jeremy Black, *The British and the Grand Tour* (London: Croom Helm, 1985); Felicity Heal and Clive Holmes, *The Gentry in England and Wales, 1500–1700* (Stanford, Calif.: Stanford University Press, 1994), 273–75; Bruce Redford, *Venice and the Grand Tour* (New Haven, Conn.: Yale University Press, 1996); Rosenheim, 195–98.

18. For a focus on the rise of the individual, see Michael Masuch, *Origins of the Individualist Self: Autobiography and Self-Identity in England, 1591–1791* (Cambridge: Polity Press, 1997); Dror Wahrman, *The Making of the Modern Self: Identity and Culture in Eighteenth-Century England* (New Haven, Conn.: Yale University Press, 2004). For interest in consumption, see John Brewer and Roy Porter, eds., *Consumption and the World of Goods* (London: Routledge, 1993); L. Weatherill, *Consumer Behaviour and Material Culture, 1660–1760* (London: Routledge, 1988); Amanda Vickery, *Behind Closed Doors: At Home in Georgian England* (New Haven, Conn.: Yale University Press, 2009).

19. For debates about the division between public and private realms and the emergence of the public sphere, see Jürgen Habermas, *The Structural Transformation of the Public Sphere*, trans. Thomas Burger with Fredrick Lawrence (Cambridge, Mass.: MIT Press, 1989); Peter Lake and Steven Pincus, "Rethinking the Public Sphere in Early Modern England," *Journal of British Studies* 42, 2 (April 2006): 270–92; Michael McKeon, *The Secret History of Domesticity: Public, Private, and the Division of Knowledge* (Baltimore: Johns Hopkins University Press, 2005), xvii–xx; Lawrence Klein, "Gender and the Public/Private Distinction in the Eighteenth Century: Some Questions About Evidence and Analytic Procedure," *Eighteenth Century Studies* 29, 1 (Autumn 1995): 97–109; David Zaret, *Origins of Democratic Culture: Printing, Petitions, and the Public Sphere in Early-Modern England* (Princeton, N.J.: Princeton University Press, 2000).

20. Sarah Pearsall, *Atlantic Families: Lives and Letters in the Later Eighteenth Century* (Oxford: Oxford University Press, 2008); Naomi Tadmor, *Friends and Family in Eighteenth-Century England* (Cambridge: Cambridge University Press, 2001).

21. Peter Barwick to Hans Sloane, 6 September 1690, BL Sloane MS 4036, f. 96.

22. Journal of James Brydges, 23 June 1698, HEH ST 26: 1.

23. Konstantin Dierks, *In My Power: Letter Writing and Communications in Early America* (Philadelphia: University of Pennsylvania Press, 2009), 189–214.

24. Robert McCracken Peck, "Bartram, William," *American National Biography Online*, February 2014.

25. Tinling, 2: 613.

26. Julian P. Boyd, ed., *The Papers of Thomas Jefferson*, vol. 4 (Princeton: Princeton University Press, 1951), 691.

27. John Perceval I to Lord Harrington, 28 April 1748, BL Add. MS 47000, f. 122.

28. Robert Brereton to John Perceval II, 13 May 1748, BL Add. MS 47009B, f. 35–36.

29. George Berkeley to John Perceval II, 14 May 1748, BL Add. MS 47014A, f. 120. For the note to reply, see BL Add. MS 47034, f. 2v.

30. John Rawdon had married the first earl's daughter, Helena, who died in 1746. John Rawdon to John Perceval II, 16 May 1748, BL Add. MS 47014A, f. 122.

31. Richard Purcell to John Perceval II, 16 May 1748, BL Add. MS 47002B, f. 13.

32. William Cooley to John Perceval II, 27 May 1748, BL Add. MS 47006, f. 21.

Index

Italics indicate pages with figures.

actor network theory, 5
addresses, 23, 28–31
Africa, 63, 158
Allen, Ralph, 24, 199
American Revolution, 203
Anglo-Spanish War, 174, 190
Antigua, 40, 59
Ashton, Peter, 67
autograph letters, 15–16

Bailyn, Bernard, 5
Banister, Mr., 133
Barcelona, siege of, 183–84
Barrimore, Lady, 153
Bartram, John, 1, 3, 197, 198, 203
Bartram, William, 203
Bath (city), 53, 55, 72, 76, 192
Berkeley, George, 15, 35, 61, 185, 204; Bermuda scheme of, 95; charitable plans of, 75; epistolary mobility of, 63–64; on news and newspapers, 172, 175, 189–90; Perceval's epistolary network and, 94, 106; SPCK and, 158
Bermuda, 38, 59, 75, 80, 95, 188
Bernard, Francis, 102
Biork, Tobias, 37–38
Blaney, Lady, 92
Blundell, Nicholas, 14–15, 16, 65, 72, 93; death of, 197; diary of, 22, 44, 65, 231n127; dining and visiting with correspondents, 73, 224n129; epistolary anchor of, 65–66, 73–74; epistolary network of, 83, *86*, 88, 92; in Flanders, 60, 65; gift giving and, 124, 128; letter book of, 29, 140; letters written for tenants, 108; letters written for wife, 110, 231n127; London correspondents of, 73; news in letters of, 177; toasts in letters and, 138; visits to Post Office, 22, 24
Blundell, Richard, 74, 88, 92
Boston, 174
Bouquet, Henry, 198
Boyle, Charles, 4th Earl of Orrery, 158
Boyle, John, 5th Earl of Orrery, 39–40, 54, 61, 95, 96, 155, 158
Bray, Thomas, 159
Brayne, Susan, 87
Brewer, John, 172
Bristol, 53, 63
British elite, 9, 15, 54, 99, 108, 170, 203–4; language used in polite society, 117; margins of, 16; mobility of, 38, 76–77, 199–200; multiple social networks among, 17; as networking society, 7; patronage and, 98; in periphery of empire, 58; shifts in socialization of, 116; social network clusters of, 79–80, *81–82*, *84–86*; trusted networks of, 43; urban life and, 53, 156; women of, 109–10, 112
Brydges, Cassandra Willoughby, duchess of Chandos, 14, 15, 59; death of, 197; ephemeral networks and, 101; on friendship, 94; gift giving and, 124–25; letter bearers and, 40; news acquisition and, 176–77, 192, 193; sending of services and, 133–34; struggle for status, 16
Brydges, James, duke of Chandos, 13–14, 15, 59, 203; contractual network of, 145, 152–54; death of, 197; in Dutch Republic, 61; employees of, 15; ephemeral networks and, 101; gift giving and, 125, 126–27; grandson of, 198; letter bearers and, 41; letter book of, 140; news acquisition and, 177, 179–80, 183, 192; Royal Society and,

Brydges, James, duke of Chandos (*continued*) 158; sending of services and, 131, 151; toasts mentioned in letters, 238n135; trading interests and, 16
Buchanan, Matthew, 104–7, 176, 180, 229n101
bureaucracy, 98
Burlington, Lady, 110–11
Butler, Richard, 67
Byrd, Warham, 93
Byrd, William, I, 3, 11–12, 15, 34, 78, 112; contractual networks and, 147–49, 153, 155; death of, 197; epistolary network of, 83, *84*, 143, *144*, 225n11; familial networks, 87, 92; letter books of, 11, 140; Perceval's correspondence with, 95–96; sending of services and, 133; shipping routes known by, 188; toasts in letters and, 138, 238n135
Byrd, William, II, 12, 13, 15, 58, 106; colonial status capitalized on by, 60; death of, 198; diaries, 64–65, 185–86, 189; dining and visiting with correspondents, 67, 68, 223n109; epistolary network of, 83, *85*; familial networks, 87, 92–93, 96; gift giving of, 124; gossip of Virginia and, 56; importance of distant correspondence to, 69–71; kissing of hand mentioned in letter, 118; letter bearers and, 38; letters treated like continuing conversations, 119; news acquisition and, 174, 176, 177, 178, 179, 182, 184–91; Perceval's correspondence with, 33–35, 57–60, 75, 76; Royal Society and, 157–58, 167; seasons and letter posting, 34, 214n96; on ship-borne letters, 34–35, 214n93; shipping routes known by, 188; silent correspondent of, 121; on slavery, 57, 219n39; toasts in letters, 136; travels of, 66; on urban centers, 53, 55; women correspondents of, 109
Byrd, William, III, 198, 203

Cadogan, Charles, Earl Cadogan, 198
Cadogan, William, Earl Cadogan, 32
Cairnes, Sir Alexander, 32, 106
Callon, Michel, 5
capitalism, 97–98
Cartwright, Capt., 153
Catholics, 14, 60, 65, 158, 198, 252n11; Maryland as Catholic colony, 159; Tumult of Thorn and, 193–94
Chamberlayne, John, 25, 106, 158, 160
Charles I, king, 21
Child, Sir Josiah, 14
children, letters of, 116
Cicero, 114, 119
cities, letters clustered in, 52
Civil Wars, English, 21, 159, 169
Clark, Peter, 166
Clogher, Bishop of, 105, 106
clubs, 7, 156–60
code, letters written in, 23
coffeehouses, 7, 27, 68, 156; letters as virtual coffeehouses, 18; news acquisition in, 183, 187, 192
Coghill, Marmaduke, 71, 195
Colden, Cadwallader, 59
Cole, Mr., 73, 74
Collinson, Peter, 2, 15, 28, 55, 117, 202; addressing of letters by, 31; botany interest of, 16; on colonies, 57; commonplace book of, 59; credit and debt references in letters, 121; and gift giving, 123, 125, 126; intimacy expressed in letter to wife, 118–19; intimate thought conveyed in letters, 18; kissing of hand mentioned in letter, 118; letter bearers used by, 37–38; on letters as company of friends, 3; letters inserted into commonplace book, 13; news acquisition and, 180, 195; news in letters of, 171; Royal Society and, 158, 159; salutations used by, 120; sharing of letters, 42–43; silent correspondent reprimanded by, 122; Sloane's correspondence with, 68; "speaking letters" to Bartram, 1, 197, 198; toasts in letters, 136; travels of, 61
colonies, British-ruled, 49, 55, 200; absentee landlords in, 71; expansion of British Empire, 197, 198; idealized picture of rural life in, 56–57
commonplace books, 12, 13, 59
community, 4, 18, 112, 156; imagined communities, 202; toasts and, 135
compliments, giving of, 116, 117
Continent (Europe), 33, 59, 74, 159, 200, 203; British elite drawn to, 60–61, 77; connections among British elite in, 58, 62; letter delivery, 31–33; letters originating from, *51*, 52, *52*; life outside urban centers, 54–55; Perceval's travels in, 28, 31–32, 34, 63, 66, 72, 95–96; postal systems in, 32, 36, 45; wars in, 191

contractual networks, 143, *144*, 145, *146*, 167; construction of contractual letters, 145, 147–49; trust in, 149–55
Convention Parliament, 21
Cork, County (Ireland), 54, 66, 77, 195
Cornwall, Velters, 63, 67
courtships, 12
Crofts, Christopher, 102
Crofts, Philip, 102
Crofts, William, 99
Curll, Edmund, 45
Custis, Daniel, 186
Custis, John, 15, 70–71, 93, 96, 151, 184–86

Davenport, William, 99
Davys, John, 18, *20*, 210n1
debt and credit, language of, 121–22
Defoe, Daniel, 14
Depagez, Colonel, 105–6
Dering, Charles, 92
Dering, Daniel, 28, 32, 33, 36, 93; death of, 89, 96; letters co-written with wife, 42; Perceval's correspondence with, 61, 88–89, 96; Perceval's epistolary network and, 83; SPCK and, 158; toasts in letters, 137; travels of, 63
Dering, Sir Edward, 83
Dering, Helena, 83
Dering family, 95
diaries, 9, 12, 66; of Blundell, 22, 44, 65, 231n127; of Byrd II, 64–65, 185–86, 189; of Perceval, 64
diasporas, ethnic and religious, 4
Dierks, Konstantin, 21
distance, 17, 118, 150, 184–91
Dockwra, William, 23
Doneraile, Viscount, 102
Donnellan, Martha Usher, 89
Donnellan, Nancy, 137
Donnellan family, 80
Dublin, 26, 27, 47, 63, 89, 212n53; British needs and expansion of, 53; as a center of British world, 76; as flourishing city, 197; letters originating in, 49
Dungannon, Lord, 11

East India Company, 14, 31, 197
Effingham, Lord, 195
elections, 97, 101–4, *103*; connected to maintain an interest, 101; female involvement, 110–11
Eliot, John, 37, 41, 60, 151
Emmerson, Mr., 131
England, 1, 28, 76, 160, 200; absentee landlords in, 71; country-city divide in, 53; printing of letter collections in, 45
English Rogue, The (Head), 2
ENGLISH School-Master Compleated, The (Hawkins), 2
epistolary networks, 71, 76, 141, 184, 203; of Byrd I and II, 83, *84–85*; constant, 22, 80; contractual networks, 143, *144*, 145, 152–53; ephemeral, 97–107, *100*, *103*, 108; fluidity of, 78–79, 112; family, 83–93; friends, 93–96; geographic map of 48–53; institutional 156–57, 161–62; mobility and, 63–64, 71; news processing, 184; of Perceval, *81–82*; permanent, 22; social hierarchy borders and, 107–12; social maps of 79, *81–82*, *84–86*, *100*, *103*, *144*, *146*, *162*
epistolary worlds, 47–48; centers and peripheries of, 48–58, *50–52*, 76–77; stability and mobility in, 58–63
Eyre, Henry, 73, 224n129

face-to-face interaction, 66–67, 117–18, 129, 201
family, 11, 74, 79; distance and strain on familial networks, 92–93; in Perceval epistolary network, 80, 83, 87–91; sharing of letters with, 41–43
Filenius, Dr., 37–38
Fisher, William, 29, 31
Fitzgerald, Captain, 95
Florida, Anglo-Spanish rivalry in, 190–91
Fothergill, John, 203
Fountaine, Sir Andrew, 39
France, 33, 49, 66
franking of letters, 27, 199, 212n52
Frankland, Mr., 131
Franklin, Benjamin, 1
Freemasons, 157
French Academy of Sciences, 166
friendship, 3, 4, 93–96, 117, 202; gift giving and, 124, 125; institutional networks and, 163–64; landlord-agent relations framed as, 151–52; money and, 126
fur trade, 12

Gelibrond, John, 73, 224n129
gender, 17, 107, 108, 111–12
George II, King, 174, 176

Georgia, colony of, 59, 75, 159–60
gift giving, 113, 114, 122–28, 138, 139, 152
Glorious Revolution, 159
Godfrey, Ambrose, 97, 107
Gooch, Governor, 68
Goodman, Dena, 110
Grafton, Duke of, 90
Grand Tour, 61, 199
Great Northern War, 176
Grymes, John, 185
Gunpowder Plot (1605), 171
Gwim, Sir Rowland, 131

Habermas, Jürgen, 21, 171
Hanbury, John, 70
Hancock, David, 5
Handel, Georg, 13
Hardy, Mr., 95
Harrington, Lord, 204
Hastings, Lady Francis, 30
Hasting, George, 4th Earl of Huntingdon, 28
Hastings, Henry, 5th Earl of Huntingdon, 171
Hastings, Lucy, Countess of Huntingdon, 18, 21, 121, 210n1
Hastings, Selina, Countess of Huntingdon, 10, 132
Hastings, Theophilus, 7th Earl of Huntingdon, 130, 171–72
Hastings family, 22, 48, 120–21, 129, 237n114
Hawkins, John, 2
Head, Richard, 2
History of the Royal Society (Sprat), 159
Hodder, Thomas, 99
Horsmanden family, 93, 94, 225n11
How, James, 21
Howet, Thomas, 67
Huntingdon, earls of, 16, 28, 115, 125
Hutchison, Archebald, 95

identities, religious, 5, 6
identity, regional, 58
India, 36, 127
Indians, North American, 59, 60
information distribution, 8
institutional networks, 156–167, *162*
intellectual networks, 5–6, 44, 54–55
interest, networks of, 6, 8, 18
Ireland, 1, 11, 16, 76; absentee landlords in, 71; British elites living in, 54, 55; British rule over, 53; elections in, *103*; franking in, 27, 212n52; letter delivery to, 24, 26–28; packet services to, 27, 212n49
Italy, 62

Jacobite Rising (1715), 14, 54, 65, 111, 175
Jamaica, 59
Jefferson, Thomas, 203
Jennings, George, *10*
Joynes, John, 130

kinship relations, 4, 6, 87–93
Knatchbull, Mary Dering, 83, 91, 92
knowledge creation, 5

laboring classes, 108–9, 116–17
landlords, 18, 23; absentee, 43, 55, 71, 108, 141, 149; agents' epistolary relations with, 149–55; circulation of letters and, 43, 44; contractual letters and, 143, 145, 147; tenants' petitions to, 108–9
Latour, Bruno, 5
le Grand, Helena, 15, 83, 90, 91–92
letter books, 9, 15, 67; of Blundell, 68, 140; of Brydges, 13, *142*; of Byrd family, 11, 12; of Byrd I, 140; of Perceval, 88, 239n4
letter delivery: to the Continent (Europe), 31–33; to Ireland, 26–28; within London, 25–26; to Scotland, 26; transatlantic, 33–36
letters: addressing of, 28–31, *30*; bonds created and sustained by, 138; of children, 116; as company of friends, 3; contractual, 145, 147–49; conversation within, 1, 119; cost of sending, 25, 212nn37, 40; courtly letters of seventeenth century, 17; creation of individual self and, 114; delayed and miscarried, 23, 36; drafts of, 9; regarding estates, 11, 19, 26–28, 43–44, 140, 143, 147, 149–53; flexibility in style of familiar letters, 114–22; gifts sent with, 122–28; hurried additions in, *20*; institutions and preservation of, 141, 160–67; laboring class production, 7, 108–9; locations of origin, 49, *50–52*; medieval, 135; merchant, 141, 143, 148–53 networking function of, 7–8, 78–80, 201; news and, 171–78, 181; as objects of study, 7–8; obliging, 120–21; official government, 145, 147–48, 151–55; opened by Post Office personnel, 23, 211n20; physical connections with, 118–19; read by family of recipient, 41; recipients found by, 24, 29; reciprocal

nature of, 120, 121; sharing of, 42–43; women writing, 109–12
Levant Company, 16
Licensing Act (1695), 172
Linnaeus, Karl, 38, 55
literacy, 8
London, 36, 48, 72; as a center of British world, 76; coffeehouses of, 187; contractual networks and, 143; country-city divide and, 53; epistolary world dominated by, 52–53; letters originating in, 49, 52; newspapers in, 174; as postal center, 21, 24, 25; rising population of, 197
Louis XIV, 184
Low Countries, 49
Ludwell, Philip, 70, 72

Magnolfi, Lorenzo, 61, 113, 123
Marlborough, Duchess of, 110–11, 127
Marlborough, Duke of, 155
Maryland, 159
Maul, Henry, 102
Mauss, Marcel, 124
merchants, 5–6, 18, 31–36, 70, 121, 140, 141, 143, 148–54, 188
migration, 5, 157, 169
Milan, 52
Mingay, John, 132
mobility, geographic, 5–6, 7, 38, 48, 58–77, 87, 106, 112, 128, 167, 169, 193, 199–200, 202
Molineux, Viscount, 67
Moore, Sir Emmanuel, 83, 102, 126, 127
Moore, Robert, 83
Muddiman, Henry, 172, 173
Muldrew, Craig, 156

Naples, 52, 104
Netherlands (Dutch Republic), 19, 24, 32, 61, 66; Perceval in, 191; postal system of, 32; Randstad, 49, 52, 218n7
networks: personal/social, 2–9, 31, 41, 45–46, 202; contractual correspondence and, 155; contemporary conception of, 2–3; institutional networks and, 158–59, 163, 168; letters as connective tissue of, 78; networks of interest, 5–6; "problem-anchored" networks, 97, 105, 107; reinforced by political realm, 45; scholars on, 4–6; "strength of weak ties," 106–7; trust in, 41–45
Newman, Henry, 25, 26, 33, 158, 161, 212n41
news, 1, 18, 169, 170–78; colonial access to, 184–91; credibility of, 178–84; as "talk," 191–96
newsletters, 169, 172, *173*, 177–79, 183, 187, 193
newspapers, 18, 170, 175–76, 177; in colonies, 187; credibility of, 179–80; ferried on ships, 190; news as "talk," 191–92; on Tumult of Thorn, 193
New York, 33
North, Arthur, 147, 152, 153
North Carolina, 33, 59
Norton, Mary Beth, 110
nostalgia, historical inquiry and, 4
notebooks, 9

Oglethorpe, James, 75
Oldenburg, Henry, 160, 163
Ormond, Duke of, 128, 130
Otway family, 83, 93, 94
Oxford, Bishop of, 39, 40

Paris, 47, 52
Parker, Catherine, 88
Parker, Mary, 88
Parker, Philip, 83, 92
Parks, William, 185, 187
Parliament, 7, 27, 72, 110, 177, 197; Exclusion Crisis and, 174; Irish absentee landlords and, 141; news of addresses in, 190
Paston letters, 48, 129, 135
patronage, 98, 104, 105, 129, 204
Pennsylvania, 16
Penny Post, 21–22, 23, 25, 35, 212n41; complications of, 26; smooth functioning of, 36
Peppard, Nicholas, 198
Perceval, Catherine Parker, Countess of Egmont, 83, 88, 106, 110
Perceval, Catherine (daugher of John), 110
Perceval, Cecil Parker, 204
Perceval, John, 3, 15, 24, 53, 87, 99, 196; as absentee landlord, 141; agents of, 149, 153–54; Berkeley's correspondence with, 94, 175, 185, 189–90; Byrd's correspondence with, 57–58, 75, 76, 189; children of, 116; correspondence forwarded by, 37; death of, 94, 197, 204; on delay in mail delivery, 31–32; dining and visiting with correspondents, 73, 222n89; ephemeral networks and, *100*, 101–2, *103*, 104–6, 229n101; as

Perceval, John (*continued*)
epistolary anchor, 75–76; epistolary network of, 80, *81–82*, 83–91, *146*, 161, 163; European postal systems and, 32–33; on face-to-face interaction, 66–67; formality of letters, 115; in France, 55; gift giving and, 113, 123–26, 128, 138; Ireland compared to America by, 57–58; Irish estates of, 49, 146; letter bearers and, 39; letter books of, 9, 10, 140, 239n4; management of local affairs through letters, 68; mobility of correspondents and, 63; Newman's correspondence with, 25–26, 212n41; news acquisition by, 172, 175–76, 179, 180–81, 183, 185; political events monitored by, 71–72; sending of services and, 128, 130, 131, 133, 134; sharing of letters with family, 41–42; SPCK involvement of, 157–58, 161, 164, 165, 242n83; Taylor as estate agent of, 26–28; tenants of, 15, 27, 40, 43, 108–9; titles held by, 9, 16, 23, 140, 204; toasts in letters and, 137–38, 238n135; travels of, 61, 66, 72–73, 76, 113–14, 191, 220n61; on Tumult of Thorn, 194
Perceval, John, II, 110–11, 116, 180, 198, 204
Perceval, Philip, 32, 37, 87, 93; brother John's epistolary network and, 80, 83, 88; on news and newspapers, 170–71; travels of, 47
Perceval, William, 83, 90, 91–92
Perry, Micajah, 151
Perry and Lane, firm of, 147, 148–50, 152–55
personal letter bearers, 37–41
Petit, Brigadier, 106
petitions, 108–9, 230n116
Petre, Lady, 15
Petre family, 31
Philosophical Transactions (journal of Royal Society), 44, 167, 196
pirates, 34
Pitt, William, the elder, 198
Plumb, John, 67
Poland, 193–94, 196
Pope, Alexander, 45
Portugal, 19, 49, 174
postal systems, 17, 46; Continental, 32; expansion of, 18; gaps in, 200; history of public postal system in England, 21–24; of Holy Roman Empire, 32; letter bearers as complement to, 40; of Netherlands, 32; newsletters and, 169; state power and, 19
postmarks, 13, 15, 16; dating of, 30; in Hastings correspondence, *10*, 22, 210nn2, 13
*Post Office, 8, 17, 37, 46, 151; in Dublin, 27; difficulties of use, 23–24; evolution of, 21, 198–99; General Post Office (Lombard Street, London), 25; income of, 198; letter writers' suspicion of, 23, 44–45; number of Post Offices in England, 24; permanence of epistolary networks and, 22; use of, 22
postscripts, 130, *132*, 137, 150, 171
power, desire for, 16
Pratt family, 83
Presbyterians, 54
privacy, 44
private sphere, 7–8; "feminine private," 110; news, 175–76; redefined as personal, 45–46
Proselyte Society, 25, 161
Protestants, 158, 161, 192–94
public sphere, 7–8, 21, 22, 45; female exclusion from, 110; in news, 171–75; overlap with private sphere, 201–2, public oversight, 154–55
Purcell, Richard, 204

Quakers, 13, 54

Rand family, 93, 94, 225n11
Randolph, Captain, 133
Randolph, Edward, 186, 188
Randolph, Isham, 186, 188
Randolph, Sir John, 188
Randolph, Lady, 65, 192
Ray, John, 14
Ray, Margaret, 15
Reformation, multiplication of religious identities in, 5
religious networks, 5–6
Restoration, 19, 24, 136
Rhode Island, 35, 37, 64, 189
Richards, Grace, 225n11
Richmond, Duke of, 28, 31, 120
Rook, Lady, 92
Royal Society, 13, 44, 59, 60, 97; Byrd II's gifts to, 124; collaboration with similar societies, 166; correspondence with multiple members of, 163; institutional networks and, 160; journal of, 44, 167; "New World" discoveries and, 159; origins of, 156–57, 158; preservation of letters and, 141; Sloane and, 157–58, 164–65; social stability and, 159
Ruddes, Captain, 78

Sacheverell, Henry, 91
salutations, in letters, 115, 119–20
Scotland, 1, 24, 26, 49; absentee landlords in, 71; British elites living in, 54, 55
seals: broken, 9, 16; opened by Post Office personnel, 23, 211n20; placement of, 16; privacy and, 44–45
secretaries, 108, 134, 161, 163
self, individual, 8, 114, 201
services, sending of, 128–35, 138, 139, 152, 237n114
Seven Years' War, 195, 197
Shapin, Steven, 182
ship captains, 34–35, 40, 186
Short, Tom, 185, 187
silence, as rejection, 122
slaves, 57, 59, 150, 186, 219n39
slave trade, 197
Sloane, Hans, 13, 15, 25, 29, 107, 202; death of, 197; epistolary network of, 161, *162*, 163; family of, 16; far-flung correspondents of, 31, 63; gift giving and, 126; letter bearers and, 38–39, 41; mobility of, 59; requests in letters and, 68; Royal Society and, 157–58, 160, 164–65, 167; sending of services and, 131, 133; sharing of letters, 42–43; supplicants and, 97; toasts mentioned in letters, 238n135
Smith, Capt. Christopher, 70
Smith, Major, 95
Smith, Mary, 70
Smith, Mr., 37, 38
sociability, urban, 199
social network analysis, 4, 17, 79–80, 225n6
Society for Promoting Christian Knowledge (SPCK), 141, 156–61, 163–67
Society for the Propagation of the Gospel in Foreign Parts (SPG), 159, 164
sociology/sociologists, 4, 6, 106–7
Sokoll, Thomas, 230n116
South Sea Bubble, 95
Southwell, Edward, 61, 64, 69, 94, 214n92; connections to powerful people, 96; death of, 72, 96; news acquisition and, 181, 191; Perceval's epistolary network and, 83, 88–90; Royal Society and, 158; son of (Edward the younger), 73, 223n123; supplicants and, 99; toasts in letters, 137; toasts mentioned in letters, 238n135
Southwell, Elizabeth, 83
Southwell, Sir Robert, 83, 101
Southwell family, 87, 95
Spain, 19, 49, 92, 174
Spencer, Alice, Countess of Derby, 28
Spotswood, Governor and Mrs., 69
Sprat, Thomas, 159
St. John, Henry, Viscount Bolingbroke, 155
Stanhope, Philip, Earl of Chesterfield, 99, 145
status, social, 107–8, 111
Steiger, Mr., 97, 107
Stratford, Mr., 153
Strong, Mr., 19
supplicants, 97, 99, *100*, 104–7

Taylor, Berkeley, 26–28, 29, 31, 36, 240n14; contractual networks and, 147, 148; letters to Perceval, 240n33
Taylor, William, 145, 147
Taylor, William (second), 71, 147, 149, 153, 240nn14, 33
Taylor family, 83, 93, 94
Temple, John, 154
tenants: circulation of letters among, 43–44; letters by, 149, 150–51; petitions from, 108–9
Thoresby, Ralph, 164
toasting, 135–38, 139, 152, 238n135
tobacco trade, 12
trading factors, 15, 18, 35
transatlantic trade, 79, 141
Trench, Henry, 104
Tschiffely, Samuel, 68
Tumult of Thorn, 193–94
Turner, William, 145, 147
Tuscany, Grand Duke of, 61, 113–14, 134

urban centers, 49, *50–52*, 58
Usher, Kit, 80

verbal messages, 39
Virginia, 11–12, 16, 17, 33, 87, 198; distance from centers of British world, 76, 77, 184–91; idealized picture of rural life in, 56–57; lack of urban centers in, 55

Wager, Charles, 69, 95
Wales, 159, 160
Walpole, Horace, 72
Walpole, Sir Robert, 101

Warner, Michael, 45
War of the League of Augsburg, 47
War of the Spanish Succession, 32, 92, 179, 182
Washington, George, 198
Webber, Daniel, 99, 101
West Indies, 13, 19, 33, 149–50, 191, 214n88
Wills, Hanna, 99
Windsor, Lord, 95
women, 79, 91, 111–12; letter writing of elite women, 109–10; limited place in epistolary world, 108
Wormeley, Col. Christopher, 152
Worth, Captain, 194
Wright, Lady, 131
Wynne, Captain, 78

Acknowledgments

This book owes its creation to networks of support perhaps even more than the lives it inspects. I was able to lean upon and look to constant nodes of assistance as well as more ephemeral webs that crystallized when needed. I sometimes sit back and visualize this network and the image humbles me and requires acknowledgment.

My first thanks goes to the major nodes of my network. First, to Keith Wrightson who has nurtured this project since the beginning. He has never flagged in his support and was always willing to go above and beyond the call of duty, reading it in all its many incarnations. I must also offer a huge thanks to Peter Mancall, not only as the editor of this series but as a colleague and mentor. When my confidence wavered, his did not, and that mattered. Volumes of appreciation are also owed to Cynthia Herrup for reading segments of the work and for being a constant voice of calm.

My web of connections, which stretched from Yale to the Huntington Library to the University of Southern California, deserves my heartfelt gratitude as well. Steven Pincus was always willing to lend support and both Brian Cowan and John Demos deserve a thank you. A big thanks also goes out to Roy Ritchie for his unflagging support and to Steve Hindle for his always solid advice. I also thank the participants of the USC-Huntington Early Modern British History Seminar and a special thanks goes out to Lori Anne Ferrell for reading parts of the manuscript at a crucial period and to Sarah Easterby-Smith for always being willing to talk about networks. I'm also grateful to Abby Swingen, Bob Morrissey, Adrian Finucane, Jason Sharples, Keith Pluymers, Mark Hanna, Emma Hart, Rosemary O'Day, Nick Rogers, Rebecca Lemon, Will Fisher, Marjorie Rubright, Amy Braden, and anyone else who has had to listen to me talk about the trouble with networks over the years. I must also proffer thanks to Phil Ethington for listening to me talk about the issues surrounding visualizing data and for directing me to the

USC Spatial Studies Institute. I thank Nina Noujdina, attached to the institute, for making me see just how dated my hand-drawn, Sharpie-made maps were, and Joshua Brown, brother-in-law extraordinaire, for transforming my networks into figures I could actually use for this book.

This book also owes its existence to the help provided by the curators and staff members at multiple libraries. I offer thanks to those who helped me at the British Library, the Bodleian Library, the London Metropolitan Library, the Lancashire Records Office, the Shakespeare Trust Record Office, the Linnean Society, and the Virginia Historical Society. But most of all, I thank everyone at the Huntington Library who has helped me over the years: Mary Robertson, who directed me to documents, and everyone in the readers services department: Catherine Wehrey, Molly Gibson, Kadin Henningsen, Juan Gomez, Sara Georgi, Claire Kennedy, Jaeda Snow, Allee Monheim, Michael Fish, Meredith Berbée, Laura Stalker, and Christopher Addé. Thanks for saying hello and giving your opinion on everything from sentence construction to maps. I also need to thank the institutions whose funding made this project possible: the Huntington Library, the USC-Huntington Early Modern Studies Institute, the Office of the Dean of USC Dornsife, the British Academy, the North American Conference on British Studies, the Institute for Historical Research, the Yale Center for British Art, and the Yale Center for International and Area Studies.

I also thank everyone involved at the University of Pennsylvania Press. Bob Lockhart has helped shepherd me through this process with great patience, and my anonymous readers provided insightful comments and helped me restructure the manuscript into what it is today. Parts of Chapter 6 appeared in "Dealing with Newsmongers: News, Trust, and Letters," *Huntington Library Quarterly* (June 2013); I thank them for allowing me to publish the material in a slightly different manifestation here.

My friend and family networks also deserve a great deal of credit and thanks. This project depended upon the support of Heather Brown, Heather and Pat Richardson, Don and Sue Hartley, Maria Garcia, Katherine Mannheimer, Anne Dewitt, Rachel Bond, Chris Bond, Jake Lundberg, Wendy Warren, Helen Veit, Charles Keith, Kaja Cook, Sarah Keyes, Michael Block, and many others. But most of all I owe thanks to my parents who experienced all the ups and downs of this process with me. For that reason this book is dedicated to them.

www.ingramcontent.com/pod-product-compliance
Lightning Source LLC
Chambersburg PA
CBHW020947310726
48980CB00001B/82

* 9 7 8 0 8 1 2 2 4 6 4 8 3 *